The Dun & Bradstreet Handbook of
Credits and Collections

The Dun & Bradstreet Handbook of

Credits and Collections

Harold T. Redding
Vice President and Secretary, Dun & Bradstreet, Inc.

Guyon H. Knight III
Project Staff, Dun & Bradstreet, Inc.

Thomas Y. Crowell Company
Established 1834   New York

Designed by Abigail Moseley

Manufactured in the United States of America

2   3   4   5   6   7   8   9   10

Library of Congress Cataloging in Publication Data

Redding, Harold T
   The Dun & Bradstreet handbook of credits and collections.

   1. Credit. 2. Collecting of accounts. I. Knight, Guyon H., III, joint author. II. Title.
HF556.R43   332.7   74-9777
ISBN 0-690-00590-3

We wish to thank the following authors and publications for permission to use or adapt their material:

Commercial Credit and Collection Guide by Bruce D. Classon. Copyright © October 14, 1968 by Prentice-Hall, Inc., Englewood Cliffs, N.J.

Credit and Collection Management (3rd Ed.) by William J. Shultz and Hedwig Reinhardt. Copyright © 1972 by Louisa V. Shultz, New Harbor, Maine 04554 & Hedwig Reinhardt, 39 Gramercy Park N., New York, N.Y. 10010.

Robert Bartels, *Credit Management.* Copyright © 1967 by The Ronald Press Company, New York.

Executive's Credit & Collection Guide. Copyright © 1972 by Executive Reports Corporation, Englewood Cliffs, N.J.

Improving Credit Practice by Donald E. Miller and Donald B. Relkin. © 1971 by the American Management Association, Inc.

Law Directory, Volume V. Copyright © 1973 by Martindale-Hubbell, Inc.

"Managing Trade Receivables," by Patrick Davey. © 1972, The Conference Board Inc.

Uniform Commercial Code Handbook: Analysis and Explanation by Garn H. Webb and Thomas C. Bianco. Copyright © 1969 by Holt, Rinehart & Winston.

Merle T. Welshans, "Using Credit for Profit-Making," *Harvard Business Review* (Jan-Feb 1967), Vol. 45, No. 1. Copyright © 1966 by President and Fellows of Harvard College; all rights reserved.

Advantages of promissory notes appearing on p. 14 from *Credit and Collection Principles and Practice* (7th Ed.) by Albert F. Chapin and George E. Hassett, Jr. Copyright © 1960 by McGraw-Hill, Inc. Used by permission of McGraw-Hill Book Company.

Classification of assets and liabilities on pp. 221-224 and Tables for Determining Collection Period on pp. 319-326 from *Practical Financial Statement Analysis* (6th Ed.) by Roy Foulke. Copyright © 1968 by McGraw-Hill, Inc. Used by permission of McGraw-Hill Book Company.

Credit characteristics on p. 2 and the classification of credit types on pp. 7-10 adapted with permission from Robert H. Cole, *Consumer and Commercial Credit Management* (4th ed.; Homewood, Ill.: Richard C. Irwin, Inc.)

PREFACE

Credit managers, like business executives in every field, suffer from a common information malady: plenty of information available but most of it difficult to pin down and use.

The Dun & Bradstreet Handbook of Credits and Collections has been compiled with the specific intention of remedying that situation.

For the first time, Dun & Bradstreet—an acknowledged leader in the field of credit and collection—presents the complete credit story in a book that is marked by its easy-to-read language and its easy-to-use format.

The Dun & Bradstreet Handbook of Credits and Collections uses a dual indexing system to save busy credit executives valuable time when looking for the answers to specific credit and collection problems.

At the beginning of this book, you will find a detailed listing of all the material contained in the book. Each section is given a number code which can be used to find that section in the book. Major topics are identified by three- or four-digit codes (100, for example, or 303 or 1104). Specific items discussed within each major section are identified by numerical subdivisions of the major code (100.3, for example, or 303.6 or 1104.4). Further refinements of the specific items are identified by another numerical subdivision of the major code (100.3.1 for example, or 303.6.2 or 1104.4.1). In this way, simply by reading the complete contents, you will be able to identify major topics of interest to you—and see how these topics are analyzed in the book.

At the end of the book you will find a complete alphabetical topical index that also identifies the page numbers where each topic is discussed. The authors have made sure that this index covers every subject so that you will have no difficulty finding the information you want.

Since 1841, Dun & Bradstreet, Inc., has been gathering credit information, establishing procedures and methods for credit analysis, defining the parameters of the acceptable and unacceptable credit risk in each industry, and developing systems to coordinate all phases of the credit operation. Each year, Dun & Bradstreet, Inc., puts its theories to practice by evaluating well over 3,000,000 businesses for composite credit and estimated financial strength ratings. Each year, too, Dun & Bradstreet personnel interview millions of businessmen in every field to discuss their thinking on various business problems and practices. The result of this activity has been an enormous amount of material on which the authors of this book have been able to draw. It forms the heart of *The Dun & Bradstreet Handbook of Credits and Collections*.

Still, it has not been enough. Authors of previous books on credits and collections have established the framework in which credit problems are discussed. We have relied on this framework and have reported the contributions these authors have made to the credit field. You will find their books listed on the copyright page and their contributions signaled in the text of this book.

More important, we have called upon many credit executives all over the country to obtain their advice and opinions on matters relating directly to this book. They have been generous with their time and unstinting in their efforts to supply material we requested and to arrive at solutions to credit problems we explored together. In a large measure, this book is a tribute to the skills of credit executives who have made their profession an honored and respected one.

In particular, we would like to thank the following individuals for their continued cooperation and assistance throughout the project: George B. Hallock of Hoffmann-LaRoche, Inc.; Frank Wey and Harry J. Flynn of American Metal Climax, Inc.; T. Cornell of Jonathan Logan Financial; Robert Forney, and Jan M. Abbott, Carl E. Effgen, and Arthur M. Hendrickson of Fortex Data Corporation.

Special thanks go to W. H. Bassett, Jr., of the Reynolds Metals Company; William C. Bruder of Steelcase Inc.; Virginia Bruns of Union Camp Corp.; George N. Christie, Ph.D., of the C.R.F.; J. R. Howells and Clint Eckstrom of PPG Industries, Inc.; James J. Kelly of Lever Brothers Co.; Bernard Kopel of First National Bank of Boston; and David M. Longobucco of Chesebrough-Pond's Inc., for their assistance.

Professor Hedwig Reinhardt of Bernard M. Baruch College (CUNY) offered much helpful advice and her substantial contributions to this book are sincerely appreciated.

In addition, we would like to thank the following people for supplying materials and discussing credit problems with us: Harold T. Hahn and A. A. Dilworth of American Credit Indemnity Company; Lloyd Sinnickson of American Cyanamid Co.; Judy Capel of First National City Bank Corporation; O. D. Glaus of Genesco, Inc.; H. L. Gomling of Lyon Furniture Mercantile Agency; Luis W. Morales of

Robert Morris Associates; Terry W. Clifford of Tektronix, Inc.; and Richard C. Hostetler and John E. Cochran of Western Union Telegraph Company.

Cooke O'Neal of the National Association of Credit Management and Joseph S. Hyde of Credit Research Foundation, Inc., were also of assistance, as was the staff of Martindale-Hubbell, Inc.

Several sections of this book deal with legal matters which you, as a credit manager, are likely to encounter. While Dun & Bradstreet has taken every reasonable precaution to insure the accuracy of this information at the time of publication, we do not guarantee its accuracy. If you are confronted with a legal problem, we urge you to consult your own attorney. There are several reference volumes—particularly the *Credit Manual of Commercial Laws* published by the NACM—which will give you more extensive coverage of legal issues.

Finally, we would like to recognize the assistance of many people here at Dun & Bradstreet for gathering material, offering solutions to credit problems, and reading portions of the manuscript. Without their help, this book could not have been written.

H. T. R.

G. H. K., III

CONTENTS

CHAPTER 10: ORGANIZATIONS RELATED TO THE CREDIT FIELD *267*

CHAPTER 1

CREDIT FUNDAMENTALS

[100]   **DEFINITION OF CREDIT.** Credit is the power to promise future consideration (in the form of goods, services, cash, or another economic value) for the present acquisition of goods, services, cash, or another economic value. In fact, however, you will also find that the word *credit* refers to:

[100.1]   **Credit Transactions.** The process by which the promise is given and the economic values received.

[100.2]   **Credit Ratings.** An estimate of a person's or a business's financial capacity and intention to repay bills promptly.

[100.3]   **Credit Records.** The evidence of how a person or business has fulfilled past obligations.

[101]   **CREDIT CHARACTERISTICS.** The concept of credit is best explained by the underlying assumptions upon which the notion of credit is based, and by the general purposes for which credit exists.

[101.1]   **Underlying Assumptions.**

[101.1.1]   CONFIDENCE. The power to effect a credit transaction results from and varies according to the confidence someone has in another person's:

1. *Willingness* to fulfill his promise, which is a reflection of his character.
2. *Ability* to fulfill his promise, which depends upon his capabilities, his financial strength, and the future of his business, his industry, and the economy in general.

[101.1.2]   FUTURITY. Credit assumes the *future* payment for goods or services, cash, or another economic value. As the future is never definite, the notion of futurity includes probability and whether the probable gain from a credit transaction is worth the risk of possible loss.

[101.2]   **General Purpose of Credit's Existence.** Because credit is the power to exchange a promise of future payment for present economic values, credit exists as a medium of exchange. As such, credit has these characteristics, which have been identified by Robert H. Cole in *Consumer and Commercial Credit Management.*

[101.2.1]   CREDIT AND MONEY. Its acceptance is more limited than that of money because of the risk and because of the future time element, but credit is faster, safer, and more convenient.

[101.2.2]   CREDIT AND TIME. Credit arises at the time of the transaction.

[101.2.3]   CREDIT AND WEALTH. It arises to facilitate one particular transaction, but the total amount of credit is elastic and limited only by the wealth of the society.

[101.2.4]   CREDIT AND FUTURE PAYMENT. Once issued, it does not close the transaction but continues into the future until payment is actually made.

[101.2.5]   CREDIT AND CREDIT LIQUIDATION. It is often self-liquidating, that is, the goods that a promise to pay procures become the means to fulfill the promise.

[102]   HOW CREDIT IS USED.

[102.1]   **Production, Distribution, and Consumption.** As you have just seen, credit exists in order to be used as a medium of exchange. As such, credit aids in the production, distribution, and consumption of goods and services. In fact, without the benefit of credit, our production, distribution, and consumption of goods and services would cease. There is not enough money in the world to cover daily business transactions now carried out on credit. Even if there were, production would cease as inordinate amounts of time and effort would be devoted to carrying money from one place to another. Distribution would cease because few could accumulate enough money in advance to pay for goods that are to be sold afterward. And, of course, consumption would cease as a natural consequence of production and distribution stoppages.

[102.2]   **Expansion.** Not only does credit aid in the production, distribution, and consumption of goods and services, credit enables production, distribution, and consumption of goods and services to expand.

[102.3]   **New Business.** Credit enables the capable businessman with little capital to begin production or distribution.

[102.4]   **Standard of Living.** Credit enables the consumer—with little ready cash —to enjoy a higher standard of living all the time.

[102.5]   **Seasonality.** Credit reduces the effects of seasonal slumps in business activity common, for example, to the fashion industry.

[103]   HOW CREDIT IS ABUSED. Although credit is a necessary ingredient in the day-to-day function of our society and has been a vital element in its growth and development, the use of credit can be abused. Here's how:

[103.1]   **Overexpansion.** An overabundance of credit—or even a small amount of credit unwisely extended—can cause overexpansion of a business, leading to its collapse.

[103.2]   **Overtrading.** A credit policy whose terms are too liberal can result in overtrading. Too much of a company's capital can be tied up in accounts receivable and bad debts.

[103.3]   **Inflation.** Too much credit within a society can raise the prices of goods and services produced, distributed, and consumed. This can lead to inflation and, eventually, recession or even depression.

[103.4]   **Extravagance.** An excess of credit can tempt the individual to lead an extravagant life—with someone else's money.

[103.5]   **Speculation.** Too much credit can mean too much temptation to speculate.

[104]   **HISTORY OF CREDIT.** Credit is probably as old as the notion of possession and certainly as old as money and trade. As early as 1300 B.C. the Babylonians and Assyrians were lending money on the basis of mortgages, advance deposits, and other security instruments. The year 1000 B.C. saw the introduction of unsophisticated bills of exchange in Babylonia. By the time of the Romans, the use of credit extended throughout the empire and credit documents had reached high levels of development.

The collapse of the Roman Empire signaled the coming of the Middle Ages but credit did not fade into some dark medieval oblivion. Instead, trade between all cities in Christendom was carried out on the basis of letters of credit. Indeed, the expanded use of credit between Italian bankers facilitated the redevelopment of production and consumption that grew into the Renaissance.

Mercantile credit use experienced even greater growth once the New World was discovered. Even though Europe's money supply increased with the import of newly discovered precious metals, trade between European colonies and their mother countries continued to be financed through credit. Nowhere was this more true than in trade relations between the American colonies and England. In fact, the Pilgrim settlement at Plymouth was financed through a loan that took twenty-five years to repay.

Originally, English merchants granted terms of twelve months and longer to colonial borrowers because money was scarce and shipping time extended. Moreover, much trade was based on the tobacco crop, which could be harvested only once a year. Bills of exchange and promissory notes, often endorsed, not only traveled between England and the colonies, but from one colony to another to finance trade.

By the 1850's the credit period had been reduced to from four to eight months and more American manufactured goods came into the trade picture. Promissory notes remained common and trade acceptances came into general use. Merchants offered cash discounts of from 5 to 30 percent.

Significant changes in credit practice reflected the significant changes in the entire country caused by the Civil War. The growth of commercial banking had facilitated the use of credit, but now money was untrustworthy and merchants wanted fast payment. Terms fell to thirty to sixty days and cash discounts became a popular way to induce quick collection of receivables. Fast-paced commercial transactions of this period contributed to the development of open-book-account terms.

Since the Civil War, the length of mercantile credit terms has varied but the long terms common in antebellum days were never to become popular again. In fact, as buying pace increased—with customers buying several times during the year or even during one month—shorter terms became the most common. Developments in transportation and communication have contributed to this process. In addition, open-book-account terms have become the predominant form of trade credit and cash discounts have been substantially reduced.

[105]   **IMPORTANCE OF TRADE CREDIT.** Trade credit has become a vital medium in financing the movement of goods and services. In fact, the amount of trade credit on the books of U.S. companies has increased substantially and at a rate more than comparable to the rate of increase in loans that commercial banks have made to business. Those who have followed Dun & Bradstreet figures through the years will notice a change in those reported below. Beginning with figures released by the U.S. government (Securities and Exchange Commission) in 1973, the types of financial and investment corporations excluded from consideration in compiling the figures were redefined. The new revised figures exclude real estate and investment trusts, personal finance companies, business finance companies, security and commodity brokers and dealers. Dun & Bradstreet has recalculated its figures, beginning with those of 1951, on the basis of the new definitions of excluded companies.

[105.1]   **Trade Credit and Bank Loans.** In terms of dollars, total loans by commercial banks rose from $57.7 billion at the end of 1951 to $455.6 billion as of December 31, 1973. Commercial bank loans to business rose from $25.9 billion to $159.9 billion in this same period.

Trade credit outstanding increased from $45.9 billion on December 31, 1951 to $252.2 billion on December 31, 1973. (See Table 1.1.)

[105.2]   **Trade Credit and Other Financial Quantities.** The importance of trade credit can be put in better perspective by comparing it with other financial quantities.

Total corporate trade notes and accounts receivable grew 449.5 percent between 1951 and 1973. On the other hand, inventories rose 272.1 percent in this period and net working capital 197.5 percent. Trade receivables—which means trade credit—grew more than twice as rapidly as net working capital. (See Table 1.2.)

[105.3]   **Trade Credit and Net Working Capital.** There is a very significant comparison between net working capital and trade notes and accounts receivable.

Aggregate net working capital of U.S. corporations rose from $81.3 billion on December 31, 1951 to $241.9 billion on December 31, 1973. On the other hand, the figures show trade notes and accounts receivable accumulated even more rapidly, from $45.9 billion to $252.2 billion.

This means, in other words, that 56.5 percent of corporate net working capital was reflected in trade receivables on December 31, 1951; but on the same date in 1973, receivables were equivalent to 104.3 percent of net working capital. (See Table 1.3.)

By 1973, U.S. corporations had concentrated their "eggs" of corporate liquidity in the "basket" of credit.

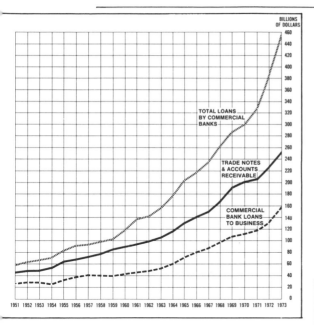

TABLE 1.1

Dollar Growth of Trade Credit

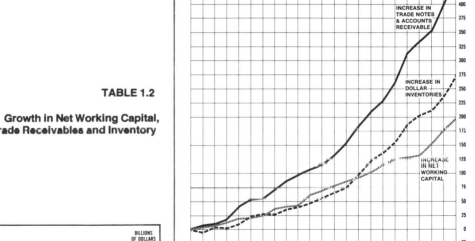

TABLE 1.2

**Growth in Net Working Capital,
Trade Receivables and Inventory**

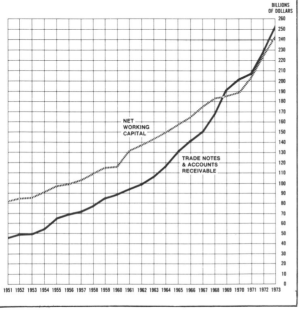

TABLE 1.3

**Dollar Growth in Net Working
Capital and Trade Receivables**

**Sources: U.S. Securities and Exchange
Commission Report on Working Capital
of U.S. Corporations.**

Differences in the Use of Trade Credit. Not all industries use trade credit to the same extent. Table 1.4 shows the variation between merchant wholesalers in the use of credit.

TABLE 1.4
Merchant Wholesalers: Credit Sales as a Percentage of Total Sales (1967)

Wholesale Trade, Total	**85.6**	Farm Products—Raw Materials:	
		Cotton	51.1
Motor Vehicles and Automotive Equipment:		Grain	56.2
Automobiles and other Motor Vehicles	62.0	Livestock	70.2
New and Used Automobiles,		Farm Products—Raw Materials, N.E.C.	(V)
Motorcycles	(V)	Hides, Skins, and Pelts	87.1
Trucks and Tractors—Road Type	70.2	Leaf Tobacco	(V)
		Wool, Wool Tops, and Mohair	(V)
Automotive Equipment	81.9	Other Raw Farm Products	(V)
Automotive Parts, Equipment			
(without Machine Shop)	85.1	Electrical Goods:	
Automotive Parts, Equipment		Electrical Apparatus, Equipment,	
(with Machine Shop)	76.3	Supplies	93.4
Used Automotive Parts and		With Major Appliances and	
Equipment	66.7	Housewares	93.2
Petroleum Products Marketing		With Housewares, but not Major	
Equipment	90.4	Appliances	91.6
Tires and Tubes	80.4	Without Housewares or Major	
		Appliances	93.5
Drugs, Chemicals, and Allied Products:		Electrical Appliances, TV and	
Drugs, Proprietaries, and Sundries	91.2	Radio Sets	91.8
General-Line Drugs	96.0	Electronic Parts and Equipment	87.5
Specialty-Line Drugs and Toiletries	86.2		
		Hardware: Plumbing, Heating Equipment	
Paints and Varnishes	89.8	Supplies:	
Chemicals and Allied Products, N.E.C.	95.0	Hardware	92.7
		General-Line Hardware	93.2
		Specialty-Line Hardware	91.3
Piece Goods, Notions, and Apparel:			
Piece Goods (Woven Fabrics)	97.4	Plumbing and Heating Equipment and	
Piece Goods (Jobbers)	96.1	Supplies	92.9
Piece Goods (Converters)	98.7	Heating Equipment and Supplies	92.5
		Plumbing Fixtures and Supplies	93.0
Notions and Other Dry Goods	97.2		
Men's and Boys' Clothing and		Air-Conditioning, Refrigeration Equipment,	
Furnishings	94.6	Supplies	90.1
Women's, Children's, and Infants'		Air-Conditioning Equipment and	
Clothing	95.9	Supplies	91.3
Footwear	97.4	Refrigeration Equipment and Supplies	88.0
Groceries and Related Products:		Machinery, Equipment, and Supplies:	
General-Line Groceries	79.1	Commercial Machines and Equipment	86.2
Voluntary Group Wholesalers	73.3	Office Machines and Equipment	84.8
Retailer Cooperative Wholesalers	89.1	Restaurant and Hotel Supplies	86.0
Other General-Line Wholesalers	78.8	Store Machines and Fixtures	88.1
		Construction, Mining Machinery,	
Frozen Foods	86.7	Equipment	88.0
Dairy Products	82.1	Farm Machinery and Equipment	87.4
Poultry and Poultry Products	86.0	Industrial Machinery and Equipment	91.7
Confectionery	68.0	Food-processing Machinery and	
Fish and Seafoods	82.4	Equipment	92.5
Meat and Meat Products	89.2	General Purpose Industrial Machinery,	
Fresh Fruits and Vegetables	85.1	Equipment	88.5
		Metalworking Machinery and	
Groceries and Related Products,		Equipment	91.4
N.E.C.	82.8	Materials-Handling Equipment	94.0
Coffee, Tea, and Spices	92.9	Oil Wells: Oil Refinery, Pipeline	
Bread and Baked Goods	75.4	Equipment	97.7
Food and Beverage Basic Materials	72.6	Other Industrial Machinery and	
Other Grocery and Related		Equipment	88.7
Products, N.E.C.	81.6		

Industrial Supplies	95.3	Paper and Its Products:	
General-Line Industrial Supplies	94.3	Printing and Writing (Fine) Paper	97.7
Mechanical Power Transmission		Industrial and Personal Service Papers	93.8
Equipment	95.3	Stationery, Office Supplies, Greeting	
Industrial Valves, Fittings, Equipment	96.9	Cards	91.5
Welding Supplies	90.7		
Other Industrial Supplies	96.0	Furniture and Home Furnishings:	
		Furniture (Household, Office)	89.8
Professional Equipment and Supplies	94.9	Household and Lawn Furniture	89.2
Dental Supplies	93.6	Office and Business Furniture	90.2
Religious and School Supplies	90.0		
Surgical, Medical, and Hospital		Home Furnishings and Floor Coverings	93.6
Supplies	95.5	China, Glassware, Crockery	94.4
Optical and Ophthalmic Goods	96.1	Linens, Domestics, Curtains, etc.	94.4
Other Professional Equipment	97.2	Floor Coverings	93.4
		Other Home Furnishings	93.1
Service Establishment Equipment,			
Supplies	86.6	Lumber and Construction Materials:	
Beauty and Barber Supplies	78.0	Lumber and Millwork	95.4
Custodial Supplies	91.5	Lumber (without yard)	97.0
Laundry and Dry-Cleaning Supplies	87.8	Lumber (with yard)	93.7
Other Service Establishment Supplies	89.3	Plywood, Millwork (Metal or Wood)	95.5
Transportation Equipment Except Motor		Construction Materials	93.0
Vehicles	81.2	Brick, Tile, Cement, etc.	93.4
Aircraft, Aero. Equipment, Parts	77.8	Glass (Flat, Brick)	92.1
Marine Machinery and Equipment	88.1	Roofing, Siding, Insulation Material	93.2
Other Transportation Equipment	90.4	Other Construction Materials	92.7
Metals and Minerals, N.E.C.:			
Coal	94.6	Other Kinds of Wholesale Business:	
Metals Service Centers	96.0	Amusement and Sporting Goods:	
Ferrous Metals Service Centers	95.9	Cameras and Photographic Supplies	92.0
Nonferrous Metals Service Centers	96.1	Sporting Goods	90.0
		Toys, Games, and Fireworks	93.2
Metals Sales Offices	90.9	Other Recreation Goods	85.9
Ferrous Metals Sales Offices	94.2		
Nonferrous Metals Sales Offices	87.3	Books, Periodicals, and Newspapers	91.9
		Farm Supplies	77.2
Petroleum and Petroleum Products	(V)	Jewelry, Diamonds, and Precious	
		Stones	87.4
Scrap and Waste Materials:		Art Goods and Advertising Specialties	93.1
Iron and Steel Scrap	91.9		
With Processing Equipment	92.0	Other Products:	
Without Processing Equipment	91.6	Flowers and Florists' Supplies	85.8
Waste and Secondary Materials	90.7	Forest Products, Except Lumber	85.1
		General Merchandise	81.2
Tobacco and Its Products	71.5	Phonograph Records, Prerecorded	
		Tape	92.4
Beer, Wine, Distilled Alcoholic Beverages:		Musical Instruments and Sheet Music	92.5
Beer and Ale	50.8	Textile Bags, Bagging, and Burlap	93.5
Wine and Distilled Spirits	89.4	Other Wholesalers	90.6
(V)-Insufficient analysis to show separately			

Source: U.S. Department of Commerce

[105.5]   **Trade Credit and the Economy.** All statistics point to the supreme importance of trade credit to the U.S. economy. In fact, between 90 and 95 percent of all business transactions are carried out on the basis of credit.

[106]   **TYPES OF CREDIT.** Credit has different uses depending on its type (adapted from *Consumer and Commercial Credit Management*).

[106.1]   **Public Credit.** Public credit is credit that municipal and state governments and the federal government and its agencies can obtain. The purpose of such credit is to enable the government to perform its functions. It is not self-liquidating, as citizens are expected to pay for it out of taxes and other payments to the government. Public credit is obtained by issuing:

1. State, municipal, and federal bonds.
2. Short-term Treasury notes.
3. Treasury certificates.
4. Treasury bills.

[106.2]   **Consumer or Personal Credit.** Observe that there are four kinds of consumer or personal credit:

[106.2.1]   RETAIL (MERCHANDISE) CREDIT. This is credit advanced by a retailer to an individual to enable him to procure goods upon promise of future payment. Retail credit takes three forms:

1. *Regular charge account.* This is a very common form of retail credit. It means that the customer may purchase any amount of goods up to the limit that a store might set and pay for them later —usually within thirty days. There is no finance or carrying charge.
2. *Revolving charge account.* This is a variation on the regular charge account. It means that a customer can buy any amount of goods up to the limit set by the store. Payment for these goods falls due at a later date—usually thirty days. If the customer does not make payment within the thirty-day period, he then will make monthly payments on the amount owing the store. In such a case, there is a finance charge.
3. *Installment plan.* Installment-plan buying differs from the two previous credit buying methods in the following three important respects:
   a. The arrangement usually involves the purchase of one item, which is paid for over a considerable period of time in equal payments.
   b. A down payment or initial payment on the goods is usually made.
   c. Installment payments may be secured by some legal instrument. Otherwise, installment credit resembles revolving-charge-account credit in that finance or interest charges are made.

[106.2.2]   PERSONAL LOAN CREDIT. Personal loan credit differs from consumer retail credit in these ways:

1. Instead of goods, cash is advanced upon promise of future payment.
2. Credit is not advanced by stores but by:
   a. Banks.
   b. Small loan companies.
   c. Insurance companies.
   d. Savings and loan associations.
   e. Credit card companies.
   f. Credit unions.

Otherwise, personal loan credit resembles retail credit in that:
1. Payments may be made by:
   a. Regular installment.
   b. Single payments.
   c. Graduated installments.
2. Interest or finance charges are usually made.

[106.2.3]   SERVICE CREDIT. Service credit means the receipt of professional services—those of doctors, lawyers, dentists, etc.—by the individual for which he promises future payment.

[106.2.4]   CONSUMER MORTGAGE CREDIT. This form of credit is extended for much longer terms than the other forms of credit and usually involves larger amounts of money.

[106.3]   **Merchandise Credit.** Merchandise credit enables a business to obtain present goods or services from another manufacturer, wholesaler, or retailer upon promise of payment at a specific time in the future. Merchandise-credit transactions may be set up in a number of ways:

[106.3.1]   OPEN ACCOUNT. Sales may be made on open-account terms or evidenced by some negotiable instrument.

[106.3.2]   CONDITIONAL SALES. Sales on a merchandise-credit basis may be conditional, that is, the title will remain with the seller until all payments are made.

[106.3.3]   LEASE-PURCHASE. Sales of capital goods can be made on a lease-purchase arrangement. In this case, the amount paid at each established interval represents an installment payment. After the equivalent to complete payment has been paid, the user may exercise an option to buy the piece of equipment. Finance charges are generally made. Lease purchase arrangements differ from conditional sales in that the buyer may charge lease payments as a current expense while conditional-sales payments must be charged as a capital expenditure.

[106.4]   **Investment Credit.** Investment credit is the extension of the means to purchase or improve land, equipment, buildings, or other fixed assets. Investment credit is often represented by bonds and debentures; it can be unsecured or secured by mortgages or liens. Investment credit is usually extended by:
1. Banks.
2. Government agencies.
3. Institutions.
4. Insurance companies.
5. Underwriters.

[106.5]   **Bank Credit.** Bank credit is of two kinds:

[106.5.1]   BANK CREDIT IN THE FORM OF CHECKS. These are drawn by depositors.

[106.5.2]   BANK LOANS. Bank loans are made to businesses (or individuals) on generally short terms, either secured or unsecured, to finance temporary or unusual needs. Some of these needs are:
1. To finance seasonal requirements.
2. To finance heavy (but temporary) receivables loads.
3. To pay taxes.
4. To pay extraordinary damage charges.
5. To obtain discounts.

Remember that cash credit (represented by bank loans) can also be extended by savings and loan associations, individuals, insurance companies, and other finance companies.

Bank credit in the form of loans differs from merchandise credit in these ways:

1. Cash is advanced instead of goods and services.
2. Repayment terms are generally longer.
3. Banks are more careful in evaluating credit risks because bank credit must be more secure.
4. Bank credit is governed by many laws.

[107]   **DOCUMENTS OF CREDIT.** The documents of credit are the records or evidence that a credit transaction has taken place. Documents of credit can be divided into two groups: nonnegotiable instruments and negotiable instruments.

[107.1]   **Differences between Negotiable and Nonnegotiable Instruments.** The differences between negotiable and nonnegotiable instruments are as follows:

[107.1.1]   RIGHTS UNDER LAW. Nonnegotiable instruments are covered by contract laws while negotiable instruments confer additional rights to the holders.

[107.1.2]   RIGHTS AND TRANSFERS. The original rights of the original holder of a nonnegotiable instrument cannot be enlarged upon transfer of the instrument. In the case of a negotiable instrument, these rights can be expanded. Except for those defenses that would completely nullify the contract, the holder of a negotiable instrument is free from all the other defenses of the maker.

[107.1.3]   PRESUMPTION OF CONSIDERATION. Nonnegotiable instruments do not carry the presumption of consideration; that is, nonnegotiable instruments do not presume that something of value was given to bind the contract. The burden of proof that something of value was given and thus that a contract exists falls upon the seller in the case of a nonnegotiable instrument. Negotiable instruments carry the presumption of consideration. In such a case, it becomes the debtor's burden to show that no consideration was involved and thus that a binding contract does not exist.

[107.1.4]   SALES AND TRANSFERS. Nonnegotiable instruments are more difficult to sell or transfer to third parties.

[107.2]   **Nonnegotiable Instruments: Open-Book Account.** The principal type of nonnegotiable instrument involved in the credit process is the *open-book account*. Open-book-account credit is extended when the seller agrees to deliver goods, services, or other economic values to the buyer upon the buyer's simple promise to pay for them at a future date. Although an invoice may be sent to the buyer, the only record of this transaction is kept on the account books of the seller (where it appears as an "account receivable") and of the buyer (where it appears as an "account payable"). The actual form of the record books may vary considerably. Some possibilities are:

1. Hand-written ledgers, which are the simplest form.
2. Machine-posted ledgers, where a machine records the sales-credit transactions on a separate card for each account.
3. Punch-card ledgers, where the sales-credit information is key-punched onto a card.
4. Computer-stored ledgers where sales-credit information is stored in a computer data bank.

Open-book-account credit is the most extensive form of mercantile credit in use. There are several reasons for this, including the following:

1. Open-book-account credit offers the least sales resistance because the buyer does not have to acknowledge debt by signing some legal instrument.
2. Open-book-account credit is the most easily adaptable to use of cash discount terms.
3. Open-book-account credit is most flexible when extensions or other adjustments are to be made.

[107.3]   **Negotiable Instruments.**

[107.3.1]   REQUIREMENTS. In order for a credit instrument to be negotiable, it must contain a promise or order to pay a fixed or easily determined sum of money and be:

1. Signed by the maker or drawer.
2. Unconditional.
3. Payable on demand or at a definite time.
4. Payable to order or to the bearer.

Note also the following requirements:

1. *Title.* In order for someone to have title to a negotiable instrument, it must be delivered to him.
2. *Liability.* In order for someone to become liable under a negotiable instrument, he must sign it. An agent may sign for a principal if he indicates the principal's name. If he does not, the agent then becomes liable.

[107.3.2]   CLASSIFICATION. The requirements of a negotiable instrument suggest two broad classifications that can be made:

1. *Promises to pay and orders to pay.*
   a. *Promises to pay* involve only two parties: the maker of the instrument and the payee. The maker simply promises to pay to the payee a certain sum of money at a certain time.
   b. *Orders to pay* involve three parties: the maker or drawer, the payee, and the agent. The maker orders the agent to pay a certain sum of money to the payee. Remember that one negotiable instrument can change from a promise to pay into an order to pay during different phases of its existence.
2. *Bearer instruments and order instruments.*
   a. *Bearer instruments* are negotiated upon simple delivery or presentation alone.
   b. *Order instruments* are negotiated upon delivery and endorsement and can involve a succession of payees in addition to the original one.

FIGURE 1.1. Check

KINDS OF NEGOTIABLE INSTRUMENTS.

    1. *Checks.* Checks (see Figure 1.1) are written orders by depositors to banks to pay a certain amount of money, which the bank is holding for that purpose, to a named person or entity.

    Checks are not commonly thought of as credit instruments since they assume that instantaneous payment will be made upon presentation. As a result, checks are virtually considered as money.

    Nevertheless, checks present credit risks because there is no guarantee that the maker has sufficient funds to cover the check when he makes it or that he will have sufficient funds to cover the check when the payee presents it. Despite the existence of bad-check laws, which make it a crime to write checks when the maker knows he has insufficient funds and thus intends to defraud the payee, thousands of checks are returned every year because of insufficient funds.

    Therefore, before accepting a check from a customer assure yourself that he is worthy of your confidence. Checking with the bank is not enough for two reasons:

    a. The maker could stop payment on the check before you cash it.

    b. The maker could have sufficient funds to cover the check at the time he makes it, but the funds could have been depleted by the time you cash it. In this connection, remember to cash checks promptly. Unreasonable delay in cashing checks may remove the maker's liability if there are insufficient funds at the time of the check's presentation.

    2. *Certified checks.* (see Figure 1.2) When there is some reason that you question the credit worthiness—or honesty—of a customer and don't want to accept a check, you can request a certified check. A certified check is a personal check upon which the bank has stamped "Certified." An authorized bank official must initial it and the money must already have been deducted from the depositor's account. In effect, a certified check signifies the bank's acceptance of the risk.

    3. *Cashier's checks.* Cashier's checks (see Figure 1.3) are checks written by the bank upon itself when a depositor has advanced the money to the bank. They rank with certified checks as

FIGURE 1.2. Certified Check

guaranteed forms of credit risks and should be required from customers of dubious credit responsibility.

4. *Postdated checks.* Postdated checks are personal checks payable later than the day on which they are written. Because of this element of futurity, postdated checks are not considered orders to pay, but promises to pay. There is no guarantee beyond the general credit worthiness of the customer that there will be sufficient funds to cover the check when it is presented. Nevertheless, postdated checks—especially a series of postdated checks—can be an effective way to encourage your customer to settle his trade debt.

5. *Promissory notes.* A promissory note is an unconditional promise in writing made by one person to another, signed by the maker, agreeing to pay on demand or at a fixed or determinable time, a definite sum of money to order or to bearer. Promissory notes may be straight, that is, there may be but a single one to cover one specific transaction (see Figure 1.4); or they may be serial, that is, a series of notes to cover one or more transactions (see Figure 1.5).

Promissory notes, though frequently used in bank credit, are rarely used in business credit transactions. When they are, it

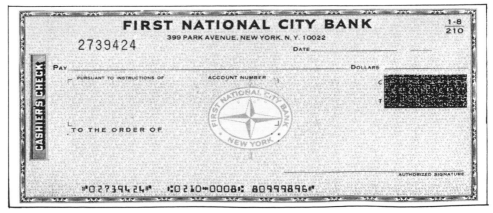

FIGURE 1.3. Cashier's Check

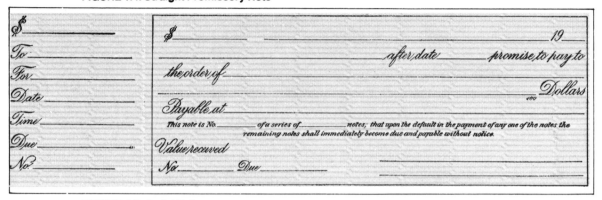

FIGURE 1.4. Straight Promissory Note

FIGURE 1.5. Serial Note

is generally to close out a past-due account for which credit was originally extended on open-account terms or to enhance the credit risk of a doubtful customer. To accomplish these goals, the promissory note has these advantages which have been identified by Albert F. Chapin and George E. Hassett, Jr., in *Credit and Collection Principles and Practice:*

a. It is positive evidence of debt.
b. It definitely fixes the time and the amount of payment.
c. It largely precludes the possibility of dispute as to quantity and quality of goods.
d. It is a more effective means of securing prompt payment.
e. It has a higher value as a salable asset than the open account.

However, remember that promissory notes are not guarantees that payments will be made. They are not even security; they are evidence of a debt. When required at the time of a sale, moreover, they can offend your customers by implying that their credit standing is poor. Finally, promissory notes can tie up your credit department in bookkeeping and legal procedures. Promissory notes come in the following forms:

a. *Single-name Paper.* Single-name paper is a note that is signed by the maker alone. His credit worthiness is the only assurance that the note will be honored.
b. *Double-name paper.* This is a promissory note signed by two or

more makers or signed by the maker and endorsed by other people. In such a case, the credit of the additional makers and/or endorsers stands behind the note. For this reason, it increases the likelihood of repayment and can be more easily discounted.

c. *Collateral notes.* Collateral notes are promissory notes secured by some form of collateral that the customer pledged to the seller. Depending on the form of the collateral, different factors should be considered in evaluating the degree to which it enhances the credit risk:

(1) *Pledge of accounts receivable.* You must appraise the credit worthiness of the customers to whom your customer has been selling. Is adequate provision made, in the accounting of receivables, for bad debts? In the event of default on the note, will you have trouble collecting the receivables?

(2) *Inventory liens.* You must appraise the true value of the inventory, taking into consideration whether it consists of finished goods, raw materials, or works in progress. Ask yourself how long it will take to convert inventory into cash, or partially completed products into finished products.

(3) *Securities.* Make sure securities are registered and fully paid for. Make sure that there is no stockholders' agreement that prohibits the stock from being used as collateral. Try to appraise accurately the market value of the stock. In appraising the value of securities as collateral, take into account voting and dividend rights as well as the speed with which you could sell the stock itself.

(4) *Fixtures and equipment.* Fixtures and equipment enhance a credit risk, when assigned as collateral, to the degree which the fixtures or equipment could be converted to cash. Verify the salability of the items; make sure that they remain in the condition in which they existed when they were evaluated. The procedures by which these different items are offered as collateral in secured transactions are specified in Article 9 of the Uniform Commercial Code, discussed more fully in Chapter 5.

d. *Judgment notes.* Judgment notes, a special form of promissory note, are given as a separate agreement in which the maker agrees to have a judgment recovered against him if he defaults in his payments. Judgment notes are negotiable—like any other negotiable instrument—but be aware that the provisions for recovery may not be enforced.

e. *Bonds.* Bonds of all kinds, government as well as private, are another form of promissory note, although they differ in respect to the extent of their regulations, the complexity of their provisions, and the quality of the protection they give.

f. *Drafts.* A draft (See Figure 1.6) is a written order made by one party directing another party to pay him a definite amount of

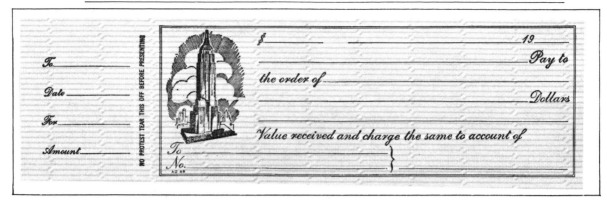

FIGURE 1.6. Draft

money. When the draft directs a party to pay someone other than the maker of the draft, the draft is then known as a *bill of exchange.*

Simple drafts are of two types:

(1) *Sight drafts.* A sight draft is one that is payable immediately upon acceptance.

(2) *Time drafts.* A time draft is one that is payable at a specified time after the draft has been accepted.

Drafts do not become valid negotiable credit instruments until they have been accepted by the buyer. He does this by writing "accepted" across the face of the draft and indicating the time (if a sight draft) and the place of payment. Drafts are usually paid through banks. Drafts are not often used in mercantile credit transactions because they imply that the buyer is a very poor credit risk. Because of this, they are most frequently used in conjunction with bills of lading and to close out past-due accounts. For this purpose, they have the same advantages as the promissory note. You will observe that they differ from promissory notes (and other legal negotiable instruments) in that they are drawn by the seller (creditor) himself and not by the debtor.

FIGURE 1.7. Trade Acceptance

Drafts can be drawn upon the buyer's bank instead of the buyer himself and this is often a good way to reduce the negative impact a draft carries.

g. *Trade acceptances.* Trade acceptances (see Figure 1.7) are the same as simple drafts with this difference: They arise out of a single transaction involving the sale and the purchase of merchandise. Because of this, a trade acceptance cannot truly be used to refinance previously existing debt, and it should not be renewed.

APPLICATION FOR COMMERCIAL LETTER OF CREDIT

FIRST NATIONAL CITY BANK
111 WALL STREET, NEW YORK, N. Y., 10015

______________________________ 19____
(PLACE AND DATE)

GENTLEMEN:

PURSUANT TO THE CONTINUING COMMERCIAL CREDIT AGREEMENT HERETOFORE EXECUTED BY THE UNDERSIGNED AND DELIVERED TO YOU, THE UNDERSIGNED HEREBY REQUESTS YOU TO OPEN YOUR ☐ IRREVOCABLE ☐ REVOCABLE CREDIT (HEREINAFTER CALLED THE CREDIT'), AS FOLLOWS:

IN FAVOR OF ______________ (NAME) ______________ (ADDRESS)

FOR ACCOUNT OF ______________ (NAME) ______________ (ADDRESS)

UP TO THE AGGREGATE AMOUNT OF ______________

AVAILABLE BY ______________ (SIGNIFY TENOR) DRAFTS DRAWN, AT YOUR OPTION, ON YOU OR YOUR CORRESPONDENTS

FOR ______________ PER CENT, INVOICE COST WHEN ACCOMPANIED BY THE FOLLOWING DOCUMENTS AS CHECKED:

☐ SPECIAL CUSTOMS INVOICE
☐ "ON BOARD" OCEAN BILLS OF LADING, (FULL SET REQUIRED IF MORE THAN ONE ORIGINAL ISSUED)

EVIDENCING SHIPMENT TO ______________ (OCEAN PORT OF DESTINATION)

DRAWN TO ORDER OF FIRST NATIONAL CITY BANK

NOTIFY ______________ (NAME) ______________ (ADDRESS)

☐ COMMERCIAL INVOICE STATING THAT IT COVERS
☐ MARINE INSURANCE POLICY OR CERTIFICATE (FULL SET REQUIRED IF MORE THAN ONE ORIGINAL ISSUED)
☐ WAR RISK INSURANCE ALSO REQUIRED
☐ OTHER INSURANCE ______________ (IF OTHER INSURANCE IS REQUESTED, STATE RISKS TO BE COVERED)

☐ OTHER DOCUMENTS ______________

INSURANCE TO BE EFFECTED BY ______________ (IF EFFECTED BY SHIPPER, INSURANCE MUST BE ISSUED IN THE CURRENCY OF THE CREDIT)

BILLS OF LADING TO BE DATED NOT LATER THAN ______________

BILLS OF EXCHANGE TO BE NEGOTIATED NOT LATER THAN ______________

ADDITIONAL PROVISIONS TO BE INCLUDED IN THE CREDIT:

ALL DOCUMENTS LISTED HEREIN ARE TO BE FORWARDED BY NEGOTIATING BANK TO FIRST NATIONAL CITY BANK, NEW YORK, N. Y. BY AIR MAIL IN A SINGLE MAILING

"We hereby certify that transactions in the merchandise covered by this application are not prohibited under the Foreign Assets Control Regulations of the United States Treasury Department and that any importation covered by this application conforms in every respect with all existing United States Government regulations."

FORTHWITH UPON THE OPENING OF THE CREDIT, KINDLY BE GUIDED BY WHICHEVER OF THE FOLLOWING IS CHECKED:

CHECK ONE

☐ FORWARD THE ORIGINAL CREDIT INSTRUMENT BY ☐ AIR MAIL ☐ ORDINARY MAIL
TO ______________ (NAME) ______________ (ADDRESS)
DIRECTLY OR THROUGH YOUR CORRESPONDENT, AT YOUR OPTION, UNLESS OTHERWISE INDICATED HEREIN.

☐ CABLE ALL THE TERMS AND CONDITIONS OF THE CREDIT TO YOUR CORRESPONDENT REQUESTING THAT THE BENEFICIARY BE NOTIFIED OF THE OPENING OF THE CREDIT, UNLESS OTHERWISE INDICATED HEREIN.

☐ NOTIFY THE BENEFICIARY BY CABLE THROUGH YOUR CORRESPONDENT THAT YOU ARE FORWARDING THE ORIGINAL CREDIT INSTRUMENT BY AIR MAIL, UNLESS OTHERWISE INDICATED HEREIN.

SHIPPING DOCUMENTS FOR CUSTOM HOUSE ENTRY ARE TO BE SENT BY YOU TO ______________ (NAME)
______________ (ADDRESS)

VERY TRULY YOURS,

____
PLEASE SIGN WITH AN AUTHORIZED SIGNATURE REGISTERED WITH US.

FOR BANK USE ONLY

LIAB. CLASS	SYMBOL	AMOUNT	TENOR DRAFT	DRAFT ON	PREPARED BY
CUSTOMERS CODE		ADVISE CREDIT THRU			DATE

SF 1358 (L) REV. 7-69

FIGURE 1.8. Application for Commercial Letter of Credit

To be a valid negotiable instrument, it must be accepted by the buyer in the same way in which he would accept any draft. Like other drafts, trade acceptances risk offending a customer because they are generally required of poorer credit risks. Nevertheless, they can be easily negotiated. If accompanied by an offer of a substantial cash discount if immediate payment is forthcoming, trade acceptances can even lead to very fast payment of trade obligations.

h. *Bank acceptances.* Bank acceptances are the same as trade acceptances with this difference: They are drawn upon the customer's bank instead of upon the customer himself. They are made at the instigation of the *buyer*, who asks the bank to accept a draft payable to a seller when the seller considers the buyer a poor risk. In effect, the bank is extending credit to the buyer and may require the buyer to pay for the service or put up collateral. As far as the seller is concerned, this form of protection is very secure indeed.

i. *Letters of credit.* Letters of credit (see Figure 1.8) are generally used to finance foreign trade, but they can be used within the United States. In effect, a letter of credit substitutes the bank's credit for the credit of a company because the bank

CHART 1.1. Import Letter of Credit Procedure

(Process is reversed in EXPORT L/C procedure in which Foreign Buyer provides L/C against which Domestic Seller draws drafts.)

Domestic Buyer

Presents Title Documents— Pays Custom Duty— Removes Goods

Foreign Seller

(4) Ships Goods Order of Bank—Customer as ultimate destination

(1) Arranges L/C with Bank

Collects from Buyer— Surrenders Shipping (Title) Documents (8)

Dock

(5) Draws Drafts against L/C— Attaches Shipping & Insurance Documents & Invoice

Notifies seller that L/C has been opened— terms, etc. (3)

Local Bank

Foreign Bank forwards Invoice, Shipping Documents, Paid Drafts, & Collateral Papers. (7)

Foreign Bank (6) pays draft against credit or funds of Issuing Bank

(2) Forwards original L/C—Authorization to accept Drafts drawn against it.

Use of Trust Receipt at Point (8)
Buyer occasionally may arrange to take in goods and process them before paying local bank. Bank then requires him to execute a Trust Receipt which states the conditions under which possession of the goods is permitted before payment.

(Uniform Domestic Straight Bill of Lading, adopted by Carriers in Official Southern, Western and Illinois Classification territories, March 15, 1922, as amended August 1, 1930, and June 15, 1941.)

UNIFORM STRAIGHT BILL OF LADING

(PRESCRIBED BY THE INTERSTATE COMMERCE COMMISSION)

ORIGINAL—NOT NEGOTIABLE

Shipper's No.________

Agent's No.________

________________Company

RECEIVED, Subject to the classifications and tariffs in effect on the date of the issue of this Bill of Lading,

AT________________, 19

FROM________________

the property described below, in apparent good order, except as noted (contents and condition of contents of packages unknown), marked, consigned, and destined as indicated below, which said company (the word company being understood throughout this contract as meaning any person or corporation in possession of the property under the contract) agrees to carry to its usual place of delivery at said destination, if on its own road or its own water line, otherwise to deliver to another carrier on the route to said destination. It is mutually agreed, as to each carrier of all or any of said property over all or any portion of said route to destination, and as to each party at any time interested in all or any of said property, that every service to be performed hereunder shall be subject to all the conditions not prohibited by law, whether printed or written, herein contained, including the conditions on back hereof, which are hereby agreed to by the shipper and accepted for himself and his assigns.

(Mail or street address of consignee—For purposes of notification only.)

Consigned to________________

Destination________ State of________ County of________

Route________________

________ Car Initial________ Car No.________

(Delivering Carrier)

NO. PACKAGES	DESCRIPTION OF ARTICLES, SPECIAL MARKS, AND EXCEPTIONS	*WEIGHT (Subject to Correction)	CLASS OR RATE	CHECK COL.

If this shipment is to be delivered to the consignee without recourse on the consignor, the consignor shall sign the following statement:

The carrier shall not make delivery of this shipment without payment of freight and all other lawful charges. *(See Section 7 of conditions.)*

(Signature of Consignor.)

If charges are to be prepaid, write or stamp here, "To Be Prepaid."

Received $________ to apply in prepayment of the charges on the property described hereon.

Agent or Cashier.

Per________

(The signature here acknowledges only the amount prepaid.)

Charges advanced:

$________

1

* If the shipment moves between two ports by a carrier by water, the law requires that the bill of lading shall state whether it is "carrier's or shipper's weight."

NOTE.—Where the rate is dependent on value, shippers are required to state specifically in writing the agreed or declared value of the property.

The agreed or declared value of the property is hereby specifically stated by the shipper to be not exceeding

per

________*Shipper.* ________*Agent.*

Per________ Per________

*Permanent Post-office address of Shipper*________

The fibre boxes used for this shipment conform to the specifications set forth in the box-maker's certificate thereon, and all other requirements of Rule 41 Consolidated Freight Classifications.

FIGURE 1.9. Uniform Straight Bill of Lading

agrees to honor drafts presented to it for the payment of merchandise shipped by a seller to a customer. (See Chart 1.1 for a description of the import letter of credit procedure.) A letter of credit is a more easily negotiated instrument if it is:

(1) *Confirmed,* that is, if the local (or American) bank that is designated to accept the draft confirms that it will in fact do so.

(2) *Irrevocable,* that is, that payment for a shipment of goods will be made regardless of subsequent difficulties the buyer might experience.

j. *Bills of lading.* Bills of lading are not actually instruments of credit, but they are often used with sight drafts so you should be familiar with them. In fact, the bill of lading is a document issued by a common carrier to a shipper and serves three purposes:

(1) Receipt for shipment of goods.
(2) Contract to deliver goods.
(3) Document of title.

Bills of lading are of two types:

(1) *Straight bill of lading* (see Figure 1.9), which is not negotiable and in which control of the goods covered is transferred to the purchaser.

(2) *Order bill of lading* (see Figure 1.10). In this case, control remains with the seller until he receives the bill of lading made out to him (or some third party) and he (or the third party) endorses it.

When a sight draft is attached to the order bill of lading (S.D.–B.L.), the procedure is as follows:

(1) You, as seller, attach the sight draft drawn on your customer to an order bill of lading that you have endorsed to that customer.

(Uniform Domestic Order Bill of Lading, adopted by Carriers in Official, Southern, Western and Illinois Classification territories, March 15, 1922, as amended August 1, 1930, and June 15, 1941.)

UNIFORM ORDER BILL OF LADING Shipper's No.________

ORIGINAL Agent's No.________

________________________**Company**

RECEIVED, subject to the classifications and tariffs in effect on the date of the issue of this Bill of Lading,

at________________________________19

from________________________

the property described below, in apparent good order, except as noted (contents and condition of contents of packages unknown), marked, consigned, and destined as indicated below, which said company (the word company being understood throughout this contract as meaning any person or corporation in possession of the property under the contract) agrees to carry to its usual place of delivery at said destination, if on its own road or its own water line, otherwise to deliver to another carrier on the route to said destination. It is mutually agreed, as to each carrier of all or any of said property over all or any portion of said route to destination, and as to each party at any time interested in all or any of said property, that every service to be performed hereunder shall be subject to all the conditions not prohibited by law, whether printed or written, herein contained, including the conditions on back hereof, which are hereby agreed to by the shipper and accepted for himself and his assigns.

The Surrender of the Original ORDER Bill of Lading properly indorsed shall be required before the delivery of the property. Inspection of property covered by the bill of lading will not be permitted unless provided by law or unless permission is indorsed on the original bill of lading or given in writing by the shipper.

(Mail or street address of consignee—For purposes of notification only.)

Consigned to **ORDER OF**________________________

Destination____________ State of____________ County of____________

Notify________________________

At____________ State of____________ County of____________

Route________________________

Delivering carrier____________ Car Initial____________ Car No.____________

No. Packages	DESCRIPTION OF ARTICLES, SPECIAL MARKS, AND EXCEPTIONS	*WEIGHT (Subject to Correction)	CLASS OR RATE	CHECK COLUMN

Subject to Section 7 of conditions. If this shipment is to be delivered to the consignee without recourse on the consignor, the consignor shall sign the following statement:

The carrier shall not make delivery of this shipment without payment of freight and all other lawful charges.

____
(Signature of consignor.)

If charges are to be prepaid write or stamp here, "To be Prepaid."

Received $________ to apply in prepayment of the charges on the property described hereon.

____
Agent or Cashier.

Per____________
(The signature here acknowledges only the amount prepaid.)

Charges Advanced:

$________

*If the shipment moves between two ports by a carrier by water, the law requires that the bill of lading shall state whether it is "carrier's or shipper's weight."

NOTE.—Where the rate is dependent on value, shippers are required to state specifically in writing the agreed or declared value of the property.

The agreed or declared value of the property is hereby specifically stated by the shipper to be not exceeding

____________ per ____________

The fibre boxes used for this shipment conform to the specifications set forth in the box maker's certificate thereon, and all other requirements of rule 41 of the Consolidated Freight Classification.

____________ Shipper. ____________ Agent.

Per____________ Per____________

*Permanent post-office address of shipper*____________

FIGURE 1.10. Uniform Order Bill of Lading

(2) Have your bank forward these papers to your customer's bank or a bank in his city.

(3) The bank in his city will present the sight draft to your customer for payment.

(4) Once the customer has accepted and paid the draft, the bank turns over the order bill of lading to him.

(5) Your customer presents the order bill of lading to the shipper and takes possession (and title) of the goods.

[108]   **TERMS OF SALE.** The terms under which a product or service is sold vary considerably from industry to industry, from region to region, and from company to company. As adapted from William J. Shultz and Hedwig Reinhardt, whose analysis in *Credit and Collection Management* is followed below, three fundamental factors govern the length of terms.

[108.1]   **Factors Determining Trade Terms.**

[108.1.1]   CIRCUMSTANCES SURROUNDING THE PRODUCT SOLD. This means inventory turnover. The length of the terms of sale varies in direct proportion to the rate of inventory turnover. Thus:

1. Raw materials are sold on shorter terms than finished products.
2. Perishable goods are sold on shorter terms than durable goods (equipment is often sold on installment terms stretching over months).
3. Standardized products and standard brands may be sold on shorter terms than unknown, slower-moving goods.
4. Cheaper products are sold on shorter terms than expensive products.
5. Nonseasonal products are sold on shorter terms than seasonal products.

[108.1.2]   CIRCUMSTANCES SURROUNDING THE BUYER. These include:

1. *Location.* Rural buyers often get longer terms than city buyers; close buyers get shorter terms than buyers located at a distance.
2. *Risk.* Good credit risks often get longer terms than poorer credit risks.
3. *Quantity.* Customers buying in small quantities often get shorter terms than those buying in larger quantities.
4. *Method of operation.* Retailers and wholesalers often get shorter terms than manufacturers.
5. *Competition.* The more competition there is to buy a scarce product, the shorter the terms are likely to be.

[108.1.3]   CIRCUMSTANCES SURROUNDING THE SELLER. These include:

1. *Liquidity.* Sellers in need of cash will require shorter terms than those with a strong liquid position.
2. *Competition.* The more competition there is to sell a product, the longer the terms are likely to be.

[108.2]   **Classification of Trade Terms.** Selling terms fall into these two groups:

[108.2.1]   NET TERMS. Net terms give no incentive for the buyer to pay before the due date. In other words, no discount privilege is extended. Regardless of when the bill is paid, the buyer must pay the full amount.

The most common net terms are those calling for payment thirty days or sixty days after the date of the invoice. These terms are expressed as "net 30 days" (or "net 30") and "net 60 days."

[108.2.2]   DISCOUNT TERMS. Discount terms—those that allow an amount of money to be deducted from the selling price as a reward for fast payment —are granted when the seller hopes to encourage the buyer to pay for his purchase in a short period of time or as an inducement for the customer to buy that particular seller's product instead of another.

1. *Reasons why a seller would want fast payment:*
    a. To eliminate the need for bank borrowing to finance receivables.
    b. To eliminate the cost of carrying receivables.
    c. To eliminate bad debts that increase as payments are delayed.
    d. To take advantage of cash discounts the seller's suppliers offer him.
2. Discount terms are expressed as a percentage of the amount of the invoice.
3. To earn the discount, the customer must pay the invoice within a stated period of time.
4. *Cash discounts* should not be confused with *trade discounts,* which are a selling or pricing device. In quoting prices in a catalog, for instance, a wholesaler may use a figure such as $27 less 15 percent less 10 percent. This means that the buyer is able to get 15 percent off the list price and an additional 10 percent off the remainder. Trade discounts are used to encourage large purchases, to save printing expenses because different trade discounts can be given while the printed list price in a catalog can remain the same, and to disguise the wholesale price from the retail price so that consumers will not know what a company's markup is.
5. In some industries, net terms and discount terms are the same provided that payments are made on time. That is, the time allowed for payment of an invoice is the same as the time allowed for payment with deduction of a discount. In such cases, the cash discount becomes, in effect, a trade discount; it is also larger than the usual trade discount.
6. *Unearned discounts.* Some companies do not pay their bills within the discount period and yet deduct the discount from their payments. Such companies, when they make a practice of this habit, are not worthy of credit confidence. In fact, they are poor credit risks.

      As a creditor, moreover, you should be aware that if you allow some companies to take unearned cash discounts in order to keep their business, but do not allow other companies to take them, you may be violating the Robinson-Patman Act.

[108.3]   **The Terms Themselves.** Following is an explanation of trade selling terms.

[108.3.1]   PREPAYMENT TERMS. These terms, which are not true credit terms because they require the customer to pay with no risk of loss to the seller, include the following:

1. *C.B.D.* (Cash before Delivery) or *C.W.O.* (Cash with Order). These terms require payment before a shipment is sent or the goods manufactured.
2. *C.O.D.* (Cash on Delivery). These terms require payment at the time of delivery. In the event that payment is refused, the seller must absorb any shipping, insurance, and related charges.
3. *S.D.–B.L.* (Sight Draft–Bill of Lading). Once again, as with C.O.D. terms, title to the goods remains with the seller—moreover, secured by the Bill of Lading held by a third party (bank)—until the buyer actually pays for the goods. If the buyer should refuse payment, however, the seller must absorb the shipping costs.
4. *Other advance payment terms.* In some industries and in some special circumstances in other industries, the very high cost of producing a manufactured article may induce the seller to require partial payment or the first of several installment payments to be made before manufacturing begins. This is not necessarily a reflection of the credit worthiness of the customer; it may also be a means of financing manufacture of the product, i.e. financing the seller's needs in order to begin it. These terms, in addition to C.B.D. terms, are the only real prepayment terms.

[108.3.2]   CASH TERMS. Cash terms in effect require payment within ten days, so they are true credit terms. These terms arise from the idea that the buyer should have time to receive and verify the order before making payment.

[108.3.3]   SPOT-CASH TERMS. These terms refer to the immediate payment upon receipt of goods. They are used most frequently in connection with the sale of smaller amounts of merchandise when the buyer and seller meet face-to-face and exchange merchandise for cash on the "spot."

[108.3.4]   INDIVIDUAL-ORDER TERMS. These open-book-account terms come into play when the customer does not order frequently enough for multiple-order billing at the end of the month.

In such cases, the period of the net terms begins on the date of invoicing. Sometimes, to allow a distant customer a fairer deal on discounts, the seller will offer his goods on R.O.G. (Receipt of Goods) or A.O.G. (Arrival of Goods) terms. These are more common when the goods are shipped by water or some other slow method.

[108.3.5]   MULTIPLE-ORDER TERMS. These open-book-account terms come into play when a customer orders frequently and one invoice covers several shipments made during a single period. These terms include:

1. *E.O.M.* (End of Month). This means that all orders are billed on a single invoice written and dated at the end of the month (usually the twenty-fifth). The payment period allowed by the terms begins on the invoicing date, or—in practice—the first day of the following month. Cash discounts are generally larger than in individual order terms but the cash-discount period usually coincides with the net-payment period (8% 10 E.O.M.). The credit period may be as long as forty days, depending on the airmail shipping dates. There is rarely a net due date.
2. *M.O.M.* (Middle of Month). This means that all orders are billed

on an invoice that is issued twice a month (or biweekly). The credit period would run to the 25th for the shipments of the first half of the month, and to the 10th of the following month for shipments during the second half of the month.

3. *Prox.* (Proximo—or at some specified date in the following month). These terms are similar to E.O.M. terms; however, a net period is generally added, the cash discount is lower and these terms are used in fields where E.O.M. terms are not (Example: 2 10 prox. net 30).

[108.3.6]   BILL-TO-BILL (Drop Delivery). On each delivery, the bill for the previous delivery is collected. Gasoline delivery to retailers is often on this basis and is called "Load-to-Load."

[108.3.7]   CONSIGNMENT TERMS. The seller, by consigning merchandise to another, transfers physical possession of the goods but not legal title to them. An element of credit is involved as the consignor (the manufacturer or wholesaler) must have faith in the integrity of the consignee (the retailer). The consignor must be sure that the consignee will (1) protect the goods in his possession and (2) make remittance to the consignor when the merchandise is sold. Important legal considerations govern consignment terms, the most significant of which are:

1. The merchandise consigned must be kept separate from other goods and clearly labeled.
2. Revenue from the sale of the consigned merchandise must be kept separate from the proceeds from the sale of other goods.
3. Insurance on the goods must be provided by the consignee for the consignor.

[108.4]   **Dating.** Dating, or the granting of longer credit periods, includes two practices:

[108.4.1]   SEASONAL DATING. Seasonal dating means that goods are sold but that the credit period does not begin until later—when the selling season for the customer begins. Seasonal dating works to the advantage of the seller, as it moves his goods, and to the advantage of the buyer, as it enables him to have goods on hand at the beginning of the selling season. This type of dating is effected by postdating the invoice to a later date.

[108.4.2]   EXTRA DATING. Extra dating means granting extended terms for some specific unusual circumstances. It is the customary way to give particularly long, identical credit and discount periods (2 10 60 extra = 2/70/70).

[108.5]   **Anticipation.** Anticipation occurs when a customer takes a deduction (it is part of the terms) in addition to the cash discount, which is usually one-half of one percent per month, when he pays before the due date of a long credit period. Thus, anticipation most often occurs when extra dating is granted, but also with E.O.M. and prox. terms, even with individual-order terms.

TERMS OF SALE
EXPLANATION OF TERMS

E.O.M.—End of Month—In trade practice, goods invoiced prior to the twenty-fifth of the month are payable or subject to discount up to the tenth of the following month. If invoiced on the twenty-fifth or later, payment and discount date is figured as the tenth day of the second following month.

PROXIMO OR PROX—Next month.

2/10/30, 2%-10 NET 30, 2/10 N 30—Are identical in meaning. A 2 percent discount is allowed if bill is paid within ten days—the full amount is due in thirty days.

10TH AND 25TH OF EACH MONTH—Purchases made between the first and fifteenth of the month are due on the twenty-fifth of that month, purchases made between the sixteenth and thirtieth are due on the tenth of the following month.

Numbers in parentheses denote standard industrial classification code numbers.

Manufacturers

Agricultural Implements: (SIC—3522) 2%—10 Net 30 and 1%—10 Net 30 on smaller items. Seasonal datings and notes up to 180 days used for larger implements.

Airplane Parts and Accessories: (SIC—3722-23-29) Principally 1/2%—10 Net 30. Also 1%—10 Net 30 and Net 30 days.

Automobile Parts and Accessories: (SIC—3714) Primarily 2%—10th Prox.

Bakeries: (SIC—2051-52) Generally cash with some weekly and monthly terms. Also some concerns report granting 1%—10 Net 30 on products such as cookies and fruit cakes.

Bedsprings and Mattresses: (SIC—2515) Mainly 2%—10 Net 30 and 2%—15 Net 30. Some concerns also report 2%—30 Net 60.

Blouses and Waists: (SIC—2331) 8%—10 E.O.M.

Bodies, Auto, Bus, and Truck: (SIC—3712-13) Mostly Net 30 days. Some Net 10th Prox and Net 10 days. Several concerns report using installment contracts in some instances.

Bolts, Screws, Nuts, and Nails: (SIC—3451-52) 1/2%—10 Net 30. Also 1/2%—10th & 25th Net 30. Some concerns report terms up to 2%—10 Net 30 and 2%—10th Prox, Net 30.

Books, Publishing, and Printing: (SIC—2731-32) Net 30 days. Extended terms given to selected accounts. Special seasonal datings granted to college bookstores for textbooks.

Breweries: (SIC—2082) Cash in most states by law. Where credit is permitted terms are usually load to load, Net 10 days, and Net 30 days.

Chemicals, Agricultural: (SIC—2871-72-79) Principally Net 30 days. Varying discount terms are also reported by some concerns. Most companies give additional time either through seasonal datings or extended terms.

Coats and Suits, Men's and Boys': (SIC—2311) Net 30 days and Net 10 E.O.M. Also some Net 60 days.

Coats and Suits, Women's: (SIC—2337) 8%—10 E.O.M. Datings granted at beginning of spring and fall seasons.

Communication Equipment: (SIC—3661-62) Mostly Net 30 days. 1%—10 Net 30 also offered by some concerns.

Concrete, Gypsum, and Plaster Products: (SIC—3271-72-73) Considerable variance depending on product with 2%—10 Net 30 most widely used. Also 2%—15 Net 30.

Confectionery Products: (SIC—2071-72-73) 2%—10 Net 30. Datings given during special seasonal promotions.

Construction Machinery: (SIC—3531-32-33) Mostly Net 30 days on smaller machinery with various contract terms given on larger equipment.

Cosmetics, Perfumes, and Toilet Preparations: (SIC—2844) 2%—30 days and 1%—30 days. Some companies still report giving 2%—10 Net 30 and 1%—10 Net 30, but because of competition and an effort to improve customer cooperation, the trend is to extend the discount period.

Cotton-Cloth Mills: (SIC—2211) Generally Net 10 days. In addition to Net 10 days, several concerns grant 60 extra days at a 1% interest charge. Seasonal datings are also reported.

Dairy Products: (SIC—2021-22-23-24-26) Mainly cash and Net 7 days. Some Net 30 days.

Dresses, Women's, Misses' and Juniors': (SIC—2335) 8%—10 E.O.M. Some Net E.O.M. also reported.

Drugs: (SIC—2831-33-34) Generally 1%—10 Net 30 and 2%—E.O.M. Some concerns report changing to Net 30 days from discount terms because of unearned discounts taken by customers.

Electronic Components and Accessories: (SIC—3671-72-73-74-79) Net 30 days. Also ½%—10 Net 30 and 1%—10 Net 30. Discount terms have but,adopted to improve payments.

Electrical Industrial Apparatus: (SIC—3621-22-23-24-29) Mostly Net 30 days with ½%—10 Net 30 and 1%—10 Net 30 also granted.

Electrical Parts and Supplies: (SIC—3641-42-43-44) Generally 2%—10th Prox Net 30 and 2% —10 Net 30. Also some 2%—15th Prox.

Electrical Transmission and Distribution Equipment: (SIC—3611-12-13) Generally Net 30 days. Some concerns report stopping discount terms because of unearned discounts taken by customers.

Foundries: (SIC—3361-62-69) Net 30 days and ½%—10 Net 30. Some 1%—10 Net 30 but mostly discontinued. Trend is toward Net terms because of unearned discounts taken by customers.

Fruits, Vegetables, and Seafoods, Canned and Preserved: (SIC—2031-32-33-34-35-36-37) 1½%—10 Net 30. SD–BL terms no longer used extensively.

Fur Garments and Accessories: (SIC—2371) Generally 8%—10 E.O.M. Also various extended terms up to 4-month notes.

Furniture: (SIC—2511-12-14-15-19) 2%—30 Net 60 and 2%—10 Net 30. Some concerns still report Net 30 days but the trend is toward granting discounts to speed collections.

Grain-Mill Products: (SIC—2041) Mostly Net 30 days and cash. Also some Net 10 days reported. Terms granted to 60 and 90 days in special cases.

Hardware and Tools: (SIC—3421-23-25-29) Principally 2%—10 Net 30. Some 2%—10th Prox Net 30.

Heating Apparatus and Plumbing Fixtures: (SIC—3431-32-33) Mainly 2%—10 Net 30 and 2% —10th Prox. Also some Net 30 days. Terms up to 90 days granted to special accounts.

Hosiery: (SIC—2251-52) Net 30 days.

Household Appliances: (SIC—3631-32-33-34-35-36-39) Mainly 1%—10 Net 30. Some 2%— 10th Prox and Net 30 days reported.

Industrial Chemicals: (SIC—2812-13-15-16-18-19) Generally Net 30 days and 1%—10 Net 30. Trend is away from granting discounts.

Iron and Steel, Producers: (SIC—3312-13-15-16-17) Mainly ½%—10 Net 30. Also some 1%— 10 Net 30 and 2%—10 Net 30.

Knitted Outerwear: (SIC—2253) Mostly 8%—10 E.O.M. Some 2%—10 E.O.M. and 3%—10 E.O.M. Several concerns report granting datings on fall merchandise.

Lumber: (SIC—2421) 2%—10 Net 30 and 2%—10 days. Several concerns also report 2%—15 Net 30.

Machinery, Industrial: (SIC—3561-62-64-65-66-67-69) Generally Net 30 days. Also ½%—10 Net 30, 1%—10 Net 30, and 2%—10 Net 30 reported. Larger machinery on contract basis usually with a percentage down, a percentage when completed, and the remainder 30 to 90 days after delivery.

Machine Shops: (SIC—3599) Primarily Net 30 days and cash.

Meats and Provisions, Packers: (SIC—2011-13-15) Weekly terms.

Mechanical Instruments: (SIC—3821) Mostly Net 30 days. Some concerns report ½%—10 Net 30 and 1%—10 Net 30.

Medical, Surgical, and Dental Equipment: (SIC—3841-42-43) Net 30 days and 2%—10 Net 30. Also 2%—10th Prox.

Metal Stampings: (SIC—3461) Generally Net 30, Net 10th & 25th. Use of discount terms is growing with 1%—10th or 25th Net 30 being the most common.

Millwork: (SIC—2431) 2%—10 Net 30 and Net 30 days. Several concerns report terms of 2%—5 days after arrival, Net 30 days on larger orders.

Office and Store Fixtures: (SIC—2541-42) Mostly Net 30 days. Progress payments are often required on large orders.

Outerwear, Girls', Children's, and Infants': (SIC—2361-63-69) 8%—10 E.O.M. Several companies report that competition has forced out 2%—10 E.O.M. terms.

Overalls and Work Clothes: (SIC—2328) Generally Net 30 days. Some concerns report discontinuing 60-day terms. Special seasonal datings are granted by most companies.

Paints, Varnishes, and Lacquers: (SIC—2851) 2%—10 Net 60 and 1%—10 Net 30. Also some 2%—10 Net 30. Most concerns give seasonal datings.

Paper: (SIC—2621) Mostly 1%—10 Net 30 and 2%—30 Net 31. Also 2%—10 Net 30.

Paperboard Boxes: (SIC—2651-52-53-54) 1%—10 Net 30. Occasionally special terms are granted of Net 30 to Net 90 days.

Paper Products, Converters: (SIC—2641-42-43-44-45-46-47-49) Mainly 1%—10 Net 30. Also some Net 30 days. A few concerns report special terms on seasonal products.

Petroleum Refining: (SIC—2911) 1%—10 Net 30 and Net 30 days.

Plastic Materials and Synthetics: (SIC—2821-22-23-24) Mainly Net 30 days. Also ¹/₂%—10 Net 30 and 1%—10 Net 30. Some concerns report changing from Net to discount terms to improve customer cooperation. Seasonal datings and extra 30 or 60 days given to special accounts.

Printers, Job: (SIC—2751-52-53) Generally Net 30 days. Also some 2%—10 Net 30. Some concerns report changing to discount terms and others have added service charges on past-due items in order to improve collections.

Scientific Instruments: (SIC—3811) Generally Net 30 days. Some Net 10 days and Net 10th Prox.

Shirts, Underwear, and Pajamas, Men's: (SIC—2321-22) Mostly 2%—10 E.O.M. Also 3%—10 E.O.M. and Net 30 days.

Shoes: (SIC—3141) Mostly 5%—30 days. Also Net 30 days and 5%—30 Net 60.

Soft Drinks, Bottled and Canned: (SIC—2086) Mostly cash. Some weekly, Net 10 days and Net 30 days granted.

Structural Iron & Steel, Fabricators: (SIC—3441-42-43-44-49) Generally ¹/₂%—10 Net 30 and Net 30 days. Some concerns report discontinuing discount terms because of unearned discounts.

Toys and Sporting Goods: (SIC—3941-42-43-49) Mainly 2%—10 E.O.M. Also 2%—10 Net 30. Most concerns give special seasonal datings.

Trousers, Men's & Boys': (SIC—2327) Generally Net 30 days and Net 60 days. Some Net 10 E.O.M.

Underwear, Women's, Misses', Children's, and Infants': (SIC—2341) Mostly Net 10 E.O.M. and 8%—10 E.O.M.

Wholesalers

Air-Conditioning and Refrigeration Equipment: (SIC—5077) 1%—10th & 25th, Net 30. Also 2%—10th Prox, and some Net 30.

Apparel: (SIC—5036-37) Men's, Boys', Women's, Children's & Infants'—Generally Net 30 to Net 60 days. Also Net 10 E.O.M. Special datings given seasonally in some instances.

Automotive Parts and Accessories: (SIC—5013) 2%—10th Prox and Net 30 days. 30-60-90 day terms given on special dating.

Beer, Wine, and Distilled Alcoholic Beverages: (SIC—5095) Net 30 days, C.O.D., and 10th Prox terms are all used. State laws differ on the terms used for the sale of alcoholic beverages.

Chemicals & Allied Products: (SIC—5029) Net 30 days and 1%—10 Net 30.

Confectionery: (SIC—5045) Net 7 days and C.O.D. Special terms given with seasonal dating on special orders.

Construction & Industrial Machinery & Equipment: (SIC—5082-84) 2%—10 Net 30 and also Net 30 days.

Dairy Products: (SIC—5043) Mainly Net 7 and Net 30 days.

Drugs & Drug Sundries: (SIC—5022) 2%—10 E.O.M. and 1% E.O.M. Seasonal dating also granted.

Dry Goods and Notions: (SIC—5034) 2%—10 E.O.M., Net 10 days E.O.M. Also Net 30 and Net 60 days.

Electrical Parts and Supplies: (SIC—5063) 2%—10th Prox, and 2%—10 Net 30. 10th Prox terms also used.

Electrical Parts and Equipment: (SIC—5065) 2%—10th Prox, and 2%—10 Net 30. Also 2%—10 E.O.M. and Net 30 days.

Farm Machinery and Equipment: (SIC—5083) 5%—10th Prox and 2%—10th Prox. Some special terms given on large pieces of equipment.

Fruits & Fresh Produce: (SIC—5048) Net 7 days and Net 30 days. Also C.O.D.

Furniture and Home Furnishings: (SIC—5097) 2%—10 Net 30. 5%—15 days, 4%—45 days, Net 46. Also 2%—30 Net 60. Some firms report extending credit terms to meet competition.

Groceries: (SIC—5041) Mostly Net 7 days and also C.O.D.

Hardware: (SIC—5072) 2%—10th Prox and 2%—10 Net 30 and Net 60 days.

Household Appliances, Electrical: (SIC—5064) Major appliances—Net cash on receipt of invoice. Net 10 and Net 30 days. Traffic appliances—2%—10 Net 30 and Net 10th Prox. Also special dating when similar terms are received from the manufacturer.

Lumber and Building Materials: (SIC—5098) 2%—10 Net 30 and 2%—10th Prox. Net 30.

Meats & Meat Products: (SIC—5047) Mainly Net 7 days. Also Net 30 days.

Metals and Minerals: (SIC—5091) ¹/₂%—10th & 25th Net 30, 2%—10 Net 30.

Paints and Varnishes: (SIC—5028) 2%—10 Net 60 and 2% Net 30. Special dating terms also given.

Paper and Its Products: (SIC—5096) 1%—10 Net 30 and 2%—10 Net 30. 2%—Prox terms also extended.

Petroleum and Petroleum Products: (SIC—5092) 1%—10 Net 30 as well as 10th Prox terms. Load to load or C.O.D. to smaller retail accounts.

Plumbing & Heating Supplies: (SIC—5074) 2%—10th Prox and 2%—10 Net 30.

Poultry and Poultry Products: (SIC—5044) Mostly Net 7 days. Also Net 30 days.

Scrap and Waste Materials: (SIC—5093) Mostly cash. Some Net 30 days.

Shoes: (SIC—5039) 2%—10 Net 30 and 2%—10 E.O.M. and Net 30 days. Many report special terms on seasonal dating. Some report dropping Net 30—60 days because of competition.

Tires & Tubes: (SIC—5014) Mostly Net 30 days. Some 2%—10th Prox terms used. Dating terms also given.

Tobacco and Its Products: (SIC—5049) Primarily Net 7 days and also C.O.D. Some concerns also use Net 30 days.

Source: Dun & Bradstreet, Inc.

CHAPTER 2

COMPONENTS OF CREDIT RISK

[200]   **THE CREDIT RISK.** As a credit manager, your primary responsibility is to make money for your company. You no longer simply pass judgment on what salesmen have accomplished by saying Yes or No to incoming orders. You look upon yourself and your department as a profit producer and a profit center. In fact, top management is now acting on what credit executives have known for a long time: Credit policies and practices directly influence sales and profits. Loosening up your credit standards will certainly increase sales—and that can lead to more profits or lower unit costs. Tightening up credit standards can easily lead to better collections and, perhaps, more cash in the bank. But it could spell lower sales and reduced profits. Although top management may determine what your company's policy will be, it's up to you alone to decide whether selling a particular company a particular amount of merchandise will carry that policy out.

[201]   **CREDIT POLICY.** Determining the degree of risk your company is willing to accept means, essentially, determining its credit policy. (For an example of one company's credit policy, see Figure 2.1.) Whether your policy is liberal or conservative, it may have these characteristics:

[201.1]   **Characteristics of Credit Policies:**

[201.1.1]   GENERALITY. Policy is general.

[201.1.2]   COMMON SITUATIONS. Policy applies to common situations.

[201.1.3]   TIME. Policy extends over long periods of time.

[201.1.4]   FORMULATION. Policy is formulated at various levels within a company.

[201.1.5]   BASICS. Policy provides basic definitions and a basic outlook for a company.

[201.2]   **Use of Credit Policy.** Credit policy is the link between the abstract goals of the company and the specific directives designed to meet them.

> The credit policy shall be consistent with overall company policies and ethics.
>
> In all phases of its activities, the credit department shall maintain a positive approach to the fulfillment of beneficial intercompany, intracompany, and customer relations. Customers will be entitled to full disclosure regarding company terms and performance requirements applicable to their class of business.
>
> The credit department shall protect and conserve the company's investment in accounts receivable through flexible and prudent credit accommodations and collection practices.
>
> Consistent with the company's fiscal policy, the credit department shall recognize company sales and marketing objectives; and as such, shall cooperate with the sales department in accepting all marginal accounts which the credit department foresees as a source of additional net profit to the company.
>
> The credit department shall fully inform company management of the investment in and the condition of accounts receivable through measurements consistent with company accounting practices.

FIGURE 2.1. Company Credit Policy

[201.2.1]   GOALS. As a credit man, you will distinguish between:
1. *Company goals,* which might include objectives for sales, profits, prestige, and employee satisfaction.
2. *Credit department goals,* which, in the broad sense, might include the protection of corporate liquidity, safeguarding a major investment, enhancing profit, and sales assistance must be translated into specific objectives. These might include the number or amount of past-due accounts, speed of collecting past-due accounts, and percentage of credit sales in relation to all sales.

[201.2.2]   SPECIFIC DIRECTIVES. Credit policy will be implemented by specific directives covering:
1. Collections—when to start, what procedures to follow, when to abandon.
2. Payments that anticipate the due date and on which discounts not included in the terms have been taken.
3. Bad debts.
4. Lines of credit.
5. Marginal accounts.
6. Slow-paying accounts.
7. Unearned discounts.
8. Guarantees.
9. Cutoff dates.
10. Incoming orders.

[201.3]   **Formulating Credit Policy.** There are three basic steps in formulating credit policy:

[201.3.1]   OBJECTIVES. Establish (or be aware of) the company's objectives and the credit department's objectives.

[201.3.2]   INFLUENCING FACTORS. Determine what factors will influence the credit department's achieving its objectives. These circumstances could be:
1. Industry conditions.
2. Competition.
3. Your company's financial position.
4. Objectives and policies of other departments with which your policy must be compatible.

[201.3.3]   ACTION. Decide what course of action will carry you to your objectives within the limitations imposed by your company, your industry, your customers, and the economy as a whole.

[201.4]   **Who Formulates Credit Policy.** A recent study carried out by the National Association of Credit Management with the *Harvard Business Review* indicates that the responsibility for establishing credit policy generally rests with the president or chief executive officer in small companies. However, as the size of the company increases, the greater the likelihood that the chief financial officer or the chief credit executive will formulate credit policy.

[201.5]   **Classification of Credit Policy.** Credit policies are generally classified as liberal or conservative. You should be aware, however, that these labels apply to two different aspects of credit policy itself:

[201.5.1]   CONSERVATIVE POLICY.

1. A company is restrictive in granting credit both in amount and in the degree of risk it is willing to accept.
2. A company requires a detailed investigation of every company before it will make a credit decision.

[201.5.2]   LIBERAL POLICY.

1. A company is lenient in granting credit both in amount and in degree of risk it is willing to accept.
2. A company requires little or no investigation of highly rated companies and minimal investigation of marginal accounts buying up to predetermined limits.

[201.6]   **Factors that Determine whether a Company Will Have a Liberal or Conservative Policy (Amount and Degree of Risk).** When reviewing these factors, keep in mind that one company can have several different policies depending on (1) the particular product and its profit margin; (2) the geographic location where the different products are sold; (3) the time of year when the products are sold. According to the survey conducted by the National Association of Credit Management with the *Harvard Business Review,* competition is the most important factor of those listed below.

[201.6.1]   FACTORS CALLING FOR A CONSERVATIVE POLICY.

1. *Competition.* If there is little or no competition for your product, you can be very selective about whom you grant credit to, on what terms, and for what amounts.
2. *Profit margin.* If there is a very narrow margin of profit on the products you sell, you cannot afford high collection or bad-debt costs. As a result, your credit policy must be conservative.
3. *Volume.* If most of your revenue comes from little volume, your credit policy must be conservative enough to assure that you collect on your sales.
4. *Customer demand.* When there is high demand for your product, you can be as selective as you like when you choose the people to whom you are going to sell.
5. *Inventory.* When your inventory is low, your credit policy can be conservative.
6. *Liquidity of your company.* When your company has a poor cash position or needs more ready cash for some specific purpose,

you cannot afford to tie up your assets in slow-moving receivables. Your credit policy must be conservative.

7. *Industry conditions.* When the conditions in the industry to which you sell are doubtful, unstable, or generally threatening, your credit policy should be more conservative.

8. *General economic conditions.* When the general situation of the nation's economy is such that the future is uncertain, your credit policy may be conservative to avoid potential losses.

9. *Specialized product.* When you produce a specialized product to your customer's specifications, your policy must necessarily be conservative.

10. *Time-consuming product.* When your product takes so long to produce that much of your operating capital is tied up in each unit, your investment must pay off. Your credit policy must be conservative.

FACTORS CALLING FOR A LIBERAL POLICY.

1. *Competition.* When there is much competition in your industry, your credit policy may be liberal for two reasons:
   a. If a liberal policy is the norm for the industry, then you may have to have a liberal policy to hold your customers.
   b. You may choose to have a more liberal policy when the industry as a whole has a conservative one in order to wield more competitive clout.

2. *Profit margin.* When the profit margin on your product is wide, you can afford to have a liberal credit policy. Collection expense and reasonable bad-debt loss will not eat your profits up.

3. *Volume.* When your company has to maintain a heavy volume to stay ahead of high overhead cost, your credit policy had better be liberal.

4. *Customer demand.* When customer demand for your product is low or falling, a liberal credit policy may be in order.

5. *Inventory.* You may have excess inventory on your hands that you want to get rid of for one (or all) of the following reasons:
   a. Technologically, it is out of date.
   b. Stylistically, it is old hat.
   c. Financially, it is too expensive to carry over to a new selling season.
   If such is the case, then a liberal credit policy may be one way to produce quick sales.

6. *Industry conditions.* When the conditions in the industry to which you sell look particularly good, you might want to have a liberal credit policy to take advantage of a marginal customer's exceptionally good prospects.

7. *General economic conditions.* Similarly, when the economy as a whole looks promising, your credit policy may be more liberal.

8. *Introduction of new products.* In order to launch a new product, you might liberalize your credit policy.

9. *Securing a particular outlet.* In order to secure an outlet in a

specific location or to attract a particular kind or class of customer, you could utilize a liberal credit policy.

10. *Collections.* When you know that your collection operation is particularly effective, you can afford a more lenient credit policy.

[201.6.3]   IMPORTANCE OF A SUFFICIENTLY LIBERAL CREDIT POLICY. Once you agree that the objective of the credit department is to make profits for the company, you will realize the importance of a sufficiently liberal credit policy. No company can avoid bad debts. In fact, if you don't have a reasonably large number of bad debts in relation to your volume, your credit policy may be too conservative. Here's a method to find out if it is: Determine your profits on additional sales after two to three times your customary losses. Do your profits improve even after the increased losses are deducted? If so, your credit policy may indeed be too restrictive.

[201.7]   **Liberal and Conservative Credit Policies (Extent of Investigation).** A credit department may institute a liberal or conservative policy in regard to the amount of investigation it requires before passing on a credit risk. The more conservative the policy, the more thorough the investigation would be on a larger number of accounts. More specifically, the extent of the investigation will be determined by these factors:

[201.7.1]   FACTORS THAT COMPRISE THE EXTENT OF THE INVESTIGATION.

1. *Number of sources checked.* The more conservative the policy, the more sources of information would be checked before a credit decision is reached. A very liberal policy could mean that only the credit rating is used as a basis for extending a line of credit. Some companies have gone a step further and sold up to a given amount on a new order without any investigation whatever. This most often occurs when the order is small, when a company wants to move inventory fast, or when there is a shortage of personnel. These companies are playing the law of averages, but the practice is hazardous. In fact, there is evidence that fraudulent overbuy operators have sometimes learned who uses this approach and have directed unsolicited orders to them.

2. *Areas of information covered.* Even a liberal credit policy would require that any investigation undertaken cover elements pertaining to the three C's of credit (see page 37). The more conservative the policy, the more areas—and the more specific points within each area—would be checked.

3. *Depth of information.* Some liberal credit policies call for a cursory review of several factors. Conservative policies, however, may demand thorough investigation of character, for example, and detailed financial analysis.

4. *Quality of information.* Information quality depends upon the integrity and knowledge of its source, the amount of time and effort the source devotes to answering your query, and the scope and completeness of the reply. As far as financial information is concerned, its quality is often revealed by the reputation of the auditors and the acceptance of the accounting principles em-

ployed. Unaudited statements or estimates—because they are based on the customer's unverified figures—could indicate that the quality of the information revealed is not high. Even a statement prepared by a certified public accountant should be examined closely. You should know whether the accountant has expressed an opinion and, if so, whether it was qualified or unqualified. If it was qualified, you should find out what the qualifications were and how they may affect the accuracy and thus the quality of the facts revealed by the figures. The more conservative the credit policy, the greater the demand for quality information.

[201.7.2]   FACTORS THAT DETERMINE THE ADOPTION OF A LIBERAL OR CONSERVATIVE CREDIT POLICY (EXTENT OF INVESTIGATION).

1. *Cost.* The basic consideration when deciding how much time and energy you can devote to credit investigation is cost. While agency service costs can be significant, the same investigation within your own department can be much more costly. Naturally, costs vary according to the number of orders a credit department processes, but as sales increase, credit-department unit costs should decrease proportionately.

   Because the costs of credit information and analysis can be high, credit executives recognize that the same amount of time and energy cannot be devoted to every account. Money saved on an investigation of one customer can be spent on the investigation of another, more difficult account. This means that instead of writing for information on all accounts, you could telephone for information on important ones. Instead of jamming your files with material on every account, you could have easy access to the material on complex ones. Instead of sending your salesmen out to investigate every account, you could use thorough, up-to-date agency reports for most of them. A liberal or conservative credit policy will be chosen, therefore, according to these criteria as well:

2. *Size of order.* The larger the order, the more information you need to make sure your credit decision is the right one. Your policy may call for extensive investigation of companies ordering more than a specified amount.

3. *Time.* Obviously, the extent of your investigation is limited by the amount of time you have to make a decision.

4. *Potential volume.* Even when an initial order is small, the potential volume a customer represents could lead you to make a more thorough investigation. Your credit policy should provide for this possibility.

5. *Risk inherent in general type or class of customer.* Other factors being equal, retailers are known to be greater risks than wholesalers, wholesalers greater risks than manufacturers. Within these general categories, too, some lines show evidence of being greater risks than other lines. Table 2.1 reveals the failure rate for some retail and manufacturing lines. (These figures, compiled annually by Dun & Bradstreet, are available at your request.) Your credit

Retail Lines Ranked By Failure Rate 1972

Line of Business	Failure Rate Per 10,000 Operating Concerns
Men's Wear	97
Women's Ready-to-Wear	88
Cameras and Photographic Supplies	85
Infants and Children's Wear	76
Furniture and Furnishings	63
Gifts	60
Books and Stationery	54
Sporting Goods	49
Appliances, Radio and Television	42
Dry Goods and General Merchandise	34
Shoes	33
Toys and Hobby Crafts	30
Women's Accessories	27
Auto Parts and Accessories	23
Jewelry	22
Drugs	22
Eating and Drinking Places	22
Bakeries	20
Lumber and Building Materials	17
Automobiles	17
Hardware	14
Grocery, Meats and Produce	13
Farm Implements	10

TABLE 2.1

Failures in Specific Retail and Manufacturing Lines (Rate per 10,000 Operating Concerns in 1972)

Source: Dun & Bradstreet, Inc.

Manufacturing Industries Ranked By Failure Rate 1972

Line of Industry	Failure Rate Per 10,000 Operating Concerns
Transportation Equipment	119
Furniture	113
Electrical Machinery	100
Leather and Shoes	88
Apparel	88
Textiles	60
Metals, Primary and Fabricated	51
Paper	47
Machinery Except Electrical	45
Printing and Publishing	41
Chemicals and Drugs	41
Food	36
Lumber	27
Stone, Clay and Glass	20

policy may direct a more thorough investigation of the higher-risk categories.

6. *Profit margin.* When the profit margin on your product is very narrow, an extensive and costly investigation could eliminate that profit altogether. If, on the other hand, your profit margin is wide, you can afford to pay for a more extensive investigation should one be needed.

7. *Your confidence in your decision.* Credit policy should permit you to extend your investigation to remove doubt about your decision if possible loss is substantial.

8. *Small possible loss.* When the possible loss from an account is insignificant, your credit policy might not call for a labored investigation that could waste the time and energy of the credit department.

[201.8] **Communicating Credit Policy.**

[201.8.1] TO WHOM. Depending upon your reasons for communicating your credit policy, you would certainly consider informing:

1. *The sales department,* whose efforts will be seconded or rejected according to the policies of the credit department.
2. *Your customers,* who will have to meet your standards or go elsewhere.
3. *Your competition,* which can instigate credit wars that often bring instability and losses to an entire industry.

[201.8.2] IN WHAT FORM: WRITTEN OR UNWRITTEN POLICY. Credit policy does not have to be written out to be effective or even quite complex. Nevertheless, an explicit written statement of credit policy does hold these advantages:

1. It forces those making up the policy to really think it out.
2. It reduces the need to rely on memory.
3. It saves time lost in discussions over what the policy really is.
4. It reveals differences of opinion and misunderstandings that could cause problems later if left unresolved.
5. It shows where policy is inadequate.
6. It makes a more precise working tool.
7. It provides a method of continuing a stable operation.
8. It forces changes to be intentional and conscious.
9. It enables a credit department to be consistent.
10. It facilitates the handling of exceptions by providing a norm from which to start.
11. It provides a basis for regular review of credit policy.

[201.9] **Reviewing Credit Policy.** Once you have established a credit policy, do not dismiss it from thought. Instead, make provisions for periodic review of the credit policy to see if changes are in order. A change in any one of the variables that determine whether your policy is liberal or conservative can mean that your policy will swing in one direction or the other. If your policy is not effective in helping you reach the goals top management has set for your company and you have set for the credit department, obviously changes will have to be made. Periodic review will help you determine whether credit policy itself is deficient or whether it is being improperly implemented. Whenever you hear of changes in your company, in your industry, or in your customers' condition, this, too, will cause you to review credit policy.

[201.10] **Changing Credit Policy.** A credit policy should be sufficiently flexible that it does not require constant change. However, there are sound reasons for changes.

[201.10.1] REASONS FOR CHANGES. According to the results of a survey taken by the National Association of Credit Management with the *Harvard Business Review,* changes in credit policy often take place to correspond to changes in the financial condition of a company's customers. Nevertheless, a combination of factors making up the seller's condition is most influential in determining credit-policy shifts.

[201.10.2] PREPARATION FOR CHANGES. The study mentioned above also shows that approximately 40 percent of those surveyed perform preliminary investigations of the anticipated results of contemplated policy changes.

Of that 40 percent about 60 percent base their preliminary studies on a "survey of competitive practice."

[201.10.3]   RESULTS OF CHANGES. Credit men are convinced that appropriate changes in credit policy are instrumental in producing more profits (though not necessarily more sales) for their companies.

[202]   **EVALUATING THE CREDIT RISK.** Several later chapters in this handbook are devoted to the technical complexities of evaluating the credit risk. All of them, however, are methods for arriving at an evaluation of the traditional three Cs of credit.

[202.1]   **The Three C's of Credit.** "Character," "Capacity," and "Capital," the traditional three C's of credit, have frequently been expanded to four with "Conditions." Some authors have added to that list with "Collateral" and even "Computers." These general terms, no longer considered a Bible, do provide a useful framework in which to view the specific areas of credit investigation and evaluation. The three C's of credit, in fact, point to the two major questions an evaluation of a credit risk tries to answer: (1) Will the customer be willing to pay his bill on time? (2) Will he be able to pay his bill on time?

[202.1.1]   CHARACTER. Character refers to the sincerity with which a customer undertakes a trade obligation and the determination he will have to see that obligation through. You will most often become familiar with a man's character through his reputation, but you should be careful to distinguish between them. A good reputation is definitely not proof of worthy character.

[202.1.2]   CAPACITY. Capacity refers to an individual's ability to formulate and carry out objectives. His business capacity means his ability to formulate and carry out profit objectives that will enable him to pay his bills.

[202.1.3]   CAPITAL. Capital refers to the financial resources that a customer has at the time he places an order and those that he is likely to have when it is time to pay for that order. Capital is often considered the most important element of the credit evaluation, but in fact, it should not rank above the others.

[202.1.4]   THE OTHER C'S.
1. *Conditions.* Conditions refer to those situations that exist or could exist in an industry (or in the total society) that might have an effect on a customer's ability to pay, or intention of paying, his bills.
2. *Collateral.* Collateral refers, in fact, to financial or other resources that a company can rely on to pay its bills. In a secured transaction, of course, collateral refers to the items pledged to guarantee a debt. Collateral provides a margin of safety for the seller.
3. *Computers.* As more and more companies install computers to handle payroll, accounting, and other office procedures, more and more credit men are beginning to use the computer for credit-department operations. They have found that computers enable them to keep more and better records, to keep those

records up-to-date, and to use them more effectively to calculate risks and returns.

[202.2]   **Classification of the Credit Risk.** The results of the credit analyst's evaluation of an account should be a classification. In fact, breaking down potential customers into general risk categories is one of the fastest and most efficient methods of processing the many orders that cross the credit analyst's desk. The following classification is quite common.

[202.2.1]   FIRST-CLASS OR PRIME (REQUIREMENTS) RISK. The first-class risk has the highest possible credit rating. Such a customer is one of the giants of his field who has proved his ability and willingness to pay time and again. The credit analyst will give automatic approval to all orders.

[202.2.2]   SECOND-CLASS RISK. The second-class risk always pays his bills reasonably promptly when he orders within his credit limit. In fact, as long as the second-class risk stays within the limits set by the credit department, order approval is automatic. If he should go beyond his limit, the credit manager must decide whether accepting or rejecting the risk is justified or not under the terms of the company's credit policy.

[202.2.3]   MARGINAL ACCOUNTS. There is very little agreement in the credit field upon what exactly constitutes a marginal account—beyond the fact that the credit analyst is not sure that he will be willing and able to pay his bills on time. Major marginal-account characteristics include the following, however:

1. Poor payment record.
2. Credit line exceeding normal credit extension.
3. Unstable finances.
4. Overtrading.
5. Continuing operating losses.

If a credit analyst classifies a customer a marginal risk, he should carefully review the case to see if some basis for a sale can be determined. By finding ways to sell marginal accounts, a credit man can most effectively increase his company's profits.

[202.2.4]   DOUBTFUL ACCOUNTS. Trading with doubtful accounts is carried on with the expectation of bad-debt losses. In fact, the possibility of loss is generally so great that the credit manager should try to persuade such customers to buy on special secured terms. If he cannot, acceptance of doubtful accounts on open-book terms means a very liberal credit policy indeed.

CHAPTER 3

THE CREDIT EXECUTIVE

[300] **THE CREDIT EXECUTIVE.** Although top management has often been slow to recognize the vital contribution credit executives can make to their companies, credit executives are now coming into their own as important participants in overall company management and as contenders for higher executive posts. Today, credit executives must be well trained, well educated, and well suited to deal with three groups of people: (1) credit personnel within their department; (2) other department heads and top management; and (3) customers and other business associates outside the company.

The increasing importance of the credit executive's role in his company and his ever-growing contact with friends and customers outside the company make it more necessary than ever that he have the proper personality-training mix to carry out successfully all his duties.

[301] **QUALIFICATIONS FOR CREDIT MANAGEMENT AT THE EXECUTIVE LEVEL.**
[301.1]   **Personal Qualities Characteristic of Credit Executives.**
[301.1.1]   JUDGMENT. The credit executive's greatest need is perhaps that of clear, dispassionate, and impartial judgment. In his rise up the corporate ladder and as the top credit executive, he is continually called upon to make decisions that will affect his customers, his company, and his own personnel. In order to make the right decisions for all concerned—including himself—the credit executive must be able to:

1. Pick out the important elements from the mass of facts, opinions, and other data with which he is presented.
2. Weigh these important elements honestly against each other and against company goals and policies.
3. Decide upon the best course of action.

This means that the credit executive must be:

1. Emotionally stable.
2. Realistic.
3. Confident of his own analytical powers.

[301.1.2]   INITIATIVE. Good judgment is essential to the success of a credit executive. Without initiative, however, he may never be fully recognized by top management for his contributions and it is unlikely he will move up in the corporate structure. One credit executive gained such recognition primarily as a result of an unusual approach to the setting of credit limits. Another designed reports to his top management which gave them a quick accurate picture of his credit operation. In the process he demonstrated clearly the key role played by the credit executive in his company. Yet another executive successfully initiated the automation of the accounts receivable and credit evaluation function. Still another improved efficiency by implementing a change in the organizational structure of the credit operation. In each instance it took the good judgment to know what was needed and the initiative to implement the necessary change rather than waiting for direction from top management.

[301.1.3]   CHARACTER. Because the credit executive makes important decisions that vitally affect companies and people, his character must be above question. The credit executive must never make decisions on any other basis than that required by company policy—honestly formulated—and that required by credit seekers—objectively, yet compassionately, appraised. The credit executive must often give customers bad news and he always wants his opinion to count with top management. Character is the foundation upon which he builds respect to maintain goodwill and advance his own causes.

[301.1.4]   PERSEVERANCE. In order to be effective, the credit executive must not only make decisions but stand by them and see them through. A credit executive who vacillates, who wavers in the face of pressure from one party and then another, renders no service to his company, his staff, nor to himself.

[301.1.5]   TACT. The credit executive's job is to make money for his company by increasing credit sales and increasing successful collections of those sales. Credit executives don't like to lose customers—and they can't afford to lose many. Therefore, when it falls to the credit executive to deliver bad news—that credit can't be granted on the terms asked by the customer or that the line of credit to an old customer is being reduced— he must have the tact to do it gracefully and maintain that customer's goodwill.

In addition, the credit executive must often tread a delicate line between the sales, production, and accounting departments. To maintain his friendships with those departments—yet to make his opinions count —the credit executive must have tact as well as judgment and character.

[301.1.6]   LEADERSHIP. Like any executive, the credit executive must be a leader. He must be able to stimulate the members of the credit department to work swiftly, efficiently, thoroughly, and with company policy in mind. He is the one who sets the tone for customer payment habits. The credit manager's leadership ability is, in large measure, a determining factor in his staff's satisfaction on the job. In addition to the other qualities listed above, leadership comprises:

1. Competence in the technicalities that subordinates must perform.
2. Strictness in performance requirements.
3. Fairness in the judgment of performance.
4. Compassion.
5. Enthusiasm.

[301.2]   **Professional Skills Required for Credit Management.** In order to function effectively as a credit executive, the credit manager must possess knowledge and skills in the following areas:

1. Accounting.
2. Financial-statement analysis.
3. Commercial law, including:
   a. Negotiable instruments.
   b. Bankruptcies.
   c. Taxes.
4. Collection techniques.
5. Economics, including:
   a. Economic indicators.
   b. Banking.
   c. Monetary policy.
6. Business management and psychology.
7. Finance.
8. Communication skills.
9. Marketing.
10. Purchasing.
11. Public relations.
12. Personnel.

[301.3]   **Management Skills Required by the Credit Executive.** As a manager, the credit executive must be able to:

1. Formulate policy.
2. Evaluate performance against policy.
3. Institute remedial action when necessary.
4. Inspire organized teamwork.
5. Delegate authority and responsibility.

[301.4]   **Training Required by the Credit Executive.**

[301.4.1]   FORMAL TRAINING. In this day of specialization and widespread education, it is becoming more and more important that the credit executive have a college education, and preferably an M.B.A. This is not to say that many credit executives, like many executives in all areas of business, have not worked their way up to the very top with little or no college training. Nevertheless, university education can offer:

1. Training in professional skills in the areas mentioned above.
2. General training that enables the credit executive to see his work and the role of business in general in perspective.

[301.4.2]   ON-THE-JOB TRAINING. No matter with what educational background the credit executive began his career, he would not have advanced to his present position without extensive on-the-job training in the credit department of his or other companies. Only experience can teach the credit manager:

1. How to develop specific routines for running a credit department.
2. How to manage his staff and deal effectively with the other businessmen.
3. How to work well under pressure.

CONTINUING PROFESSIONAL TRAINING. Credit executives, like all business executives, recognize that fast-paced business changes make continuing professional training a necessity. Credit executives are particularly fortunate in having many professional training programs at their disposal. These include:

1. *The National Institute of Credit.* In association with the Credit Research Foundation and neighboring colleges and universities, local chapters of the National Institute of Credit offer correspondence courses and classes leading to the award of two certificates:

   a. Associate Award.

   b. Fellow Award.

These awards are presented for successful completion of study in such areas as:

   a. Credit and collection principles.

   b. Accounting.

   c. Business correspondence.

   d. Law.

   e. Management techniques.

2. *The Graduate School of Credit and Financial Management.* The Credit Research Foundation, together with Dartmouth College, Stanford University, Williams College, and the London Graduate School of Business Studies, sponsors an annual two-week program that brings together top credit executives for advanced training in credit, finance, and management for three years. In order to successfully complete this program, the credit executive must submit an acceptable research thesis. Once he does, the credit executive receives the Executive Award, the highest honor given by the credit profession.

3. *Dun & Bradstreet Correspondence Courses.* Dun-Donnelley Publishing Corporation and the National Credit Office (a D & B company) offer a three-level correspondence course in credit and financial analysis that has been written—and is graded—by top analysts in the credit field.

   a. Level One—*The Fundamentals of Credit.* This course introduces the beginning credit analyst to the fundamentals of his field: accounting, financial-statement analysis, and the role of credit and the credit manager in the company and in the economy.

   b. Level Two—*Credit and Financial Analysis.* Beginning where the Fundamentals of Credit left off, Credit and Financial Analysis continues with detailed examination of risk evaluation; financial-statement composition; internal, comparative, and working-capital analyses; evaluation of marginal risks and bankruptcy and other financial embarrassment situations.

c. Level Three—*Advanced Credit and Financial Analysis.* This course is unique, for no other covers the same ground in the same way. Advanced Credit and Financial Analysis is aimed directly at the problem of judgment. While judgment is partially based on experience, it is heavily dependent upon analysis. This means that the credit executive must have a sound knowledge of how his actions affect sales and profits, how to handle risk in a meaningful way, and how to balance expected profit against increased risk. The course uses both traditional and highly advanced techniques and integrates them through the application of text to cases. Students are presented with approaches to the resolution of credit decisions and are given a series of cases to which to apply these approaches. The cases become increasingly difficult and increasingly less obvious. Thus, a very important part of this case learning is the search for the real problem and the selection of the appropriate analytical tool. By this means, the student is given both immediate experience in the application of the approaches described in the text and experience in determining the real problem and most important considerations.

4. *Credit-Management Workshops.* The Credit Research Foundation sponsors credit-management workshops lasting two to three days which explore in depth very specialized areas of credit management.

5. *American Management Association Seminars.* The A.M.A. frequently sponsors seminars devoted to credit problems that would be of particular interest to the credit executive. In addition, the A.M.A. gives many seminars throughout the year on other management topics that attract credit executives.

6. *National Credit Congress.* Every year, the National Association of Credit Management holds the National Credit Congress. This is an important opportunity for credit executives to hear respected leaders of the profession and to participate in study and social events with comembers of the credit field.

7. *Publications.* Magazines such as *Credit and Financial Management, Dun's, Business Week*; research papers published by the Credit Research Foundation; and newspapers such as the *Wall Street Journal* are a continuing source of credit-management ideas and general economic and business information essential to the credit executive.

[302]   **ROLE OF THE CREDIT EXECUTIVE IN HIS BUSINESS.** The role of the credit executive in his business depends, of course, on many particular factors beyond those of his personality and his ability.

[302.1]   **Factors Determining the Role of the Credit Executive.**

[302.1.1]   SIZE OF COMPANY. In a large company, the credit executive may be confronted with these two extremes—or, more likely, he will find his role situated somewhere between them:

1. His role is very restricted to management of the credit department, as the company has sufficient personnel to take care of other areas.
2. His role has greatly expanded beyond management of the credit department because he is recognized as an overall manager whose opinion is of value on many different areas in the business. As a result, he is asked to become a member of management committees (marketing and finance, for example) and his advice is sought by members of the following departments:
   a. *Sales*—because they recognize that credit is fundamental in making a sale and in collecting the money from a sale.
   b. *Purchasing*—because they recognize that the credit executive (or his department) can give valuable appraisal of supplier stability and responsibility.
   c. *Finance*—because they recognize that the credit executive is adept at forecasting cash needs and cash flow.
   d. *Legal*—because they recognize that the credit executive is greatly versed in bankruptcy law and laws dealing with negotiable instruments and taxes.
   e. *Public relations*—because they recognize that the credit executive and his department are in frequent contact with customers and thus constitute a good medium for sales and public-relations efforts.

In a small company, the credit executive will have to become involved with all of the departments listed above because the intelligence and skills of all executives will be needed for any given problem. In fact, in very small companies (and some not-so-small ones) the credit executive's role is actually performed by someone whose primary responsibility lies somewhere else. Some likely candidates are:

1. *Accountants*—because they are familiar with ledgers, financial analysis, and the company's own financial situation.
2. *Sales managers*—because top management realizes that credit is a sales function and because the sales department has the personnel to maintain contacts with customers.
3. *The company president himself*—in many very small companies, the president has retained the credit executive's job for himself. This is often because he wants to have a very close watch over his receivables and cash position and because he realizes that granting credit is one of the most delicate management functions.

[302.1.2]   LOCATION OF THE CREDIT DEPARTMENT IN THE ORGANIZATIONAL STRUCTURE. The location of the credit department within the company's organizational structure often is a determining factor in the role the credit executive will play. Traditionally, the credit department is located as follows:

1. *Under the treasurer-comptroller and his department.* The credit executive usually reports to the treasurer or vice-president and treasurer. This placement has resulted from top management's recognition that credit can be a treasury function in that:
   a. Receivables are one step away from cash.

b. Receivables represent an investment of the company's resources.

2. *Under the sales or marketing department.* An ever-growing number of companies have acknowledged credit's marketing function by placing the credit department under the sales department. This is more often the case in a dynamic, sales-oriented company where profit margins are small and competition large.

3. *Independent credit department.* Still other companies have an independent credit department whose manager, the credit executive, is on the same level as other department heads. An independent credit department is essential if final credit authority is in danger of residing elsewhere—in the sales or finance departments, for example—than with the credit executive. When the credit department is independent, the credit executive reports to a vice-president or the president.

4. *Others.* Although the above three situations describe the majority of credit departments, the credit department and the credit executive can be responsible to almost any other company official, including:
   a. Executive vice-president.
   b. Secretary.
   c. General manager.
   d. Vice-president of finance.
   e. A management committee.

[302.1.3]   LINE, FUNCTIONAL, OR STAFF POSITION. Whether the credit executive and his department are in a line, functional, or staff position has an even greater effect on the role the credit executive will play in the company.

1. *Line position.* A line organization has these characteristics:
   a. There is a chain of command with authority extending directly to immediately subordinate positions and indirectly to more subordinate positions.
   b. Each member of the department is responsible to a single person.
   c. Authority means the power to act or to have action taken on your behalf.

   A credit executive in a line operation is responsible for—or does himself, depending on the size of the operation—the following operations:
   a. Determination of credit risk.
   b. Setting of credit limits.
   c. Approval of customer orders.
   d. Collection of accounts.
   e. Supervision of lower-level personnel.

2. *Functional position.* A functional position has the same credit responsibilities as a line position but an individual can report (or be responsible) to more than one person. Such a system is particularly advantageous when some member of the credit department has a particular specialty that is to be used and directed by different departments. This position is also common

when one credit department serves more than one product or territory division of the same company.

3. *Staff position.* A staff position is characterized by responsibility but no authority to act or to command action. As a result, staff responsibilities fall into the following areas:
   a. Administration.
   b. Recommendation.
   c. Advisory.
   d. Research.
   e. Planning.

[302.1.4]   BRANCH OFFICE OR HEADQUARTERS POSITION. Whether the credit executive manages a branch office of a large corporation or manages the headquarters credit office of a corporation with branch credit offices can greatly influence the role the credit executive will play. If he manages a branch office, he will be more actively involved in day-to-day credit decisions on individual accounts than if he were at the headquarters office. If he is at the headquarters office, he will be more involved in establishing procedures and policies that will be directly implemented by the branch offices.

[302.1.5]   TOP MANAGEMENT'S VIEW OF CREDIT. The role of the credit executive is determined somewhat by the viewpoint held by top management. If the credit operation is never even thought about except when there are receivables difficulties, then obviously the credit executive will not carry much weight within the company. His role will be limited to running his own department. When management regards credit as a vital marketing tool, however, the credit executive's duties—and opportunities—expand. The credit executive's actions and the nature of his reports to top management can influence their viewpoint.

[302.2]   **Responsibilities of the Credit Executive.** Within the limits imposed by the considerations discussed above, the credit executive may become involved in any of the following operations:
1. Formulation of credit policy.
2. Formulation of general company policy.
3. Staffing of the credit department.
4. Training of the credit department.
5. Administration of the credit department, including:
   a. Budgeting.
   b. Promotions and terminations.
   c. Reports and meetings.
   d. Actual credit and financial analysis.
   e. Development and use of controls.
   f. Inter-company relations.
   g. Development and maintenance of credit records systems.
   h. Decisions on credit limits.
   i. Decisions on marginal accounts.
   j. Supervision of collections.
6. Maintenance of good customer relations through:
   a. Correspondence.
   b. Personal visits.

c. Financial counseling.
7. Cash forecasting.
8. Economic forecasting.
9. Protection of company interests through:
   a. Detection of customer stockpiling.
   b. Anlaysis of industry trends to determine whether the industry can absorb increased production.
   c. Aid in negotiating offset arrangements, security, and settlements with suppliers.
10. Maintenance of bank relations, including:
    a. Handling deposits of cash and securities.
    b. Exchange of credit information.

[303]   **MEASURING CREDIT-GRANTING EFFECTIVENESS.** Credit managers are now well aware of the vital role they play in contributing to the successful operation of their companies. All information points to the fact that the investment in trade receivables is growing significantly; the return on this investment has thus become one of the most important responsibilities in financial management. And the credit manager's stature has grown because it is his. In addition, the sales arm of an organization now often realizes that profitable sales to marginal risks—although they require the greatest skills of analysis and forecasting by the credit department—are a major source of increased company revenue. Salesmen—once natural enemies of the credit department—have come to recognize credit men as their allies.

But the credit manager's own awareness of this responsibility is not enough. Top management can only evaluate a credit performance that is effectively communicated to them and to others in the company. In fact, the more forceful and convincing the presentation of credit operation results, the greater the respect, responsibility, and reward that the credit manager will obtain.

It is the credit executive's responsibility to determine what reports best reflect the progress being made in reaching the goals set down by the credit policy.

The sections that follow are designed to give you the tools you need to present the credit story to your management. You may choose some or all of these methods, according to your individual requirements. Whatever you do select, however, you will know that you are more effectively communicating your department's results by doing so.

[303.1]   **Collection Results.** There are three measurements that can be used to determine collection results. The best results are obtained when all three are taken into consideration.

[303.1.1]   AGING OF RECEIVABLES. Obtained at monthly intervals, agings reflect the total receivables, the amount that is current and the amount that is past due (usually broken down into thirty-day categories up to 180 days, with everything over 180 days grouped together). Variations of this approach are made to suit individual circumstances.

[303.1.2]   TURNOVER OF RECEIVABLES. There are a number of ways to make this evaluation. Some of them are the following:

1. *Net sales to accounts receivable.* This may be calculated by dividing the closing balance sheet accounts receivable (after deducting the reserve for bad debts) into the net sales for the year. A refinement averages the receivable position semiannually, monthly or otherwise in lieu of simply using the closing figure.

2. *Collection index.* This may be calculated by dividing receivables outstanding at the beginning of a fiscal period into collections realized during that period. Collection trends can be determined by making a comparison with similar indexes for comparable periods in the past.

[303.1.3]   DAYS' SALES OUTSTANDING (D.S.O.). This measure of credit-department efficiency is calculated by dividing the closing accounts receivable balance by the average daily credit billings. By comparing current D.S.O. with that of the preceding month, year—or whatever period desired—the credit manager can evaluate the trend of his department's performance. D.S.O. is also useful in comparing your credit department's performance with that of other companies in your field. (The data is available from the Credit Research Foundation's *National Summary of Domestic Trade Receivables.*) If the D.S.O. is considerably longer than the period provided by the terms of sale, the credit manager will know that his collection efforts must be improved.

[303.2]   **Bad Debt Losses.** This measurement can be made in two ways:

[303.2.1]   ACTUAL NUMBER AND DOLLAR AMOUNT. This may be used as an absolute measure of your credit-granting operation but it must be viewed in perspective. Comparisons of bad debt trends of other companies in the same industry can be made by using statistics derived from U.S. government sources and published by such organizations as Dun & Bradstreet and CRF. Company credit policy determines what risk categories can be accepted and thus influences the bad-debt figure. If company policy changes from one reading to another, this fact should be taken into account. General economic and industry conditions can also greatly affect a company's bad-debt losses even when credit-department operations remain constant. Bad-debt losses per risk category can be a more useful measure of your credit-granting operation.

[303.2.2]   BAD-DEBT RATIOS. Generally, bad debts are measured as a percentage of total sales or, more usefully, as a percentage of total credit sales. One drawback is that frequently bad debts for one period are matched with sales of a different period. Appropriate sales averages can be used to overcome this difficulty.

[303.3]   **Credit Rejections.** This figure can be calculated on the basis of orders, total dollar amounts or both. A ratio can be determined by dividing the rejection figure by the number of credit orders or the dollar amount of the total credit orders, as the case may be. Guidelines can be set up to review credit policy or its implementation if there is significant upward or downward fluctuation.

[303.4]   **Return on Investment in Receivables.** A few companies, usually those operating on a profit center approach, attempt to maintain receivables at an optimum level and use the R.O.I. approach to accomplish that end. It is difficult to administer but has been done with a degree of success in some cases. One method provides for an interest charge by the credit operation assessed to the appropriate profit center. Another method is to apply the concept more loosely with the investment in receivables measured in the over-all context of the investment in other assets. It would appear that much refinement is needed in order to make this a viable approach in a wide segment of industry, but there are dividends to be reaped by the credit executive who can successfully apply such innovative concepts.

[303.5]   **Measurement of Administrative Efficiency.** There are several ways to make this evaluation.

[303.5.1]   COST COMPARISONS. A traditional approach is that of making a comparison of current year's cost of operating the credit department with the cost of prior years and against budgeted costs. While this has some value, credit executives have been searching for more meaningful tools.

[303.5.2]   VOLUME OF WORK. One way to measure the effectiveness of the credit staff and credit systems is to calculate the number of orders processed, letters written, calls made, etc., and compare it with the volume of work during a previous equivalent time period. This can be a useful way to measure such "nonquantitative" functions as customer relations and inter-departmental cooperation.

[303.5.3]   VOLUME OF ACTIVE CREDIT ACCOUNTS. This figure can be used to calculate the following performance indicators:

1. Average sales per account.
2. Average profit per account.
3. Average accounts receivable per account.
4. Average credit-department cost per account.

When compared with previous figures, these calculations can give you a good measure of your department's effectiveness.

[303.6]   **Sophisticated Quantitative Tools.** Credit executives are becoming aware of the opportunities offered by the application of sophisticated quantitative tools to accounts receivable management. Regression analysis, decision theory and other such tools offer opportunity for further breakthroughs. Mathematical models have been devised to assist in the determination of acceptable risks and to help maximize return on investment in receivables. In his book *Analysis for Financial Decisions,* William Beranet gives detailed treatment to a variety of trade credit models. This area offers new and potentially rewarding challenges to the credit executive.

CHAPTER 4

ORGANIZATION OF THE CREDIT FUNCTION

[400] **ORGANIZATION OF THE CREDIT FUNCTION.** To achieve maximum efficiency in serving the company and its customers, a credit department must be carefully and thoughtfully organized. The particular credit-department organization you develop—the lines of authority and responsibility adopted, the various mechanical (or manual) systems used, the place of the credit department within the structure of the company as a whole— depends upon the functions assigned to the credit department. These, of course, vary from company to company, industry to industry. Nevertheless, certain basic functions are common to all.

[401] **FUNCTIONS OF THE CREDIT DEPARTMENT.** In addition to those functions common to all company departments—hiring, training, budgeting, payroll administration, etc.—the functions of the credit department can be broken down into these five areas:

[401.1] **Extending Credit.** The credit department evaluates the credit worthiness of its company's customers and decides, in accordance with company policy and its goal of making money, whether merchandise or services can be sold on credit terms. To expedite processing subsequent orders, the credit department then may establish a credit limit for the customer. More precisely, the credit department's extension of credit involves these operations:

[401.1.1] DETERMINATION OF COMPANY POLICY. The credit department either formulates credit policy in cooperation with top management or, if top management alone is responsible for this task, the credit-department personnel make sure that they understand what company policy is and how they can implement it.

[401.1.2] COLLECTING CREDIT INFORMATION. The credit department is responsible for collecting all available credit information about a customer that is needed to make a credit decision. The sources and methods of collecting information (all discussed in detail in Chapter 6) include:

1. The company's salesmen.
2. Interviews or telephone calls with the customer.
3. Banks.
4. Factors.
5. Other suppliers.
6. Credit agencies (including D&B).
7. Public records.
8. Newspapers.

The information needed to make the credit decision depends upon those variables discussed in Chapter 6, but can include these facts, treated extensively in Chapter 5:

1. Composition of the business.
2. Its antecedents.
3. The history of the business.
4. Its operation.
5. Industry conditions.
6. Economic factors.
7. Finances—as reflected by financial statements, profit-and-loss statements, interim statements, estimates, and other financial information.
8. Paying habits.
9. Banking relationships.

How the information can be stored for fast retrieval and confidential handling will be discussed in Section 403.4.1.

[401.1.3]   REVISING CREDIT INFORMATION. Not only must the credit department collect the information necessary to make an initial credit decision, it must also make sure that the credit information it has is up-to-date. Revision of credit information should include an automatic check of customer credit ratings as well as collecting new financial (and other) information as it becomes available.

[401.1.4]   SETTING OF CREDIT LINES AND LIMITS. On the basis of an evaluation of the information it collects, the credit department must establish a credit line for the customer. The methods used to perform this operation are discussed in detail in Chapter 7. As part of its job setting credit lines, the credit department must also establish the terms of sale, and any special conditions to be met by a customer in order for a sale to go through. Periodically, the credit department must review the credit lines of its customers in light of new information to make sure that they are reasonable. A credit line that is too liberal could expose your company unnecessarily to credit risk, while a line that is too conservative could drive good business opportunities away to your competition.

[401.1.5]   CHECKING OF ORDERS. As sales orders come in, the credit department must check them against the customer's line of credit, the terms that have been established, and any conditions that have been set up to make sure that the sale represents an acceptable credit risk. If the customer is a new one, the credit department must evaluate the risk it represents. Depending on the credit worthiness of the customer, the credit department will either:

1. Pass the order and set a line of credit.

2. Reject the order.

3. Mark the customer as a marginal account and establish special terms for it and/or note that payment practice must be followed closely.

If the customer is an old one, but if the order goes beyond the established line or if there are unpaid bills outstanding, the credit department must decide whether to OK the order on the basis of the information it has or make a new investigation.

[401.2]   **Collecting Receivables.** Once your company's goods or services have been sold to a customer on the basis of open-book-account terms, then the function of the credit department is to make sure that the bill is paid. In the best of circumstances, this task—as far as the credit department is concerned—will involve no more than registering the payment on the customer's ledger card and checking to make sure that no unearned cash discounts were taken. When payments prove a problem, then the credit-department function is expanded to include the following tasks, outlined here and discussed in detail in Chapter 12.

[401.2.1]   DETERMINATION OF COMPANY COLLECTION POLICY. Either in cooperation with top management or by itself, the credit department determines the collection policy that must be followed to collect past-due accounts.

[401.2.2]   ESTABLISHMENT OF COLLECTION SCHEDULE. Usually, the schedule followed for the use of various collection devices is a part of company policy. Nevertheless, the credit department will want to review that schedule for each individual collection case to see if effective variations could be made to speed collection.

[401.2.3]   FORMULATING AND ADMINISTERING COLLECTION DEVICES. Once an account is identified as delinquent, the credit department must make the necessary telephone calls, write the necessary letters, or go on the necessary visits to bring the money in. Often this involves use of standard material that is part of the credit department's files. If these techniques prove ineffectual, the credit department may consider granting extensions, placing the account for collection with a professional agency, or writing the account off as a bad debt.

[401.3]   **Performing Intercompany Credit Services.** One of your credit department's functions is its cooperation with the credit departments of other companies, with credit associations, and with credit agencies.

[401.3.1]   CREDIT DEPARTMENTS OF OTHER COMPANIES. Your credit department maintains contact with the credit departments of other companies for three reasons:

1. *In order to obtain credit information about your customers.* One of the best sources of credit information—and one of the best analytical tools for use in credit evaluation—is a customer's payment record with other trade suppliers. Lines of communication must be kept open so that this information is available to you.

2. *In order to give credit information about your customers.* If you expect to receive credit information about prospective customers from the credit departments of other companies, you must be prepared to give credit information about your customers to other credit departments. Customers should be aware that this ex-

change of information is essential to a smoothly running economy and that all information exchanged is handled confidentially.

3. *In order better to evaluate conditions within the industry and the economy as a whole.* One element in your analysis of a credit risk is industry conditions and the general economic picture when credit is granted and as it can be predicted for the duration of the credit. The information you obtain from other credit departments can be of great value in analyzing these situations. In addition, the *National Summary of Domestic Trade Receivables,* a listing of days' sales outstanding for the country's leading industries, is a valuable indicator of the business health of those industries important to you as well as the economy as a whole. It is published quarterly by the Credit Research Foundation.

[401.3.2]   CREDIT ASSOCIATIONS. Your participation in the activities of local and national credit associations can be of great help to successful performance of the credit department. Credit associations are a vital source of information about:

1. Your current and potential customers.
2. The latest collection and analytical techniques.
3. Special problems your credit department may be facing, such as automation or intercompany relationships.
4. The economy as a whole.

Moreover, credit-association activities give credit personnel in your company the opportunity to meet and get to know credit-department personnel in other companies. Development of cordial—personal—relationships between the staffs of different companies goes a long way toward opening up valuable lines of communication between departments.

[401.3.3]   CREDIT AGENCIES. The importance of your credit department's cooperation with credit agencies, especially Dun & Bradstreet, cannot be overstressed. Credit agencies are the only source of completely impartial credit information. Trained agency specialists in credit and industry fields can often provide more accurate, better-thought-out analyses than members of credit departments. This is because often they have more time, experience, knowledge, or information than credit managers themselves. When Dun & Bradstreet, the National Credit Office, Lyon Furniture Mercantile Agency or any other credit agency contacts your firm for your ledger experience on a company, be sure to give them your best, most prompt cooperation. If you have your receivables in computer storage, you may wish to pursue the possibility of providing such information on tape to the credit agency. A representative of Dun & Bradstreet would be happy to discuss it. Remember, too, that it is in the best interests of your own company to provide Dun & Bradstreet with your latest financial statement and other information, and this should be brought to the attention of the corporate treasurer.

[401.4]   **Providing Customer Service.** The credit department is in the unique position of being able to provide perceptive, useful services to the customers of its company. In fact, not only *can* the credit department do this, it *must.* One of the credit department's most important functions is to establish and maintain goodwill with customers. The credit department can perform this task in the following ways:

[401.4.1]   ASSISTING FINANCIALLY TROUBLED CUSTOMERS. Because of their extensive financial and collection experience, credit-department personnel can often help a customer solve his temporary financial and collection problems. Credit men can suggest sources of funds, methods to control accounts receivable, better methods of cash forecasting, and other financial techniques that can turn a troubled business around. Drawing upon their wide collection experience, your credit-department personnel can pass on the latest techniques and any special pointers they have acquired.

[401.4.2]   PLEASANTLY HANDLING REGULAR CREDIT ACTIVITIES. The credit department rarely has the opportunity to deal closely with its company's best customers since these pay promptly and without dispute. Nevertheless, credit personnel can, whenever the occasion arises or according to a pre-established schedule, take the time to write a letter of appreciation to these customers, thanking them for their continued patronage.

[401.4.3]   TAKING SPECIAL CARE IN DIFFICULT CREDIT SITUATIONS. Whenever the credit department must refuse credit, require special terms, or lower a customer's credit line, it should take special care to explain carefully its viewpoint to the customer and work with him to reach a buying arrangement satisfactory to all concerned. Where possible, the credit department can, as indicated in Section 404.4.1, offer financial advice that may result in a better credit situation for the troubled customer. Even when an account must be placed for collection, the credit department must remain fair and dignified.

[401.5]   **Maintaining Good Interdepartmental Relationships within The Company.** One of the credit department's most vital functions is establishing and maintaining good relationships with other departments in its company. Credit men no longer sit isolated in a back room where they merely accept or reject salesmen's orders. Their training and experience enable them to provide exceptionally useful services to many areas of a company.

[401.5.1]   CREDIT DEPARTMENT–SALES DEPARTMENT RELATIONSHIP. The old cliché that sales are not sales until the money is collected illustrates the vital connection between the sales and credit departments. Now, however, credit men and salesmen realize that mutual cooperation must go far beyond simple approval or rejection of credit sales.

    1. *Credit department's obligations to the sales department.*
       a. The credit department must inform the sales department immediately of any change in the credit standing of one of the company's customers. This includes any change—positive or negative—in the line of credit, credit terms, any special restrictions, or the withdrawal of credit. For an example of one company's change-notification slip, see Figure 4.1.
       b. The credit department has the obligation, through its analyses of a company and its industry, to notify the sales department of any sales opportunities it is able to identify.
       c. Where possible, the credit department should evaluate the

F2205-5

CREDIT STATUS CHANGE NOTICE

TO ORDER DEPT.	FROM CREDIT DEPARTMENT	DATE

☐ DALLAS   ☐ DECATUR   ☐ BELVIDERE   ☐ SAN LEANDRO   ☐ DES PLAINES

☐ AMES   ☐ DELMAR   ☐ FORT WORTH   ☐ PASADENA   ☐

SUBJECT

A/R NO.

CUST. NO.

☐ ALL ORDERS SHOULD BE REFERRED TO CREDIT DEPT. FOR APPROVAL PRIOR TO SHIPPING

☐ IT WILL NO LONGER BE NECESSARY TO REFER ORDERS.

☐ ESTABLISH CREDIT LIMIT OF $ _____ PER ORDER

☐ DO NOT SEND INTRODUCTORY SHIPMENTS

☐ YOU MAY SEND INTRODUCTORY SHIPMENTS

☐ FUTURE ORDERS SHOULD BE FILLED ONLY ON A COD OR CWO BASIS

☐

REMARKS

☐ REPRESENTATIVE   ☐ M.I.S.   ☐ DIV. SALES MGR.   ☐ CREDIT   ☐

FIGURE 4.1. Credit Status Change Notice

credit worthiness of any potential customers *before* an order is placed.

d. In order to ensure good cooperation between the two departments, the credit department must communicate the credit policy of the company to the sales department. If a salesman knows in advance whether an account is likely to be accepted or rejected because of company credit policy, he can save much time and effort for himself and the credit department before making a "sale." Advance knowledge of credit policy can also spare hard feelings, which are likely to arise when a sales order is rejected.

e. The credit department can help the sales manager by aging accounts receivable according to salesman. This will provide an additional measure of a salesman's ability that the sales manager might find useful.

2. *Sales department's obligations to the credit department.* Because of their close contact with customers and the industry, salesmen are in a good position to help the credit department in its work. The sales department's responsibilities thus include the following:

a. Salesmen can gather information about customers that will help the credit department to analyze the credit risk.

b. Salesmen can assist the credit department in making collections. Often salesmen are so well acquainted with a customer that a few words from the salesman will be all that's needed to speed payments. (This is a basic policy decision, however, and there can be reasons for not doing so.)

c. Salesmen can give the credit department useful information about the industries with which the company deals so that the credit department will be better able to determine the state of the economy as a whole.

[401.5.2]   CREDIT DEPARTMENT–ACCOUNTING DEPARTMENT RELATIONSHIP. Although the credit department normally has no direct accounting responsibility, close cooperation between the two departments is essential. Very often, customer ledgers are kept in the credit department itself and thus accounting-department personnel must go there for the information they need. When the accounting department maintains those records, the credit department should make sure that they are in a form that the credit department can easily use for its purposes. In addition, the credit department often assists in legal (bankruptcy) proceedings and auditing procedures that might involve the accounting department and handles credit corrections and adjustments.

[401.5.3]   CREDIT DEPARTMENT–PRODUCTION DEPARTMENT RELATIONSHIP. The credit department can help the production department in three significant ways:

1. By analyzing the operations of its company's customers, the credit department can tell if any customer is stockpiling and thus help the production department avoid overproduction or overexpansion.

2. The credit department, as a result of its continual analyses of the economy as a whole and the industry served by its company in particular, can help the production department forecast product need.

3. The credit department can help the production department evaluate the necessity or utility of plant expansion.

[401.5.4]   CREDIT DEPARTMENT–PURCHASING DEPARTMENT RELATIONSHIP. The credit department has an important role to play in helping the purchasing department operate efficiently. Indeed, the vital necessity for a continual supply of raw materials at reasonable costs makes the credit department's contributions to this operation of utmost utility. Specifically the credit department can:

1. Evaluate the financial stability of suppliers to determine whether they will be capable of producing the required supplies over the required period of time.

2. Establish security arrangements with suppliers who may show financial instability.

3. Analyze purchase terms, conditions, and offset rights to make sure that its company is getting a fair deal.

[401.5.5]   CREDIT DEPARTMENT–DATA-PROCESSING-SYSTEMS DEPARTMENT RELATIONSHIP. Although credit managers were once reluctant to become involved with the data-processing departments of their companies, now they recognize that cooperation is vital. More and more companies are computerizing their credit operations and credit managers must become intimately involved in setting up the systems and procedures that will meet their credit objectives. Even when the credit operation itself is not computerized, credit managers must make sure that computerized ledger and accounting systems are designed to furnish the information needed by the credit department.

[402]   **CREDIT DEPARTMENT PERSONNEL.** The makeup of the credit-department staff will vary, of course, according to the size of the credit department, the complexity of its operations, and the kind of organizational framework in which it exists.

[402.1]   **Staff Titles and Responsibilities.** Depending upon the size and complexity of the credit department and its operations, the department's personnel may be composed of any or all of the following job categories:

[402.1.1]   CREDIT MANAGER. Every company that sells its products or services on credit should have a credit manager—or someone who assumes the credit manager's role. The duties and qualifications of the credit manager were discussed in detail in Chapter 3.

[402.1.2]   ASSISTANT CREDIT MANAGER(S). When the credit operation is very large or complex, a credit department may have one (or more) assistant credit managers. These men and women ideally should have the same qualifications as the credit manager himself because their function is to share his responsibilities. When hiring an assistant credit manager you should try to obtain one who is capable of taking over the credit operation—either in an emergency or permanently in the event of the credit manager's leaving the post. If not, training should be quickly directed toward that end.

[402.1.3]   CREDIT SUPERVISORS. When the company's operations are large, credit departments may have credit supervisors. These staff members usually are responsible for all credit functions for a certain product, a certain territory, or a certain division of the company. They report to the credit manager or the assistant credit manager. Theoretically, they should be as well qualified as their managers but as a minimum, they should have two years of college training in relevant subject matter and at least a year of experience. Credit managers have found that inexperienced personnel who lack formal training do not have the skills or judgment called for in the credit office.

[402.1.4]   CREDIT ANALYSTS. Credit analysts are found in two varieties:

1. *Those responsible for all credit transactions involving certain customers.* These credit men must gather all the necessary credit information, analyze the credit risk represented by an account, establish a line of credit (or, if a line of credit is not feasible, then devise alternate terms or conditions, or reject the order), keep check to see that the account is paying properly, and devise and administer any collection devices that may be needed. They report to the credit manager, his assistant, or credit supervisors.

2. *Those responsible for a certain credit operation for all (or a group of) customers.* When a company's credit department does not have individuals responsible for all credit functions for certain custom-

ers, then they must have the personnel to perform certain credit functions for all customers. They report to the credit manager, or credit supervisors. Such personnel include:

   a. *Investigators*—who are responsible for collecting credit information.

   b. *Credit editors*—who are responsible for analyzing the credit risk.

   c. *Authorization agents*—who decide whether the risk can be accepted.

   d. *Collection correspondents*—who are responsible for devising and administering collection procedures.

[402.1.5]   TECHNICAL SPECIALISTS. When the credit operation is very large and complex, it is not unusual for technical specialists in law, economics, or computers to be found as members of the credit-department staff. When there are no technical specialists of this sort, then other members of the credit department perform these functions or call upon the resources of outside specialists.

[402.1.6]   OFFICE PERSONNEL. There are two types of office personnel you can find in credit departments throughout the country:

   1. *General office personnel.* This category includes:

     a. Secretaries.

     b. Stenographers.

     c. Filists.

     d. Messengers.

   2. *Office personnel skilled in credit-related fields.* This category includes:

     a. Statisticians—who compile credit records and aid in credit analysis.

     b. Posting clerks—who record payments and verify that orders shipped are within credit limits.

     c. Reference clerks—who maintain current files of credit information and collection results.

[402.2]   **Number of Staff Members.** The number of credit-department staff members a company will have depends, of course, on how many orders it must process, the depth of investigation required by company policy, and to a certain extent, by the abilities and skills of the department members themselves.

[402.3]   **Training of Credit-Staff Personnel.** Credit managers must do their best to select staff members who are innately honest, loyal, attentive, judicious, and possessing the necessary analytical abilities to develop into good, thorough credit men. These qualities cannot be taught, although they may be stressed, complimented, and commented upon by credit managers in day-to-day operations. Furthermore, credit managers would do well to select staff members who are good verbal and written communicators and have had formal training in the areas most related to credit work:

   1. Credit.

   2. Accounting.

   3. Economics.

   4. Financial management.

5. Business law.
6. Marketing.
7. Public relations.
8. Management.

Company training programs are often necessary to develop the necessary talents in credit personnel or to tune them up.

[402.3.1]   KINDS OF TRAINING PROGRAMS.

1. *Orientation programs.* These are the simplest types of training programs a credit staff member can receive. Generally they are limited to an explanation of company credit policy, the credit department's role in the company, and the new employee's role in the department; basic instruction in the use of credit-department systems, procedures, equipment, and materials; and clarification of the company's personnel policies, pay scales, vacations, and other benefits.

2. *On-the-job training.* On-the-job training means that the new employee learns the operation of the credit department by actually performing credit functions under the supervision of more senior credit personnel.

3. *Formal training programs.* Formal training programs have been instituted in many companies for the following reasons:
   a. *Purpose of formal training programs.*
      (1) To reduce the amount of time credit-department personnel must spend with new employees.
      (2) To develop skills in:
         (a) Financial statement analysis.
         (b) Written and verbal communications.
         (c) Commercial law.
         (d) Data interpretation.
      (3) To train lower-level credit men for higher executive positions.
   b. *Subject matter of formal training programs.* In addition to the academic fields listed previously, formal training programs can also include instruction in company policies and practices and thus complement on-the-job training.
   c. *Methods of formal training.* In addition to workshops, seminars, and classroom instruction given at the company by more experienced credit men, formal training programs can include any of the training programs discussed under continual professional training for credit managers (see Chapter 3, Section 301.4.3).

[402.3.2]   TRAINING-PROGRAM PARTICIPANTS. Virtually all new employees receive some sort of orientation program.

[403]   **STRUCTURAL ORGANIZATION OF THE CREDIT DEPARTMENT.** Credit-department personnel are faced with the problem of making accurate credit decisions in a short amount of time. Credit-department organization is designed to achieve maximum efficiency in this decision-making process

by developing standard procedures relating to how decisions are to be made and who is to make them. In addition, more specific goals of the credit-department organization are as follows:

[403.1]   **Goals of Credit-Department Organization.**

[403.1.1]   EFFICIENT HANDLING OF PAPERWORK. Credit operations depend upon the availability and accuracy of recorded information. Therefore, the department's organization should ensure that all information is complete, accurate, up-to-date, and easily accessible.

[403.1.2]   CUSTOMER CONTROL. In order to make the most money for its company and to ensure customer goodwill, the credit department must maintain adequate control of customer payments. This means that payments must be recorded as soon as they come in so that customers will not be antagonized by incorrect dunning or allowed to become seriously delinquent in payments. It also means that accurate records of collection progress must be maintained.

[403.1.3]   DEPARTMENT STABILITY AND CONTINUITY. Credit-department organization aims to make the running of the credit department as orderly as possible. When procedures and staff functions are carefully determined and explicitly communicated, the department is less susceptible to disruption caused by the departure of any staff member. Credit-department organization should also insure that operations can continue if some records or credit information are lost. A well-organized credit department also means that credit operations can be handled more efficiently when the work load is high and pressure is heavy.

[403.2]   **Variables of Credit-Department Organization.**

[403.2.1]   SIZE OF THE COMPANY. The larger the company, of course, the larger the credit department tends to be and the stricter credit-department organization must be to insure effective performance of credit functions. In a small company, frequently only one or two men are responsible for credit operations and little formal organization is needed. They know their customers well and can individually check up on payments and credit information through their contacts with banks, credit agencies, and other suppliers.

[403.2.2]   METHOD OF OPERATION. Whether a company is a wholesaler, a service organization or a manufacturer influences the degree of formal organization required of its credit department.

1. *Wholesalers.* Credit-organization problems tend to be less complicated for wholesalers than for manufacturers, as wholesalers generally know their customers well. Moreover, complicated terms or discounts are usually those decided upon by manufacturers and merely passed on by wholesalers. Naturally, the degree of organization will depend on the volume handled.

2. *Service industries.* Service industries have less to lose in a credit transaction, are in a position to cut off their service immediately in the event of nonpayment (without loss of goods or expense of recovering them), and thus have the fewest credit problems of all. Their credit organization need not be rigidly structured.

3. *Manufacturers.* Manufacturers usually have the most complex credit problems and thus the strictest credit-department organi-

zation. The variables that influence a manufacturer's credit organization are as follows:

a. *Number of products.* If a manufacturer produces a large number of products, he will frequently need a credit operation organized around each one.

b. *Number of distributors.* If the number of distributors is large, then a manufacturer will often require a credit operation organized around a certain group of them. Certainly, more credit men and credit women will be needed as the number of distributors increases.

c. *Quality of distributors.* A company selling a large number of products but only to the automobile producers would obviously need a less strict credit-department organization and a smaller credit department than a company selling direct to thousands of small retail outlets.

[403.2.3]   LINE OR STAFF. A major factor determining precisely how the credit department will be organized is whether the department under consideration performs a line or staff function. If the department has a staff function, organization can be looser, as the department is not responsible for day-to-day credit decisions and the routine paper and detail work that such an operation requires. Each credit manager can decide for himself what organizational structure will best enable the staff department to provide its advisory services. Line credit departments, however, are responsible for the day-to-day credit decisions. Within a line operation, credit responsibilities can be grouped around customers—one credit man responsible for all functions involving only some customers assigned by product, territory, or alphabet—or around functions with one credit man responsible for each function for all customers.

[403.2.4]   CENTRALIZED OR DECENTRALIZED CREDIT OPERATION. The responsibilities and duties of the credit department vary according to whether the credit operation is centralized or decentralized. Credit executives emphasize that the decision to have a centralized or decentralized structure depends on the particular circumstances, facilities, and personalities of each individual company. They are convinced, moreover, that neither a centralized nor a decentralized credit structure is perfect in itself. Effective credit operations result from the imagination and skill with which credit managers compensate for each system's deficiences. See Charts 4.1, 4.2, 4.3, 4.4, which illustrate the lines of authority for centralized and decentralized line and staff credit operations.

1. *Centralized operation.* A centralized operation is one in which credit policy is set, credit procedures are established and the actual work of gathering credit information, analyzing credit risks, setting credit limits and collecting receivables is carried out for all customers at one central location. Credit managers point out that the advantages of this set-up include the following:

a. *Advantages of centralized organization.*

(1) Close control over the credit-extension and collection functions.

(2) Better training of credit personnel.

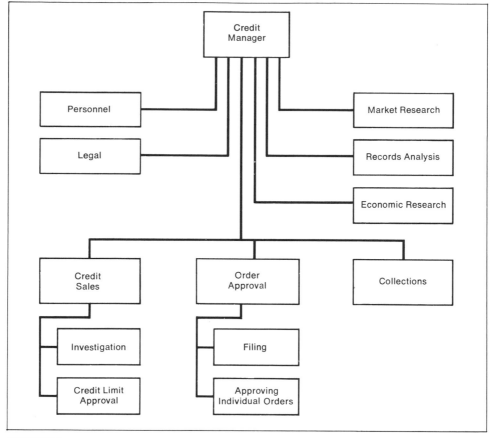

CHART 4.1

Organization of a centralized line credit operation, where responsibilities are grouped by function. If responsibilities were grouped by customers, then one man would be responsible for all functions for a certain group of customers, as in Chart 4.2.
Chart adapted from *Credit Management* **by Robert Bartels**

     (3) Greater consistency in interpreting and carrying out credit policy.

     (4) Lower costs of running the department.

     (5) Few reports necessary for credit management and top management.

  b. *Disadvantages of centralized organization and possible solutions.*

     (1) One of the most disconcerting problems encountered in a centralized credit operation is slow action on order approval and credit problems. Credit managers suggest that a possible solution is to utilize order limits at shipping points and other local outlets. Some advanced credit systems use computer terminals at shipping points and local outlets for fast communication with headquarters data.

     (2) Perhaps the most prevalent problem encountered in a centralized system is poor and infrequent contact with customers. Successful credit executives overcome this problem by making those visits they do have with customers pay off. In addition, they have found that telephone

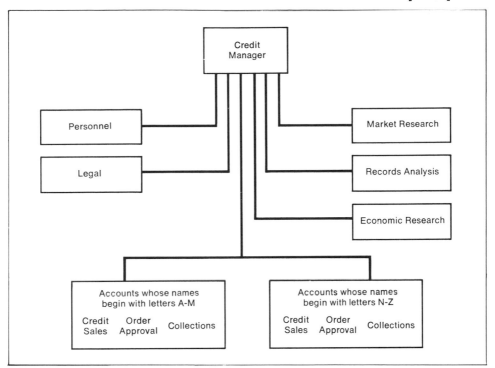

CHART 4.2

Centralized line credit department where responsibilities are grouped by customers.
Chart adapted from *Credit Management* **by Robert Bartels**

contacts, which are easier and cheaper, can often accomplish the tasks at hand.

2. *Decentralized operation.* A decentralized operation is one in which credit policy and general procedures are set at one headquarters location but specific directives and the actual work of gathering credit information, analyzing credit risks, setting credit limits and collecting receivables is carried out at various geographical locations. Credit managers have signalled these advantages of the decentralized system:

a. *Advantages of decentralized organization.*
   (1) Better credit department relationships with customers.
   (2) Better relationships between the credit staff and the sales and financial staff.
   (3) Better credit information.
   (4) Better collections as customers know and respect credit department personnel and procedures.
   (5) Faster action on credit approval and credit and collection problems.

b. *Disadvantages of decentralized organization and possible solutions.*
   (1) One of the most difficult problems credit managers are likely to face under a decentralized system is the inability of local credit managers to withstand the pressure exerted by local office management. Too often the credit manager at a local office will be asked to disregard his own judgment of a case in favor of a potentially profitable sale. The key

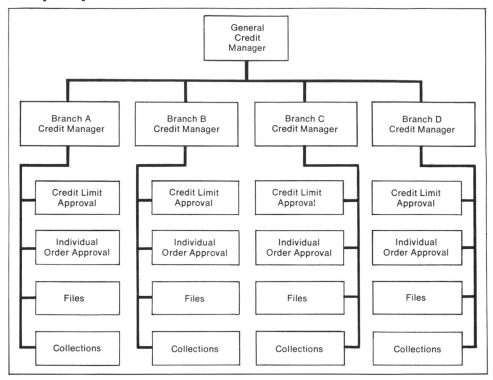

CHART 4.3

Organization of a decentralized line operation.
Chart adapted from *Credit Management* by Robert Bartels

solution to this problem according to credit managers interviewed is to give the local credit manager complete financial responsibility for those sales made at his location —and final authority for approval of credit risks. If credit personnel have been well trained, top credit management finds that credit decisions are rarely contested and if they are, top credit management is able to support local judgment in most cases.

(2) Another hard problem for top credit management in a decentralized system is keeping close control over local activities. At the same time, local credit managers tend to forget that top credit management is available to help solve credit problems until those problems reach the serious stage. For both problems, effective credit managers suggest periodic visits of top credit management to local offices to review (1) fulfillment of staff requirements, (2) equipment and facilities, (3) customer relations, (4) sales department relations, and (5) relations between local and headquarters credit management.

[403.2.5]   WHO HANDLES THE ORDERS AND VERIFIES THE CREDIT. Although the credit department may formulate credit policy, evaluate credit risks, and establish credit limits, the credit department does not necessarily handle all orders. Possible variations include the following:

1. *Sales department handles orders.* Frequently, especially when perishable or seasonal goods are involved, the sales or production

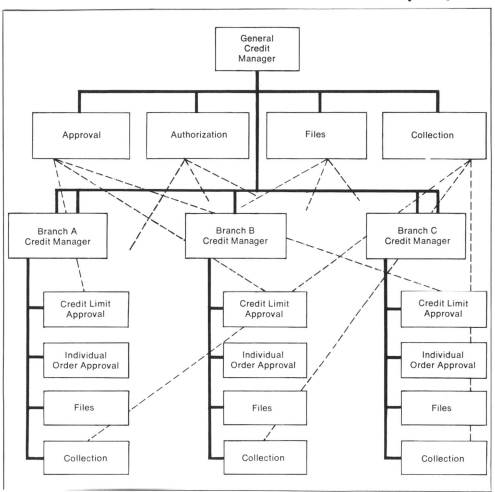

CHART 4.4

Line/staff organization of a decentralized credit operation.
Chart adapted from *Credit Management* by Robert Bartels

department will process orders without referring them to the
credit department for verification. In this situation, the credit
department issues specific instructions that the sales department
must follow. The procedure might work as follows:

a. After evaluating the account, the credit department issues
   specific instructions (credit line or limit, terms, special conditions if any, etc.) to the sales department, where they are filed
   in the customer's folder.

b. Periodically, the accounting department issues a statement of a
   customer's account (an accounts-receivable trial balance, for
   example).

c. As remittances come in, a copy of the remittance advice is sent
   to the sales department, where it is filed in the customer's
   folder.

d. As new orders come in, the sales department adds them to all
   other amounts owing as indicated by the balance shown on the
   accounting department's statement plus all other billed or
   unbilled orders made since the statement. From this total, the

sales department subtracts all remittances as indicated by the remittance advices. If the resulting amount falls within the credit line established by the credit department, then the sales department ships the order. When the order exceeds the credit limit, the credit department is so advised and the latter takes over the case.

2. *Sales or shipping department ships orders without specific credit department approval.* In such a situation, the credit department receives copies of new orders and checks them for credit purposes. The sales department (or shipping department) waits a specified period of time and then ships the order *unless* they have been told not to by the credit department. This procedure does save time.

[403.3]   **Organization of Credit Decision-Making** One of the major reasons that careful organization of the credit department is important is so that credit decision-making can be handled accurately, quickly, and, wherever possible, in a routine way by the lowest possible level of credit personnel. Routinization of credit decision-making results in better customer service and greater employee efficiency. It involves the organization of three credit operations.

[403.3.1]   ORGANIZATION OF INFORMATION GATHERING AND CUSTOMER RE-EVALUATION. The credit department must ensure that credit information is obtained and a new evaluation made of customers at regular intervals. This can be done by setting up a chronological index file listing the customers to be researched and evaluated every month. Such a system not only ensures that credit lines will be up-to-date; it also spreads out evenly the work load of evaluating customers. The file could be so arranged that the customer's name appears twice: It would appear one month as a reminder that a request for the latest financial statement, Dun & Bradstreet report, and other information that is requested and received by mail should be obtained. The second listing the following month could be a reminder that the evaluation and analysis should be undertaken.

Depending upon the complexity of the operation, this file could be maintained and the information-gathering operation carried out by:

1. A special person or group with that responsibility alone.
2. The credit analyst, who maintains a file and performs the operation on his own customers.

Remember that part of the regular Dun & Bradstreet report service is automatic notification of any new information or revisions of previous reports that occur during a one-year period from the original request for a report. Receipt of a D&B Special Notice or a revised report could be your signal, too, to make a new customer analysis.

[403.3.2]   ORGANIZATION OF CREDIT APPROVAL FOR FIRST ORDERS. In order to ensure the fastest possible credit decisions, organization of credit approval can be based on the factors listed below.

1. *Automatic approval of small orders.* Many companies have found out that if they must process many small orders, it is cheapest to establish an upper limit (to be determined by company policy, previous experience, business conditions, etc.) and automatically

ship all orders up to that limit. If a company adopts this procedure, it will want to keep close watch on its receivables.

2. *Approval based on Dun & Bradstreet ratings.* Many companies set up dollar limits according to Dun & Bradstreet ratings. (see Table 4.1). Orders up to these limits are automatically approved without credit investigation. (Table 4.2 is an example.) If a company has different product lines, then different scales can be established. Frequently, the first-order scale becomes a monthly limit.

3. *Disposition of large or unusual orders.* When a company receives a large order, an order exceeding the limit merited according to the Dun & Bradstreet rating or an order requesting special terms, handling, or other conditions, the credit analyst must decide these issues:

   a. Whether the order should be rejected outright because it violates company policy.

   b. Whether the size of the order, the potential of the customer, the desire to secure him as an outlet mean that a credit investigation is in order.

   c. Whether, on the basis of the results of the investigation, credit can be extended on the company's terms or the terms desired by the customer.

   d. Whether the account can be sold on special terms, if not acceptable on standard terms.

   e. Whether the account should be accepted as a marginal risk.

   f. Whether the account should be rejected.

Personnel who handle each class of order listed above could be as follows:

1. *Order clerks.* Order clerks could screen incoming orders and automatically approve those orders falling within limits set by the company or established corresponding to Dun & Bradstreet ratings.

2. *Credit analysts.* Orders exceeding the limits mentioned above (or in cases where order clerks do not screen orders, then all orders) can be referred to credit analysts who decide whether an investigation is necessary, carry the investigation out, and decide whether credit can be granted and on what basis. Accounts can be assigned to credit analysts according to product, territory, or division and, within those categories, by alphabet, credit limit, or complexity of the case. As indicated before, credit analysts can be responsible for all credit functions involving a certain number of customers or they can merely be assigned the evaluation-approval-of-credit task.

3. *Credit managers.* A company can establish an upper limit of credit beyond which credit analysts must seek management advice before granting credit. Managers, of course, must be available for consultation on difficult or special cases.

[403.3.3]   CREDIT AUTHORIZATION OF REPEAT ORDERS. In order to facilitate processing of a customer's repeat orders, the credit department must develop two standard procedures:

1. *Setting credit limits.* At the time of his first evaluation, the credit analyst should assign a credit limit or line of credit. The procedure and methods of carrying this out are discussed in detail in Chapter 7. Here it can be said that credit lines, set for a specified period of time, can be based on these factors:

   a. Amount of credit possible to grant within a given time period.
   b. Size of an individual order.
   c. Outstanding balance.

2. *Determining authorization procedure.* These steps in the handling of repeat orders are common:

   a. Accounts-receivable ledger card is made up for each customer.
   b. The purpose of this card is to show clearly the balance owing by the customer at any one time. In addition, the terms of sale and any special conditions and other information are recorded.

ESTIMATED FINANCIAL STRENGTH			COMPOSITE CREDIT APPRAISAL			
			HIGH	GOOD	FAIR	LIMITED
5A	Over	$50,000,000	1	2	3	4
4A	$10,000,000 to	50,000,000	1	2	3	4
3A	1,000,000 to	10,000,000	1	2	3	4
2A	750,000 to	1,000,000	1	2	3	4
1A	500,000 to	750,000	1	2	3	4
BA	300,000 to	500,000	1	2	3	4
BB	200,000 to	300,000	1	2	3	4
CB	125,000 to	200,000	1	2	3	4
CC	75,000 to	125,000	1	2	3	4
DC	50,000 to	75,000	1	2	3	4
DD	35,000 to	50,000	1	2	3	4
EE	20,000 to	35,000	1	2	3	4
FF	10,000 to	20,000	1	2	3	4
GG	5,000 to	10,000	1	2	3	4
HH	Up to	5,000	1	2	3	4

CLASSIFICATION FOR BOTH ESTIMATED FINANCIAL STRENGTH AND CREDIT APPRAISAL

FINANCIAL STRENGTH BRACKET

1 $125,000 and Over

2 20,000 to 125,000

EXPLANATION

When only the numeral (1 or 2) appears, it is an indication that the estimated financial strength, while not definitely classified, is presumed to be within the range of the ($) figures in the corresponding bracket and that a condition is believed to exist which warrants credit in keeping with that assumption.

"INV." shown in place of a rating indicates that the report was under investigation at the time of going to press. It has no other significance.

Absence of a Listing
The absence of a listing is not be construed as meaning a concern is non-existent, has discontinued business, nor does it have any other meaning. The letters "NQ" on any written report mean "not listed in the Reference Book."

Year Business Started
The numeral shown is the last digit of the year date when the business was established or came under present control or management. Thus, 8 means 1968; 9 means 1969. No dates go past ten years. Thus the absence of a numeral indicates ten years or more. This feature is not used in connection with branch listings.

ABSENCE OF RATING DESIGNATION FOLLOWING NAMES LISTED IN THE REFERENCE BOOK
The absence of a rating, expressed by two hyphens (--), is not to be construed as unfavorable but signifies circumstances difficult to classify within condensed rating symbols. It suggests the advisability of obtaining a report for additional information.

EMPLOYEE RANGE DESIGNATIONS IN REPORTS OR NAMES NOT LISTED IN THE REFERENCE BOOK
Certain businesses do not lend themselves to a Dun & Bradstreet rating and are not listed in the Reference Book. Information on these names, however, continues to be stored and updated in the D&B Business Data Bank. Reports are available on these businesses but instead of a rating they carry an Employee Range Designation (ER) which is indicative of size in terms of number of employees. No other significance should be attached.

KEY TO EMPLOYEE RANGE DESIGNATIONS

ER 1	Over 1000 Employees
ER 2	500 - 999 Employees
ER 3	100 - 499 Employees
ER 4	50 - 99 Employees
ER 5	20 - 49 Employees
ER 6	10 - 19 Employees
ER 7	5 - 9 Employees
ER 8	1 - 4 Employees
ER N	Not Available

TABLE 4.1. Key to Dun & Bradstreet, Inc., Ratings

c. Approved orders are recorded on a customer ledger card.

d. When a new order is received a credit analyst or an order clerk checks the order against the ledger card to verify the terms and the amount of the new order against the balance owing to see if the total falls within the limit set by the credit analyst.

e. Orders that exceed this amount are given to credit analysts or the credit manager for review.

f. If an order is rejected, then someone in the credit department is responsible for informing the sales department of that fact.

[403.4]   **Organization of Credit Support Systems.** In order that credit approval and authorization may be carried out with maximum efficiency and minimum confusion and wasted effort, you must develop organized support systems and mechanical aids. These can be classified as follows:

[403.4.1]   CREDIT FILING SYSTEMS. Every credit department will have a file of customer ledger cards. These cards are filed alphabetically or by code

	1	2	3	4
5A	REQUIREMENTS			
4A	REQUIREMENTS			
3A	REQUIREMENTS			
2A	25,000	15,000		
1A	10,000	5,000		
BA	7,500	3,500		
BB	5,000	3,000		
CB	4,000	2,500	I N Q U I R E	
CC	3,500	2,000		
DC	3,000	1,500	O N A L L	
DD	1,500	1,000		
EE	1,000	750		
FF	800	500		
GG	500	300		
HH	100	100		

1   2,000
2   500

IMPORTANT NOTE:

The average lines indicated above are not intended to suggest limits, but are offered merely as a guide to help process orders. It is suggested inquiry be made on orders in excess of these amounts or when slowness or past due item exists.

Most credit executives consider it good business to inquire on all first orders.

TABLE 4.2. Reference Book Suggested Credit Limit Chart for Processing Orders

and can be broken down by product, division, territory, etc. Depending upon the complexity of the credit operation and the volume of orders a credit department must process, other credit department files can be set up in a multitude of ways. (Note that tickler and collection files will be discussed in Chapter 12, devoted to collection practices and procedures).

1. *Filing methods.*
   a. *Customer file.* In companies that do not collect a great deal of information about each customer, all material—including all credit material—relating to each customer can be filed in one folder.
   b. *Subject file.* In companies with few customers, all material on one subject for all customers can be kept in one folder. All files, including the credit file, would be located in one central place. These two methods have the disadvantage that credit information, which should be kept confidential, is available to all. To help overcome this problem, credit-department files (and the material in them) could be of a different color than other filed material.
   c. *Sectionalized (accordian) credit file.* If a company carries out extensive investigation of its accounts, it might consider maintaining an accordian file for each customer. These folders are divided into eight sections that can be labeled:
      (1) Financial statements.
      (2) Credit analysis.
      (3) Ledger experience.
      (4) Customer history.
      (5) Correspondence.
      (6) Agency report.
      (7) Miscellaneous.
      (8) Interoffice commentaries.
   d. *Credit department subject files.* The credit department can maintain a file for each subject in which all material from all customers pertaining to that subject can be placed. More likely, the credit department will maintain a set of files for each customer.
2. *Special-purpose files.* Credit departments often have one or more of these special files, depending on the complexity of their operation.
   a. *Index file.* This file is used if code numbers or some other method of customer identification not readily apparent is used.
   b. *Summary file.* This file can contain basic credit information about each customer and can be used for initial screening of incoming orders.
   c. *Duplicate invoice file.* Many credit departments receive automatically a duplicate invoice from each order. These can be stored separately.
3. *Microfilm-microfiche systems.* When the material gathered in the credit department is so extensive that it takes up much space, is

hard to retrieve and store quickly, and is subject to loss, the credit manager would be wise to consider a microfilm or micofiche system. Such a system reduces the amount of space that records take up and greatly increases retrieval and storage speeds.

   a. Microfilm generally comes in a roll or cartridge form. Although it is not particularly well suited to files that must be frequently updated because the film must be spliced, records can be indexed and stored for easy, fast access.

   b. Microfiche is a type of microfilm that is produced directly from computer records that are stored in the form of magnetic tape.

   c. Microthin jackets resemble microfiche except that they can be produced manually. Because of a mechanism known as a jacket reader-filler, splicing is unnecessary and records can be easily updated.

[403.4.2]   CREDIT FORMS. All credit departments use a variety of forms to expedite the operation of their work. The following list suggests some possibilities:

1. Financial-statement forms.
2. Customer-summary cards.
3. Credit-terms notice.
4. Statement-comparison forms.
5. Ledger cards.

[403.4.3]   FORM LETTERS. Credit departments should develop form letters to speed up the work flow at every possible level. Many times, form letters can be devised that can be adapted to individual cases. Some form-letter possibilities are:

1. Requests for financial statements.
2. Letters that acknowledge and express appreciation for a new order.
3. Letters that inform customers that credit has been refused or cannot be granted on regular terms.
4. General letters of appreciation for long patronage.
5. Letters that give advice to customers on financial or other matters. These letters will, of course, have to be adapted to each individual case, but the format can be standardized.

[403.4.4]   CREDIT LIBRARY. In order to have helpful credit material readily at hand, the credit manager should attempt to build a credit library. This library does not have to be extensive—or expensive. But it should include some standard credit texts, publications of credit associations, legal and economic information, and helpful Dun & Bradstreet publications, many of which are available at only a nominal charge.

[404]   **CREDIT DEPARTMENT EXPENSES.** While it would, of course, be impossible to specify what credit-department expenses would be for any one company, studies have provided information on the relative importance of different credit-department expenses. This information is available from CRF.

CHAPTER 5

CREDIT INVESTIGATION

[500]   **CREDIT INVESTIGATION.** As credit manager, you know your job is to determine whether a prospective customer will pay his bills to your company—on time, without excessive disputes. When you're right, your company's profits rise and you stand out in the eyes of top management. When you're wrong, you lose and your company loses—in bad debts, which is money thrown down the drain; in potential sales, which is a profit opportunity your company has missed because of your bad judgment.

Making your job tough is the fact that businessmen sometimes say they will pay their bills to you on time and then they don't. You cannot begin and end your investigation with a customer's promise. You have to know what questions to ask, what information to find in order to know how good a customer's promise is likely to be. Knowing the areas of credit investigation is the first step to making the right credit decision.

Not every customer will warrant a thorough examination in each area. The cost of credit information in time and effort can be high. You should devote more attention to the investigation of marginal accounts than you do to established customers in healthy financial condition. Nevertheless, you should be aware of every potential trouble spot a detailed credit investigation can expose. Here they are:

[501]   **OWNERSHIP.** The first thing to find out is who owns the business. "That's obvious," you might say. But remember: About 20 percent of the businesses operating at the beginning of this year will either have vanished or changed their ownership by the end of the year. Remember, too, that things are not always what they seem. The sign on the store might say "Johnson's Hardware," but the store may be owned by Johnson's Hardware, Inc., and its operation actually may be directed by the local bank—not by friendly George Johnson, who signed your order.

Ownership is a legal matter. Whoever holds title to the assets of a business is legally the owner and is legally responsible for paying the bills. You should therefore be aware of the following two situations:

1. *Agent or manager.* An agent is a person appointed to transact the business of another. The manager or agent derives his authority from the owner. Frequently, the owner confers written authority upon the agent by means of a power of attorney, but often informal, spoken authority is given.

   The owner may confer only limited power or he may confer very broad power. The owner may even confer such wide power that he practically loses control over his own assets. An agent or manager, therefore, may become the person who most influences the success, failure, or payment policies of the business. If this is the case, you must investigate the character, integrity, and abilities of the agent or manager before reaching a credit decision.

   Nevertheless, it is the owner who is legally liable and responsible for the debts incurred by the company.

2. *Hidden ownership.* Hidden ownership occurs when someone who has a very strong interest in a business, who has provided all or part of the capital, and who actually shapes the policies, wishes someone else to assume technical ownership. This is done by transferring the assets to the name of the technical owners. The technical owners are often referred to as "straw owners" or "straw names."

   Again, the hidden owner may be the one who determines the success, failure, and payment policies of the company. If that is the case, then he's the one you should investigate.

   Nevertheless, it is the technical owner who is legally liable and legally responsible for the company's debts.

   Here are the questions to ask to determine if someone is a hidden owner:
   a. Does he make important decisions?
   b. Is he authorized to sign on the bank account?
   c. Does he buy substantial amounts of merchandise?
   d. Does he fight the battles of the business?

[501.1]   **Composition of the Business.** The owner's liability—the extent of his responsibility under law—depends upon the legal composition of the business. You must be able to identify and understand the seven principal forms of business organization listed below:

[501.1.1]   SOLE PROPRIETORSHIP.

1. *Definition.* The sole proprietorship is a business enterprise owned by one person. The person is usually the manager, as well as its owner. The individual owner does business directly.

2. *Responsibility.* In a sole proprietorship, the owner has both his business and personal assets at stake. If he runs up debts, and he doesn't have enough business assets to pay, you may sue and attach whatever personal assets he may have over and above personal exemptions. (A personal exemption is the legal right of a debtor to retain a specified portion of his personal property free

from sale on execution. The size of exemption is prescribed by state laws and therefore is not uniform in amount.)

[501.1.2]   GENERAL PARTNERSHIP.

1. *Definition.* A partnership is an association of two or more persons to carry on as co-owners of a business for profit. (Note that there may be other types of partnerships and partners—limited or special partners, for example. These will be discussed under Section 501.1.3.)

2. *Responsibility.* Members of a general partnership are jointly and severally liable for debts of the firm. This means that each partner stands to lose not only what he put into the business, if the enterprise fails, but if the assets of the firm are insufficient to cover the debts, each partner is also *personally* liable for the debts of the firm. Thus, a man with means may be called upon to pay all the debts of the partnership if it develops that his partner or partners have no outside resources.

   This element of unlimited liability is the principal disadvantage of the general partnership from the partners' point of view. *As a creditor, however, you can recognize that personal wealth of any one of the general partners adds to the attractiveness of the credit risk.* The general wealth of a limited partner is of no credit significance.

   When any partner does something in or for the business, he automatically binds the whole partnership. Even if a debt is contracted by one partner without the consent of the other partners, the others become personally liable. This is because as far as outsiders are concerned, each partner has a right to act for the partnership. Each partner is said to be an "agent." But if a partner contracts a debt or acts outside the business (places a mortgage on his house, for instance), he does not bind the partnership.

3. *Establishment.* When two or more persons form a partnership, they enter into a contract. The terms of the contract are carefully outlined in a partnership agreement. The agreement is usually written, although an oral agreement is binding. Such points as the division of profits or losses, and the procedure to be followed in case of the death of any partner are clearly defined in the agreement.

4. *Kinds of partnerships.* Partnerships may be set up in various ways. There may be one single partner who supplies all the capital and who, through the partnership agreement, "controls" the policies of the firm even though there are eight or ten other partners. If such is the case, you investigate with special care this partner's abilities and intentions. At times, a partner may come in who provides no capital, but who works on a profit-sharing basis. A good salesman is sometimes given such an interest.

[501.1.3]   LIMITED PARTNERSHIP.

1. *Definition.* A limited partnership is a partnership having as members one or more general partners and one or more limited partners. A limited partner contributes cash or property to the

firm but does not enter into the actual operation of the business. He would, of course, receive a share of any profits the partnership earned but he would *not* be personally liable for debts beyond his capital contribution.

2. *Responsibility.* The *general* partners have all those rights and powers and are subject to all restrictions and liabilities of partners in a general partnership and are jointly and severally liable for the partnership debts and obligations. The *limited* partners are not liable beyond the capital contributed to the firm. Dealings between the firm and third persons are to be carried on by the general partners. The general participation of a limited partner in the conduct of the firm may subject him to liability as a general partner.

3. *Agreement.* Because of the limitation feature, you, as a creditor, have to know exactly with whom you are dealing. Clearly, disaster could strike if you granted credit because a well-to-do man was a "partner" in a firm, but later you found out he was only a limited partner. To protect against such situations, most states require the filing of a limited partnership certificate signed by all the partners and which contains the following information:

   a. Name of the partnership and principal place of business.
   b. Character of business partnership will engage in.
   c. Names and addresses of each partner, with specification as to who are general and who are limited partners.
   d. Amount of cash and description of other property contributed by each limited partner.
   e. Duration of partnership.

   Unlike a general partnership, which is a common-law form of organization, the authority for the existence of a limited partnership is derived from statutes. Before a legal limited partnership contract can be drawn up, the partners must comply with state regulations.

   Notice of the formation of limited partnerships is frequently published in legal or daily newspapers.

4. *Limited partnership names.* You should be aware that various state laws contain provisions as to the use of firm names and names of partners so that the public knows that a limited partnership exists. In some states, the name of at least one general partner must appear in the firm name. According to the Uniform Limited Partnership Act itself, the name of a limited partner is not to appear in the title except under certain unusual conditions, such as the name of the limited partner is *also* the name of a general partner.

5. *Undistributed profits.* A limited partner may let profits accumulate in the business. There is some question whether you should consider them liabilities due the limited partner or whether you should consider them part of the firm's capital when you evaluate the credit risk. Such a situation requires careful investigation of the circumstances existing in the particular state.

CORPORATION.

1. *Definition.* A corporation is an artificial body created by law and endowed by law with the power of acting in many respects as a single individual and to carry on business as authorized in its articles of incorporation. Nevertheless, as an enterprise created out of the power of the law, a corporation stands on its own feet, has its own assets and liabilities, and its own rights and privileges and responsibilities apart from the individuals who run it or hold stock in it.

2. *Responsibility.* Unlike sole proprietorships and partnerships, shareholders and managers of a corporation are *not* liable for the debts of the corporation. The corporation is responsible for its own debts. Its stockholders may lose whatever they paid for the stock in the corporation as the stock diminishes in value due to losses, but the stockholders are not called on to meet the debts of the corporation should the assets of the corporation not cover its debts.

(There are a few exceptions to the above. In some states, shareholders are personally liable to the employees of the corporation for unpaid wages. In practically all states, stockholders of banks and financial institutions may under certain circumstances be liable beyond the shareholders of the ordinary business corporation.)

Because members of the corporation are not liable, you must not confuse the assets of a corporation with the assets of either its stockholders or its management in your evaluation of the credit risk. A small corporation, for example, has an entity separate and distinct from its president—even though the president may own all the stock and may be the day-to-day manager. He may, it is true, buy merchandise, but he does so as an officer and employee of the corporation. He signs the purchase order as president, not as owner of the assets. *He* is not the owner, but rather the *corporation* controlled by him is the owner.

3. *Establishment.* When a corporation is formed, a certain number of people are asked to provide the capital. Those who contribute are known as shareholders or stockholders. They hand over certain assets, usually cash, and get in exchange a certificate of stock for the capital provided. (The amount of stock a corporation is authorized to issue is fixed by its charter.) Thus a stockholder who owns ten shares of stock in a corporation which has 1,000 shares of capital stock outstanding, owns 10/1,000 or 1/100 of the corporation.

All assets acquired by a corporation are owned exclusively by the corporation, and it is the corporation that holds legal title to such property. The property of a corporation is not subject to the control of individual members, but only to the control of the corporation itself, which acts through its officers, subject to the conditions prescribed by law.

Again, the stockholders have no *personal* responsibility for the debts of the corporation (beyond the exceptions listed above). It is only the corporation that can be looked to for satisfaction. A stockholder, unlike a member of a general partnership, risks only his equity interest in a corporation.

Because of this legal situation, look to the balance sheet to define the limits of the responsibility of the corporation. As a creditor, you cannot look beyond to the personal assets of the stockholders. On the other hand, if you are a private creditor of one of the stockholders, you can attach the *stock* owned by that stockholder because that is a personal asset. This does not in any way change the status of the corporation. That share of the corporation ownership merely passes from one person to another.

The typical procedure for forming a corporation is as follows:

a. The incorporators, having met the requirements as to number and citizenship, prepare or have prepared articles of incorporation that set forth the detailed information required by the state law.

b. Upon being properly executed, the articles (along with the necessary fees) are submitted to the secretary of state.

c. When satisfied that the articles are in proper form, that they meet the requirements of the law, and that the object of the corporation is lawful, the secretary of state will file the articles in the proper state records and issue a certificate of incorporation.

d. The articles of incorporation are then placed on public record.

e. The incorporators and directors hold their first meetings for the purpose of taking the necessary steps for getting the corporation under way, such as adoption of bylaws and election of officers.

f. Sometimes, incorporators must give public notice of the incorporation by newspaper and submit proof that they did so to the secretary of state.

4. *Management.* Control of a corporation rests with the holders of a majority of the stock. The stockholders of a corporation elect a board of directors. The board directs the general policies of the corporation and elects the officers who control the day-to-day activities of the company. In evaluating the credit risk, you must investigate the abilities of a corporation's operating managers as well as the determination of the board to set the corporation's goals and see that the managers meet them.

5. *Charter.* A corporation comes into being only when the state or federal government grants a charter. A charter confers the right to exercise corporate powers. *Until a charter is actually granted, the business does not exist as a corporation and is therefore not responsible.*

6. *Bylaws.* Supplementary and subordinate to the charter is a set of rules that regulate the internal management of the corporation. They relate to such matters as the powers of the officers, the time

of stockholders' meetings, and the handling of funds. They usually designate the number of directors the board will have.

7. *Subsidiaries.* One development peculiar to corporations is the formation of subsidiary concerns. One company may form a second company, or may buy the stock of a second company. The first is known as the "parent" and the second is known as the "subsidiary." A subsidiary is any corporation with more than 50 percent of its voting stock owned by another corporation.

Subsidiary companies are formed for several purposes. The subsidiary may carry on a business somewhat different from that of the parent company, or at a different location. At times the subsidiary is formed to split up the liability, particularly when some new undertaking is to be started.

Although courts have held that the subsidiary corporation is, in fact, an extension of the personality of the parent company, there is no automatic assurance that the parent company will cover all or part of the debts of its subsidiary in the case of financial embarrassment. The existence of a strong parent company does not necessarily strengthen the credit risk represented by a subsidiary. In fact, for the parent to become legally liable for the debts of the subsidiary, formal guarantees must be signed.

8. *Affiliates.* When one concern has an interest in another, although that interest is 50 percent or less, the second concern is said to be affiliated or associated with the first. One concern may also be affiliated with another merely because the stock of the one is owned by the officers of another. You should remember, however, that there is not necessarily a direct financial connection between affiliated companies as far as responsibility is concerned. A corporation is not responsible for the debts of its affiliates. Nevertheless, failure of an affiliate, especially when the parent company holds a large interest, can threaten the financial stability of the parent.

[501.1.5]   ESTATES.

1. *Definition.* An estate of a decedent is not another form of business organization in the strict sense of the word, but it presents unique problems in evaluating the credit risk. When a person dies, that which he owned at his death—his estate—must be disposed of in some manner. If he leaves a will, the will is probated (that is, tested or proved) and "letters testamentary" are issued to the "executor" named in the will. If the decedent left no will (dies "intestate"), an administrator rather than an executor is appointed by the court.

2. *Will.* The will is the "charter" under which an estate is directed. The will is the document in which the decedent has outlined what he wants done with his property, and the court will do everything in its power to see that the wishes of the "will" of the decedent are carried out. In many cases, the will outlines very definitely what is to happen to the interest of a decedent in a business.

3. *Responsibility.* The question of responsibility of an estate is of vital importance. As a credit man, you should make sure that you know where it lies. In the ordinary, nonestate business situation, the responsibility is clearly outlined. That is, you can determine who is responsible and the degree of responsibility as measured by legal prescriptions and financial strength. In the case of an estate, however, the property or the assets may be owned by the estate, but because of one legal restriction or another, it may be that the executor or the administrator will be unable or unwilling to satisfy your claim. You must remember that unless the will shows very clearly that it is the wish of the decedent that his property shall be put at the risk of the business, the courts will usually see to it that the executor or the administrator remove the property from the risk of the business as soon as possible.

In all cases, when a business principal with whom you are doing business dies, you should contact the executor or the administrator of the estate immediately to find out how it will be disposed.

[501.1.6]   MASSACHUSETTS OR VOLUNTARY TRUST.

1. *Definition.* A Massachusetts or voluntary trust exists when title to the company's property is vested in trustees, and the persons interested in the trust have received certificates showing their interest in the property. The management of the business is entrusted to the trustees whose powers are limited by the declaration of the trust. It involves the separation of the ownership of property into two parts: (1) the legal title being held by one (a trustee) for the benefit of (2) others called beneficiaries. Incidentally, this form of business organization is called a Massachusetts trust because it became popular in that state, where the law prohibited organization of corporations whose purpose was to own and deal in land.

2. *Responsibility.* Whether such an organization constitutes a partnership and carries with it partnership liabilities has been the subject of numerous court decisions in many states. When evaluating a credit risk, however, consider common-law trusts as corporations. The beneficiaries are in a similar position to that of stockholders of a corporation, except that beneficiaries have only minor control over the trustees. If a court finds that it is vested in beneficiaries, the business entity may be judged a partnership. In determining the risk of such an organization, find out who really makes the decisions.

3. *Deed of trust.* The deed of trust outlines the duties, powers, and liabilities of the trustees; the right of the beneficiaries; and the duration of the association. The deed of trust is open to public inspection.

[501.1.7]   JOINT VENTURE.

1. *Definition.* A joint venture is an association of two or more persons or business organizations to carry out a single business transaction for profit. In order to do this, they combine all or part of their

property, money, efforts, skill, and knowledge. These arrangements are becoming more frequent, particularly in the construction field.

2. *Responsibility.* Legal responsibility is similar to that of partnerships and, in most court decisions, the law of partnerships is being applied. There is a difference, however, in that one coadventurer does not bind the other by his acts in the same manner as in the ordinary partnership. Also, the joint venture covers but one particular transaction.

3. *Contract.* The contract of joint venture should show the intent of the contractors and will use appropriate words to bind the promisors to complete the whole of the obligation—either together or separately, if one or the other fails to perform. The fact that often joint adventurers do not realize they have actually formed a joint venture, subject to special laws, makes careful investigation of such a situation, when suspected, essential.

[501.1.8]   SUMMARY OF SPECIAL CREDIT FEATURES OF CERTAIN FORMS OF BUSINESS ORGANIZATION.

1. *Individual proprietorship.*
   a. Credit risk is enhanced or weakened depending on the personal assets of the proprietor, which are available to creditors.
   b. Management skills must be possessed by one man. In some cases the proprietor may have all the needed abilities but partnerships and corporations provide a greater opportunity for diversified management skills of a number of people.
   c. The life span of the business is less stable since it often depends upon the well-being of the proprietor.
   d. The proprietor is his own boss, so decisions—both wise and unwise—can be made quickly with no review or control.

2. *Partnerships.*
   a. Credit risk is enhanced or weakened depending on the personal means of the partners (if they are general partners), which are available to creditors.
   b. Existence of several partners means that necessary business skills are more likely to be available to the firm.
   c. Existence of several partners also means that dissension is possible; therefore, sudden breakup of the partnership is possible.

3. *Corporation.*
   a. A corporation has no assets beyond those listed on its balance sheet. Creditors cannot look to management's or the stockholders' assets to satisfy the debts of the firm.
   b. The board of directors can review management's performance and make speedy changes in personnel if not satisfied. This, of course, would not be true if the company is closely held with one or two people running it.
   c. Corporations have perpetual life. Changes in stock ownership

and changes in management have no effect on the duration of the business.

[501.2]   **Verification of Ownership.** In order to verify the form of business organization—and thus ownership and responsibility—use the following devices:

[501.2.1]   REGISTRATION. Most states have laws requiring that any person or persons, before carrying on any business under an assumed or fictitious name (such as ACE Trucking Company), first file a signed certificate revealing:

1. Their real names and addresses.
2. The name under which they will do business.
3. The name of the agent who has authority to represent them, and his address, if the owners live outside the state.

[501.2.2]   FINANCIAL STATEMENT PROPERLY SIGNED. If you require a customer to submit a financial statement, request that he have the owner of the company sign it and indicate his title. In a partnership, all partners must sign the statement in order for you to consider it valid assurance of ownership.

[501.2.3]   WRITTEN ACKNOWLEDGEMENT. A letter, properly signed by the owner or owners, will assure you of ownership. Remember that the letter must be signed by the person who acknowledges ownership and responsibility. One man cannot vouch for the assumption of responsibility of another.

[501.2.4]   OTHER PUBLIC RECORDS. These include recorded bills of sale, general- and limited-partnership agreements on record, records of litigation, filings under the Uniform Commercial Code—all of which reveal true ownership.

[501.2.5]   ADVERTISEMENTS AND ANNOUNCEMENTS IN THE PRESS. Announcements of ownership changes and advertisements showing ownership can be read in newspapers, magazines, and trade publications.

[501.2.6]   BANK RECORDS. Banks will generally have records of ownership.

[501.2.7]   ACCOUNTANT'S STATEMENTS. Accountant's statements will sometimes reveal ownership either in the certificate or in the capital accounts of the statement.

[501.2.8]   LEASES, FIRE-INSURANCE POLICIES, AND OTHER FORMAL DOCUMENTS. When you can procure them, these documents sometimes disclose ownership.

[501.2.9]   OTHER SUPPLIERS. Your industry colleagues can tell you who hold themselves out as owners of a business.

[501.2.10]   LOCAL AUTHORITIES. Chambers of commerce and local trade associations can confirm your understanding of ownership.

[501.2.11]   CREDIT REPORTS. Business information reports, such as those issued by Dun & Bradstreet, generally disclose ownership.

[502]   ANTECEDENTS. Once you have determined who the owners and managers of a business are, the next step is to investigate their antecedents. All credit men recognize how important it is to know what their potential customers have done in the past. Many credit men consider that that is the most important element of the credit investigation. The reason?

There is no better prediction of the future than the lessons of the past. If a man has proven himself honest, conscientious, and skillful in the past, that is your best assurance that he will be honest, conscientious, and skillful in the future. If, on the other hand, he has been dishonest, lazy, and incompetent before, you had better be on your guard against the possibility that he will be again. Businesses do not run themselves. Their policies and results are shaped by people. Most companies rely completely on the abilities of a very few men. Find out what they are like. Even though large corporations are run by management teams, which reduce the influence of any one man, you should determine the ability and honesty of those in charge.

Antecedent information is important not only in helping you forecast the future of a business; it may also be important in determining the accuracy of other information you may receive—especially financial information which is not in the form of audited figures prepared by a CPA. Has management generally been accurate in the past with sales and profit predictions? Or have they been off the mark? More generally, past experience will help you decide whether a financial statement is (1) an incorrect representation dishonestly made, (2) an honest representation incorrectly made, or (3) an adequate representation honestly made according to accepted accounting procedures.

[502.1]   **Preliminary Examination of Antecedents.** Before you begin evaluating a businessman's antecedents, make sure that you have them all. Do this by verifying:

1. That there are no gaps in a man's history.
2. That you have examined all previous business ownerships and employment.
3. That you are not overlooking any of a businessman's activities because they were conducted under a different name. A change of name is usually made through petition to a court and the court order becomes a matter of public record. Remember that there is nothing improper in a man's changing his name (without going to court), provided no fraud is involved.

[502.2]   **Information Relevant to a Man's Character.** This information will tell you whether a man has been willing and determined to pay his bills in the past, and thus how likely he will be to do so in the future. When trying to evaluate a man's character, remember that the absence of incriminatory factors is just as revealing—if not more so—than the appearance of accolades. Drawing upon your own experiences and those of others whom you are able to contact, look for:

[502.2.1]   PAST HISTORY OF LAWSUITS AND CRIMINAL PROCEEDINGS. When a man is called upon to defend himself in a court of law, he may be charged with a crime or he may be the defendant in a civil proceeding. With few exceptions, alleged violations of private rights constitute civil actions, whereas alleged violations of public laws constitute criminal actions. The exceptions are those public laws that have both civil and criminal sections, such as the antitrust laws.

1. *Civil proceedings.* When a suit is entered, it means that one party (the plaintiff) claims that he has been wronged. The mere fact

that a businessman (or a business) is sued does not mean that he is guilty. Nevertheless, a pattern of suits brought against or brought by a customer can be a good indication that you might encounter payment problems of one sort or another.

When a case goes through a court and a judgment is returned against the prospective customer, that means that in the opinion of the court, he has breached the legal right of another. You should be on your guard that the same thing does not happen to you. For these reasons, you should find out if the businessman you are investigating has been involved in any civil proceedings and what their nature was. Be particularly attentive to these features:

a. Whether satisfaction (payment) of a judgment has caused or indicates an impairment of financial condition in an otherwise healthy company.

b. Whether judgments or court opinions have been entered against the businessman that are based on matters that reflect significant deviation from expected behavior or business practice such as judgments awarding damages for assault and battery, civil antitrust activities, violation of trade secrets, and misappropriation of funds. Such circumstances would reveal a potential customer of considerable moral uncertainty.

c. Whether a suit was for damages to collect insurance, which is often the only method to collect a completely legitimate, nonincriminating claim.

2. *Criminal proceedings.* As in civil proceedings, the fact that a man is brought before a court of law and charged with a criminal act is no proof of guilt. However, at the time it occurs it can have an effect on the business for several reasons, including possible excessive time away from the business or a drain on finances. If he is found guilty, however, that is a strong warning that his subsequent actions must be carefully examined before you grant credit. If he is judged innocent or pardoned, but if there is a pattern of criminal charges against a man, that is an indication that the credit risk could be high. A man who is repeatedly defending himself in court, regardless of his guilt or innocence, can certainly not devote the necessary time and energy to his business affairs. As a creditor, you stand to lose.

3. *Crime commissions.* In addition to civil and criminal proceedings, governmental or civic crime commissions and legislative committees can launch investigations into the business activities of a man. You should be aware if your prospective customers have been subject to such investigations because such investigations, too, can detract from a businessman's devotion to his business.

[502.2.2]   PAST HISTORY OF FIRES. Fires represent particular hazards to business operations. Even the most innocent fires cause delayed collections for creditors and can often result in credit losses. This is because fire-insurance policies, even where they are held and even though they do cover damage, do not always result in 100 percent coverage of loss.

Losses occur because business stops and payments such as salaries, rent, and interest on borrowed money continue. Business comes to a halt and the fire-stricken company never gets the opportunity to recover in the slow season what it lost in the busy season. The time it takes to determine the value of lost merchandise and to collect insurance can also mean that finance charges accumulate and debt rises. More serious, fires sometimes occur and losses are suffered because desperate businessmen turn to arson to solve their problems. Therefore, it is imperative that you determine if a businessman has suffered a fire and, if so, you should establish the following:

1. Date of fire.
2. Assets damaged.
3. Whether it was a total or partial loss.
4. The amount of loss to merchandise, fixtures, buildings, and other assets.
5. Amount of insurance carried.
6. Amount of insurance recovery.
7. Salvage value of merchandise, fixtures, equipment, buildings, or other assets.
8. Cause of fire.
9. Whether the business is continuing in operation at the same location and, if so, under what conditions.
10. Whether operations have been temporarily suspended.
11. Criticism of the cause of the fire, if any.

Knowing the above will help you determine the part the business-man played in the fire, his responsibility in protecting himself against fire loss, his ability to remain in business, and his ability to pay his bills on time.

[502.2.3]   EVIDENCE OF A BUSINESSMAN'S STABILITY, including:

1. His age.
2. His marital status.
3. Participation in church and civic affairs, which strengthens the credit risk.
4. General reputation as to honesty, integrity, and conscientiousness.
5. Any history of involvement with drugs or alcoholism.

[502.3]   **Information Relevant to a Man's Ability.** These facts will enable you to determine whether, if willing, a man will be able to pay his bills on time. Therefore, investigate:

[502.3.1]   PAST EXPERIENCE IN THE SAME FIELD IN WHICH HE NOW OPERATES. This includes the answers to such questions as:

1. When?
2. Where?
3. What the responsibilities were?

[502.3.2]   PAST EXPERIENCE IN OTHER FIELDS. Determine what, if anything, is relevant to the man's current activities.

[502.3.3]   SPECIAL FACTORS WHICH COULD INFLUENCE THE RELATIVE IMPORTANCE OF PAST EXPERIENCE. Factors include:

1. Success when working for someone else, if the man is now self-

employed (or ability to work on a management team if previous success came when the man was self-employed).

2. Success in operating a small-size company where problems were more simple and easily handled, when the company has now grown and the problems are difficult, complex—and different.

3. The existence of a contract or some other agreement that might inspire complacency.

Remember: A man's previous success is properly valued only when it is compared with his current activities.

[502.3.4]   INVOLVEMENT IN OTHER ENDEAVORS. Government posts or other jobs could siphon off a man's time and energy as well as create conflicts of interest or financial weakness in your potential customer. To evaluate a businessman's participation in other activities, you must determine:

1. The name of the related concern and the percentage of his participation or ownership.

2. The activities of the affiliated concern, where it is located, and when it was started.

3. Any intercompany relations, such as:
   a. Whether one business buys or sells from another.
   b. Whether there is money borrowed or advanced.
   c. Whether there are any guarantees or endorsements.

4. The financial strength of the related company as evidenced by tangible net worth and other facts.

The separate activities of individual proprietors and partners are of particular importance. You might be including their personal assets in your evaluation of the risk when, in fact, they could already be pledged through another business.

[502.3.5]   ANY HISTORY OF BUSINESS FAILURE. A business failure occurs when there has been a loss to creditors. Although a loss of equity or invested capital without a loss to creditors is not a business failure, any involvement of a businessman that necessitates the halt of a business should spur careful investigation. Actual failures include bankruptcies, general compromises and extensions, whether or not they are court-supervised, and informal discontinuances when there is a loss to creditors.

Whenever a man is associated with a business failure, you should determine:

1. *Type of failure.* A "voluntary" bankruptcy may reflect a lack of confidence management had in itself or at least manifests their opinion that the plight was hopeless. An "involuntary" bankruptcy gives evidence that those selling goods or services to the business were doubtful that management could or would turn the business around.

2. *Cause of failure.* If you don't know the cause, you won't be able to judge the significance of the failure. In fact, failures must attract your immediate attention because all evidence reveals that the principal cause of failures is management deficiency. Dun & Bradstreet investigations show that management deficiencies were responsible for 93.5 percent of all manufacturing failures and 93.4 percent of all wholesale failures (See Table 5.1). Even

Percent	Manufacturers	Wholesalers	Retailers	Construction	Commercial Services	All	Underlying Causes
	1.8	1.6	2.3	2.5	1.1	2.0	**Neglect**
	1.5	3.1	1.2	1.1	1.5	1.5	**Fraud**
	8.2	8.1	16.9	8.7	13.9	13.0	**Lack of Experience in the Line**
	11.9	12.8	14.9	20.7	14.8	15.0	**Lack of Managerial Experience**
	22.0	21.5	23.5	27.5	23.0	23.6	**Unbalanced Experience***
	51.4	51.0	37.4	37.3	41.1	41.5	**Incompetence**
	1.1	0.9	1.3	—	0.6	0.9	**Disaster**
	2.1	1.0	2.5	2.2	4.0	2.5	**Reason Unknown**
	100.0	100.0	100.0	100.0	100.0	100.0	Total
	1,576	965	4,398	1,375	1,252	9,566	Number of Failures
	$486,669	$258,694	$126,937	$140,749	$185,154	$209,099	Average Liabilities Per Failure

*Experience not well rounded in sales, finance, purchasing, and production on the part of the individual in case of a proprietorship, or of two or more partners or officers constituting a management unit,

TABLE 5.1. Causes of 9,566 Business Failures in 1972
Source: Dun & Bradstreet, Inc.

when a business stops with no loss to creditors, you must recognize that proven inability in the past is the strongest possible warning against inability in the future.

3. *Amount of liabilities.* A failure with large liabilities should cause more concern than one with few debts outstanding.

4. *Final settlement with creditors.* If you know the amount of liabilities, but not the final settlement, you know only half the story. Determination to pay off creditors—and success in doing so—is strong assurance that a man has a strong sense of obligation to creditors. Providing that he acquires the needed abilities to run a business, or employs those who compensate for his deficiencies, a man with a past failure who subsequently paid all his debts can become a good credit risk.

When a man who has had a business failure asks you for new credit, ask yourself these questions:

1. Does he have adequate capital?
2. Does he have a reasonably good knowledge of the line?
3. Is he watching liabilities? Excessive debt is present in most failures, so you should check carefully for:
   a. Excessive volume for capital employed.

Apparent Causes	Percent	Manufacturers	Wholesalers	Retailers	Construction	Commercial Services	All
Due to .... Bad Habits		0.4	—	0.5	0.9	0.2	0.5
Poor Health		1.2	1.1	0.9	1.2	0.8	1.0
Marital Difficulties		—	0.1	0.4	0.1	0.1	0.2
Other		0.2	0.4	0.5	0.3	—	0.3
On the part of the principals, reflected by .... Misleading Name		0.1	0.1	0.0	—	—	0.0
False Financial Statement		0.2	0.4	0.2	0.5	0.2	0.3
Premediated Overbuy		0.1	0.1	0.1	—	—	0.1
Irregular Disposal of Assets		1.1	2.2	0.8	0.5	1.1	1.0
Other		—	0.3	0.1	0.1	0.2	0.1
Evidenced by inability to avoid conditions which resulted in .... Inadequate Sales		48.9	50.0	45.7	35.9	46.9	45.4
Heavy Operating Expenses		11.6	8.1	6.3	12.4	8.4	8.5
Receivables Difficulties		16.1	18.9	4.1	16.0	6.5	9.6
Inventory Difficulties		4.4	9.4	7.9	1.6	1.4	5.7
Excessive Fixed Assets		6.5	2.5	2.5	3.7	6.1	3.8
Poor Location		1.3	2.3	7.3	1.0	2.7	4.3
Competitive Weakness		20.4	20.9	27.8	32.3	26.8	26.4
Other		10.2	8.6	4.7	5.2	8.2	6.5
Some of these occurrences could have been provided against through insurance .... Fire		0.7	0.6	0.8	—	0.2	0.6
Flood		0.1	—	0.1	—	—	0.1
Burglary		—	0.1	0.2	—	—	0.1
Employees' Fraud		0.1	—	0.0	—	—	0.0
Strike		—	0.1	0.0	—	0.2	0.0
Other		0.2	0.1	0.2	—	0.2	0.1
Per Cent Of Total Failures		16.5	10.1	46.0	14.3	13.1	100.0

Because some failures are attributed to a combination of apparent causes, the totals of these columns exceed the totals of the corresponding columns on the left.

    b. Operating losses.

    c. Too liberal withdrawals.

  4. Has he put too much capital in fixed assets?

  5. Is inventory in line with sales?

  6. Has he granted credit too liberally so that capital is tied up in slow receivables?

  7. Is he investing or lending money that should be retained in the business?

  8. Is he controlling expenses?

  9. Is he building sales on adequate markup?

If your prospective customer provides satisfactory answers to these questions, if there is other evidence that the new business is running well (such as healthy sales, employee contentment, and operation over an extended period of time), you might look more favorably on the credit risk. Remember, however, that failures are signals that management has failed. Don't be fooled by explanations such as "lack of working capital, strong competition, changes in demand," and the other old saws. These things are the result of—not the justification for—management failure.

[502.3.6]   PROVEN EXPERIENCE IN THE FOUR AREAS NECESSARY FOR BUSINESS SUCCESS:

1. Finance.
2. Sales.
3. Purchasing.
4. Production.

[502.4]   **Special Considerations for Management Teams.** Individual managers of larger corporations and other enterprises where management teams control the day-to-day operations should, of course, be investigated with respect to the qualities and abilities listed above. As a team, however, it is the composite of abilities that counts, not the overall abilities of one man. Thus, management teams, not individuals, must be versed in sales, finance, production, and purchasing. In addition:

[502.4.1]   DELEGATION OF AUTHORITY. Management teams must make adequate provision that the necessary authority for decision-making has been distributed among responsible people.

[502.4.2]   SPIRIT. Management teams must have spirit.

[502.4.3]   BALANCE. Management teams must have balance. Look for teams where:

1. The optimism of youth balances the pessimism of age.
2. The adaptability of youth balances the conservatism of age.
3. The ambition of youth balances acceptance of the status quo.
4. The energy of youth balances the perspective of age.
5. The experience of age balances the immaturity of youth.

[502.5]   **Special Considerations for Family Management.**

[502.5.1]   HUSBANDS AND WIVES. The business activities of a theoretically nonactive husband or wife often can have a bearing on the business you are investigating. Where they do appear important (extensive activity of one spouse when the other is the technical owner, for instance), get the details.

[502.5.2]   FATHERS AND SONS. Be aware of the activities and abilities of the father when the son has recently gone into business for himself. Often, the father is supplying the capital and knowhow for the enterprise. His continued aid might be necessary for the business's survival. Remember, too, that the success of the father is no assurance of the success of the son when he takes over the family business. This is certainly more true in the case of the founder's grandchildren.

[502.6]   **When Management Changes.** Management changes occur because of death, departure, retirement, and termination. Depending on the circumstances, you should determine the following:

[502.6.1]   DEATH. When a proprietor, partner, or important stockholder dies, find out:

1. Amount of life insurance and name of beneficiary.
2. Whether the estate has been probated.
3. Names of heirs and their interests.
4. Name of the executor, if there is a will; the bond required and the limit of the executor's authority.
5. Name of the administrator, if there is no will.
6. Provisions for continuing or winding up the business, or disposing of the interest of the deceased.

The death of a stockholder, director, or officer of a corporation has no effect upon the corporate entity itself, which continues. It will have an effect upon the stock ownership and possibly on the management.

[502.6.2]   RETIREMENT OR VOLUNTARY DEPARTURE. When management retires or quits, you should learn:

1. The degree to which the retiring management was responsible for the company's success (or lack of success).
2. Whether the departures were foreseen and whether replacements had been hired and trained.
3. Whether the new management is composed of men capable of operating the business or whether they represent investors or "business executioners."

[502.6.3]   TERMINATION. When management is terminated, find out:

1. If the new management will remedy incompetence.
2. Whether the new management is composed of men who represent investors or "business executioners."
3. If the business will continue the same operation according to the same principles.

[503]   **HISTORY OF THE BUSINESS.** Just as you investigate the background of the principals of a business, so, too, must you investigate the history of the business itself. Like the individuals who run them, businesses have past histories of success and failure that are our best guides to their future. Here are the facts you need.

[503.1]   **Length of Time in Business.** Length of time in business refers to length of time present ownership has been in control of the business. Knowing this fact is essential because the first years of a business are critical. The latest Dun & Bradstreet figures show that more than half of the businesses that fail do so during the first five years. And of this half, most fail during the first three years. If you know when a business began, you can better gauge its probability of survival.

[503.1.1]   NEW BUSINESSES. New businesses pose the most critical problems of evaluation for credit managers. As a first step toward evaluating the new business, find out:

1. *Amount of starting capital.* Starting capital must be sufficient to finance the kind and extent of operation planned by the management.
2. *Source of starting capital.* Starting capital is usually derived from:
   a. Savings.
   b. Borrowings.
   c. Gifts.
   d. Inheritance.
   e. Sale of real estate.
   f. Sale of a prior business.

Knowing the source of the starting capital tells you if the owner had the ability to earn and accumulate his own capital. The attitude of a man risking his own money can differ from that of a man using somebody else's. If the money has been borrowed, find out how much and the source of the funds. This often reveals significant details about the future operations and financing of the business.

You should recognize that the problems of a brand-new business and a business that has come under new management will be different. An old business with new management will at least have an established market and customers. It will have some kind of image with the public. A new business must start from scratch.

After the first year, however, all new businesses will face the same problems and possibilities. These include the following, which have been adapted by permission of the publisher from *Improving Credit Practice* by Donald E. Miller and Donald B. Relkin, copyright 1971 by the American Management Association, Inc.:

1. Original funds will have been dissipated.
2. The business can be judged on performance.
3. Rapid changes are possible.

Age in Years	Manu-facturing	Wholesale	Retail	Construction	Service	All Concerns
One Year or Less	2.0%	1.6%	1.9%	1.3%	2.4%	1.9%
Two	11.8	8.9	16.0	10.3	10.8	13.0
Three	13.5	12.5	20.4	14.8	16.6	17.0
Total Three Years or Less	27.3	23.0	38.3	26.4	29.8	31.9
Four	13.3	12.4	13.8	12.4	16.0	13.6
Five	9.9	10.7	10.1	8.8	11.8	10.2
Total Five Years or Less	50.5	46.1	62.2	47.6	57.6	55.7
Six	5.8	6.1	6.9	7.7	8.4	6.9
Seven	4.7	6.5	4.3	6.2	5.5	5.0
Eight	4.5	4.6	3.5	5.1	4.2	4.1
Nine	2.7	3.4	3.4	5.2	3.0	3.5
Ten	3.1	2.5	2.7	3.5	2.9	2.9
Total Six-Ten Years	20.8	23.1	20.8	27.7	24.0	22.4
Over Ten Years	28.7	30.8	17.0	24.7	18.4	21.9
Total	100.0%	100.0%	100.0%	100.0%	100.0%	100.0%
Number of Failures	1,576	965	4,398	1,375	1,252	9,566

TABLE 5.2. Age of Failed Businesses by Function (1972)
Source: Dun & Bradstreet, Inc.

Year	% In Business 5 Years or Less	% In Business 6 to 10 Years	% In Business Over 10 Years
1945	59.1%	19.8%	21.1%
1946	71.8	13.9	14.3
1947	77.6	13.3	9.1
1948	76.5	12.5	11.0
1949	74.6	14.5	10.9
1950	68.2	19.0	12.8
1951	63.2	23.5	13.3
1952	59.9	25.8	14.3
1953	58.5	26.7	14.8
1954	57.2	27.3	15.5
1955	56.6	26.0	17.4
1956	58.6	23.1	18.3
1957	58.9	21.8	19.3
1958	57.2	21.4	21.4
1959	57.1	22.3	20.6
1960	58.6	20.8	20.6
1961	56.2	22.4	21.4
1962	55.4	22.2	22.4
1963	55.4	21.7	22.9
1964	56.0	21.5	22.5
1965	56.9	21.4	21.7
1966	57.1	21.5	21.1
1967	55.3	22.5	22.2
1968	53.9	23.3	22.8
1969	53.2	24.4	22.4
1970	54.9	22.7	22.4
1971	54.2	22.2	23.6
1972	55.7	22.4	21.9

TABLE 5.3

Age Failure Trend (1945–72)
Source: Dun & Bradstreet, Inc.

For all "new" businesses three to five years old, Miller and Relkin warn:

1. The capital structure will usually be much less than that of the average firm that has been in existence longer.
2. Past industry conditions that were abnormally favorable and allowed a new company to "ride the crest of a wave" may subside.
3. There may be management differences over future objectives that could cause disruption.
4. Management's unwarranted confidence or dissatisfaction could unjustly influence your credit decision.

[503.1.2]   OLD BUSINESSES. Although old businesses (those that have been in existence more than five years) have been statistically better credit risks, you cannot assume that an old business is a good risk. The trend is now toward a greater number of failures in companies older than ten years. Although such companies have endured the rigors of the first critical years, dry rot, nepotism, or general stultification bring many companies to the brink of financial embarrassment (see Tables 5.2 and 5.3).

[503.2]   **Length of Time in Present Line.** If a business established its success and financial strength in one line—or performing one type of operation—you cannot count on continued success if it switches. Make sure you know how long a company has been doing what it currently does.

[503.3]   **Fires and Lawsuits.** Businesses, as well as individuals, suffer fires and lawsuits. Regardless of whether the management sustaining them is the current management or not, investigate the history of fires and lawsuits.

[503.4]   **Involvement with Federal or Other Governmental Regulatory Agencies.** Often a company will generate ill will because of violations of consumer codes, food and drug codes, antitrust regulations, or any other "cause." You should find out how lingering ill will may affect a company's future.

[503.5]   **Effects of Mergers and Acquisitions.** If the business you are investigating has been acquired in a merger—or if it has acquired another company—find the answers to these questions proposed by Bruce D. Classon in his *Commercial Credit and Collection Guide.*

1. What was the purpose of the combination? Expanded sales? Markets? Profits? Talent? Product? Plant? Cash?
2. Does the acquiring company have the desire and ability to manage the company or is it "raiding" it?
3. Will the net result benefit the standing of both entities, or is one of them so weak as to pull the other down?
4. Does the combination tend to balance or increase seasonal risk?
5. Is the combination for tax purposes, to offset losses against earnings, and if so, will it stand up under examination?
6. Is the combination for the purpose of obtaining a public listing or going public?
7. What sort of reputation has the new entity and how has it conducted its affairs in the past?
8. Are there operating or overhead savings to be made by sharing facilities and services?
9. Are the two products compatible?
10. Is the merger likely to start antitrust action?

[504]   **OPERATION.** Without an understanding of a firm's operation, you will find it impossible to evaluate the credit risk it represents. Knowing what a company does—its size, scope, and characteristics—is the basic ingredient in your analysis of its figures, management, and future.

Are the receivables high, low, or just right? You can't tell without knowing the terms of sale and the company's seasonally active and low points. Does the manager have the necessary talents for success in his line? You couldn't say without knowing what the line is. What's the competition like and is your potential customer meeting it? To answer that, you would have to know what the product is and to whom your customer sells it. This is the information you need to have about a company's operation:

[504.1]   **Method of Operation.** There are four primary methods or kinds of operation, commonly referred to as functions. Each one suggests different capital and managerial requirements. Determine the amount of business your potential customer transacts under each of the following before evaluating his staff and strength:

[504.1.1]   FOUR PRIMARY METHODS OF OPERATION.

1. *Retailing.* A retailer sells goods in small quantities for personal or household consumption. Often he is called a "dealer."
2. *Wholesaling or jobbing.* A wholesaler buys goods in quantity, breaks them down, and distributes them in their original state to manufacturers, processors, or retailers. A wholesaler is sometimes called a "jobber," especially if he sells in odd lots or directly to industrial consumers.
3. *Manufacturing.* A manufacturer transforms materials or products and, in the process, adds value by applying labor. He may also process, slaughter, fabricate, or reclaim.
4. *Service.* A service industry is one that handles products only incidentally as it performs a service for its customers or clients.
5. *Other.* Other functions include such activities as agriculture, construction, mining, and transportation, but most of these functions have similarities to the basic four, such as manufacturing in the case of the first three and service in the latter instance.

[504.1.2]   HOW TO DETERMINE A COMPANY'S METHOD OF OPERATION. This information is not difficult to obtain. Get it from:

1. The company's name (but this can be uninformative or even misleading).
2. Business information reports.
3. Salesmen.
4. Standard Industrial Classification (SIC) number. The SIC system has been developed by the federal government to classify American industries. Every industry group (indicated by the first two digits) and most kinds of products within an industry have been assigned a SIC number. Should you find out a company's SIC number, you can find out what that company does by looking up the number in the SIC Manual or in the Introduction to the *Dun & Bradstreet Reference Book.* Where possible, check the date that the SIC number was assigned because of periodic major revisions in the system.

The major classifications recognized by the SIC system are the following:
   a. Agriculture, Forestry, and Fishing (0111–0971).
   b. Mining (1011–1499).
   c. Construction (1521–1799).
   d. Manufacturing (2011–3999).
   e. Transportation, Communications, Electric, Gas, and Sanitary Services (4011–4971).

    f. Wholesale Trade (5012–5199).

    g. Retail Trade (5211–5999).

    h. Finance, Insurance, and Real Estate (6011–6799).

    i. Services (7011–8999).

    j. Public Administration (9111–9721).

[504.2]   **Influence of Method of Operation on Financial Statements.** The method of operation produces the following effects on statements. Whenever there is a significant variation from these norms in your potential customer, find out why.

[504.2.1]   MANUFACTURERS.

1. Principal costs are labor and materials.
2. Working capital must be adequate to meet these costs.
3. Financing for permanent (and fixed) capital needs must be available.
4. Gross profits vary widely, but as a percentage of sales they are higher than those of wholesalers.

[504.2.2]   WHOLESALERS.

1. There are no manufacturing costs.
2. Most revenue is used to purchase merchandise.
3. What remains is used for overhead, selling, and profits.
4. Moderate investment in fixed assets is the norm.
5. Profits are greatly influenced by general business conditions and fluctuations in price of materials.
6. Profit margins are narrow.
7. Compared to manufacturers, there is a heavy volume per dollar of invested capital.

[504.2.3]   RETAILERS.

1. Retailers have higher expense to sales ratios than wholesalers.
2. Additional expenses include advertising, high rents, display and service costs.
3. The major expense is materials.
4. Gross-profit margins are higher than those of wholesalers.
5. Capital turnover is slower than that of wholesalers.

[504.2.4]   SERVICE INDUSTRIES.

1. They have very little inventory and most of it is incidental goods and supplies.
2. There is a high ratio of labor costs to sales.
3. Collection periods must be short, as labor costs call for quick cash outlays.
4. Credit terms are therefore shorter.

[504.3]   **Seasonal Characteristics.** Most businesses are affected to some degree by seasons, although seasonality is not so pronounced now as formerly because businesses have diversified and now do summer and winter business. Nevertheless, you should be aware of what effect seasons have on your prospective customers. Pay particular attention to the following:

[504.3.1]   EFFECTS OF SEASONALITY ON BALANCE SHEET. Businesses affected by seasons obtain radically different operating results depending on what season they are in. When you're examining a balance sheet—or any set of figures—find out at what point in the season they were drawn up. Be able to recognize at least these three major seasonal periods:

1. *Inventory buildup.* During this period, merchandise is bought and processed into manufactured goods or collected for distribution in the major selling period. Often, especially in the garment industry, losses can be expected during this period.

2. *Major selling season.* During this period, the inventory must be liquidated and profits must come into the company to pay off debts. The cash position must be strong.

3. *Interim season.* Inventory and receivables should be low. The cash position should be strong. Very often statements drawn up at this point show no bank borrowing.

[504.3.2]   EFFECTS OF SEASONALITY ON FUNCTION OF CREDIT. As a credit man, be sure that when credit is required for inventory buildup, you are providing true trade credit and not equity financing.

[504.3.3]   EFFECTS OF SEASONALITY ON AMOUNT OF CREDIT. You must be aware of seasonal needs so that the amount of credit you extend will be proportionate to true need. If you are unaware of seasonal variations, you may become unjustly alarmed or falsely confident about a credit risk.

[504.3.4]   EFFECTS OF SEASONALITY ON TIME OF REPAYMENT. If a company is influenced by seasonality, you must expect to be repaid during the major selling period or the interim period. Failure to receive payment during these periods is a warning that payment problems could be on their way.

[504.3.5]   EFFECTS OF SEASONALITY ON COLLECTION TIMING. It could be unwise to bring legal collection proceedings during the inventory buildup season. Your seasonally affected customer might not have the money to pay. A forced bankruptcy at this time would solve no one's problems.

[504.4]   **Product.** Knowledge of what product or products a potential customer makes, sells, or utilizes is essential knowledge for the credit decision. You have to know whether his product will sell to predict future financial strength. Determine:

[504.4.1]   CONSUMER TENDENCIES. Find out what consumer tendencies are and whether a company's product will match them.

[504.4.2]   ADVANTAGES AND DISADVANTAGES. Find out the advantages and disadvantages of a company's product and how they stack up against those of the competition.

[504.4.3]   NUMBER. Find out how many different kinds of product a company produces so that you'll know what will happen if materials become unavailable or the product's popularity fades.

[504.4.4]   SEASONALITY. Determine whether a company's products are seasonally balanced so that the company can avoid cash shortages.

[504.4.5]   NATURE. Your final evaluation of a company's product should take into account its nature as determined by whether the company makes or sells:

1. *Competitive consumer goods,* in which case competition will be strong and product life span short.

2. *Component parts for capital goods,* in which case the product's fortune will depend upon that of capital goods manufacturers.

3. *Faddish products,* which might disappear overnight.
4. *Standard products made on a mass-production basis.* If this is the case, then these factors usually apply:
   a. An uncertain market exists.
   b. Production must be planned to keep the plant in operation at a profitable level.
   c. Financing must be sufficient to provide enough stock to meet anticipated demand. Still, production must be scheduled so as to avoid overproduction.
5. *Products made to customers' specifications on a special production basis.* This would suggest the following:
   a. A certain market exists, so obsolete inventory is not a threat.
   b. Availability of raw materials and component parts is a determining factor in a company's ability to produce the product.
   c. Financing of the contracted job must be available.
6. *Products that require readily available materials so that supply delays are not frequent.*
7. *Products that have been adequately tested and marketed.*
8. *Products that comply with government regulations.*

[504.4.6]   PRICE. Check the price range of the company's products to find out whether they are competitive in their class and line, whether the markup is sufficient to cover expenses and profit, and whether the price is proportionate to the life expectancy of the product.

[504.5]   **From Whom the Company Buys.** The significance of this piece of information varies with the method of operation.

[504.5.1]   WHOLESALERS AND RETAILERS. For wholesalers and retailers, it is important to know whether the products of the companies from which the company buys are as reputable and well known as your company's product that he will sell.

[504.5.2]   MANUFACTURERS. Find out if your manufacturing customers have established sources of supply that can guarantee shipment of essential supplies at reasonable prices—even during shortages. Knowing a manufacturer's suppliers also clues you in on the quality of his own product.

[504.6]   **Number of Active Accounts on the Books.** Determine the number of active accounts a company has and you will be on the way to determining the popularity of its product. You will also be able to see if the company is dependent on the fate of a relatively small number of accounts or on that of a particular industry.

If a potential customer sells an important part of his product to one company or industry, you must be aware of its condition and trend. In particular, if a manufacturer or wholesaler sells an important percentage of total sales to a subsidiary, parent, or affiliate, establish the following to evaluate your customer's financial health:

[504.6.1]   PARENT, SUBSIDIARY, OR AFFILIATE ACCOUNTS. Determine:
1. Name of the company.
2. Selling terms.
3. Percentage of total sales represented.
4. Any other intercompany relations.

[504.6.2]   UNRELATED COMPANY ACCOUNTS. If a manufacturer or wholesaler sells an important percentage of total sales to one or just a few unrelated concerns, determine the terms and percentage of total sales for each class.

[504.6.3] MANY ACCOUNTS. If your customer sells to a large number of accounts, make sure that he has the necessary staff, facilities, and procedures to handle the load.

[504.7] **Type and Class of Trade Sold.** Determine the class and type of trade sold to evaluate the quality of the company's receivables and the particular situations and problems that your customer—if a manufacturer—might encounter according to whether his output is distributed by jobbers, retailers, or sent directly to consumers. Collection periods, selling expenses, and product prices will all vary.

You should be alert to the chance that a customer sells to the government (federal, state, or local) because continued demand for the product can be uncertain at best and payment is often drawn out and dependent upon successful completion of the project.

[504.8] **Terms of Sale.** Your potential customer's terms of sale give you an indication of how fast you can expect his payment to you. If he sells on very short terms, you should expect that he will be collecting money rapidly and that your payment will be quickly forthcoming. Any deviation should draw your immediate attention.

If, on the other hand, his selling terms are extended, seasonal, or based on completion of a contract, payment to you could be slower.

A change in selling terms merits an examination. If they become more liberal, it could mean the company has a lot of slow-moving inventory. If they tighten up, it could mean product demand is high.

Selling terms that differ from industry standards should prompt you to ask why.

[504.9] **Territory in Which Sales Are Made.**

[504.9.1] INFLUENCE OF TERRITORY ON PRODUCT. Where a customer sells his product has a bearing on these product features:

1. Its cost.
2. The terms for which it is sold.
3. Length of time required for shipment.
4. Quality and speed of service.

Any of the above could contribute or detract from sales and the financial health of the company.

[504.9.2] REGIONAL VARIABLES. Regional variations in taste and payment practices can also influence the success of a company's products and the speed with which you get paid. Pay attention to political, industrial, and natural events that occur in the territory where your customer's product is sold. Local strikes, fiscal and budget policies, floods, and shutdowns can affect anyone's financial picture.

If your customer sells to foreign clients, you must, of course, be attuned to political and monetary situations.

[504.10] **Number of Employees.** Although the size of a company, as represented by the number of employees, is no guarantee of its success, larger companies are better risks than smaller ones. They have proven their ability to survive and grow.

[504.10.1]   CREDIT DETRACTIONS OF SMALL COMPANIES.

1. They are more easily affected by the death or departure of key personnel.
2. They tend to be more lax about keeping financial records and are therefore less able to spot upcoming danger and prevent it.
3. They have less capital (even though they also probably have less debt).

[504.10.2]   NUMBER OF EMPLOYEES AND INDUSTRY STUDIES. Finding out the number of employees is important for another reason. Many industry figures are published on a "per-employee" basis—for instance, the number of salesmen and sales managers for each $100,000 in sales; or the number of machine operators for x number of units. If you don't know the number of employees, you won't be able to compare your customer's company with others in the field. Industry Studies on a number of industries are available from Dun & Bradstreet. (See Figure 5.1) In addition, the Bank of America, in its "Small Business Reporter" series, publishes very useful industry studies.

[504.11]   **Competition.** No prediction of a customer's success can hope to be accurate without taking into account the competition. Not only must your customer's product be evaluated with reference to that of the competition, but also his paying habits, his selling terms, his pricing, his profit margins, and his trend must be analyzed in light of what others in his field are doing. Other points of comparison include research talents and budget, technological sophistication of equipment, extent of advertising and marketing, and availability of financing.

[504.12]   **Location.** Inappropriate or mistaken locations cause business failures every year. Make sure that location doesn't do your customers in. What the proper location is depends upon the kind of operation.

[504.12.1]   MANUFACTURERS. The location of a manufacturer should assure:

1. Adequate labor.
2. Adequate transportation.
3. Plentiful raw materials.
4. Sufficient power.

[504.12.2]   WHOLESALERS. Wholesalers must be located at a workable distance both from their customers and their sources of supply. Transportation facilities must be adequate for fast, convenient shipments.

[504.12.3]   RETAILERS. Retailers must be located where buying traffic can reach them easily. Studies have shown that stores have a better chance of success when located in communities or shopping centers with other stores carrying comparably priced merchandise and catering to similar trade.

The possibility of future expansion at the current location can be a factor to consider when you evaluate the location of a company.

[504.13]   **Facilities and Equipment.** To be successful and, therefore, to be able to pay bills, a company must have adequate facilities and equipment.

[504.13.1]   CRITERIA FOR JUDGING FACILITIES AND EQUIPMENT:

1. Technological soundness.
2. Age.
3. Production efficiency (especially in straight-line operations).

INDUSTRY STUDIES
Dun & Bradstreet, Inc.

FINANCIAL REPORT ON: FURNITURE MANUFACTURERS

The dollar value of shipments by manufacturers of household furniture is expected to rebound in 1968 to $4.1 billion, up 3.5% over 1967 shipments of $3.96 billion. Shipments in 1967 were 2% below the high of $4.04 billion recorded in 1966 after 5 successive years of growth. The decline in 1967 was due principally to a drop-off in residential construction, tight credit, the reluctance of wholesalers and retailers to carry high inventories in an uncertain market and the diversion of a higher percentage of disposable income into savings.*

During 1967, furniture manufacturers experienced declining profit ratios when compared with prior years. This decline was largely the result of rising labor costs, raw materials, advertising and administrative expense as well as increased transportation rates.

PROFITS DOWN - The median ratio of net profits on net sales declined from 3.04% in 1966 to 2.41% in 1967. In addition, net profits on tangible net worth dropped to 7.87% from 10.94%. Net profits on net working capital were also below the 1966 level.

DEBT POSITION IMPROVED - In 1967 the ratio of current debt to tangible net worth, total debt to tangible net worth and funded debt to net working capital showed slight improvement over the 1966 figures.

CONDITION SATISFACTORY - The financial condition maintained by furniture manufacturers has been satisfactory for the most part. The median ratio of current assets to current debt of 2.85 showed improvement over the past few years and is the highest level reached since 1962. Inventory turnover as measured by net sales to inventory continues at a satisfactory level as illustrated by the 1967 median of 6.9 times.

*U.S. Department of Commerce

FINANCIAL RATIOS (MEDIAN)   FURNITURE MANUFACTURERS

NUMBER OF CORPORATIONS	1958	1959	1960	1961	1962	1963	1964	1965	1966	1967
	141	139	134	93	105	104	105	106	119	114
Current Assets to Current Debt ♦	3.24	2.82	3.00	2.77	2.86	2.15	2.67	2.62	2.73	2.85
Net Profits on Net Sales (%)	1.79	2.12	1.92	2.03	3.01	1.83	2.84	2.73	3.04	2.41
Net Profits on Tangible Net Worth (%)	5.63	8.94	4.91	5.90	7.94	6.75	9.69	11.74	10.94	7.87
Net Profits on Net Working Capital (%)	8.90	15.34	9.03	9.45	12.94	10.43	14.92	17.15	17.55	13.80
Net Sales to Tangible Net Worth ♦	2.78	3.05	2.70	2.81	2.97	4.11	3.49	3.25	3.04	3.11
Net Sales to Net Working Capital ♦	4.27	5.34	4.20	5.34	4.55	6.11	5.19	4.94	4.95	5.12
Collection Period Days	48	41	43	44	47	40	43	44	42	43
Net Sales to Inventory ♦	6.2	6.3	5.3	5.9	5.5	7.6	7.3	7.1	6.7	6.9
Fixed Assets to Tangible Net Worth (%)	29.8	33.8	34.5	32.1	31.2	32.8	33.2	35.2	35.7	36.0
Current Debt to Tangible Net Worth (%)	28.8	33.6	28.9	32.6	33.7	48.8	41.5	38.7	36.6	35.7
Total Debt to Tangible Net Worth (%)	54.8	66.8	63.0	59.2	68.7	93.0	75.9	66.3	64.6	64.3
Inventory to Net Working Capital (%)	68.2	79.2	70.0	75.0	75.9	79.3	74.0	75.5	81.7	79.2
Current Debt to Inventory (%)	67.4	67.9	70.6	74.6	76.8	93.4	79.2	80.7	74.6	78.6
Funded Debt to Net Working Capital * (%)	26.9	22.7	23.9	21.4	24.0	38.8	29.4	26.1	37.6	30.9

♦ Times   * Applies only to concerns with long term debts.

FURNITURE STORES - 1967

Number of Corporations - 187	Upper Quartile	Median	Lower Quartile
Current Assets to Current Debt #	5.74	3.07	1.79
Net Profits on Net Sales (%)	4.86	2.16	0.69
Net Profits on Tangible Net Worth (%)	11.20	6.01	2.01
Net Profits on Net Working Capital (%)	11.94	6.33	2.05
Net Sales to Tangible Net Worth #	4.72	2.49	1.60
Net Sales to Net Working Capital #	5.03	2.71	1.65
Collection Period (Days)	57	111	209
Net Sales to Inventory #	6.6	4.8	3.7
Fixed Assets to Tangible Net Worth (%)	3.8	9.2	22.0
Current Debt to Tangible Net Worth (%)	20.4	46.3	105.6
Total Debt to Tangible Net Worth* (%)	47.2	98.2	165.2
Inventory to Net Working Capital (%)	32.2	60.2	106.5
Current Debt to Inventory (%)	55.5	90.2	143.7
Funded Debts to Net Working Capital* (%)	9.1	20.0	41.5

* Applies only to concerns with long term debt.
# Times

FAILURES - There were 271 furniture stores failures during 1967 with liabilities totaling $16,096,000. Managements inability to meet competition and unbalanced experience in sales, purchasing and finance continue as the major causes for these failures. The number of failures the past few years has been fairly constant. Six-month figures for 1968 indicate a decline in the number of failures, but the average liabilities are at a peak amount and considerably higher than in 1967.

FAILURES OF FURNITURE STORES
1958 - 1968

YEAR	NUMBER	LIABILITIES	AVERAGE LIABILITIES
1958	441	$ 19,280,000	$ 43,718
1959	304	13,475,000	44,325
1960	396	20,876,000	52,717
1961	450	27,688,000	61,528
1962	369	20,468,000	55,444
1963	295	21,599,000	73,186
1964	296	20,457,000	68,774
1965	278	19,741,000	71,011
1966	250	14,892,000	59,568
1967	271	16,096,000	59,395
1968 (6 Mos.)	85	6,236,000	73,365

COMMENTS - The dollar size of the typical sale by a furniture store is substantially larger than for most retail lines. Also, most sales are on credit terms frequently providing for installment payments over an extended period. As a result, accounts receivable are a major asset and generally constitute from 40% to 50% of total current assets. The ability of the management of a furniture store to keep its receivables in good condition is of major importance in maintaining the business in a sound financial condition.

INDUSTRY STUDIES   October 18, 1968
General Reporting and Service Department

Dun & Bradstreet, Inc.
99 CHURCH STREET · NEW YORK, N. Y., 10007

BUSINESS INFORMATION SYSTEMS, SERVICES and SCIENCES
Economics · Marketing · Sales · Credit · Finance · Education · Research

---

FIGURE 5.1

Sample Dun & Bradstreet Industry Study

4. Shipping efficiency.

5. Inventory-control facility.

[504.13.2]   OWNERSHIP. It goes without saying that you should find out if facilities and equipment are owned or leased. The amount of rent and the identity of the landlord could be important facts to ascertain.

[504.14]   **Housekeeping.** The physical appearance of the premises can often be your guide to an operation—especially when other information is missing. The quality of the housekeeping can tell you:

1. Employee attitudes.

2. Risk of fire and accident (and thus whether insurance rates are in line).

3. Efficiency of management.

4. How well inventory is controlled.

[504.15]   **Insurance and Physical Hazards.**

[504.15.1]   INSURANCE. All businesses should carry insurance of two kinds:

1. *Liability insurance,* insurance to cover damage suits.

2. *Fire insurance,* covering:

   a. Buildings.

   b. Plant and equipment.

   c. Furniture and fixtures.

   d. Merchandise.

   e. Business interruption.

Automobile and truck insurance should also be carried where appropriate, and employees who handle money should be bonded. Failure to carry adequate insurance is a strong warning that the account must be carefully watched. For example, low coverage in relation to the valuation of the assets could reveal that assets are overstated. It could also reflect vulnerability to unforeseen losses from fire, flood, and other disasters.

[504.15.2]   PHYSICAL (FIRE) RISKS. Fire-insurance underwriters have identified certain flagrant fire risks. As a credit man, you must know what they are and guard your company against dealing with those companies that present them.

1. *Untidy premises.* A slovenly place of business is a poor fire risk. Such a place not only facilitates the spread of fire, but it indicates an attitude of indifference and carelessness on the part of the owner toward normal fire prevention.

2. *Vacant or unoccupied buildings.* A vacant building that has been boarded up for some time will, if unwatched, occasionally become a haunt for hoodlums or a neighborhood gang. A carelessly thrown match can cause such a place to go up in smoke, especially if it's an old building. The length of time a place has been vacant is directly proportionate to the risk.

3. *Dilapidation.* Many an old building is a tinderbox, particularly buildings in which there are accumulations of litter, worn-out wiring, or wiring overloads. These conditions are frequently found in slum areas.

4. *Changing neighborhoods.* When a neighborhood begins to deteriorate, fire losses climb. In some instances, buildings lose their

utility and thus are abandoned. Other times, businesses move away and customers follow—only the fire hazards remain.

5. *Lack of fire protection.* If a fire breaks out in a locality in which there is a paid fire department, and the building is reasonably close to fire hydrants, the chances are that the fire can be brought under control within a reasonably short time. The extent of dollar loss is thereby minimized. But in suburban or rural localities, served at best by volunteer fire departments, there are business premises that are sometimes as much as half a mile from a fire hydrant. A fire in such a locality can be quite damaging.

6. *Neglect of proper building maintenance.* Neglect of proper building maintenance is one of the surefire causes of fire. A crumbling chimney, dilapidated roof, lack of paint, or need for repairs are some signs of poor maintenance.

7. *Delayed demolition.* This hazard is similar to that of a vacant or unoccupied building, except that a building that is waiting to be torn down generally contains flammable rubble and is less likely to be locked or boarded up than one that is merely vacant while awaiting future tenants.

8. *Intrinsic hazards.* Certain types of business, because of the nature of the products they process or sell, are naturally highly susceptible to fire. They include:
   a. Plastics.
   b. Chemical products.
   c. Explosives.
   d. Paper.
   e. Advertising novelties.
   f. Mattresses and bedding.
   g. Woodworking plants.
   h. Firms using excelsior and similar packing materials.
   i. Lumberyards.
   j. Retailers of secondhand merchandise.
   k. Junk dealers.
   l. Restaurants.
   m. Bowling alleys.
   n. Dance halls.
   o. Third- and fourth-rate hotels.
   p. Vacant theaters.
   q. Paint-spraying establishments.

In all cases, not only should you investigate your customer as a potential fire hazard, you should also investigate the businesses adjacent to his.

[505] **INDUSTRY CONDITIONS.** In order to evaluate successfully the credit risk of a customer, you must keep up-to-date on the conditions that exist in the industry to which that customer belongs and in the industry to which that customer sells.

[505.1] **Importance of Industry Conditions to Credit Analysis.**

[505.1.1] INDUSTRY SUCCESS. With few exceptions, no company can be more successful in the long run than the industry itself. Without making fundamental changes in its product line, a company in a dying industry will eventually die itself.

[505.1.2]   INDUSTRY INFLUENCES. With few exceptions, no company can remain independent of the influences affecting the industry as a whole. For example:

1. An industry coming under increased governmental control means that your customers in that industry will come under increased governmental control, too.
2. An industry switching to automation or computers means that your customer will probably switch if he is going to survive.

[505.1.3]   INDUSTRY PECULIARITIES. Every industry has peculiarities that are reflected in its financial statements, paying habits, selling terms, and seasonal variations. You can't put a company into proper perspective if you don't know the industry forces to which it is subjected.

[505.1.4]   COMPETITION. In order to judge the future success or failure of a company, you must be aware of its competition within its industry.

[505.1.5]   FINANCIAL STRENGTH. In order to judge the financial strength and operating efficiency of a company, you must compare it with those in its industry.

[505.2]   **Components of an Industry's Condition.**

[505.2.1]   LOCATION AND THE REGIONAL INFLUENCES IT RECEIVES.

[505.2.2]   STATUS IN THE EYES OF GOVERNMENT, LABOR, AND CONSUMER GROUPS.

[505.2.3]   STAGE OF BUSINESS MATURITY.

[505.2.4]   SENSITIVITY TO ECONOMIC CONDITIONS.

[505.2.5]   REQUIREMENTS FOR TECHNICAL SKILLS AND THEIR AVAILABILITY.

[505.2.6]   GENERAL STRENGTH OF COMPANIES IN THE INDUSTRY.

[505.2.7]   GENERAL STRENGTH OF THOSE THAT BUY AND SELL THE INDUSTRY.

[505.2.8]   REQUIREMENTS FOR RAW MATERIALS AND THEIR AVAILABILITY.

[505.3]   **Special Features Which Can Cause Distortions in the Financial Statements of Companies Throughout an Industry.**

[505.3.1]   THE INDUSTRY'S TERMS OF SALE. These can reduce the importance of the accounts-receivable entry.

[505.3.2]   UNUSUAL ALLOWANCES OR OFFSETS.

[505.3.3]   UNUSUAL BILLING PRACTICES. These include bill-and-hold, and goods held at the processors that must be accurately identified and recorded in the inventory and accounts-receivable entries.

[506]   ECONOMIC FACTORS. Just as one company is influenced by developments in its industry as a whole, so, too, is an industry influenced by developments in the economy as a whole. As a credit man, you don't have to know about complicated, esoteric theories. But you should be familiar with basic economic trends. The survival and success of your customers depend on them. Here is what you should know:

[506.1]   **Business Cycles.** As a minimum, you can identify which period of the business cycle you are in, whether it be a period of:

1. Prosperity.
2. Crisis.

3. Depression.
4. Recovery.

[506.2]   **Direction of the Economy.** You should also identify toward which period the economy is moving and how fast.

[506.3]   **Variables of the Economy.** You should determine the state of these variables in order to measure the health of the economy:

1. Amount of disposable consumer income.
2. How much of this is being saved.
3. The rate of inflation.
4. The level of unemployment.
5. Stock-market activity.
6. The health of key industries, such as cars and steel.
7. The tax situation, including:
    a. Changes in corporate tax structures.
    b. Tax credits for capital investment.
    c. Fluctuations in specialized taxes.
    d. Exemptions for pension funds.
    e. Tax loss carry-backs and carry-forwards.
8. Interest rates, remembering that:
    a. Rising rates slow expansion and cause tightening throughout the economy. Slow payments from marginal accounts can be expected.
    b. Falling interest rates can cause overexpansion and the appearance of speculators.
9. What government controls are in effect or are pending.
10. Status of tariffs and quotas.
11. Presence of any economic interruptions, including those caused by:
    a. Labor troubles resulting from strikes, slowdowns, contract negotiations, wage talks, unionizing movements.
    b. Natural disasters.
    c. Commodity availability and pricing.
    d. International factors including wars, quotas, embargoes, nationalizations.
    e. Political factors including elections, legislation, agency and judicial review.

Remember that in an expanding economy, the truly progressive company will grow at least as fast as the economy itself. In a shrinking economy, the poorly run company will fail faster.

[507]   **FINANCES.** This is the heart of your evaluation of the credit risk. By using all available financial information—statements, trial balances, interim figures, profit-and-loss statements, estimates—find out whether a customer will be able to pay his bills to you on time. (Turn to Chapter 9 to find complete details on the methods of financial analysis.)

[508]   **PAYMENTS.** For business to run smoothly—in fact, for it to run at all—men must make promises and keep them. The record of a customer's

payments is the record of how he keeps his commercial promises. Here's what payment information can do for you.

[508.1]   **Information Obtained by Reviewing the Payment Record.**

[508.1.1]   CONFIRMATION. The payment record can confirm your evaluation of management—or stir you to a new investigation.

[508.1.2]   COMPARISON. The payment record lets you compare your policy with that of other companies selling to the customer.

[508.1.3]   SPECIAL FINANCING. The payment history informs you of any special financial arrangements a company may have.

[508.1.4]   DISCREPANCIES. The payment record can disclose any discrepancies between industry norms and customer practice.

[508.1.5]   SOURCES OF SUPPLY. The payment record may reveal any unusual sources of supply that could raise questions in your mind.

[508.1.6]   BUYING HABITS. It can also tell when, what, and where a company buys. Nevertheless, a payment record does have limitations as far as a credit investigation is concerned. A payment record is historical. It tells what was done in the past. Your problem is to predict what will happen in the future. Keep in mind, therefore, that as your customer's business changes, his payment practices might also change. But don't forget that honesty and willingness to pay, once demonstrated, are reliable guides to the future. So are dishonesty and reluctance to pay.

[508.2]   **Components of the Payment Investigation.**

[508.2.1]   RECENT AND LONG-RANGE CREDIT HISTORY. The payment history involving recent and current suppliers is among your most important information because it is a better indication of a customer's ability and willingness to pay now and in the future. Still, his long-range payment history, especially his practices when business was bad or money tight, can tell you a story about his future attitudes.

The trend of payments will also tell a revealing tale about the financial condition of a company.

Note: When developing a customer's credit history, make sure that you are basing it on the people or policies that will determine payments to you. Corner Hardware, when owned by Joe Smith, might have paid promptly. But now that it is owned by Henry Scokes, payments could become slow. On the other hand, the payment practices of a business that has changed its name or form of organization, but which is still run by the same people, are likely to remain the same. Beware of a situation in which a business is placed under the jurisdiction of a court. From that moment on, the court—not the business—will determine payment policy. If your company had been receiving favorable treatment at the expense of other suppliers, that situation could change abruptly.

[508.2.2]   REPRESENTATIVE SAMPLING OF SUPPLIERS. A company's payment record with different suppliers can vary widely. Although your experience might be good, this could be because he is slow with others. Some concerns in trouble maintain a few accounts prompt for reference purposes. Unless you are aware of such a situation, the customer could suddenly go bankrupt and you could be left holding the bag. Similarly, a customer could be prompt with others but slow with you. If that is the case, you must find out why and what can be done about it. If your terms, experience, or line of credit are out of line with those of other suppliers, you'd better do some checking.

Therefore, in order for your examination of payments to be truly meaningful, make sure you have the ledger experience of a representative sample of a potential customer's current suppliers.

The sample should be representative with respect to:

1. *Number.* If a customer is buying from hundreds of suppliers, the ledger experience of three or four would be insufficient. When possible, attempt to procure as many ledger experiences as possible, but never stop your investigation before you can reach a definite conclusion about paying habits. If you have two experiences that show prompt payments and two that show slow payments, you need more.

2. *Primary and secondary suppliers.* Your payment history should include both primary and secondary suppliers. Your customer could be giving preferential treatment to one or the other. If he is, how does your company stand?

3. *Large and small suppliers.* Likewise, your customer might be favoring large or small suppliers with prompt payments and you have to determine what your company can expect.

4. *Location.* Often a customer—particularly one located in a small town—will pay his local bills on time because he sees and deals personally with local suppliers (who might also be his friends). At the same time, his payments to suppliers located at a distance could be slow. Where do you fit in?

5. *Amount of indebtedness.* Some companies pay off small bills promptly while falling behind on large ones. The reverse is equally possible. Calculate how the size of a customer's debt to you will influence his payments.

6. *Old and new suppliers.* Beware of the company that pays its new suppliers quickly to establish good credit—and then lets its older suppliers wait.

7. *Amount of discount offered.* Some companies time their payments to coincide with the amount of discount they will obtain. You must decide whether the presence or absence of a discount will affect a potential customer's payments to your company.

8. *Customer-supplied and independently developed references.* It goes without saying that the supplier references that a customer furnishes will generally be good, particularly in the period immediately after the references have been furnished. Whenever possible—and always if there is any suspicion in your mind about a payment record—seek out suppliers not mentioned by the customer and find out what they have to say.

[508.2.3]   HIGH CREDIT. The high credit extended to a customer is a good indication of the confidence that other suppliers have in an account. The trend of the high credit is an even better indication of where suppliers think the account is going. The amount of credit that a customer has been granted from different suppliers also indicates what he is buying and from whom. Any difference from the industry norms as to amount of credit and type of supplier should alert you to a more careful analysis.

[508.2.4]   AMOUNT CURRENTLY OWING. This figure reveals the amount of purchasing a customer is doing from his sources. This figure assumes even more importance when compared to the high credit. The current amount owing should logically coincide with the time of season when the ledger experience was taken. That is, if your customer is in the middle of his manufacturing period or stocking period (if a wholesaler), the amount owing would represent a large percentage of the high credit. If the ledger experience was taken at the end of the selling season, the amount currently owing would represent a small percentage of the high credit. Any deviation from what should be expected for the industry of that customer should provoke your examination.

[508.2.5]   AMOUNT PAST DUE. Past-due accounts are always cause for concern. Your responsibility as a credit man includes finding out not only how much of an account is past due to other suppliers—a large amount past due will alarm you more, of course, than an insignificant amount—but why. The reasons for slowness are practically infinite. In addition to simple lack of funds, be alert to these possible causes:

1. Strikes or other labor troubles.
2. Lawsuits.
3. Management turmoil or changes.
4. Thefts and embezzlement.
5. Fires.
6. Natural disasters.
7. Owner withdrawals.
8. Sickness.
9. Bank calling in loans.
10. Overbuying.

Not all slowness results from an inability to pay. Consider these factors that could cause *temporary* slowness:

1. Disputes about the quality or accuracy of a shipment.
2. Shipment was never received.
3. Differences between invoicing date and date of receipt of shipment (a seller may start calculating the payment period from the date of invoice while his customer might begin the calculation on the day he receives shipment. This will occasionally lead to a slowness record and the charge that unearned discounts are taken).
4. Required information was not included on the invoice.
5. Invoice was misdirected to the wrong department.
6. Person who must authorize payment is temporarily out of the office.
7. Temporary overflow of work in the accounts-payable department.

If any of these situations become habitual, however, you should follow the account more closely.

[508.2.6]   TERMS OF SALE. It may be important to know the terms of sale for several reasons. Your customer may be failing to take advantage of discounts. He may be getting "special terms" that result from liquidity problems. He may be such a volume buyer (discount department stores) that he can virtually set his own terms. To know that he is paying another supplier promptly may not be particularly significant if that supplier is granting terms well beyond those you extend or even the industry norm.

[508.2.7]   GENERAL PAYMENT EXPERIENCE. Suppliers usually will report that an account either:

1. *Discounts,* meaning that it pays in time to earn cash discounts offered by the supplier for fast payments.
2. *Is prompt,* meaning that it pays its bills on time.
3. *Is slow,* meaning that the account is late.
4. *Anticipates,* meaning that it pays in advance to get a discount (rarer than others).

If an account is slow, find out how long. If an account occasionally runs a few days slow, this is no cause for alarm. If an account runs consistently a few days slow, this serves notice that more strict supervision of the account might bring prompt payments to your company. If an account is very slow, examine it very carefully before granting credit. Make sure, too, that notes are not given to close out slow or past-due accounts; or that prompt payment is not required from *all* of a supplier's customers if they are to remain his customers.

The trend of a potential customer's payments is of particular interest. If the trend is favorable, why not congratulate the company? If the trend is favorable, but the customer still pays a few days slow, this could be a sign that business is nevertheless improving. But it could also be a sign that suppliers are insisting on prompt payments (or better payments) because of a *lack* of confidence in the account. Therefore, find out the reasons for improved payments. They could be:

1. Improved sales and income.
2. New or additional funds borrowed.
3. Better collections.
4. Selling of receivables.
5. Seasonal phenomena.
6. New capital investment.
7. Inventory reductions.

A change in payment trend for the worse should be a strong cause for concern. Even the best companies run slow on occasion, but a trend from prompt to slow payments requires your most careful investigation.

[508.2.8]   LENGTH OF TIME SOLD. A long history of satisfactory relations between a customer and other suppliers can be a good indication that a profitable account can be developed by your company, too. A history of many short-term relationships should raise questions in your mind. Is the customer just unstable or do suppliers deal with him for a short period of time because he doesn't pay his bills or because he causes them other difficulties? Both situations should arouse your suspicions.

Once again, the trend is important. A sudden influx of new suppliers may indicate that a customer is expanding operations or it may mean that old suppliers have cut him off. Find out what the situation is.

[508.2.9]   STATUS OF EQUIPMENT-DEBT PAYMENTS. If you are selling to an industry where, because of the nature of the operation, an important part of the investment is in equipment and other fixed assets, determine the status of the payments for these items. Make sure your investigation reveals:

1. Date of the financing arrangement.
2. Items covered.
3. Name of creditor.
4. Terms of repayment.
5. Status of payments.
6. Trend of payments.

[509]   **BANK INFORMATION.** Your customer's relations with his bank are among the most important that he can have. His standing at the bank is one of the most important credit indicators that you can have. Because banks are so intimately involved with the activities of a company, moreover, they can often furnish ownership, trade, and operating information that you have been unable to locate elsewhere. Here is the banking information you should get to make correct credit judgments.

[509.1]   **How Long the Bank Has Had the Account.** You need this information to put the bank's evaluation of your customer in perspective. If the account is new (and the business isn't), find out why the company changed banks or needed additional banking services. If it is a new account and a new company, find out who introduced the account. Bank accounts are generally introduced through a bank officer or another depositor who could be a source of much information.

[509.2]   **What the Average Balance Is.** Knowing what average balance a customer keeps in his account helps you judge his liquidity and financial picture in general. This figure, when compared with that of other companies in the field, can alert you to an unnatural situation that would require closer investigation. If your customer is a new business, knowing the opening balance can help you determine if there is adequate financing to launch the enterprise. Finding out the *current* balance is always necessary to determine—or verify—a company's cash position. Once again, the trend of the average balance can often be a clue to a company's credit picture.

[509.3]   **Whether It Is a Borrowing or Nonborrowing Account.** If the account is nonborrowing, you should find out why. It could be that you are getting information from the wrong bank; that is, a company's secondary bank. More serious, however, is the possibility that the customer is considered a poor credit risk by the bank and has had to resort to other, more costly forms of financing. Financing from nonbank sources is not necessarily a poor reflection on a customer's credit picture because additional funds from whatever source can mean that bills will be paid on time or discounted. Nevertheless, outside financing and no bank borrowing can indicate that a customer's situation is serious. For instance, Small Business Administration loans with no bank participation, while still not necessarily unfavorable, should stir you to additional investigation.

If the account is a borrowing one, find out the following information and compare it with what you know about the industry and what this company has done in the past.

[509.3.1] WHEN THE CUSTOMER BORROWS. A company should borrow at appropriate times. A loan taken out long past the selling season to pay trade bills, for example, merits an investigation.

[509.3.2] HOW OFTEN DOES THE ACCOUNT BORROW. A regular borrowing account, if payments are promptly met with no damage to the trade record—or if a company periodically cleans up its loans—can be a good indication that the account deserves your confidence. Frequent large borrowing, however, could mean that the company is undercapitalized.

[509.3.3] THE REASONS WHY THE ACCOUNT BORROWS. Short-term financing is generally used to obtain cash when there is a gap between trade collections and the due dates of trade (and other) bills. Such a situation is common in seasonal operations when manufacturing or stocking activity must be carried on far in advance of the selling periods. Borrowing for other reasons should be justified.

[509.3.4] THE AMOUNT BORROWED. You should determine how much is owing to the bank and whether payment of bank obligations might interfere with payments to your company. You should compare how much is owing with the maximum amount of credit extended by the bank in the past. The amount a bank is willing to lend to a customer is often a good indication of the bank's confidence in him.

The amount of a loan should be proportionate to a company's business capacity. If it isn't—if it is too small, for instance—then the company may have to resort to other cash sources.

[509.3.5] LENGTH OF TIME ALLOWED TO REPAY LOAN. The length of time granted to repay a loan represents the minimum amount of time the bank expects that that company will remain in business, although normally, of course, the bank would not make the loan if it expected the company to fail in that short a time.

[509.3.6] AMOUNT AND FREQUENCY OF INSTALLMENT PAYMENTS. Determine whether the bank's requirements for repayment are such that they are likely to interfere with a company's trade payments. Moreover, the particular terms a bank sets are often a reflection of its confidence in an account.

[509.3.7] WHETHER THE LOAN IS SECURED OR UNSECURED. An unsecured loan (also called "straight paper" or "own" paper) is granted upon simple promise to repay. There is no collateral. Make sure that an unsecured loan is truly unsecured and that the bank has not required (or the company volunteered) an endorser. If there is an endorser, determine who he is, what part he plays in the business, and his general business honesty and integrity. Be particularly attentive to the possibility that when a corporation has borrowed money, an officer of that corporation has signed the note as an individual and is thus guaranteeing the loan.

That the bank has required an endorsement—especially when other companies in the same field and of the same size receive open, unsecured lines of credit—should alert you to the fact that closer examination of the company may be required.

Note that the following items may be used to secure loans:
1. Securities.
2. Cash surrender value of life insurance.
3. Accounts receivable.
4. Merchandise.
5. Warehouse receipts.
6. Trust receipts.
7. Discounted notes receivable.
8. Real estate.
9. Equipment.

[509.3.8] WHETHER, IF THERE ARE BANK LOANS AND LOANS FROM OFFICERS, THE OFFICERS HAVE SUBORDINATED THEIR LOANS TO THE BANK'S. When banks ask for such subordinations—and they often do—the officer's claim is usually assigned to the bank.

[509.3.9] WHETHER THERE ARE EVER ANY OVERDRAFTS. If there are, find out why.

[509.3.10] WHETHER DRAFTS ARE EVER PRESENTED TO THE BANK FOR COLLECTION. Find out if they are honored by the customer.

[509.3.11] THE GENERAL ATTITUDE OF THE BANK TOWARD THE CUSTOMER.

[509.4] **Interpreting Bank Information.** Bankers may generalize when they give you figures on either bank loans or deposits. Thus, rather than an exact figure, you will hear the number of figures. Ranges can vary depending on the bank and its location, but the following terms are now recommended by banks:

low four figures	1,000 to 2,000
moderate four figures	2,000 to 4,000
medium four figures	4,000 to 7,000
high four figures	7,000 to 9,999
low five figures	10,000 to 12,000

Don't forget to interpret the bank's information in light of its general class of customer and its location.

[510] **PUBLIC RECORDS.** Few important things happen to either a human being or a business that do not find their way into the public records. Births, deaths, marriages, suits, judgments, real-estate transfers, and mortgages make up only a part of the steady stream of record items. Public records are therefore a valuable area of investigation that can reveal significant facts about a business or a businessman. As a credit man, you will find occasion to check the following public-record items:

[510.1] **Financial Statements.** There are five federal agencies that require certain companies to file financial statements:

[510.1.1] SECURITIES AND EXCHANGE COMMISSION. Any concern that proposes to offer securities for sale to the public, if the aggregate value of those securities is $500,000 or more, must register the securities with the S.E.C. A part of the registration is a prospectus that includes financial statements.

If any one of a company's securities is listed on one of the national security exchanges, the listed corporation is required to file annual statements of condition and income with the Commission. Periodic reports must also be filed by companies whose securities are traded "over-the-counter" if they have over $1 million in assets and 500 or more stockholders.

Any company that proposes to issue securities for sale valued at *less* than $500,000 is required under "Regulation A" to file a "notice of intent" with the commission. The notice of intent does not always contain financial statements, but it includes most of the normal information in a full prospectus. Such companies do not have to file any further statements with the S.E.C. except for one notice, six months following the original, which covers the actual use of proceeds from the securities sale.

[510.1.2]   INTERSTATE COMMERCE COMMISSION. The I.C.C. regulates the activities of any transportation enterprise carrying goods or people between states. The filing of annual financial statements by railroads, bus and trucking companies, and others is required.

[510.1.3]   FEDERAL POWER COMMISSION. This agency regulates utilities producing electricity and gas. Such producers (which are also regulated by state public-utility commissions) are required to file annual financial reports.

[510.1.4]   FEDERAL COMMUNICATIONS COMMISSION. This regulatory agency develops rules and policies for licensing and implementation of rules for:

1. Community antenna television.
2. Radio and television stations.
3. Communications satellites.

Applications for broadcasting licenses and renewals of licenses (triennial basis) must be accompanied by financial information.

[510.1.5]   RURAL ELECTRIFICATION ADMINISTRATION. This agency administers the federal loan program for rural electrification and telephone service in rural areas. All R.E.A. loans are at 2 percent interest and the loan period is up to thirty-five years. Statements on R.E.A. Telephone & Electrical Cooperatives are available.

[510.2]   **Other Financial Information— States.** The following states require corporations operating in those states to file balance sheets and, in some instances, profit-and-loss statements that are classified as public records. These states, with applicable information, are as follows:

STATE REQUIREMENTS FOR FILING FINANCIAL INFORMATION

State	Latest Permissible Date for Filing	Remarks
Arizona	Three months after corporation fiscal closing date	No profit-and-loss statement
Colorado	March 15	Not uniform
Hawaii	May 1	Complete
Kansas	March 31	Complete
Massachusetts	Three months after date filed for annual meeting	Not released until approved
Michigan	May 15	Latest fiscal financial statement
New Hampshire	April 1	Highly condensed
Vermont	April 1	Highly condensed

[510.3]   **Other Public Records.**

[510.3.1]   MORTGAGES.

[510.3.2]   REGISTRATION OF FICTITIOUS TRADE NAMES.

[510.3.3]   CERTIFICATES OF INCORPORATION.

[510.3.4]   PARTNERSHIP AGREEMENTS, including:
1. Identity of partners.
2. Duration of partnership.
3. Contribution of limited partners.
4. Distribution of profits and provisions for dissolution.

[510.3.5]   WILLS, including:
1. Names of beneficiaries.
2. Provisions for continuation of a business.
3. How the estate will be settled.
4. Eventually, inventory of the estate and the amount distributed to heirs.

[510.3.6]   DEEDS.

[510.3.7]   LICENSES.

[510.3.8]   TAX ARREARAGES AND LIENS.

[510.3.9]   MECHANICS LIENS.

[510.3.10]   BANKRUPTCY PETITIONS.

[511]   **RELATED COMMERCIAL LAWS.** As a credit man, you must be familiar with three kinds of commercial laws. Each kind has an important effect on the way you evaluate the credit information at your disposal and the way you enforce your credit judgments.

[511.1]   **Mail Laws.** There are federal and state laws prohibiting the sending of false financial information through the mails and the submitting of false financial information in the hope of getting credit.

[511.2]   **Collections.** Every state has collection laws that relate to:

[511.2.1]   STATUTE OF LIMITATIONS.

[511.2.2]   GARNISHMENT EXEMPTIONS.

[511.2.3]   OTHER EXEMPTIONS.

[511.2.4]   REPOSESSION.

[511.2.5]   PROCESS SERVING.

[511.3]   **The Uniform Commercial Code.** The Uniform Commercial Code is the title of an act that has been adopted by forty-nine states and the District of Columbia to simplify, clarify, and modernize the body of law governing commercial transactions. The Uniform Commercial Code normally includes these ten basic articles:
1. General provisions.
2. Sales.
3. Commercial paper.
4. Bank deposits and collections.
5. Letters of credit.
6. Bulk transfers.
7. Warehouse receipts, bills of lading, and other documents of title.
8. Investment securities.

9. Secured transactions.

10. Effective date and repealer.

The most important article of the Uniform Commercial Code from the standpoint of the credit investigation is Article 9, which covers secured transactions (the principal exception being real estate). This article made far-reaching changes in existing law, and it has an important impact on credit decisions. It is important that you be familiar with its general provisions so that you will recognize existing claims on a company's assets and in order that you know the procedure to follow should you decide that credit must be extended on a secured basis.

Under precode law, if a creditor wanted to obtain a secured interest in the assets of a business, he could use a number of different security devices, such as chattel mortgage, conditional sales contract, or factor's lien.

Each of these devices covered only a particular type of asset. For example, a chattel mortgage covered fixed assets, and a factor's lien covered inventory (although normally receivables or other proceeds from the sale of such inventory also would be subject to this lien).

Article 9 has simplified secured financing by recognizing that in every secured transaction (regardless of what it may have been called under precode law), the debtor gives to the secured creditor a secured interest in specified collateral.

[511.3.1]   THE SECURITY AGREEMENT. The Uniform Commercial Code adopts a functional approach to secured transactions. Thus, Article 9 abolishes arbitrary differences between old types of security devices and substitutes in place of all of them a single security device called the security agreement. It is still permissible to use the old security forms such as a chattel mortgage as the security agreement.

The security agreement creates or provides for a secured interest and sets forth the specific details of the secured transaction. It can secure future as well as present debt. Provisions for the repayment of the secured interests are defined and the collateral on which a lien is given by the debtor to the secured party is listed.

In code states, a security agreement may list such a variety of assets that it will give the creditor a lien on all assets of a company. Prior to the code, this could only be done through several separate security devices.

Because of the paperwork and expense involved in perfecting separate secured interests, a creditor was not likely, under precode practice, to take more collateral than he felt was reasonably needed to secure his claim. As a result, the company usually would be left with some unpledged assets that would be available (if needed) to pay unsecured creditors. *Since the code makes it relatively easy to tie up all the assets of a business, some creditors in code states may be more inclined to oversecure their claims.*

Of course, in instances where the security agreement covers the entire inventory of a company, you may hesitate shipping the account since the merchandise they sell may become subject to the lien of the existing secured creditor.

You can prevent the existing secured creditor from automatically obtaining a lien on the goods you are selling by filing a financing statement, which represents public notice of the security agreement covering these goods, before the customer gets possession of them, and by notifying the existing secured creditor of the transaction.

If the financing statement filed by the existing secured creditor covered all equipment rather than all inventory, you could follow essentially the same procedure to prevent the existing secured creditor from automatically obtaining a lien on the new equipment being sold.

Instead of following the above procedure, as a subsequent merchandise or equipment supplier, you may be able to induce the existing secured creditor to subordinate his claim or to release a part of his collateral.

[511.3.2]   PERFECTING A SECURED INTEREST—THE FINANCING STATEMENT. In a few types of secured transactions, the signing of a security agreement alone will give you adequate or even complete protection.

But, for most transactions, you will have to file a document known as a financing statement to perfect your secured interest; that is, to make sure that your claim prevails over those of other creditors. Generally, the security agreement is not a matter of public record, although most states permit its filing instead of the financing statement.

A financing statement is a brief document that will not contain as much information about the secured transaction as the underlying security agreement. It need only contain:

1. The names, addresses, and signatures of the debtor and secured party.
2. A brief description of the collateral identified in the security agreement.
3. A statement as to whether the proceeds and products of the collateral are covered.

Usually, the financing statement contains no information regarding the amount of indebtedness (if any), the due date, or the terms of repayment. Also, while the security agreement will probably contain a precise description of the collateral, the description shown in the financing statement normally will be much briefer and less precise. For example, a security agreement may list as collateral specific items of equipment, but the financing statement, which is the public record of the transaction, may simply describe the collateral as "specified equipment" or only "equipment."

Ordinarily, the financing statement is filed after the security agreement has been signed, and a debt exists. However, you can also file a financing statement to give notice of secured financing that may occur in the future. In such an instance, the financing statement can be filed before the security agreement is signed, or if one has been signed, before a debt exists.

A financing statement, when it has been filed, constitutes public notice to all concerned about the existence or possible future existence of a secured claim. Also, a single financing statement can cover a series of separate transactions with the debtor so that the secured party does not have to file a new financing statement each time he signs a new security agreement with the debtor, provided that the type of collateral remains unchanged.

[511.3.3]   FLOATING LIENS. The term "floating lien" does not appear in the code, although the concept still exists. It can be described as applying to a situation where the description of the collateral covers after-acquired property and enables a secured creditor, without any further action on his part, to obtain automatically a secured interest in assets that the debtor acquires in place of those held when the security agreement was signed. In effect, the lien floats from one asset to another.

What is referred to as a floating lien can be created when the collateral is inventory or accounts receivable, where the debtor needs considerable freedom in selling or otherwise dealing with the collateral. The term "floating lien" is applicable when the financing statement covers the proceeds and products of the collateral. For example, when collateral is inventory and proceeds are also named, the lien in effect floats from the inventory to the receivables.

[511.3.4]   CONTINUATION STATEMENTS, TERMINATION STATEMENTS, AND OTHER FILINGS. Once a financing statement is filed, it is effective for five years even though no maturity date is shown. An effective period of less than five years may be specified. Before the expiration of the filing, a continuation statement can be filed extending the interest of the secured party for another five years or a shorter specified interval.

If the debt covered by a financing statement is paid, the debtor can ask the secured party for a termination statement and this statement, when filed, will terminate the secured interest.

Other types of code filings include a "release," which is a statement releasing part of the collateral named in an existing financing statement; an "assignment," which is a statement assigning to a new secured party a secured interest perfected by an existing financing statement; and an "amendment," which is a statement amending certain provisions in an existing financing statement. (In some instances, the name of the new secured party to whom assignment of the secured interest is being transferred is combined in the original financing statement.)

[511.3.5]   CREDIT SIGNIFICANCE. The credit significance of secured transactions is determined by the following factors:
1. Size of the secured debt.
2. Nature and extent of the collateral.
3. Overall financial strength of the debtor and his ability to generate funds to retire the secured debt.
4. Interference of a secured debt with your own wishes for security or the ability of the customer to pay your company's invoices.

Before reaching a credit decision, make sure you have determined these four facts.

State	Open Accounts	Contracts Written	Contracts Oral	Domestic Judgments
colspan info	[N.B. In all states where the Uniform Commercial Code is in effect, the statute of limitations specified by the code is four years for sales contracts.]			
Alabama	3	6	6	20
Alaska	6	6	6	10
Arizona	3	6	*	5
Arkansas	3	5	3	10
California	4	4	2	10
Colorado	6	*	*	20
Connecticut	6	6	3	21
Delaware	3	3	3	*
District of Columbia	3	3	3	12
Florida	3	5	3	20
Georgia	4	6	4	*
Hawaii	6	6	6	10
Idaho	4	5	4	6
Illinois	5	10	5	20
Indiana	6	*	6	10
Iowa	5	10	5	20
Kansas	3	5	3	*
Kentucky	*	15	5	15
Louisiana	3	10	10	10
Maine	6	6	6	20
Maryland	3	3	3	12
Massachusetts	6	6	6	*
Michigan	6	6	6	10
Minnesota	6	6	6	10
Mississippi	3	6	3	7
Missouri	5	10	5	10
Montana	*	8	5	10
Nebraska	4	5	4	*
Nevada	4	6	4	6
New Hampshire	6	6	6	20
New Jersey	6	6	6	20
New Mexico	4	6	4	*
New York	6	6	6	20
North Carolina	3	3	3	10
North Dakota	6	6	6	10
Ohio	*	15	6	21
Oklahoma	3	5	*	*
Oregon	6	6	6	10
Pennsylvania	6	6	6	*
Rhode Island	6	6	6	20
South Carolina	6	6	6	10
South Dakota	6	6	6	20
Tennessee	6	6	6	10
Texas	2	4	2	10
Utah	4	6	4	8
Vermont	6	6	6	8
Virginia	3	5	3	20
Washington	3	6	3	6
West Virginia	5	10	5	10
Wisconsin	6	*	*	20
Wyoming	8	10	8	*

*In these cases the state laws are too complicated to be summarized in this fashion.

Statutes of Limitations by States

CHAPTER 6

SOURCES OF CREDIT INFORMATION

[600]   **SOURCES OF CREDIT INFORMATION.** Your credit decisions can only be as good as the information upon which they are based. The most careful, elaborate analysis of a financial statement is worthless if the statement is old or unreliable. The most considered prediction of future paying habits can be sadly off the mark if the ledger experience upon which it is based is nonrepresentative or ancient history. Worst of all, no amount of agonizing over a credit decision will remedy a lack of information on which to base it. The preceding chapter pointed out the things you had to know to make the right credit decision. You may do much of the investigative work yourself, you may have subordinates do it or you may go to reporting agencies. Nevertheless, you must always be mindful of the fact that the final responsibility for the credit decision rests with you and you must always weigh the relative merits of the various pieces of information you obtain. This chapter will tell you where to go to find them, but the first step is to review these principles of gathering credit information.

[601]   **PRINCIPLES OF CREDIT-INFORMATION GATHERING.** To be effective, your credit-information-gathering activities must be governed by principles of good sense and fair play. These have been codified by the National Association of Credit Management and the Robert Morris Associates in a "Statement of Principles in the Exchange of Credit Information Between Banks and Mercantile Creditors" (see Figure 6.1). The principles expressed are applicable to all exchanges of credit information between all types of credit-information sources. The main points are outlined below.

[601.1]   **Confidentiality.** The credit information you gather—as well as that which you give to others—is confidential. This means that you should not divulge the information or its source to unauthorized personnel within or without your company or credit department. Inconsiderate disclosure

In recognition of the importance of confidence and considerateness in the proper exchange of credit information, Robert Morris Associates and the National Association of Credit Management adopted the following Statement of Principles in November, 1955, amended in 1971.

THE STATEMENT

1. The first and cardinal principle in the exchange of credit information is absolute respect for the confidential nature and accuracy of inquiries and replies of the identities of inquirers and sources.

2. Written inquiries should be by direct communication, manually and responsibly signed, and should correctly give name and address of the subject of inquiry. When an inquiry is made in person or by telephone, the inquirer should satisfactorily identify himself.

3. Every inquiry should indicate specifically: amount involved, reason, terms, availability of other background information, and whether source was given as reference. If inquirer's bank is used, the subject's bank of account should be named if known. When multiple bank inquiries are made, it should be so stated, and if to banks in the same locality, their names given.

4. File revisions should be undertaken only when necessary, and such inquiries should contain an expression of experience if appropriate, and in compliance with federal and state statutes.

5. When inquiries are made on behalf of third parties, it should be clearly stated but the identity of the other party must not be disclosed without permission.

6. Replies should be prompt. If written, they should be manually and responsibly signed, and as complete as possible, consistent, however, with the amount and nature of the inquiry. Specific questions should be answered if practicable, and in compliance with federal and state statutes.

7. If confidential nature of relationship with subject prevents disclosure of desired information, answers should so state.

This Statement of Principles applies to the exchange of credit information of a business or trade nature. The Fair Credit Reporting Act (Public Law 91-508), by contrast, is intended to apply to credit information exchanged and used in a nonbusiness relationship affecting individuals. Generally, the exchange of credit information between banks and mercantile concerns is unrelated to the provisions of the act. Nevertheless, exchangers of credit information should be familiar with the existence, intent, and provisions of the Fair Credit Reporting Act and/or other applicable federal or state laws that may regulate the exchange of information.

FIGURE 6.1

Statement of Principles in the Exchange of Credit Information Between Commercial Banks and Mercantile Concerns

will not only harm those who supplied you with the information, it will eventually impair your ability to get the facts you need in the future. Without complete assurance that all credit information is handled confidentially, many businessmen would stop communicating their credit experience, the free flow of credit would cease, and the entire economy of the country would be drastically affected.

[601.2]   **Consideration.** Being considerate takes very little time and brings great rewards. In collecting credit information, consideration means:

[601.2.1]   VERIFYING NAMES AND ADDRESSES. When you ask someone for credit information, make sure that the name and address of the subject of your inquiry are right. This saves everyone time and expense—including yourself.

[601.2.2]   FORMULATING SPECIFIC QUESTIONS. By asking specific questions, you save your sources time and you benefit from the precise, pertinent information you will receive.

[601.2.3]   LIMITING REQUESTS TO IMPORTANT ACCOUNTS. Put someone to the trouble of finding and communicating credit information only when you really do need it. Unnecessary requests will annoy your sources and eventually dry them up.

[601.3]   **Reciprocity.** If you expect to get credit information from others, you must be prepared to give the credit information you have about your customers in return. This means that you must respond promptly, cheerfully, and completely to any legitimate credit inquiries made to your credit department.

[602]   **FACTORS THAT INFLUENCE WHICH SOURCES YOU TAP.** Not every customer warrants a thorough investigation based upon all information available from all possible sources. Some accounts can be accepted—or rejected— without any investigation at all. The amount of information you need and the number of sources you must contact are determined by:

[602.1]   **Amount of Risk.** If the credit exposure is great, you may wish to tap more sources for more information.

[602.2]   **Time.** A fast decision often means that you must contact fewer sources.

[602.3]   **Location.** If the sources of information for any particular account are located far away, you might conclude that it is too inconvenient, expensive, or time-consuming to contact them.

[602.4]   **Cost.** Cost is really the summation of the above factors. Credit information—and collection information—can be expensive in time, energy, and money itself. Before launching a big investigation covering many sources, make sure that the account is financially worth it in terms of present or future opportunities.

[603]   **STANDARDIZING INFORMATION COLLECTION.** In order to have an efficient credit operation, you must develop a set of procedures for gathering and storing your credit information. Not only will this enable you to have the facts for a credit decision automatically at hand, it will also enable you to determine the cost of credit-information collection in advance. For instance, for each order over a certain limit you receive by mail, you might order a D&B report, make a bank check, and file for an interchange bulletin. Or you might require that each salesman fill out a credit-information form for each order he sells. The information can be stored in a standard way on a customer-history form or in compact form on an index card. The important thing is that the procedure be the same for every customer of the same class ordering the same amount of merchandise.

[604]   **DIRECT SOURCES OF INFORMATION.** Direct sources of credit information are, in effect, your customers themselves. Customer-supplied information should be your first step in your credit investigation.

[604.1]   **Advantages of Direct Contact with Customers.** By whatever method you choose (and the methods are discussed below), direct contact with customers offers these advantages:

[604.1.1]   GOODWILL. One of the credit department's most important functions is to build goodwill for its company. Direct contact with customers gives you the chance to develop a friendly, cooperative, and understanding relationship that can lead to more sales, fewer collection headaches, and greater profits for you. Once a customer knows you or your company personally, he is more likely to respect you and your problems—and give you whatever cooperation he can.

[604.1.2]   PERTINENT INFORMATION. Direct contact with a customer is usually the best means to obtain information for these reasons:

1. You can ask for precisely what you want and will know immediately if the customer has misunderstood you or is unable to furnish what you need.
2. People find it harder to turn down requests when they are delivered in person than when they are received impersonally.
3. You can explain why you need information to the customer's satisfaction. People are hesitant to divulge facts about themselves or their businesses if they don't know why the information is being sought.

Direct contact with customers gives you the opportunity to set precedents that will make credit investigation, evaluation, and collection easier for both yourself and your customer in the future. A conscious effort to set the patterns you desire, moreover, eliminates haphazard contact with the customer, which could mislead him about your policies and practices. Credit men have discovered that it is easier to set precedents at the beginning of a customer-client relationship than to try to change them later. Specifically, direct contact will enable you to set standards concerning:

1. *Amount of information.* You can let your customers know how much information you require as a matter of policy before you grant credit. You would do well to insist at the beginning that full disclosure of all pertinent details is a necessity.
2. *Kind of information—financial statements.* As part of a precedent establishing the amount of information you will want from a customer, you can also establish the kind of information you require—particularly financial statements. If a customer develops the habit of furnishing a financial statement regularly from the beginning, your credit operations are that much easier.
3. *Your terms of sale.* If you take an early opportunity to explain your terms of sale directly to a customer, you can avoid any confusion and disagreements that often arise later. Not only is your customer more likely to pay promptly—because he respects your firm policy and has one less excuse for delay—he will be much less likely to take unearned cash discounts. One way to make your point is to use a printed terms schedule. If your terms are one of the selling features of your company's product, don't forget to play this up.

[604.2]   **Methods of Direct Contact.**

[604.2.1]   SALESMEN. Credit managers have often acknowledged that salesmen could be a prime method of obtaining credit information directly from customers. Often they are on the best personal terms with their clients, visit them frequently, and are in a good position to evaluate them in relation to their competitors in the field. Specifically, salesmen are ideally suited and placed to measure the following:

1. *What salesmen can evaluate:*
   a. *Plant and equipment.* Salesmen visit the plants of many different companies and can get a good look at their equipment. A salesman's experienced eye can determine its condition and thus its value. He can get an idea of the plant's efficiency by the arrangement of the equipment and the attitude of its personnel. If the customer is a retailer, the salesman can evaluate the merchandising abilities of the managers as well as the quality of the products sold.
   b. *Location.* A salesman can easily tell if a company has a suitable location with or without competitive advantages.
   c. *Industry conditions.* Because salesmen frequently sell to many companies in the same industry, they can get an idea of how that industry in general is getting along.
   d. *Local conditions.* Salesmen most often sell one particular geographic area. As a result, no one is in a better position to foresee or measure local conditions such as natural disasters, strikes, product tastes, etc.
   e. *Management.* A salesman's success is in a large part determined by his ability to understand and to "read" people. His personal opinion of a customer's management's attitude and capability can be an extremely useful analytical tool.
2. *Other information salesmen can obtain.* In addition to the evaluations discussed above, salesmen can also procure:
   a. *Financial statements.* Salesmen can record financial statements or leave forms for customers to fill out and return.
   b. *References.* As a matter of habit, salesmen can procure trade references from their customers.
   c. *Changes.* Because they are in frequent contact with their client companies, salesmen are in a good position to find out about changes in management and operation (such as strikes, fires, etc.).
3. *Credit applications.* In order that salesmen may procure the information that you, as a credit manager, need in a form that is most easily accessible, you should develop a credit-application form. (See Figure 6.2 for an example of such a form that a large pharmaceuticals manufacturer uses.)
4. *Salesman resistance.* Although it is generally agreed that salesmen are in a magnificent position to provide vital credit information, salesmen are often reluctant to do so. Their objections embrace the issues of (1) time, (2) the desire not to offend or antagonize customers by asking for possibly unpleasant information and (3) the desire not to see a hard-earned sale go down the credit drain because of information they discover. Because of these objections, the credit manager must work to persuade the salesmen that cooperation with the credit department is in the salesmen's best interests. At the same time, the credit manager must evaluate

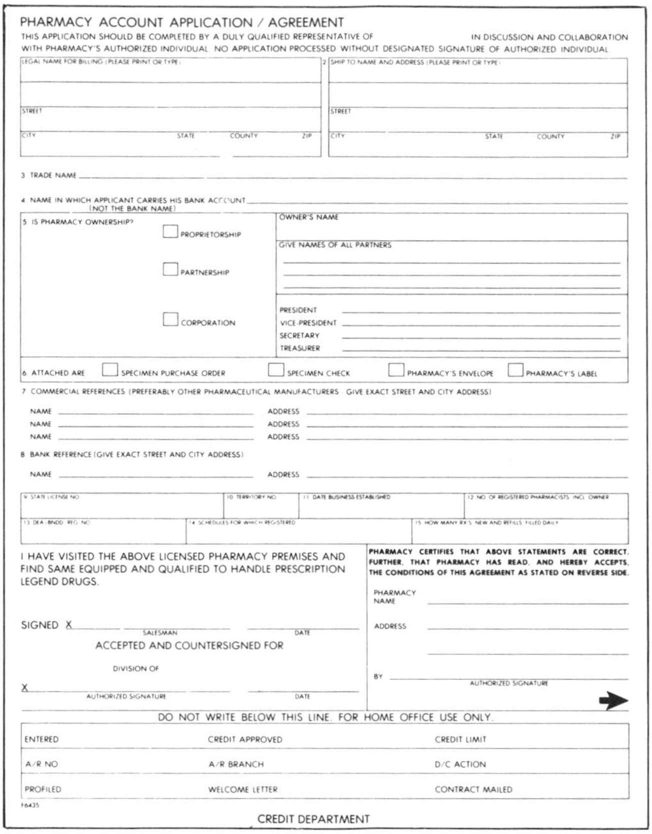

PHARMACY ACCOUNT APPLICATION / AGREEMENT

THIS APPLICATION SHOULD BE COMPLETED BY A DULY QUALIFIED REPRESENTATIVE OF IN DISCUSSION AND COLLABORATION WITH PHARMACY'S AUTHORIZED INDIVIDUAL. NO APPLICATION PROCESSED WITHOUT DESIGNATED SIGNATURE OF AUTHORIZED INDIVIDUAL.

1 LEGAL NAME FOR BILLING (PLEASE PRINT OR TYPE)
STREET
CITY STATE COUNTY ZIP

2 SHIP TO NAME AND ADDRESS (PLEASE PRINT OR TYPE)
STREET
CITY STATE COUNTY ZIP

3 TRADE NAME

4 NAME IN WHICH APPLICANT CARRIES HIS BANK ACCOUNT (NOT THE BANK NAME)

5 IS PHARMACY OWNERSHIP? PROPRIETORSHIP / PARTNERSHIP / CORPORATION

OWNER'S NAME

GIVE NAMES OF ALL PARTNERS

PRESIDENT
VICE-PRESIDENT
SECRETARY
TREASURER

6 ATTACHED ARE: SPECIMEN PURCHASE ORDER / SPECIMEN CHECK / PHARMACY'S ENVELOPE / PHARMACY'S LABEL

7 COMMERCIAL REFERENCES (PREFERABLY OTHER PHARMACEUTICAL MANUFACTURERS · GIVE EXACT STREET AND CITY ADDRESS)

NAME ADDRESS
NAME ADDRESS
NAME ADDRESS

8 BANK REFERENCE (GIVE EXACT STREET AND CITY ADDRESS)

NAME ADDRESS

9 STATE LICENSE NO. | 10 TERRITORY NO. | 11 DATE BUSINESS ESTABLISHED | 12 NO. OF REGISTERED PHARMACISTS INCL. OWNER

13 DEA (BNDD) REG. NO. | 14 SCHEDULES FOR WHICH REGISTERED | 15 HOW MANY RX'S NEW AND REFILLS FILLED DAILY

I HAVE VISITED THE ABOVE LICENSED PHARMACY PREMISES AND FIND SAME EQUIPPED AND QUALIFIED TO HANDLE PRESCRIPTION LEGEND DRUGS.

SIGNED X SALESMAN DATE

ACCEPTED AND COUNTERSIGNED FOR

DIVISION OF

X AUTHORIZED SIGNATURE DATE

PHARMACY CERTIFIES THAT ABOVE STATEMENTS ARE CORRECT. FURTHER, THAT PHARMACY HAS READ, AND HEREBY ACCEPTS, THE CONDITIONS OF THIS AGREEMENT AS STATED ON REVERSE SIDE.

PHARMACY NAME

ADDRESS

BY AUTHORIZED SIGNATURE

DO NOT WRITE BELOW THIS LINE. FOR HOME OFFICE USE ONLY.

ENTERED	CREDIT APPROVED	CREDIT LIMIT
A/R NO	A/R BRANCH	D/C ACTION
PROFILED	WELCOME LETTER	CONTRACT MAILED

F6435

CREDIT DEPARTMENT

FIGURE 6.2

Pharmacy Account Application

in a more skeptical way the information submitted by the sales force.

5. *Overcoming salesman resistance.* In order to develop a relationship in which the salesman is willing—indeed, anxious—to help the credit department, the credit manager should follow these steps:
   a. *Get to know salesmen personally.* If a salesman knows (and likes) a credit man, he will be more interested in helping him out. Moreover, later disputes about credit risks can be handled more easily.
   b. *Explain credit policy carefully.* If a salesman can come to feel himself a part of the credit department in that he is responsible for fulfillment of credit policy, then you have come a long way toward ensuring good salesman–credit-department cooperation. In order for this to happen, however, the salesman must be made aware of what company credit policy is, the reasons for it, and the ultimate advantage to the salesman in seeing that it is followed—increased company profits leading to higher salaries, commissions, and benefits.
   c. *Cooperate with salesmen in letting them know of your credit decisions.* This means as fast a decision as possible and immediate notification of the salesman in the event of an unfavorable decision. Nothing is more embarrassing to a salesman than calling on a customer only to find out that the credit department has turned him down.

[604.2.2]   INTERVIEW WITH SUBJECT. A well-planned, well-executed interview with a customer by the credit man can be the most effective means of getting credit information. It gives the man who must make the credit decision firsthand knowledge of the subject. A direct interview can supply all of the information listed above but, more important, it can furnish those almost intangible clues that make the difference between accepting or rejecting a marginal risk. From the customer's point of view, a direct interview is the means to clear up any misunderstandings that have arisen in the past, to get any advice an experienced credit man has to offer, and to size up the man who makes decisions vital to his business success. The direct interview may be the only way, moreover, to retain a customer to whom you've denied regular credit.

1. *Cost of interviews.* Interviews are extremely expensive in time and money. They should be reserved, therefore, for those accounts that present the greatest credit problems. You must make sure, furthermore, that each interview results in getting the information you need—as well as in building goodwill for your company. A wasted interview is doubly expensive.

2. *Planning the interview.* The key to the success of an interview is in planning. Make sure you follow these steps:
   a. *Decide what you must find out.* This is the first step. You must determine precisely the information you need to get.
   b. *Review the information you have.* Don't waste your time tracking down information that you already have. This will annoy the customer considerably.
   c. *Check alternative, less costly methods of finding out.* Agency reports, above all, often have the information you are searching for.
   d. *After reviewing the information you have, decide on the right tactics with which to approach your subject.*
   e. *Jot down the specific questions you intend to ask.* A businessman will answer your questions more rapidly and more directly if he recognizes that they are well thought out. Even if you don't jot them down, remember the pertinent points you want to investigate.
   f. *Know specifically with whom you wish to speak—by name.* You should always interview a principal of the business.
   g. *Get the right time.* Use the timing of your calls to your advantage. Nearly everyone is more amiable early in the day— and more accessible, too.

3. *Interviewing techniques.*
   a. *Attitude and approach.* Experienced interviewers feel there are two qualities most helpful to a man in getting information. The first can be described as a "positive" attitude. The other is a certain casual manner, which is really the absence of strain or tenseness.

   The "positive" feeling is the inner confidence you gain from interviewing experience. It arises from the recognition that you expect and you will obtain the information you want. This feeling carries with it an attitude of firm determination.

Some tension is generally present in an interview, but too much of it, unrelieved by a quality of easy getting along, might make you seem too aggressive and prevent a down-to-earth, valuable interview. No one being interviewed likes to feel that he is being pushed. The best way to get this casual feeling is to make up your mind before going to a place of business that you are going to like the man you will interview—that you are going to enjoy your call and that the interview will be friendly and productive.

In addition to being positive and friendly, your attitude should be straightforward and frank. There is no reason why you should not face the businessman squarely, explain what you want, why you want it, and why it is to the mutual advantage of both of you that he give the information, rather than resorting to matching wits with him.

b. *Logic.* Use a logical sequence in your interviews and you will cover all essential points.

c. *Record your information.* Every businessman will respect you more and be more helpful if he recognizes that you are interested enough in what he has to say to write it down.

d. *Don't dilly-dally.* Stick to the point of your interview and you will use your time more effectively.

[604.2.3]   LETTERS. Letters are one of the cheapest and most effective methods of obtaining credit information directly from customers. They can be used, of course, to find out the answers to any kind of credit question but they are most often used to procure financial statements. (For an example, see Figure 6.3.) To get results, use these techniques:

Dear

Thank you for your interest in our products as evidenced by your recent direct wholesale application.

Since one of our prerequisites for considering wholesale applicants is an opportunity to review financial statements, we would appreciate your sending us by return mail a current audited balance sheet and operating statement on your business.

You may be sure that this information will be held in strict confidence and used only for credit purposes.

Cordially,

FIGURE 6.3

Letter Requesting Financial Statement

1. *Enclose a financial-statement form.* This makes it easy for customers to give you the information you want in the form that suits you best.
2. *Enclose a self-addressed, stamped envelope.*
3. *Assure confidentiality.*
4. *Make the request seem ordinary.* This can be done by saying that you require the information from all customers so that an intelligent evaluation of each account can be made.
5. *Point out advantages of supplying credit information to the customer.* You could point out that adequate information means that you will be able to provide enough credit. You could also suggest, for instance, that the information he supplies will be used for noncredit purposes such as assuring adequate production of your company's product.

[604.2.4]   TELEPHONE. Although generally more effective as a collection tool, the telephone can be advantageously used by credit men to obtain information from customers. It has the advantage of enabling the credit analyst to judge the frame of mind of the customer and to adapt his arguments to the specific reaction of each one. Often, the analyst will get the information he needs right over the phone. As a minimum, he can obtain a promise that the necessary details will be mailed.

[605]   **INDIRECT SOURCES OF INFORMATION.** Indirect sources of information are those you consult to find out about a customer without going directly to the customer himself.

[605.1]   **Advantages of Indirect Sources.** Although direct contact with customers is the surest way to get some credit information, indirect sources offer certain advantages.

[605.1.1]   VERIFICATION. Indirect sources can often verify the information a customer has given you. Needless to say, indirect sources will point out those negative facts the customer himself naturally overlooks or fails to disclose.

[605.1.2]   OBJECTIVITY. Indirect sources of information are more likely to be objective in their evaluation of customers or in the records they keep. The opinions they offer, therefore, can be of great value.

[605.1.3]   TIME-COST SAVINGS. Some indirect sources of information can save you much time and effort in procuring accurate, up-to-date information. Credit agencies in particular provide services far beyond those which the means of average companies enable them to provide for themselves.

[605.2]   **Methods of Contacting Indirect Sources.** All the methods of directly contacting customers can be used to contact indirect sources of information. The principles and procedures are the same.

[605.3]   **Types of Indirect Sources.**

[605.3.1]   YOUR OWN RECORDS. This is not necessarily an indirect source as the information you might have could be the fruit of direct contacts. Nevertheless, you should be aware that your own experience with a customer is one of the best, most reliable guides to his future action. A quick check in your own files could save you much time and effort in reaching credit decisions. See Section 403.4 for information on how to set up accessible, usuable records systems.

[605.3.2]   BANKS. The kind of information banks are able to furnish was discussed in detail in Section 509. Here is a brief summary:

1. *Bank Information.*
   a. Amount and security of bank loans.
   b. Average balances.
   c. Paying habits.
   d. Financial condition.
   e. General opinion and verification of other information.
2. *Techniques of obtaining bank information.* A bank's primary responsibility is to its depositors. For that reason you must use care in requesting information from banks.
   a. *Develop personal contacts.* Bankers are much more likely to give you the information you need if they know and trust you.
   b. *Limit your requests.* Don't be a burden on your banker contacts. Use them only when necessary.
   c. *Be specific.* Ask bankers specific questions and you are more likely to get useful answers.
   d. *Verify subjects.* This means that you check to make absolutely sure that the name, address, and account number you furnish the bank are correct.
   e. *Deal through your own bank.* Often it is better to have your own bank make requests to other banks about their depositors. Bankers know and trust each other.
   f. *Communicate by letter only on company stationery above the signature of an authorized employee.*
   g. *Be open and honest.* You will obtain better results if you tell banks why you want the information you have requested. This is one of the responsibilities enumerated in the RMA-NACM code presented at the beginning of this chapter.
3. *How to find out your customer's bank.*
   a. Ask him.
   b. Examine your customer's checks.
   c. Have salesmen obtain this information automatically.

[605.3.3]   TRADE. Your customer's other suppliers can often provide vital information on many aspects of his operation. Most important, these suppliers can give you their ledger experience with a customer and this can be one of your most authoritative guides to what his payment performance is likely to be in the future.

1. *Ledger experience.* As pointed out in Chapter 5, ledger experience includes the following:
   a. How long sold.
   b. High credit.
   c. Amount owing.
   d. Amount past due.
   e. Paying habits.

f. Terms.

g. Last order.

h. Additional comments.

2. *Methods of obtaining trade experience.* There are several methods of obtaining trade experience. Make your selection according to your time and cost requirements.

   a. *Direct Interchange.* This means communicating in some form (letter, telephone, etc.) directly with one supplier to obtain his ledger experience on one (or more) customers. Obviously, this method is most expensive if you are to contact more than one supplier for each customer. Moreover, if your primary purpose in contacting a supplier is to find his ledger experience, direct interchange is likely to be more costly than other methods even though it can be faster. Limit your direct-interchange requests, therefore, to:

    (1) Large, risky accounts.

    (2) Accounts for which information is not available from other sources.

    (3) Accounts for which other information is out of date.

When making a direct inquiry, remember to ask specific questions, verify the account name before investigating, tell the other supplier the amount involved, and be prepared to reciprocate.

   b. *Group meetings.* Group meetings are less expensive than direct interchange because they supply more information about more customers at the same time. In addition, group meetings provide you with the opportunity to meet fellow credit men, exchange information on the latest collection and credit granting techniques, and review general industry and economic conditions. Sponsors of group meetings are:

    (1) National Association of Credit Management.

    (2) Credit associations.

    (3) Local trade associations.

    (4) Dun & Bradstreet.

    (5) National Credit Office.

   c. *Credit interchange bureaus.* Local credit interchange bureaus are organized in a system headed by the Credit Interchange Bureaus of the National Association of Credit Management. Although contact is less personal, the information supplied by participation in your local bureau is extensive, accurate, and up-to-date. Moreover, it is one of the least expensive methods of obtaining ledger experiences of suppliers from broad geographic areas. The system works as follows:

    (1) You furnish information on the customers you are selling to your local bureau.

    (2) When you want information on a customer, you send a request to your local interchange bureau.

    (3) The interchange bureau sends you a copy of any report it has on file.

(4) Your request is circulated through the system to produce responses from all of the subject's suppliers.

(5) These responses are tabulated and distributed in a new report that is then placed on file.

d. *Dun & Bradstreet.* Ledger experience is just one of the many pieces of information contained in a Dun & Bradstreet Business Information Report. The complete services of D&B are described below.

DUN & BRADSTREET. Dun & Bradstreet, Inc., has traditionally been the best source for extensive credit information at reasonable cost. Because D&B has easy access to credit information that individual suppliers often find difficult to obtain, because Dun & Bradstreet has many trained analysts who are experienced in evaluating this information, and because Dun & Bradstreet is totally impartial, most credit men use the Dun & Bradstreet ratings and reports as a source of information for their credit decisions.

1. *History.* Dun & Bradstreet was founded as The Mercantile Agency by Lewis Tappan in 1841 in response to unsettled business conditions following the panic of 1837. Tappan's idea was to assemble a central reservoir of information on country traders accessible to city suppliers. He enjoyed the friendship and confidence of New York's lending "big houses," to whose representatives he outlined his proposal that credit facts be pooled for mutual benefit to decrease risk. The proposal was heartily accepted and operations of the agency began. At first it was necessary to visit the Mercantile Agency office to look up a credit report—quite different from today's reports produced on minicomputers for individual subscribers. Tappan stayed in the business until 1849, when he retired in favor of his nephew, Arthur Tappan, and Benjamin Douglass. Douglass brought Robert Graham Dun into the firm. By 1859 Dun had bought out the other interests and the agency became known as R. G. Dun and Company.

John M. Bradstreet, meanwhile, had founded a competing firm in Cincinnati in 1853. The Bradstreet Company concentrated more on cities, however, than did the Agency, a fact reflected by its larger *Reference Book.* The first one was published in 1857 and contained over 200,000 listings.

Both companies expanded rapidly, and finally they merged in 1933.

Since that time, Dun & Bradstreet Companies, Inc., as the parent company is now known, has continued to expand—always providing more and better services to the business community. Highlights include the acquisition, in 1942, of the Credit Clearing House; of the National Credit Office in 1933; of Moody's in 1962; and the merger with the Reuben H. Donnelley Company in 1961. Today Dun & Bradstreet is involved in virtually every phase of gathering and communicating business information to its customers.

2. *Services.* Dun & Bradstreet provides scores of services for many business needs. Of specific interest to the credit man are the following:

  a. *The Dun & Bradstreet Reference Book.* The names and ratings of nearly three million businesses located throughout the United States and Canada are contained in the *Reference Book.* They are arranged alphabetically, by city or town within their particular state or province; and the book is published every two months—in January, March, May, July, September, and November—to keep the information continuously updated. This revising every sixty days is necessary to keep pace with business changes, which occur at the rate of about 5,000 during each and every working day. The names listed are commercial enterprises—manufacturers, wholesalers, retailers, business services, and other types of businesses buying regularly on credit terms.

  A line in the *Reference Book* (see Figure 6.4) tells you:

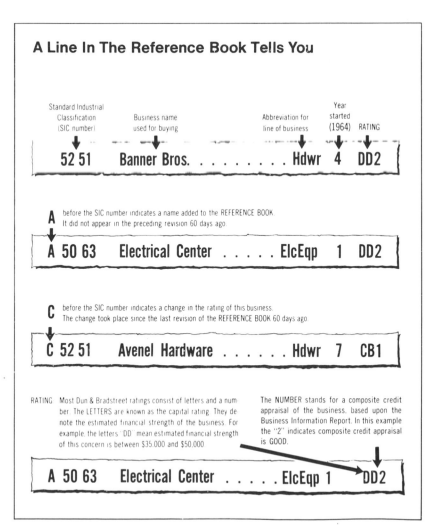

FIGURE 6.4. Information Contained in a Line of the Dun & Bradstreet Reference Book

(1) *Dun & Bradstreet rating.* Most ratings consist of letters and a number. The letters are known as the capital rating and denote the estimated financial strength of the business. The number stands for the composite credit appraisal of the business based upon information contained in the Business Information Report.

(2) *Standard Industrial Classification (SIC) Code Number,* denoting function and line of business.

(3) *Name of city, town, or village.*

(4) *Town population* (if more than 1,000 according to the 1970 U.S. Census).

(5) *County name.*

(6) *Code number of the D&B office.*

(7) *Year started.* The numeral preceding the rating indicates the year the business was established or came under the present control or management. Thus, "9" indicates 1969. The absence of a date indicates a concern in business ten years or more under its present control.

(8) *A* before the SIC code number indicates a name added to the *Reference Book.* It did not appear in the preceding edition sixty days previously.

(9) *C* before the SIC code number indicates a change in the rating of this business.

(10) The branch listing where the headquarters is located in a different state. The rating is given at the branch when the headquarters is out-of-state.

(11) The branch listing where branch and headquarters are located in the same state. No rating is given for the branch.

(12) An asterisk (*) following the buying name indicates that the business is incorporated.

(13) A town without a post office is entered with a reference to the nearest post office town, where the businesses are listed.

(14) "Inv" signifies an investigation was incomplete when this edition went to press.

(15) The name of the local bank, or banks, officers, and its capital.

b. *The Dun & Bradstreet Report.* Credit decisions are not easy to make; they require detailed and reliable information. Your company does not profit when you have to refuse an order because of insufficient information. Dun & Bradstreet reports are designed to give you the information you need. (For an example, see Figure 6.5.)

There are seven basic elements in a Dun & Bradstreet Report:

(a) *D-U-N-S (Data Universal Numbering System).* A D-U-N-S Number is a nine-digit code that identifies a specific business name and location. This code, developed and maintained by Dun & Bradstreet, is widely used throughout industry to simplify record keeping through dataprocessing applications. It is also the "address" of the detailed marketing and credit facts for each business listed in the *Reference Book* and in the Dun & Bradstreet Business Information Center.

(b) *Summary.* The summary section, in capsule form, analyzes the report. It consists of two parts. The first part, upper left to right, shows SIC (Standard Industrial Classification) Code number, D-U-N-S (Data Universal Numbering System) Number, buying name and address, ownership, line of business, year business started or came under

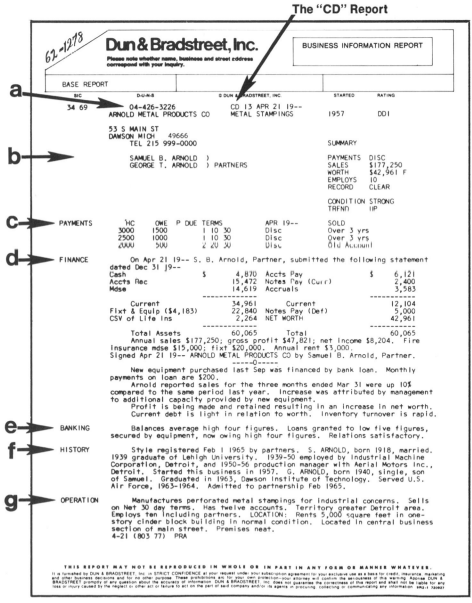

FIGURE 6.5. The Dun & Bradstreet, Inc., Business Information Report

present management or control, and Dun & Bradstreet Rating (see "Key to Ratings," Figure 6.6). The second part of the summary, to the right and beneath the rating, shows highlights of the data in the report: payments, sales, worth, number of employees, record, condition, trend. In simpler cases, the summary section provides a condensation of information needed by the credit or sales manager to reach a decision regarding the desirability of a customer or prospect. In more complicated cases, this section introduces the detailed information in the sections of the report described below.

(c) *Payments.* This section records the manner in which the subject of the report pays his bills. It gives a complete listing of his trade record, and indicates approximations of the highest credit granted during the past year (HC), amount owing, amount past due (if any), terms of sale, manner of payment, and supplier comments about the account, such as how long sold. This information is obtained directly from a representative number of suppliers and is tabulated so the reader of the report can determine how obligations are being met.

The payments section serves several important functions: If a supplier intends to open a new account, he can tell from the previous paying experiences of others what to expect in his dealings with the prospective customer. He can also determine selling terms and amount of credit granted by other suppliers and how they compare with his own selling activity or credit policy. For example, a study of this section might occasionally reveal that one creditor is receiving prompt payment at the expense of slow payments to others.

(d) *Finance.* The balance sheet gives the essential facts for determining the financial "health" of a business. The purpose of this financial statement is to show the amount of capital in use, how it is applied, and what borrowed money is involved. Most reports contain a financial statement. The weight to be given statement information depends heavily on the source. A fiscal statement prepared by a CPA with an opinion expressed without qualification is to be preferred. Any stepping down in the quality of information should be given appropriate weight. Accountants' qualifications, interim figures, unaudited figures, estimates provided by the management, all mean an increased possibility of inaccuracy as to the true financial picture of the business. The credit analyst must use whatever financial information is available, recognizing that some is better than none, but he must not fail to evaluate the level of confidence he can give depending on the foregoing considerations.

The balance sheet is usually supplemented by profit-and-loss figures, plus informaton regarding leases, insurance coverage, and other pertinent details. The comment following the statement is devoted to further necessary explanation of the figures and a description of sales and profit trends. The rating is based to a large extent upon the degree of financial stability and the trend as reflected in this section.

(e) *Banking.* This section contains additional independent, or outside, information of credit relevance. This information concerning banking relations includes indications of average balances, previous and current loan experience including manner of repayment, whether loans are secured or unsecured, and length of time relations have been conducted.

(f) *History.* The history section reveals the names, ages, and past business experience of the principals or owners of a concern. Basic features covered include the length of time the individuals have been in the line in which they are currently engaged, length of time in other lines, outside business affiliations, and information about financial successes or difficulties that may have been experienced in the past. D&B reports criminal proceedings that it learns of. Those resulting in convictions are reported indefinitely, but in the other instances, including expungements and pardons, the information is ultimately eliminated from its reports.

There are a number of important uses for this antecedent information: verifying orders, identifying owners, partners, or officers, and revealing outside interests of the principals. The information in this section decisively affects many credit decisions.

(g) *Operation.* This section describes what a concern does and, under the subheading "location," describes the nature of the premises and the neighborhood, the size of the floor space, and the types of equipment. Also described under the heading "operation"—wherever applicable—are the lines of merchandise sold or kinds of services rendered, price range, classification of customers, selling terms, percentage of cash and credit sales, number of accounts, seasonal aspects, and number of employees.

By describing the machinery of production and the distribution, the operation section helps the reader of the report to a better understanding of the balance-sheet and profit-and-loss figures. With the principal operating features, the reader is better able to judge whether capital is adequate or debt excessive. Also, sales departments use this section to determine whether the subject would make a profitable outlet for their particular lines of merchandise. Purchasing departments find this information useful in determining the ability of a manufacturer to deliver an order, or to support guarantees.

c. *Special Dun & Bradstreet reports.* The same basic elements are contained in all Dun & Bradstreet reports, but some have been developed in specialized form to fit the credit and sales requirements of various subscribers. The Arnold Metal Products report (Figure 6.5) is the type written on the majority of the names listed in the *Dun & Bradstreet Reference Book.* Other types of reports are as follows:

(1) *Analytical reports* written by a staff of analysts familiar with the complicated financial structure of larger concerns.

(2) *Key account reports* written with a view to solving particular credit and management problems and containing highly detailed information.

(3) *International reports* written on overseas business concerns in the principal Free World markets.

(4) *Municipal reports* written "in depth" on most major governmental units that issue tax-exempt bonds.

d. *The Dun & Bradstreet rating.* See Figure 6.6 for an explanation of D&B ratings.

e. *Relationship between reports and the Reference Book.* The *Reference Book* provides, in your office, credit and marketing information for a quick credit check:

(1) When an order comes to your desk.

(2) When a buyer visits your showroom.

(3) When your salesman needs information.

(4) On an account before a call is made.

The *Reference Book* is not intended as a substitute for detailed credit reports, but as an auxiliary facility to be used for ready reference where light risk is involved, and for other convenient and useful purposes. Each subscriber uses his service in the way that best fits into his own circumstances and his own situation. A concern selling small orders may rely upon the *Reference Book* alone more frequently than the concern that sells in larger amounts or on a continual basis.

Therefore, the subscriber works out the system that seems most advantageous to him. Those who have used the service over a period of years generally ask for detailed reports in the following circumstances:

(1) New accounts, particularly where there will be continuing interest.

(2) Slow accounts.

(3) Concerns recently established; for example, those that are going through their first year or two.

(4) Accounts where unsolicited orders come to you from people unknown to you.

(5) When the rating in the *Reference Book* suggests the desirability of getting more details. For example, the

ESTIMATED FINANCIAL STRENGTH			COMPOSITE CREDIT APPRAISAL			
			HIGH	GOOD	FAIR	LIMITED
5A	Over	$50,000,000	1	2	3	4
4A	$10,000,000 to	50,000,000	1	2	3	4
3A	1,000,000 to	10,000,000	1	2	3	4
2A	750,000 to	1,000,000	1	2	3	4
1A	500,000 to	750,000	1	2	3	4
BA	300,000 to	500,000	1	2	3	4
BB	200,000 to	300,000	1	2	3	4
CB	125,000 to	200,000	1	2	3	4
CC	75,000 to	125,000	1	2	3	4
DC	50,000 to	75,000	1	2	3	4
DD	35,000 to	50,000	1	2	3	4
EE	20,000 to	35,000	1	2	3	4
FF	10,000 to	20,000	1	2	3	4
GG	5,000 to	10,000	1	2	3	4
HH	Up to	5,000	1	2	3	4

FIGURE 6.6

Dun & Bradstreet, Inc., Key to Ratings

CLASSIFICATION FOR BOTH ESTIMATED FINANCIAL STRENGTH AND CREDIT APPRAISAL

FINANCIAL STRENGTH BRACKET

EXPLANATION

1 $125,000 and Over

2 20,000 to 125,000

When only the numeral (1 or 2) appears, it is an indication that the estimated financial strength, while not definitely classified, is presumed to be within the range of the ($) figures in the corresponding bracket and that a condition is believed to exist which warrants credit in keeping with that assumption.

"INV." shown in place of a rating indicates that the report was under investigation at the time of going to press. It has no other significance.

Absence of a Listing

The absence of a listing is not be construed as meaning a concern is non-existent, has discontinued business, nor does it have any other meaning. The letters "NQ" on any written report mean "not listed in the Reference Book."

Year Business Started

The numeral shown is the last digit of the year date when the business was established or came under present control or management. Thus, 8 means 1968; 9 means 1969. No dates go past ten years. Thus the absence of a numeral indicates ten years or more. This feature is not used in connection with branch listings.

ABSENCE OF RATING DESIGNATION FOLLOWING NAMES LISTED IN THE REFERENCE BOOK

The absence of a rating, expressed by two hyphens (--), is not to be construed as unfavorable but signifies circumstances difficult to classify within condensed rating symbols. It suggests the advisability of obtaining a report for additional information.

EMPLOYEE RANGE DESIGNATIONS IN REPORTS OR NAMES NOT LISTED IN THE REFERENCE BOOK

Certain businesses do not lend themselves to a Dun & Bradstreet rating and are not listed in the Reference Book. Information on these names, however, continues to be stored and updated in the D&B Business Data Bank. Reports are available on these businesses but instead of a rating they carry an Employee Range Designation (ER) which is indicative of size in terms of number of employees. No other significance should be attached.

KEY TO EMPLOYEE RANGE DESIGNATIONS

ER 1	Over 1000 Employees
ER 2	500 - 999 Employees
ER 3	100 - 499 Employees
ER 4	50 - 99 Employees
ER 5	20 - 49 Employees
ER 6	10 - 19 Employees
ER 7	5 - 9 Employees
ER 8	1 - 4 Employees
ER N	Not Available

credit rating of a concern may be "good" or "high," yet the order from that concern may seem quite large considering the size of the business as indicated by the rating.

(6) Where the buyer is seeking to increase lines of credit.

(7) Where there are changes in paying habits (if, for example, a retailer has been discounting, then starts to run past-due with you), call your Dun & Bradstreet office and explain the situation. They will try to find out what has caused the change in paying habits.

(8) And, finally, where you are selling regularly in amounts to justify the expense, you should be registered for continuous service on all accounts. If regular sales of over $100 a month are made, the cost of a report is quite insignificant for a year's service, considering that sales will exceed $1,200 a year.

f. *Change Notification Service.* This is an effective way to manage receivables. A subscriber's customers' names are registered for this service annually. Confirming this is a "List of Registrations" sent to the subscriber—which includes business name and address (where D&B records differ from those of the subscriber), the D-U-N-S Number, and, at the subscriber's option, his customer identification number and the latest D&B rating. This information can be used to update the historic data a subscriber maintains on each of his customers. Each week thereafter, a change notice is sent to you on any of your registered accounts on which a change of credit significance has been reported. On the average, six or seven change notices are issued weekly for each 1,000 registered names. This holds paperwork to a minimum while assuring the subscriber of credit coverage on all his customers.

Types of change notices are as follows:

(1) *Rating changes.* Both former and new ratings are shown (see Figure 6.7).

(2) *Special changes.* These include liquidations, voluntary bankruptcies (not reorganizations), relocations to another state, and discontinuances.

(3) *Successor changes.* These indicate that control or ownership of a business has changed (see Figure 6.8).

There are two Change Notification Options:

(1) *Option A.* The subscriber receives the "List of Registrations." Each week thereafter he receives change notices. The D&B report concerning each change is automatically sent.

(2) *Option B.* The subscriber receives the "List of Registrations." Each week thereafter he receives change notices. He may order the D&B report concerning the change by using a preprinted inquiry ticket attached to the change notice. The inquiry is charged to the regular D&B subscription.

Computer use of the Change Notification System is described later in this chapter.

g. *Special handling services.* D&B subscribers may also use any of the following special handling services:

(1) *Priority Service.* When time is at a premium and a report must be obtained in less than normal handling time, subscribers use priority service. There are two types:

(a) *Two-Way Priority Service.* Inquiry is received by telephone, taken out of routine, and wired to the D&B reporting office that covers it. A reply summary is wired back and the information is transmitted to the subscriber by telephone—usually the same day. A full report is airmailed in confirmation. There is a small charge for taking an inquiry out of routine handling.

(b) *One-Way Priority Service.* This is the same as (a) without the return wire and telephone call.

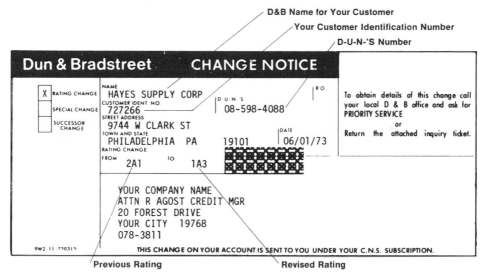

FIGURE 6.7. Dun & Bradstreet Change Notification Service—Rating Change

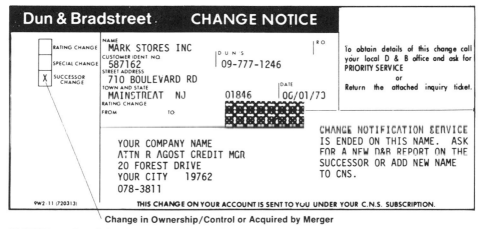

FIGURE 6.8. Dun & Bradstreet Change Notification Service—Successor Change

(2) *Consulting Service.* When time is at a premium and it is necessary to talk directly with the business analyst who actually knows the account, subscribers use this service to get firsthand insight. The analyst who receives the inquiry by a private wire network telephones information directly to the inquiring subscriber—possibly within minutes—always within twenty-four hours.

(3) *Key Account Report Service.* This provides a custom report in depth, exclusive to the inquiring subscriber. Inquiry is discussed before investigation is made to ensure coverage of the specific needs of the subscriber.

h. *Specialized reference books and directories.*

(1) *Reference Book of Manufacturers.* This book is designed for

those who buy from or sell to manufacturers. Published in two volumes in the spring and fall, it covers about 355,000 listings, including sales, credit, and purchasing data on all manufacturing establishments, their headquarters, and branches where manufacturing is done.

(2) *State Sales Guides. State Sales Guides* travel along with salesmen wherever they go. They contain the same information as the *Reference Book* but in brief, condensed editions for individual states as well as several large cities.

(3) *Million Dollar Directory.* The *Million Dollar Directory,* published by the Marketing Services Division, is designed for those buying from, selling to, or researching the largest business firms. Essentially a marketing service, this directory lists all U.S. businesses with a net worth of $1 million or more. Published annually, with May and September supplements, it lists 39,000 companies with 350,000 officers and directors, and shows interlocking affiliations where they exist. There is a new D-U-N-S Number listing section for easier identification.

(4) *Middle Market Directory.* This is similar to the *Million Dollar Directory* but extends the market down to businesses worth $500,000 or more. The directory is published annually, by the Marketing Services Division, and about 34,000 companies are listed.

(5) *Metalworking Directory.* For those who buy from or sell to the metalworking industries, this directory contains pertinent marketing facts on all U.S. metal-producing and metalworking plants with twenty or more employees, as well as important metal distributors. Approximately 39,000 plants and wholesalers are listed in this marketing service, published annually by the Marketing Services Division, in May.

(6) *Reference Book of Corporate Managements.* Published annually, this directory contains biographical sketches of about 30,000 executives in over 2,400 large corporations of greater investor and general business interest. It also identifies directors.

i. *D&B international services.* Dun & Bradstreet's 117 offices in twenty-three foreign countries stand ready to provide subscribers with up-to-date, accurate, fast credit services. These include:

(1) *International Business Information Reports.* (see Figure 6.9). International reports provide a ready gauge of credit risk and market potentials. They include:

(a) *Summary.* The summary condenses the information needed for a sales or credit decision and highlights significant facts. Credit data, on the right, shows the year the business started, the trend of payments, annual sales, net worth, and number of employees.

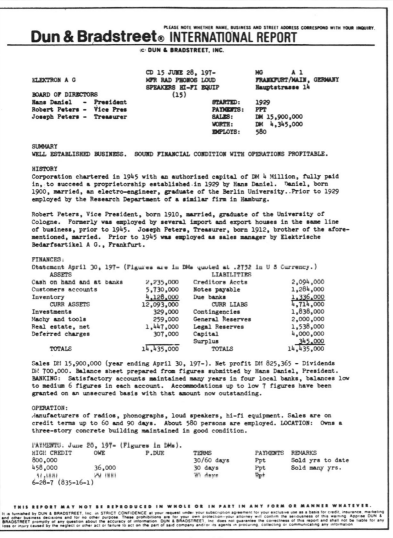

FIGURE 6.9. Dun & Bradstreet International Report

The rating, upper right, indicates the estimated financial strength and composite credit appraisal.

(b) *History.* The history identifies the owners and their commercial experience and describes the background of the business. It enhances understanding and makes it easier to establish confident business relations.

(c) *Finances.* The financial condition—how a firm is progressing, capital in use, and borrowing record—is reported here. The analysis covers the ability of the concern to meet its obligations.

(d) *Operation.* The operation section reports what the concern does, lines of merchandise and class of trade sold, facilities and equipment.

(e) *Payments.* How companies pay their bills, the answer to one of your most important questions, is indicated. A concise record of trade payments, high credits received, amounts owing and, if any, past due, terms and pertinent comments from suppliers, are listed.

(2) *International Reference Books and Market Guides.* Dun & Bradstreet International publishes the following reference books and market guides:

(a) *Argentine Reference Book.*

(b) *The Australian Key Business Directory.*

(c) *Australian Market Guide.*

(d) *Brazil Synopsis.*

(e) *British Middle Market Directory.*

(f) *Canadian Key Business Directory.*

(g) *Dun & Bradstreet Marketing Directory of Principal International Businesses.*

(h) *Dun & Bradstreet Register* (U.K.)

(i) *Exporters' Encyclopaedia—United States Market Guide.*

(j) *Exporters' Encyclopaedia—World Market Guide.*

(k) *Guide to Key British Enterprises.*

(l) *International Market Guide—Continental Europe.*

(m) *International Market Guide—Latin America.*

(n) *Republic of Ireland Register.*

(o) *Seyd's Commercial Lists (U.K.).*

(p) *South African Credit Rating Service.*

(q) *Stubbs Buyers' National Guide* (U.K.).

j. *Building and construction industries services.* Dun & Bradstreet's Building and Construction Division credit services include specialized consultants, monthly consolidated ledger abstracts (listing past-due accounts), the *Dun & Bradstreet Reference Book* and D&B Business Information Reports. Specialized services such as bonding reports, real-estate searches, and retainage reports are also available.

k. *Credit Clearing House.* Credit Clearing House, the specialized division of Dun & Bradstreet, provides an entire line of credit services for the apparel and allied fields throughout the United States. As a credit agency, CCH is unique—and thus particularly effective—for these three reasons:

(1) *It is devoted to one industry:* apparel and allied lines. Because their efforts are concentrated in one field, the staff of CCH is particularly sensitive to the buying and paying patterns of apparel retailers. Their knowledge of the industry coupled with their access to all the resources of Dun & Bradstreet means that the information they supply is the most up-to-date and incisive you can obtain.

(2) *Credit Clearing House will recommend—or not recommend—shipping an order of a specific dollar amount.* Before exposing yourself to a credit risk, you can have the expert advice of CCH analysts about your chances of collecting a particular order for a particular amount. More precisely, when you telephone CCH, they will provide you with one of these five recommendations:

(a) Credit is recommended for this transaction.

(b) Credit is recommended for this transaction to a specified amount.

(c) Credit is recommended for this transaction provided that certain specified conditions are met.

(d) Credit is recommended for this transaction to a specified amount provided that certain specified conditions are met.

(e) Credit is not recommended for this transaction.

(3) *Credit Clearing House can provide information instantaneously.* CCH subscribers who telephone their requests into New York benefit from the instantaneous retrieval and display—via cathode-ray tube—of credit facts stored in CCH computers. Here's how the system works: The inquiry is taken by a CCH cathode-ray tube operator who communicates with the computer via a keyboard located right in front of the CRT viewer. The operator "locates" the subject of the inquiry and the following information flashes on the CRT screen:

(a) D-U-N-S Number.

(b) Legal Business Name.

(c) Street Address.

(d) Additional Street Addresses (if any).

(e) City, State and Zip Code.

(f) *Apparel Trades Book* Rating.

(g) Dun & Bradstreet Rating.

(h) Transaction Decision (Recommended, Not Recommended, Exceeds Dollar Guideline).

(i) Reason Codes.

(j) Dollar Guideline.

You get this information immediately as the operator reads it from the CRT screen. Depending upon the type of contract a subscriber has, this oral report will be followed up by a recommendation slip with or without a Dun & Bradstreet Business Information Report on the subject of the inquiry. There are four types of recommendation slips:

(a) In the New York area, the form illustrated in Figure 6.10 will be provided in response to all inquiries to the CCH Business Information Center in New York City. In the "summary" box, a detailed narrative credit opinion is given. (Outside the New York area, forms are provided by CCH branch offices to answer inquiries originating from local subscribers. These offices use a special "microfiche" answering index produced by the CCH Business Information Center in New York that is continuously updated to ensure that CCH recommendations are uniform throughout the country.)

(b) A green slip (Figure 6.11) indicates that credit is recommended for the transaction. As noted on the

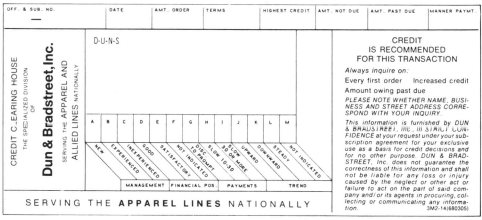

FIGURE 6.10

Credit Clearing House Recommendation Slip Used in New York Area

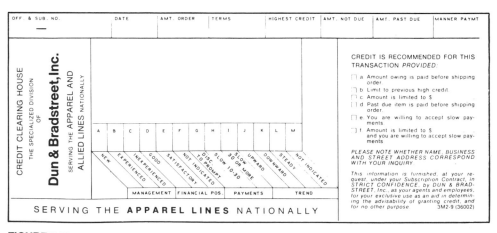

FIGURE 6.11

Credit Clearing House Recommendation Slip: Credit Is Recommended for This Transaction

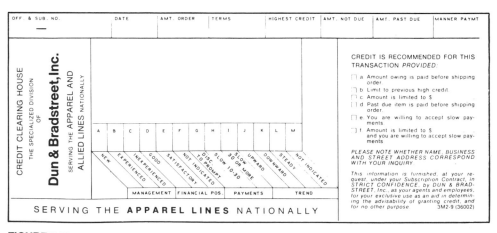

FIGURE 6.12

Credit Clearing House Recommendation Slip:
Credit Is Recommended Provided Conditions Indicated Are Acceptable

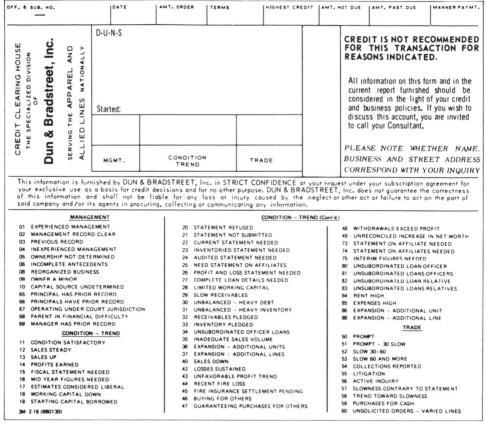

FIGURE 6.13

Credit Clearing House Recommendation Slip: Credit Is Not Recommended for This Transaction

slip, this opinion is based upon an appraisal of management, financial position, payments, and trend.

(c) A white slip (Figure 6.12) indicates that credit is recommended to a specific amount for the transaction, or credit is recommended for the transaction provided that certain conditions are met, or both. In other words, credit is qualified by some factor noted on the right-hand side of the slip.

(d) A yellow slip (Figure 6.13) means that credit is not recommended for the transaction for specific reasons given. A current Dun & Bradstreet report is included to aid the subscriber in determining the degree of risk involved. If you choose, you may receive a D&B report for *every* inquiry you make, plus continuous service—all updating information compiled within a year from the date of your first inquiry.

Credit Clearing House suggests that you use this apparel recommendation service on new accounts and reorders when:

(a) A new order exceeds the credit limit you would normally set.

(b) You receive orders from accounts that are past due.

(c) An order exceeds previous high credits assigned.

(d) Orders are received from problem accounts where the risk exposure is high.

Other Publications and Services of the Credit Clearing House.

(1) *Apparel Trades Book.* The *Apparel Trades Book* is designed to keep pace with a dynamic industry. Revised and published four times annually—February, May, August, and November—it lists over 110,000 retail and wholesale outlets with lines of merchandise handled. Each listing, moreover, includes a "three-dimensional" rating indicating financial strength, payments appraisal, and composite appraisal (Figure 6.14).

(2) *Microfiche file.* The microfiche file, an extension of the Business Information Center in New York, was developed for internal use by CCH to ensure that all subscribers to CCH services benefit equally from the information available. Data on each of the more than 110,000 retail and wholesale names in the business file are continuously updated and produced on film transparencies called "microfiche." These transparencies are sent to all branch offices serving CCH subscribers; the service representative, using a viewer, is thus able to answer local inquiries with the same information available in the New York area. This means that all offices provide the same recommendation on a given account at the same time.

(3) *Consultation service.* The staff of Credit Clearing House consultants is available to assist subscribers. These analysts, specialized in the apparel and allied lines, can help

		Estimated Financial Strength	Payments Appraisal				Composite Appraisal			
B	A	Over $1,000,000	1	2	3	4	A	B	C	D
		....(See Note¹)....	1	2	3	4	A	B	C	D
	C	Over 500,000	1	2	3	4	A	B	C	D
F	D	Over 300,000	1	2	3	4	A	B	C	D
	E	Over 200,000	1	2	3	4	A	B	C	D
		....(See Note¹)....	1	2	3	4	A	B	C	D
	G	Over 100,000	1	2	3	4	A	B	C	D
K	H	Over 50,000	1	2	3	4	A	B	C	D
	J	Over 30,000	1	2	3	4	A	B	C	D
		....(See Note¹)....	1	2	3	4	A	B	C	D
	L	Over 20,000	1	2	3	4	A	B	C	D
	M	Over 10,000	1	2	3	4	A	B	C	D
S	O	Over 5,000	1	2	3	4	A	B	C	D
	R	Over 3,000	1	2	3	4	A	B	C	D
		(See Note¹).	1	2	3	4	A	B	C	D
	T	Up to 3,000	1	2	3	4	A	B	C	D

X....Not Classified..........See Note ²

$ The dollar sign ($) preceding a rating indicates that an important part of the total worth consists of real estate or other assets not usually considered working capital.

Note¹ The letters B, F, K, and S in the Estimated Financial Strength column, indicate in a general way what is considered relative in size. To illustrate: the letter B indicates size comparable to concerns classified in the range A to C inclusive; the letter F, comparable to those from D to G inclusive; the letter K, comparable to those from H to M inclusive; and the letter S, comparable to those from O to T inclusive.

Note² The letter X is not to be construed as unfavorable but, in the column or columns in which used, signifies circumstances difficult to definitely classify within condensed rating symbols and should suggest to the subscriber the advisability of reading the detailed report.

FIGURE 6.14
Apparel Trades Book Key To Ratings

CREDIT CLEARING HOUSE	A SPECIALIZED DIVISION OF	**Dun & Bradstreet, Inc.**		RECOM-MENDED	CONDTLY RECOM.	NOT RECOM.
OFF & SUB. NO.	DATE	AMT. ORDER	HIGHEST CREDIT	AMT. NOT DUE	AMT. PAST DUE	PAYMENT			

IN ANSWER TO YOUR INQUIRY ON: D-U-N-S NO.

PLEASE NOTE WHETHER NAME, BUSINESS AND STREET ADDRESS CORRESPOND WITH YOUR INQUIRY

All information furnished should be considered in the light of your credit and business policies. If you wish to discuss this account, you are invited to call your consultant.

SUMMARY

```
THE RECORDS INDICATE YOU HAVE PREVIOUSLY INQUIRED ON THIS NAME.
        A NEW RECOMMENDATION IS AVAILABLE
IF STILL INTERESTED IT IS SUGGESTED THAT YOU MAKE INQUIRY IN THE
USUAL MANNER OR RETURN THIS NOTICE WITH THE INFORMATION REQUESTED.
WE WILL SEND YOU A NEW RECOMMENDATION.
```

This information is furnished by DUN & BRADSTREET, Inc. in STRICT CONFIDENCE at your request under your subscription agreement for your exclusive use as a basis for credit decisions and for no other purpose. DUN & BRADSTREET, Inc. does not guarantee the correctness of this information and shall not be liable for any loss or injury caused by the neglect or other act or failure to act on the part of said company and/or its agents in procuring, collecting or communicating any information.   3M 2-1 (670811)

FIGURE 6.15
Credit Clearing House Change Notification Slip

you make credit decisions on recommended accounts, not-recommended accounts—or solve just about any credit problem. The service manager in any local Dun & Bradstreet office can arrange to put out-of-town subscribers in touch with the New York analyst when the amount inquired on exceeds the credit limit recommended or when you have a specific problem you wish to discuss.

(4) *Change Notification Service.* (See Figure 6.15). The Change Notification Service for the apparel industry is designed to keep you posted on changes that take place in accounts that, for one reason or another, you do not follow closely. Old-established accounts would be an example. Here's how it works:

(a) You supply D&B with a list of your customers' names and addresses. Include your customer identification numbers if you wish.

(b) D&B will screen your accounts against its exclusive Credit Clearing House Business Information Base.

(c) Your customer names that match or are substantially similar to the names in the Credit Clearing House Business Information Base are registered for Change Notification Service.

(d) You will receive a "List of Registrations" confirming those names on which D&B will supply you with Change Notification Service. This master list gives you the means of updating the historical data you maintain on each of your customers. It provides the current name and address of each business where it may differ from yours, the D-U-N-S Number, and—at your option—the apparel trades rating at the time the names are registered for service. Dun & Bradstreet ratings are also available. Each week thereafter, you will receive "change notices" that cover any significant credit changes reported on your registered accounts.

Weekly change notices include:

(a) Rating changes.
   (i) Upward.
   (ii) Downward.
   (iii) To "Investigating." (Example: A rating could move to "Investigating" owing to civil or natural disorders.)

Change notices include former and new ratings.

(b) *Special changes:*
   (i) Voluntary bankruptcies (not reorganizations).
   (ii) Discontinuances.
   (iii) Liquidations.
   (iv) Relocations from one state to another.
   (v) A change in ownership and/or control of business (whether the business name changes or not).
   (vi) Acquisition through merger.

When a special change is issued, Change Notification Service on that name is ended. The price of the service is based on the number of accounts registered. This service offers you two options:

(i) *Option A.* You receive a change notice—plus the current D&B Business Information Report on that account, which provides the details behind the change notice.

(ii) *Option B.* You receive a change notice. D&B reports can be ordered and charged to your Credit Clearing House subscription. When a D&B report is ordered under the Credit Clearing House service, the subscriber receives Continuous Service reports (as written) for one year following the date of the inquiry providing the Credit Clearing House subscription is continuous. Should the Credit Clearing House subscription lapse, the Change Notification Service agreement would be terminated.

(5) *Apparel Outlook.* Published quarterly by the Credit Clearing House, *Apparel Outlook* magazine covers developments and trends in the apparel and allied lines. Of special interest is the annual statistical issue containing information on sales, prices, failures, businessmen's expectations, and other pertinent topics of interest to all in the industry.

3. *Commercial collection.* The Commercial Collection Division of Dun & Bradstreet is an efficient, successful professional collection agency. See Chapter 12 for a full discussion.

4. *Facilities.* Dun & Bradstreet operates 140 offices in the United States, 17 offices in Canada, and 100 offices in 22 other

countries. These offices are linked by the largest private teletype system in existence to provide D&B subscribers with the most accurate, up-to-date information possible. Dun & Bradstreet has nearly 2,000 reporters and experienced business analysts, who collect and evaluate credit information on businesses throughout the world. Installation of the Advanced Office System, now under way, will allow information obtained by D&B reporters to be stored and reproduced by computer.

5. *Dun & Bradstreet's computerized credit and receivables management system.* Dun & Bradstreet has developed a new concept for computerized credit and receivables management. It is called "Exception Credit Update Service," or ECUS, and is designed to provide the credit executive with a means of assigning instant credit limits, establishing credit by exception routines, and maintaining updated computerized customer files.

   a. *Instant credit limits.* ECUS provides current D&B ratings in machine-readable format for your computer-stored customer files. With the current D&B ratings in your system, you are in a position to instantaneously convert them to credit limits by use of your own conversion tables, which are also part of the system.

   b. *Credit by exception.* With credit limits assigned to each account, so long as orders pass your programmed tests, and outstanding balances do not exceed the limits, they are checked automatically as received. When orders or balances do exceed the limits, the situation is referred to a credit executive for decision.

   c. *Updated customer files.* D&B supplies information of changes in your accounts every four weeks. These changes are reflected in new ratings and adjustments (up or down) to old ratings. As these changes in ratings are fed into your computers, they are instantly converted into new credit limits by your conversion tables. And as the credit limits on the changing accounts ebb and flow, orders continue to be approved or referred, depending upon whether or not the outstanding balances remain within the credit limits.

   d. *How Exception Credit Update Service works.* Your customer account numbers and the D-U-N-S Numbers are the links between your credit system and the D&B Business Information Center. You provide D&B with your customer account numbers and the corresponding D-U-N-S Numbers on magnetic tape or eighty-column punched tabulating cards. D&B matches the D-U-N-S Numbers of your accounts to the data about the accounts in its Business Information Center and provides you with the current Dun & Bradstreet rating for each one. Output is on magnetic tape or eighty-column punched tabulating cards in standard format sequenced by your customer account number.

   Every four weeks thereafter your ECUS-registered

accounts are screened against changes reported to D&B's Business Information Center, and each of your customers on whom a change of credit significance has been reported is identified.

Significant changes are defined as those affecting ratings, ownership and, of course, discontinuances. These changes are sent to you in machine-readable form sequenced by your customer account numbers.

At the time of the original match of your accounts with the D&B Business Information Center, those bearing D-U-N-S Numbers no longer in the Business Information Center are returned to you matched to your customer account numbers. Invalid D-U-N-S Numbers are also returned to you. These two groups of accounts are those not being monitored through ECUS.

As you add accounts to ECUS, they are processed on a four-week cycle.

[605.3.5]   SPECIALIZED CREDIT AGENCIES.

1. *NCO (National Credit Office).* The National Credit Office, or NCO as it is usually called, is one of the largest specialized credit-reporting agencies. Started back in 1900 as The Credit Office, NCO is now a Dun & Bradstreet company with branches in ten U.S. cities.

   a. *Lines reported.* Instead of covering all fields of business, NCO concentrates on relatively few. This specialization has given NCO unique knowledge in the fields that it serves   knowledge that over the years has prompted increasing inquiry from clients for business information that goes far beyond ordinary credit needs. The lines covered by NCO are listed in Figure 6.16.

FIGURE 6.16. Lines of Business Covered by NCO Reporting

Menswear	Coats, Suits, and Intimate Apparel
Men's Tailored Clothing	Coats, Suits
Boy's Woolen Clothing	Woolen Sportswear
Uniforms	Snow Suits and Leggings
Tailored Trousers	
Hats and Caps (Men's)	Underwear, Negligees
Womenswear and Menswear—Woolens	Corsets and Brassieres
	Women's Neckwear
Work Clothing, Bathrobes	
Slacks	Children's Headwear
Dress Shirts, Sportswear,	Laces and Embroideries—Jobbers
Men's Underwear, Pajamas	Men's Neckwear
	Miscellaneous Synthetic Products
Wash Suits, Rompers (Boys)	
Men's Outerwear and Rainwear	
	Converting and Household
Dresses	Cottons—Converters
	Synthetics—Converters
Cotton Dresses and Sportswear	Tents and Awnings
Infants and Children's wear	Bonding and Laminating
Dolls—Stuffed Toys	Canvas—Gloves
Nurses' Uniforms	Bags and Greige Goods, Covers
Synthetic Fabrics—Dresses	Handkerchiefs
Synthetic Fabrics—Blouses—	Bias Binding Manufacturers, Shoulder Pads
Sportswear	

Converting and Household (cont.)

Other Greige Goods Products
Curtains and Draperies
Mattresses
Art and Table Linens
Sheets, Cases, Quilts
Slipcovers
Other Household Products
Upholstered Furniture

Mill

Dealers and Processors
  Wool and Worsted
Dealers-Processors
  Thread and Twine
Jobbers Woolen-Worsted Yarns
Jobbers and Converters, Cotton and Rayon
  Yarns

Woolen and Worsted Mills
Woolen and Worsted Weavers
(buy Yarn)
Woolen and Worsted
Spinners
Woolen Worsted—Synthetic Knit Fabrics
Carpet and Rug Mills
Belts, Hats, and Hat Bodies

Broad Synthetic Fabrics
Drapery, Upholstery and Pile Fabrics
Knitted Fabrics—Cotton
Narrow Fabrics
Elastic Fabrics
Cotton Yarn Spinners
Cotton Mills

Women's Hosiery
Half Hose
Wool Hose

Knitted Cotton—Synthetics
Underwear
Knitted Outerwear—Sportswear Manufacturing

Laces, Veilings, Nettings
Braids and Trimmings
Other Mill Products

Wholesale and Retail

Wholesalers, General Merchandise
Wholesalers, Hobbies
Wholesalers, Toys
Linen Service—Laundry
Supplies, Cotton, Rayons, Acetates
Drapery—Upholstery Pile Fabrics
Textile Exporters
Retail and Department Stores
Retail Piece Goods
Floor Coverings—Wholesale-Retail
Mass Merchandisers
Catalogue Showroom Retailers

Metals

Autos, Trucks, Buses
Commercial Trailer Bodies
Aero and Auto Parts
Batteries
Motorcycles and Juvenile Vehicles
Airplanes and Missiles

Metals (cont.)

Airlines
Aero Distributors Services
Aero Instruments Manufacturers

Heating Equipment
Washing Machines
Office Machines, Traffic
Appliances

Farm Equipment
Lawn Mowers and Garden Tractors
Construction Machinery
Materials Handling Equipment

Electronics

Electronic Parts Distributors
Radio-TV Parts Distributors
Hi-Fi
Electric Motors and Generators
Laboratory Equipment
Welding Equipment
Connectors plus Sockets, Switches, Relays,
  Circuit Breakers, Assemblies, Harnesses
Electronic Wiring Devices
Antennas and Antenna Systems
Controls—Electric, Mechanical, Electronic
Radio and TV Receivers
Communication Equipment
Capacitors, Filters, Rectifiers, Condensers
Phonographs, Amplifiers, Speakers
Test Equipment Instruments
Electrical and Electronic Components
Transformers, Coils, Transistors, Diodes
Semiconductors
Tubes, Tube Rebuilding, Tube Parts
Research and Development (Electronic)
Computers: Digital, Analog and Hybrid
Memory Units and Devices: Drums, Cores,
  Heads, Tapes, etc.
Display Devices
Other Peripheral Equipment
Input-Output Devices

Leather

Slippers, Manufacturers
Footwear, General Line, Manufacturers
Footwear, Men's, Boys, Manufacturers
Footwear, Women's, Girls, Manufacturers
Footwear, Children's, Manufacturers
Footwear, Novelty, Manufacturers
Sporting Goods, Manufacturers
Leather Goods, Miscellaneous, Manufacturers
Shoe Trimmings, Manufacturers
Gloves, Leather, Manufacturers
Pelts, Manufacturers
Personal Leather Goods, Manufacturers
Luggage, Manufacturers
Garments, Leather, Manufacturers
Handbags, Manufacturers

Chemical

Rubber Products, Manufacturers
Resins
Dyers-Finishers (Commission)
Printing Inks
Paints, Varnish, Lacquer

FIGURE 6.17. NCO Report

b. *Services provided.* NCO provides an extensive array of credit services for those lines it covers. These include the following:

(1) *NCO Reports.* NCO Reports (see Figure 6.17) are similar to D&B Business Information Reports with two major exceptions:

(a) NCO will provide a suggested dollar credit limit for those companies on which it reports.

(b) NCO gives a list of the subject concern's major suppliers and banks.

NCO reports are divided into three sections:

(a) Specialized credit reports giving financial and trade information and the credit suggestion.

(b) Management and products report giving information

nco. specialized credit report
MANAGEMENT & PRODUCTS

```
FEMINA FOOTWEAR CO., INC.           MFR. SLIPPERS & PLAYSHOES
123 West Kerry Ave.                 Dept. 964
Buffalo, N. Y. 14020                Analyst: Jeffrey Jones
Phone: 716-477-3602

JUNE 5, 197-

    John W. Sussler, Chairman of Bd.    Edwin W. Delray, Pres.-Treas.
    Peter G. Field, Vice-Pres.          Rosanne S. Dooley, Vice-Pres.
    F. J. Richman, Secy.

DIRECTORS: John W. Sussler, Edwin W. Delray, George H. Lee, and
    Ronald Lockhart.

HISTORY - Established as partnership 1935 as Adorable Shoe Co.  Succeeded
    1936 by Femina Footwear Co., N.Y. Corp.  1938 change in control
    occurred and certain of former interests retired.  Charter surrendered
    and business re-incorporated under N.Y. laws under present style.
    Plant formerly operated at Manchester, Vt., was discontinued 1949.
    Moved to caption address 1955.

PERSONNEL - Sussler, born 1910, principal financially, maintains general
    supervision over entire operation.  Long associated with this
    line and officer with subject since 1938.  Previously Vice-President
    and General Manager of Adorable Shoe Co.  Originally employed by
    others as an auditor.  $50,000 insurance carried on his life with
    company as beneficiary.  Elected Chairman of the Board 1962.

    Delray, born 1921, associated with subject since 1938, in charge of
    production.  Elected Director 1950.  Shortly thereafter elected
    Secretary and assumed the additional office of Vice-President 1959.
    Elected President and Treasurer 1962.

    Richman, born 1930.  Employed by subject since 1950.  Elected
    Assistant Secretary 1955 and Secretary 1962.  In charge of purchasing.

    Field, born 1928.  Associated since 1954.  Sales Vice-Pres. since 1963.

    Dooley, born 1929.  Employed as stylist and designer since 1956.
    Elected Vice-President 1959.

    Lee, is a local attorney.  Lockhart, is also President of Lockhart
    Gear Works, Buffalo, N.Y. and has been associated with that company
    throughout his business career.

METHOD OF OPERATION - LINE - Manufacture women's and children's turn
    process padded sole and cement process hard sole house slippers and
    playshoes.  Retail price range from $3.95 to $10.95 a pair.  Approx-
    imately 50% of production is for in-stock and 50% against orders.
    DISTRIBUTION - Direct, nationally, about 75% to department stores and
    25% to individual retailers.  Terms of sale 3/10EOM.  Use trade styles,
    "Femina", "Kittens", and "Play-Cats".
    EQUIPMENT = Lease quarters on first floor of three-story building.
    Rents 30,000 sq. ft.  Output 2,000 pairs daily.  Employs about 125.

BANKS - First Marine Bank, Buffalo, N.Y.
        Manufacturers Bank of Buffalo, Buffalo, N.Y.

    hl
```

FIGURE 6.17. NCO Report (cont.)

on the management and operation of the subject concern.

(c) A complete financial statement if it has been obtained.

When circumstances warrant, NCO will compile an extensive trade clearance on a particular company, which is made available to NCO subscribers as a special report.

(2) *Consulting service.* Consultation with its subscribers is an important feature of the NCO service. NCO has specialists in every field it covers who provide useful, precise credit answers to specific subscriber inquiries.

(3) *Group meetings.* NCO sponsors and moderates eighteen different group meetings.

(4) *Special lines service.* The special lines service evolved as an extension of NCO's basic credit reporting. Where the risk

FINANCIAL STATEMENT SUBMITTED TO **NATIONAL CREDIT OFFICE**

Name FEMINA FOOTWEAR CO. INC. Business Mfr. Slippers & Playshoes
Street and No. 123 West Kerry Avenue City Buffalo State N.Y. Zip 14020

STATEMENT OF (DATE) DECEMBER 31 196–

ASSETS		
CASH IN BANK	$ 502.51	
ON HAND	$ 19,400.00	$ 19,902.51
U.S. GOVERNMENT SECURITIES		
RECEIVABLES for Mdse Sold to Customers (Age at Foot of Page)		
ACCOUNTS	141,363.89	
Less Res. for Discounts	2,680.00	
Less Res. for Doubtful	2,800.00	133,883.89
NOTES & TRADE ACCEPTANCES (Less $ discounted)		
DUE from FACTOR or FINANCE CO.		
PHYSICAL INVENTORY OF MDSE. (Valued at lower of Cost or Market)		
Raw Materials	$ 51,987.11	
In Process	$ 61,075.71	
Finished Mdse	$ 70,912.10	183,974.92
CURRENT ASSETS		337,761.32
Due from Partners, Officers, or Employees		
Due from Affiliated or Assoc. Companies		
LAND & BUILDINGS $		
Less Depreciation $		
MCHY., EQUIP., FURN. & FIXT. $ 79,231.58		
Less Depreciation 46,804.91		32,426.67
INVESTMENTS (Describe on opp. page)		
PREPAID & DEFERRED	6,000.00	
Life Ins. - C.S. Val	77,389.97	
Goodwill	1.00	
TOTAL ASSETS		$453,578.96

LIABILITIES	
ACCOUNTS PAYABLE	$ 19,989.81
DUE CONTRACTORS (without offset)	2,222.42
UNSECURED LOANS PAYABLE	
To Banks	
To Partners or Officers	
To Others	
SECURED LOANS PAYABLE	
Owing to	
ACCRUED WAGES & EXPENSES	16,190.91
TAXES—Accrued and Payable: a. Withholding & Payroll	13,368.18
b. Federal & State Income	10,897.02
c. All Other	2,213.00
RESERVE for Income Taxes since last closing	
MORTGAGE—DEFERRED DEBT— Due within 12 mos.	
CURRENT LIABILITIES	65,233.22
MORTGAGE—DEFERRED DEBT— Due after 12 mos.	
LOANS Subordinated until (date)	
TOTAL LIABILITIES	65,233.22
IF CORPORATION	
Capital Stock Pfd. $	
Com. $ 30,000.00	
Capital Surplus $ 308,345.74	
Undist. Earnings (Sub-Chapter S) $	
Deficit (red) $	
CORPORATE, PARTNERSHIP or INDIVIDUAL NET WORTH	388,345.74
TOTAL LIABILITIES & CAPITAL	453,578.96

ACCOUNTANT—Was above statement prepared by an outside accountant? Yes ☒ No ☐ Is he C.P.A.? ☒ Registered? ☐ Licensed? ☐
Accountant's Name Paul D. Hartman & Co.
Address Buffalo, N.Y.
On what date are your books closed? 12/31
How often are books audited? Annually

MERCHANDISE—If not valued at Lower of Cost or Market, state basis used
Is original inventory record retained by you ☒ or outside auditor ☐
Is any merchandise pledged as security for any debt? No
If so, state amount so pledged. $

INSURANCE—Fire: Mdse. $ Full Bldg & Fixt $ Full
Use & Occup. $; Burglary $; Life, Benefit
Business $ 50,000 on John Sussler

RECEIVABLES
For goods shipped during months of:
a. Dec.	$ 85,561.45
b. Nov.	$ 45,212.21
c. Oct.	$ 3,110.23
d. Prior Months	$

Do these include any consigned goods, uncredited returns, or unshipped merchandise? Yes ☐ No ☒
Have all bad accounts been charged off? Yes ☐ No ☐
During the past year have any pledged, or assigned any receivables? Yes ☐ No ☒ If so describe transaction

RECONCILIATION OF SURPLUS OR NET WORTH

PROFIT AND LOSS STATEMENT

FOR PERIOD FROM Jan. 1 196– TO Dec. 31 196–		
GROSS SALES		$ 1,471,188
Less RETURNS $ 25,347		
Less DISCOUNTS $ 22,734		
NET INCOME FROM SALES		$ 1,423,107
Inventory—begin'g $ 239,479		
Purchases—Net $ 603,105		
Labor $ 360,522		
Factory Overhead $ 119,370		
Total $ 1,322,476		
Inventory at end $ 183,975		
Cost of Goods Sold		$ 1,138,501
GROSS PROFIT ON SALES		284,606
Selling & Ship. Exp. $ 90,226		
Salaries—Officers or Principals $ 65,200		
Adm. & Gen. Exp. $ 51,140		
Bad Debts $ 1,705		
Depreciation $ 5,103	213,374	
INCOME or (LOSS) ON SALES	71,232	
Other Income (exclude discount earned) $		
Total $	71,232	
Deductions from Income		
NET PROFIT or (LOSS) before Income Taxes	71,232	
Provision for Fed. & State Income Taxes	33,179	
NET PROFIT or (LOSS)	38,053	

Beginning (date)		$ 369,293
ADD: Profit for Period	$ 38,053	
Other Credits to Surplus	$	
	$	
Total	$ 407,346	
DEDUCT: Loss $		
Div & Withdr'ls $ 19,000		
Other Charges $		
NET WORTH or SURPLUS at end		$ 388,346

INVESTMENTS—Describe (If subsidiary or affiliated state % owned)
a. $
b. $

LIABILITIES—Merchandise received or charged to you but not included in Assets or Liabilities $
Amount of Contingent Liabilities $
Are any liabilities secured in any way? If so, state amount, creditor, and nature of security.

Annual Rent $ Lease Expires
NET WORTH—Has this been decreased since statement date by withdrawal, retirement of capital, payment of dividends, bonuses, or personal income Taxes?
If so, by what amount? $
TAXES—Have all Federal, State, and Local tax assessments been paid or shown accrued on statement? YES
Tax Closing date? Dec. 31 Date of latest return examined by Internal Revenue Service?

OWNER—PARTNERS—OFFICERS AND DIRECTORS

Name	Title	% Ownership	In charge of
John Sussler, Ch. of the Bd.		60%	Genl. Superv.
Edwin Delray Pres.-Treas.		30%	Production
F. J. Richman Secy.		10%	Purchasing

TO **NATIONAL CREDIT OFFICE**, a division of Dun & Bradstreet, Inc. The undersigned warrants that the foregoing figures and answers are true and accurate in every respect and orders this statement mailed to you with the intention that it shall be relied upon in the extension of credit or insurance by such concerns, including factors or agents, who may subscribe to your service now or hereafter. My (Our) accountants are authorized to supply you with any supplementary information that may be required

Dated at Buffalo this 20th day of April 196–
Signed in the presence of: Femina Footwear Co., Inc.
Name C. J. Davis By Edwin Delray
Address 2 Sunset Ave. Edwin Delray, Pres.
(Signature of Officer, Partner & Owner) (Title)

INDEPENDENT ACCOUNTANT'S OPINION (Please use your own Letterhead if additional space is necessary)
We have examined the above balance sheet and profit and loss statement. Our examination was made in accordance with generally accepted auditing standards and included such tests and procedures as we considered necessary. In our opinion the statements present fairly the position of the company in conformity with generally accepted accounting principles applied on a basis consistent with that of the preceding year.

Signature Paul D. Hartman Address Buffalo, N.Y. Date 4/19/6–

FIGURE 6.17. NCO Report (cont.)

is extremely large or exposure abnormally heavy, this service will consider a special line of credit for the individual member requesting it. The special lines manager has had many years of analytical and consulting experience and is noted for his sound credit judgment.

(5) *Guides and directories.* NCO regularly issues the guides and directories listed below. Each directory lists the company name, address, and such data as rating, line, net worth, sales, SIC number, employees, purchasing agent, payment record, divisions, and branches.

(a) *The NCO Survey.*

(b) *The NCO Electronic Marketing Directory (EMD).*

(c) *The NCO Credit & Marketing Guide to Wholesale/Retail Markets.*

(d) *The NCO Credit & Marketing Guide to the Chemical Coatings Industry.*

(e) *The NCO Credit & Marketing Guide of Leather Goods Manufacturers.*

(f) *The NCO High Fidelity & Sound Specialists Credit Guide.*

(g) *The NCO High Fidelity & Sound Specialists (Geographic Listing).*

(h) *The ACS Mobile Home & Recreational Vehicle Dealers Credit Guide.*

(i) *The ACS Mobile Home & Recreational Vehicle Dealers* (Geographic Listing).

(j) *The ACS Mobile Home & Recreational Vehicle Manufacturers* (Geographic Listing).

(6) *Specialized Claims Service.* NCO's Specialized Claims Service is a complete collection service reserved for the use of its subscribers.

(7) *Automotive & Mobile Homes Service.* This is an integrated credit service on the wheel-goods industry. Automotive Credit Service, headquartered in Detroit, issues specialized reports on all manufacturers of automobiles, trucks, tractors, buses, truck trailers, and mobile homes. It is used by the industry's leading suppliers, including steel mills, parts and tire manufacturers.

(8) *Specialized credit education.* Here is where experience is supplemented through the NCO Course in Credit and Financial Analysis, on either a correspondence or a lecture basis.

(9) *Research studies.* NCO has a highly developed and trained research staff capable of preparing multiclient and individual research reports on all phases of business activity in the lines it covers. Topics have ranged from "The Pacific Coast Fabric Market" to "The Use and Marketing of Textiles in Environmental Control."

2. *Trinc Transportation Consultants.* Trinc Transportation Consultants is the Dun & Bradstreet division that specializes in providing data on the federally regulated sector of the transportation industry. From its Washington, D.C., offices, Trinc serves both national and international accounts with publications, analytical studies, and management and marketing aids.

a. *Trinc's directories.*

(1) *The Dun & Bradstreet Reference Book of Transportation.* A geographical listing of motor carriers of property with operating revenues of $50,000 or more annually, motor carriers of passengers, Class I railroads, pipelines, water carriers, freight forwarders, air carriers, and air freight forwarders. Each listing includes company name, address, name of principal, financial operating data, D-U-N-S Number, and the D&B Rating. In addition, listings of motor carriers of property include data on revenue equipment owned. It is issued twice a year.

(2) *Trinc's Blue Book of the Trucking Industry.* A compilation of selected balance sheet, operating revenue, and expense data, based on the annual reports filed with the Interstate Commerce Commission, on approximately 3,700 Class I and Class II motor carriers of property. The *Blue Book,*

published annually, includes a management control section, as well as regional and commodity group summaries.

(3) *Trinc's Red Book of the Trucking Industry.* A compilation of selected income, expense, and shipment statistics, based on quarterly reports filed with the I.C.C. by Class I and Class II motor carriers of property. Fourth quarter edition contains five-year comparative data of cumulative figures, and supplements for first, second, and third quarters contain two-year comparative data of quarterly figures. In addition, the *Red Book* contains summaries by region and commodity grouping, and information concerning sales, leases, and acquisitions of the carriers listed.

(4) *Trinc's Green Book of Air Freight and Freight Forwarders.* A biannual publication of selected balance sheet, operating revenue, income, and expense data compiled from the reports filed with the Civil Aeronautics Board by air freight forwarders and with the I.C.C. by freight forwarders. Each listing includes shipment and tonnage statistics.

The management section contains names of principal officers.

b. *Trinc's management and marketing aids.*

(1) *Special studies.* These use data stored on computer tape as taken from reports filed with the I.C.C. Requests range from comparative analysis of carrier operations to breakouts of incremental costing elements by carriers.

(2) *Trinc's Transportation Record Service.* An individualized inquiry service providing copies of publicly available reports and documents on file with federal regulatory agencies located in the nation's capitol and government publications. Service is available on a per-inquiry basis, with continuous service provided upon request.

(3) *Trinc's Fleet Data Card Service.* A marketing data service providing identification of truck fleet operation prospects in the federally regulated sector of the transportation industry. Data includes fleet operator's name, address, telephone number, principal, revenue equipment inventory, leased equipment data, and estimated annual fuel consumption on Class I and Class II motor carriers of property. Data is available on over 11,000 regulated operators on magnetic computer tape or visual records. Future plans call for similar data on private truck fleet operators.

(4) *Computer Data Service.* The computerized development of tapes, data cards, printouts, labels, cards, etc. of data contained in Trinc's Business Information Base for use in mailing aids, studies, lists, or analysis.

3. *Lyon Furniture Mercantile Agency.* What began in 1876 as a specialized agency providing credit information on furniture

manufacturers has now grown into an organization with seven branch offices coast to coast, reporting on these lines:

a. *Lines reported*

  (1) Contract furnishings.

  (2) Furniture trade, including:

    (a) Baby carriages.

    (b) Bedding.

    (c) Bedsprings.

    (d) Carpeting.

    (e) Floor coverings.

    (f) Juvenile furniture.

    (g) Upholstery.

  (3) Interior decoration, including:

    (a) Draperies.

    (b) Home furnishings.

    (c) Lamps.

    (d) Lamp shades.

    (e) Mirrors.

    (f) Picture frames.

  (4) Lumber, including:

    (a) Hardwood.

    (b) Plywood.

    (c) Veneers.

  (5) Major home appliances.

  (6) Mobile home trades.

  (7) Stores, including:

    (a) Department stores.

    (b) General stores.

b. *Lyon Red Book.* The *Lyon Red Book*, published semiannually in

CAPITAL RATINGS Estimated Financial Worth	PAY RATINGS Based on suppliers' reports
A ....$1,000,000 or over B .... 500,000 to $1,000,000 C .... 300,000 to 500,000 D .... 200,000 to 300,000 E .... 100,000 to 200,000 G .... 75,000 to 100,000 H .... 50,000 to 75,000 J .... 40,000 to 50,000 K .... 30,000 to 40,000 L .... 20,000 to 30,000 M .... 15,000 to 20,000 N .... 10,000 to 15,000 O .... 7,000 to 10,000 Q .... 5,000 to 7,000 R .... 3,000 to 5,000 S .... 2,000 to 3,000 T .... 1,000 to 2,000 U .... 500 to 1,000 V .... 100 to 500 Z-No financial basis for credit reported.	1—Discount. 2—Prompt. 3—Medium. 4—Variable, prompt to slow. 5—Slow. 6—Very Slow. 7—C. O. D. or C. B. D. 8—Pay rating not established, but information favorable. 9—Claims to buy always for cash.

FIGURE 6.18

Lyon Red Book Rating Key

January and July, is a rating book covering the firms reported on by the agency. The format resembles that of the *Dun & Bradstreet Reference Book.* The ratings, however, are different. (Refer to Figure 6.18 for the *Lyon Red Book* Rating Key.) There is a capital rating, a payments rating, and, in contrast to Dun & Bradstreet, a rating for special conditions.

The *Lyon Red Book* is kept up-to-date by a *Weekly Supplement and Report* informing subscribers of rating changes and other significant events such as fires, lawsuits, failures, and successions.

c. *Tracer sheets.* Each week, the Lyon Agency distributes to cooperating subscribers a "tracer sheet" soliciting information on a number of accounts of particular credit interest. Subscribers are asked to report the customer's payment habits, amount owing, and amount past due. The nationwide results are compiled in the "Result of Tracer," which is available to all participating subscribers. This is a unique service of the Lyon Agency and of great importance to the industries it serves.

d. *Credit reports.* The Lyon Agency issues credit reports that relate the following business information:

(1) Corporation name, address, and telephone number.

(2) Management and management antecedents.

(3) General information.

Form 20

LYON CREDIT REPORT

This report compiled from our records is sent to you confidentially, for your exclusive use, in accordance with the terms of your contract.
The Lyon Furniture Mercantile Agency shall not be liable for any loss or injury consequent upon its negligence or that of its agents, in obtaining, compiling or communicating this information; and said Agency does not guarantee correctness of same.

(SAMPLE REPORT - NAMES & ADDRESS FICTITIOUS)

DOE, JOHN CORPORATION   FC&APL   NEW YORK.......N. Y. 10016
629 West 34th Street
Tel. MU 6-7429

Morris Doe, Pres., Age 50, Md.
Frank Blank, Treas., Age 47, Md.
John Smith, Sec., Age 49, Sgle.

Directors: The officers

REV: (ml-31) July 1, 1973

ANTECEDENTS:

Incorporated under New York State Laws March 15, 1949, continuing the business of the former John Doe Furniture Co., which had conducted business at this same address as a partnership between Morris Doe and Frank Blank.

Morris Doe is a son of the late John Doe, who started in the furniture business Feb. 6, 1910 as John Doe Furniture Co., at 1600 Dodge St., New York, N. Y. John Doe died May 5, 1965 at which time a partnership was formed between his son, Morris Doe, and Frank Blank, a son-in-law, as John Doe Furniture Co., to continue the business which at that time moved to 629 W. 34th St. Morris Doe had been assisting his father in the conduct of this business, working part time, while attending school and after graduation, giving his full time to the business. Frank Blank had been employed by the late John Doe for about ten years.

The partnership between Frank Blank and Morris Doe continued until Dec. 1, 1948, when they executed an Assignment for the Benefit of Creditors. On Dec. 5, 1948, an Involuntary Petition in Bankruptcy was filed against them and at the Trustee's sale in bankruptcy, the assets were purchased by the present corporation, the unsecured creditors of the partnership receiving a first and final dividend of 50% on Nov. 28, 1949. The partners received their discharge from Bankruptcy Jan. 12, 1950.

Control of this corporation is divided equally between Morris Doe, Frank Blank and John Smith. John Smith joined with Morris Doe and Frank Blank in forming this corporation to acquire the assets at the sale in Bankruptcy, previous to which time he had been employed for about eight years as a furniture buyer by the New York Department Store, New York, N. Y.

On Dec. 16, 1954, a fire which occurred here as a result of the faulty operation of an oil burner, caused damage to stock of about $10,000 with insurance adjustment being received in that amount.

FIGURE 6.19

Lyon Report

Form 20   LYON CREDIT REPORT   1-64

This report compiled from our records is sent to you confidentially, for your exclusive use, in accordance with the terms of your contract.
The Lyon Furniture Mercantile Agency shall not be liable for any loss or injury consequent upon its negligence or that of its agents, in obtaining, compiling
or communicating this information, and said Agency does not guarantee correctness of same.

DOE, JOHN CORPORATION   - 2 -   NEW YORK.....N. Y.

July 1, 1973

GENERAL INFORMATION
        Principals of corporation experienced and attentive, although
the President and Treasurer have been identified in the past with an
unsuccessful venture.

        Company occupies a three-story building which it owns in a good
shopping center, each floor having about 10,000 sq. ft. of display
space, the basement being used for warehouse and storage purposes.

        Corporation carries a complete line of home furnishings and has
a good sized electrical appliance department, handling only major
appliances. Deals in medium to low-priced lines, with about 90% of
sales made on the installment payment plan. Company has enjoyed a
fairly good sales volume during the past few years. However, there
appears to have been some falling off in volume during the past several
months, with prospects at this time for a continuance of previous
satisfactory sales volume appearing not favorable, local conditions of
strikes resulting in unemployment of some weeks having curtailed sales
volume in general.

FINANCIAL INFORMATION
        Company has an authorized capital of $300,000. in preferred
stock, divided into 3,000 shares with a par value of $100. each. The
paid-in capital is $150,000, $50,000 each having been contributed by
the three principals.

                    COMPARATIVE SUMMARIZED STATEMENTS
DATE   ASSETS   LIABILITIES   RESERVES   NET WORTH   SALES
Dec. 31, 1968   261,724.   101,827.   2,428.   157,468.   -
Dec. 31, 1969   217,067.   122,670.   7,060.   187,187.   888,647.
Dec. 31, 1970   370,085.   138,864.   14,537.   216,683.   250,128.
Dec. 31, 1971   384,117.   147,824.   17,027.   219,266.   270,877.
June 30, 1972   371,780.   138,473.   18,236.   215,070.   125,608.

        The following statement, received by mail, showing condition
from books and physical inventory as of June 30, 1972:-
                            ASSETS
Current Assets:
    Cash on hand and in bank $ 5,096.28
    Accts. rec., install.   220,174.05
    Mdse. inventory   50,650.00
                        Total Current Assets $275,920.33
Fixed Assets:
    Real estate   75,000.00
    Furn., fixt. & signs   15,427.18
    Del. equip.   4,908.76
                        Total Fixed Assets   95,335.94

FIGURE 6.19

Lyon Report (cont.)

Form 20   LYON CREDIT REPORT   1-64

This report compiled from our records is sent to you confidentially, for your exclusive use, in accordance with the terms of your contract.
The Lyon Furniture Mercantile Agency shall not be liable for any loss or injury consequent upon its negligence or that of its agents, in obtaining, compiling
or communicating this information, and said Agency does not guarantee correctness of same.

DOE, JOHN CORPORATION   - 3 -   NEW YORK....N. Y.

July 1, 1973

FINANCIAL INFORMATION (cont'd)
Deferred Charges:
    Prepaid ins. & interest   524.51
                    TOTAL ASSETS 371,780.78
                    LIABILITIES & CAPITAL
Current Liabilities:
    Accts. pay.   89,452.02
    Notes pay. bank, secured by
        endorsement of Pres.&Treas.   15,000.00
    Taxes pay.-Federal & State   1,521.87
            Total Current Liabilities   105,973.89
Fixed Liabilities
    Real estate mtg.   32,500.00
Res. for deprec. of fixed assets   18,236.20
                                                156,710.09
Capital:
    100 shares preferred stock   150,000.00
Surplus   65,070.69
            TOTAL LIABILITIES & CAPITAL................. 371,780.78

Sales for six months ending June 30, 1972 - $125,608

    Ins. on mdse. $45,000; on bldg. $60,000

                (SIGNED) JOHN DOE CORPORATION
                     By: Frank Blank, Treas.

ANALYSIS
        Summarized statements show net worth has been steadily increas-
ing from 1968 to 1971 but for the six months ending June 30, 1972, there
has been some reduction in net worth.

        Comparison of current statement with that of Dec. 31, 1971
shows a reduction in cash of about $47,500, with accounts receivable
having increased about $25,000. and inventory has increased about
$10,000. Accounts payable have increased about $28,000. Bank indebtedness has increased about $5,000, while taxes have been reduced by
about $2,400. and an item of about $40,000, previously shown owing to
officers, no longer appears in the statement. Frank Blank stated upon
interview that this had been paid to officers, which also explained a
good part of the reduction in cash position.

Form 20   1-44

LYON CREDIT REPORT

This report compiled from our records is sent to you confidentially, for your exclusive use, in accordance with the terms of your contract.
The Lyon Furniture Mercantile Agency shall not be liable for any loss or injury consequent upon its negligence or that of its agents, in obtaining, compiling or communicating this information, and said Agency does not guarantee correctness of same.

DOE, JOHN CORPORATION   - 4 -   NEW YORK......N. Y.

July 1, 1973

ANALYSIS (cont'd)
      Current statement shows a liquid ratio of about .57 to 1. and a current ratio of 1.05 to 1. both of which are well below accepted standard. Sales compared with receivables indicate average collection period of about 313 days which is slower than accepted standard, indicating that some of the accounts are becoming old on the books. Inventory, compared with sales, indicates a fairly satisfactory turnover of about 2.4 times a year.

      While the current and liquid positions are below accepted standard, the net worth ratio, which is about 1.4 to 1., is satisfactory and there is indicated some margin of ratable worth placed at slightly better than $60,000. after allowing for adjustments and depreciations.

BANK INFORMATION
      Satisfactory account maintained for several years. Balances previously averaged in moderate five figures, but at present average in moderate four to high four figures. Accommodations extended in high four to low five figures, secured by endorsement of principals and cared for as agreed.

TRADE INVESTIGATION
NATIONAL INTERCHANGE OF TRADE EXPERIENCE

May 25, 1972 - Result - 18 Houses Reporting

PAYMENTS	OWING	PAST DUE
1-Discount	125.	----
2-Discount	----	----
3-Discount	77.	----
4-Medium	340.	----
5-Medium	260.	----
6-Medium	180.	180.
7-Medium	410.	----
8-Medium	----	----
9-Medium	100.	----
10-Slow	600.	320.
11-Slow	390.	175.
12-Slow	740.	650.
13-Slow	367.	367.
14-Slow	239.	140.
15-Very Slow	842.	842.
16-Very Slow	726.	560.
17-Very Slow	163.	163.
18-Very Slow	639.	160.
Totals	6,198.	3,557.

FIGURE 6.19

Lyon Report (cont.)

Form 20   1-44

LYON CREDIT REPORT

This report compiled from our records is sent to you confidentially, for your exclusive use, in accordance with the terms of your contract.
The Lyon Furniture Mercantile Agency shall not be liable for any loss or injury consequent upon its negligence or that of its agents, in obtaining, compiling or communicating this information, and said Agency does not guarantee correctness of same.

DOE, JOHN CORPORATION   - 5 -   NEW YORK......N. Y.

July 1, 1973

TRADE INVESTIGATION (cont'd)
Inquiry of June 4, 1973

Manner of Payment	Now Owing	Past Due	#Days Slow	High Credit	Period Last Sold
1-Medium	125.	-	-	400.	6/73
2-Medium	680.	110.	-	725.	6/73
3-Slow	319.	284.	30	667.	6/73
4-Slow	723.	416.	30	981.	6/73
5-Slow	1,276.	962.	30-60	1,519.	5/73
6-Slow	693.	487.	60	724.	5/73
7-Very Slow	981.	876.	90	1,263.	5/73
8-Very Slow	1,547.	1,029.	90	1,849.	4/73
9-Very Slow	820.	820.	180	1,057.	4/73
10-Very Slow	716.	616.	120	716.	4/73

COLLECTION RECORD

Mar. 7, 1973 - Claim (H-35782) for $420.50 placed with High Point Office for inv. 11/6/72. Collected by Agency 4/1/73.
Apr. 22, 1973 - Claim (C-48581) for $232.60 placed with Chicago Office for goods sold 1/73. Collected by Agency 4/26/73.
May 15, 1973 - Claim (H-36784) for $195.80 placed with High Point Office for inv. 2/6/73. Collected by Agency 6/7/73.
May 16, 1973 - Claim (H-36787) for $527.00 placed with High Point office for inv. 1/5/73. Collected by Agency 6/8/73.
May 23, 1973 - Claim (N-57602) for $947.18 placed with New York Office for goods sold Dec. through March 1973. Collected by Agency 6/26/73.

SUMMARY
      PRINCIPALS EXPERIENCED AND ATTENTIVE. HOWEVER, PRESIDENT AND TREASURER HAVE BEEN IDENTIFIED IN THE PAST WITH UNSUCCESSFUL VENTURE. CURRENT STATEMENT SHOWS SUB-STANDARD WORKING POSITION, ALTHOUGH SOME RATABLE NET WORTH IS INDICATED. TRADE PAYMENTS DURING THE PAST FEW MONTHS HAVE BECOME SLOW WITH SOME CLAIMS APPEARING FOR COLLECTION.

Rate 13-H-5-116

N: (s.i.)

(4) Financial information, including current financial statement and comparative summarized statements.

(5) Analysis, including ratio analysis.

(6) Bank information.

(7) Trade investigation.

(8) Summary.

(9) Lyon rating.

An example is shown in Figure 6.19.

e. *Collection services.* The Lyon Specialized Collection Service has a staff of trained collection specialists supported by assistants whose training and experience equip them for this area of credit management. In addition, the collection-service staff has all the credit resources of the Lyon Agency to draw upon. Collection services include:

(1) *Prestige Letter Authorization Coupons.* These are supplied to patrons in book form. When received by the agency, a forceful and effective letter, written on the Lyon letterhead, is sent to the debtor. There is no collection charge for payments reported within ten days.

(2) *First Demand Service.* Unless circumstances or conditions as disclosed by the agency's records suggest more forceful measures, a usual first demand is made for immediate payment.

(3) *Special Service.* Claims not paid to the agency or to the creditor as specified in the Prestige Letter or First Demand Service remain under the supervision of Lyon's credit specialists. Claims are aggressively handled according to the circumstances surrounding each one.

(4) *Forwarding Service.* Upon authorization of its clients, Lyon's will forward claims to attorneys for collection.

4. *Others.* There are many other specialized credit agencies covering one or more industries or geographic areas. The quality and quantity of information provided varies considerably —ranging from written reports, an "abstract" (Lumberman's Credit Association), to reports given by telephone only. Some of the more important agencies are the following:

a. *National Jewelers Board of Trade,* which serves the jewelry industry.

b. *Manufacturers Clearing House,* which specializes in plumbing, heating, and air-conditioning lines.

c. *Pack Produce Mercantile Agency,* covering the fruit and vegetable markets.

[605.3.6] PUBLIC RECORDS. The federal and state governments all collect information on companies that can be useful in making credit decisions. The information available from public records is discussed in detail in Chapter 5, Section 510.

[605.3.7] NEWSPAPERS AND TRADE PUBLICATIONS. Newspapers are a useful means of learning about changes in business ownership, management, and operation. In addition, newspapers provide valuable information about industry and general economic conditions. Trade publications furnish vital in-depth information about specific fields. Here are some examples:

1. *Wall Street Journal.*
2. *The New York Times.*
3. *Daily News Record.*
4. *The Journal of Commerce.*
5. *Bullinger's Postal & Shippers Guide.*
6. *New York Stock Exchange Directory.*
7. *Women's Wear Daily.*
8. *Home Furnishings Daily.*
9. *Supermarket News.*
10. *Footwear News.*
11. *Fur Age Weekly.*
12. *New York Law Journal.*
13. *Lloyd's Register of Shipping.*
14. *Marine Engineering Log.*
15. *Dun's Review.*
16. *Business Week.*
17. *Barron's.*
18. *Fortune.*
19. *Nation's Business.*
20. *Harvard Business Review.*

[605.3.8]   OTHER SOURCES OF INFORMATION. Sources of information about your customers are limited only as much as your own imagination. See Figures 6.20 and 6.21 (a list of potential sources by line of business) for a few ideas. Some of the more important ones are discussed below.

1. *Investment services.* Moody's Investors Service, Inc. (a member of the Dun & Bradstreet Companies, Inc., group) and Standard &

Abstract companies	Merchandise suppliers
Better Business Bureaus	Merchant's associations
Bonding companies	Newspapers, reporters, columnists, and their
Bulk oil dealers	files
Chambers of Commerce	Newspapers doing job printing
City agencies and bureaus	Newspaper morgues
City directories	Pastors
Clerks of local, state and federal courts	Police records
Competitors	Postal inspectors
Corporation records	Probate courts
Courthouse records and employees	Production credit associations
Family doctors	Railroad agents in small towns
Farmer cooperatives	Real-estate agents
Finance companies	Real-estate directories
Fire-insurance agents	Retail merchants and retail merchants associations
Fire-insurance patrol	Salesmen
Fixture and supply house stores	Sheriff's offices
Insurance adjustors, agents, and fire	State agencies and bureaus
company adjustment bureaus	State and local fire marshals
Investment houses	Statehouse
Justices of the peace	Street and telephone directories (yellow pages)
Key men in the community	Town or county assessors
Landlords	Truckers and haulers in small towns
Light, power, and telephone companies	Trustees and trust officers

FIGURE 6.20. Checklist—Sources of Information

1. **Air carriers.** Ownership and operational information is obtained as filed by air carriers applying for registration under Civil Aeronautics Board regulations. Except for the "scheduled air carriers," however, no financial statements are available.

2. **Banks.** Banks are required to publish statements of financial condition at least once annually in newspapers. Statements are also readily available in printed form at the bank. State banking departments exercise authority over state-chartered banks.

3. **Brokers—securities.** Except for a limited number of brokers and dealers, every security broker or dealer in the United States has filed a registration statement and one or more balance sheets with the Securities and Exchange Commission. The registration statement gives details concerning the date of formation, ownership, type of business conducted, and ten years of antecedents for each partner, officer, and director.

4. **Builders.** A realty development is usually financed through a bank or other lending institution that provides construction funds. The real-estate records give basic information, and a further check with the lender should develop details to round out the story. Bonding companies are helpful. Sub- or prime contractors are good sources. (See Construction, heavy.)

5. **Building and loan associations.** These are state-regulated (except federal savings and loan associations) and are required to publish statements of condition. Such statements are readily available from the secretary or any official or director of the association.

6. **Bus transportation.** See Trucking.

7. **Coal mining.** Coal producers are subject to some degree of regulation by both state and federal governments. The governmental interest is concerned largely with the maintenance of safe working conditions in the mines. Coal producers are not required to file financial statements but there are two important sources of general information: (1) *The Keystone Coal Buyers Manual* lists the names of coal-mining companies, addresses, officers, mines operated, details concerning mining and hauling equipment, employees, daily capacity of mines, and annual tonnage produced. (2) Production statistics published in booklet form by the bureaus or departments of mines of the various states.

8. **Construction, heavy.** In some states, construction contractors (roads, bridges, and public buildings) are required to file financial statements with the public service or utility commission of the state.

9. **Cooperatives, farm.** Such organizations are usually chartered by states as "nonprofit" companies. Farm cooperatives fall into two main groups—marketing and purchasing. Most states have enacted laws requiring cooperatives to file financial statements with the state department or secretary of agriculture. In actual practice, however, it has been found that a number of states do not enforce the laws relative to the filing of financial statements.

10. **Cooperatives, rural electrical.** These cooperatives are formed under state laws as nonprofit organizations. They are financed principally by funds advanced by the Rural Electrification Administration, to which the cooperatives submit monthly financial reports. Statements for REA telephone and electrical cooperatives are published annually in booklet form. In some instances, it will be possible to obtain detailed figures direct from the management of the cooperatives. The Rural Electrification Administration has urged the management of cooperatives to make figures available to credit agencies.

11. **Finance and small loan companies.** Most of these are regulated by state governments. In some states, finance and small loan companies (and even pawnbrokers) are required to file financial statements with the department of banking of the state (or an agency similarly named).

12. **Fraternal organizations.** If a fraternal organization, such as the Elks, maintains an insurance, health, or accident fund, or performs any other insuring function for the benefit of its members, the organization falls under the jurisdiction of the state banking or insurance department. It is therefore required to file financial statements with the insurance or banking agency of the state.

13. **Freight forwarders.** Freight forwarders engaged in interstate commerce are required to file annual reports with the Interstate Commerce Commission.

14. **Hospitals.** Most hospitals solicit funds from the public so that financial statements are usually available in printed form. Reference to *Hospitals*, published by the American Hospital Association, will prove helpful. The directory contains information of a financial nature, mostly on expenses, description of patient facilities, and the number of personnel. In a city or community where a hospital receives financial aid from a united charity fund—such as the Community Chest—it may be found in some cases that detailed financial information would be made available at fund headquarters.

FIGURE 6.21. Potential Sources of Information by Line of Business

15. **Insurance companies.** Life, health, casualty, and other kinds of insurance companies fall under the jurisdiction of state governments. While the name of the department exercising control in the various states may vary, it is usually the function of the department of banking or insurance to regulate the activity of insurance companies. Usually, the states require insurance concerns to file financial statements and the figures are readily available, usually in printed form. An important source is *Best's Insurance Reports*. *Best's Insurance Reports* on (1) fire and casualty and (2) life insurance companies contain comprehensive information on the financial position, operating details, and history of many companies together with their comparative position in the insurance field.

16. **Investment advisers.** The activities of investment advisers are regulated by the Securities and Exchange Commission. While advisers are not required to file financial statements, they are required to register with the commission. The registration includes information pertaining to (1) form of organization, (2) names and antecedents of the officers and directors, and (3) a description of the type or types of services rendered.

17. **Liquor, package stores and dispensers.** In some states, the sale of liquors and alcoholic beverages is handled by the state itself through the operation of its own package stores. In other states, however, liquor is sold by privately owned stores licensed by the state. The liquor or alcoholic control boards require licensees to submit varying amounts of information and, in one state at least, licensees are required to submit considerable information concerning antecedents, capital, etc. In the case of bars and taverns, the owners are required to obtain a liquor license. Here again, the state control boards do not require the filing of statements. The information on file is not considered a public record. Nevertheless, a general requirement is that the licenses be posted on the premises in a prominent place so that, during a visit, it is possible to confirm (1) the name of the owner and (2) the license number.

18. **Manufacturers, general.** The *Thomas Register* of manufacturers, an annual publication in two volumes, contains lists of manufacturers in the United States. Most states publish a directory that gives the name, number of employees, and other data for each factory.

19. **Pawnbrokers.** In some states, pawnbrokers and small loan concerns must file financial statements with a state authority. Usually, where a state exercises regulatory power over small lending concerns, the power is vested in the state banking department.

20. **Pipeline operators.** Pipeline operators engaged in interstate commerce are required to file annual operating and financial reports with the Interstate Commerce Commission.

21. **Public utilities, general.** There are overlapping regulations of states and the federal government with regard to the regulation of companies in the electric power, gas, transportation, and communications fields. Detailed financial and other information is available from (1) the Interstate Commerce Commission, (2) the Federal Power Commission, and (3) the Maritime Administration. If the desired information is not available from one of these federal agencies on the small companies in the utility fields, investigation should be completed with the public service or utility commission of the state in which the utility operates.

22. **Radio and TV stations.** These are regulated by the Federal Communications Commission. All broadcasting stations are required to file detailed reports pertaining to ownership and finances when applying for broadcast privileges and thereafter on a triennial basis when licenses are renewed. Financial information filed is available to the public only in connection with applications to (1) construct a station, (2) obtain a broadcasting license, (3) acquire a license or construction permit from another concern (4) acquire over 50 percent ownership of a licensed station, or (5) renewal of a license.

23. **Railroads, interstate.** All railroads engaged in interstate commerce are regulated by the Interstate Commerce Commission and are required to file annual financial reports. The reports are supplemented by quarterly reports on operating revenues.

24. **Railroads, intrastate.** See Trucking, intrastate.

25. **Schools and school districts.** In many sections of the country it is possible to obtain the financial reports and information concerning the officials of public-school districts or systems at the county courthouse. See also Moody's *Municipal & Government Manual*.

26. **Telephone companies, interstate.** A company maintaining telephone lines between states and having an annual operating revenue of $50,000 or more is required to file annual statements with the Federal Communications Commission.

27. **Telephone companies, intrastate.** These are usually subject to state regulation regardless of the size of annual operating revenues. Such companies are, in most instances, required to file annual financial reports with a state agency or commission. In most states, the information may be available through the state public utility or public service commission.

FIGURE 6.21. Potential Sources of Information by Line of Business (cont.)

28. **Trucking, Interstate.** Any common or contract motor carrier in interstate commerce obtaining annual gross operating revenues of $1 million or more is known as a Class I motor carrier. Such a company is required to file detailed annual statements of operations and condition with the Interstate Commerce Commission and must also file quarterly income statements. Motor carriers with gross annual revenues of $200,000 to $1 million are classified as Class II motor carriers, and those with gross annual revenues of $50,000 to $200,000 are classified as Class III motor carriers. Class II and Class III motor carriers are required to file annual statements of operations and conditions with the I.C.C. See *Trinc's Blue Book, Trinc's Red Book,* and *D&B's Reference Book of Transportation.*

29. **Trucking, Intrastate.** Common carriers are frequently regulated by an agency of the state in which they operate. Some states require carriers to file financial statements that are available at the state capital from the state public service or utility commission.

30. **Water Carriers.** Ship-operating companies engaged in interstate commerce, regardless of the size of operating revenues, are required to file financial reports with the Interstate Commerce Commission. A few water carriers receiving subsidies file financial statements with the United States Maritime Administration.

FIGURE 6.21. (cont.)

Poor's provide useful information for the credit manager on companies listed on the nation's stock exchanges, or those which offer bonds or other investment securities.

2. *Collection agencies.* Collection agencies are in a position to know what companies do not pay their bills. You should develop cordial relations with those servicing your industry as well as those servicing many different kinds of businesses across the entire country.

3. *Factors.* Because factors' responsibility is to collect trade receivables, they can provide much information on the paying habits of many businesses.

4. *Trade associations.* Trade associations provide much information by means of regular publications, occasional papers, and opportunities for personal contact within the industry. Trade associations are, moreover, continually making studies about the operations, management, and finances of their industries which can be an invaluable source of information with which to compare your customer with his competitors.

5. *Individual inquiry agencies.* Such agencies as Retail Credit Co., the Hooper-Holmes Bureau, O'Hanlon Reports, and local bureaus of the Associated Credit Bureaus of Houston, Texas, can provide information on individuals that could be useful to measure the value of personal guarantees or the capabilities of management.

6. *Leasco.* Leasco Information Products, Inc., is a private company which provides financial information on companies which file financial reports with the U.S. Securities and Exchange Commission. Reports distributed by Leasco include:
   a. Annual reports to stockholders.
   b. Proxy statements.
   c. Registration statements.
   d. Final prospectuses.
   e. Semi-annual reports.
   f. Annual reports.
   g. Special situations reports.

CHAPTER 7

SETTING CREDIT LIMITS

[700]   **SETTING CREDIT LIMITS.** Credit managers do not agree on whether they should use credit limits, how credit limits—if they are used—should be formulated, whether the customer should be informed of his credit limit, or even what the term "credit limit" really means. All of this indicates that setting credit limits is one of the most confusing areas that credit managers are likely to encounter. This chapter is designed to clarify the issues and give you helpful information about setting and using credit limits.

[701]   **WHAT ARE CREDIT LIMITS?** Confusion exists about the distinction between credit lines and credit limits. Some credit managers, referring to exactly the same figure, use "credit lines" with customers because that implies a positive customer-supplier relationship; and "credit limits" within the credit department because that discourages granting too much credit. Other managers reserve the term "credit line" for the amount of credit their companies are currently extending to a customer, and use "credit limit" for the maximum amount of credit their companies would extend to a customer if the customer requested it. Still other credit managers inform customers of their "credit lines"—the amount of merchandise they can buy on credit—and set a higher "credit limit" for departmental use, which, once surpassed, stops shipment of orders until payments are made. Finally, some credit managers will continue to ship orders after the credit limit has been passed, but will signal those accounts for careful collection follow-up. For the purposes of this discussion, however, no distinction between the terms will be made. Therefore, observe the following:

[701.1]   **Credit Limits.** Credit limits are the maximum amounts of credit a supplier will grant to a customer automatically without a review of his credit picture.

[701.2]   **Credit Lines.** Although credit managers do make the distinctions outlined above, in this discussion there is no difference between credit lines and credit limits.

[702]   **ADVANTAGES OF USING CREDIT LIMITS.** Those companies using credit limits point out these advantages:

[702.1]   **Speeds Order Processing.** The use of credit limits means that many—if not most—orders can be approved automatically. This reduces paperwork and the amount of time and attention that credit men must devote to each order. As a result, orders are shipped faster and customer relations are improved.

[702.2]   **Frees Credit Men for Harder Cases.** Because many orders are processed automatically without review, credit men need concern themselves only with difficult cases or accounts in the process of change.

[702.3]   **Frees Credit Managers for Policy Decisions.** Just as the use of credit limits frees credit men for work on harder or changing accounts, so, too, does the use of credit limits release managers from day-to-day credit decisions so that they can devote their attention to matters of policy and particularly difficult cases. As a result, credit managers become more useful to top management and their position within their companies rises.

[702.4]   **Cuts Cost.** Using credit limits can cut credit-department costs in these two ways:

[702.4.1]   OPERATING COSTS. Because of the time, effort, and paperwork saved when credit limits are used, the department can operate more efficiently with fewer people.

[702.4.2]   MARGINAL-RISK COSTS. Credit limits can restrict the number of marginal risks a company accepts. If company policy is conservative, this is a good way to save money.

[702.5]   **Improves Collection.** Credit limits prohibit shipments whose value would carry a customer over them. As a result, the customer is required to make a payment (or reduce his order) unless the credit department raises the limit. This can encourage a customer to pay his trade bills to you promptly.

[703]   **DISADVANTAGES OF USING CREDIT LIMITS.** The disadvantages of using credit limits are few when compared to the advantages. Nevertheless, you should be aware of the following possible pitfalls:

[703.1]   **Overextends Credit.** If the method used to set the credit limit is faulty, the result could be that you grant too much credit to a risky customer.

[703.2]   **Underextends Credit.** Likewise, a faulty credit-limit-fixing system can mean that you are turning away good business.

[703.3]   **Offends Customers.** When referring to credit limits, your credit-department personnel must exercise judgment and tact or they risk offending your customers. This becomes especially critical when an order must be held up until payments are made—or be rejected. Some companies prefer not to mention credit limits until a problem arises.

Others inform the customer of the line that has been set up and indicate that if the customer should feel subsequently that his requirements are greater, they will review it.

[703.4]   **Reduces Marginal Risks.** Credit managers now recognize that effective handling of marginal risks is the best way to increase credit profits. Any system that tends to reject marginal risks could therefore be detrimental to credit-department effectiveness.

[704]   INFORMING CUSTOMERS OF THEIR CREDIT LIMITS. There is much disagreement about informing customers of their credit limits. Before you decide, consider these advantages and disadvantages:

[704.1]   Advantages of Informing Customers of Their Credit Limits.

[704.1.1]   PROMOTES SALES. If the credit limit you set is higher than the customer has requested or is likely to have expected, this might induce him to buy more and more often from your company. It could also be an important selling point on his first order with your company.

[704.1.2]   PREVENTS MISUNDERSTANDINGS. If a customer knows what his credit limit is, it is unlikely that he will request orders whose value will exceed the limit without offering some explanation or supporting evidence for an increased limit. Thus, it is rare that a credit department must reject an order without a reason apparent to the customer.

[704.1.3]   PROVIDES OPPORTUNITIES FOR CUSTOMER COUNSELING. The time you choose to inform a customer of his credit limit is also a good time to build his goodwill toward your company. This can be done by showing him how he can improve his financial picture in order to merit a larger credit limit. It also provides an opportunity to congratulate him on his present credit worthiness.

[704.1.4]   SIGNALS CHANGES IN BUYING AND PAYING PRACTICES. Credit limits will immediately signal any change in a customer's buying habits as orders exceeding the credit limit begin to come in regularly. This provides the credit man with an opportunity to review the line of credit, offer financial or purchasing advice to the customer if it is warranted, and inform the sales and production departments of his estimates of future demand. If credit limits are exceeded—not because of increased orders but because of slower payments on previous orders—this will alert the credit department to the need for a renewed investigation.

[704.2]   Disadvantages of Informing Customers of Their Credit Limits.

[704.2.1]   OFFENDS CUSTOMER'S SENSE OF FINANCIAL RESPONSIBILITY. If a customer should be assigned a credit limit lower than he thinks he should get, he is very likely to be offended at your view of his financial responsibility and may take his business elsewhere.

[704.2.2]   DISCOURAGES PURCHASES. If a customer knows what his credit limit is, he may automatically take his orders for additional supplies to other companies instead of submitting information that would increase his limit at yours.

[704.2.3]   DISCOURAGES PROMPT PAYMENTS. If a customer knows what his credit limit is, he may buy up to that limit and delay payment until he wishes to place additional orders.

Timing or Occasion of Revision	Number of Mentions		
As conditions warrant	27	Quarterly to annually depending on risk classification	3
Annually	25		
On a continuing basis	18	Semiannually	3
In response to changes in paying or buying habits	14	Quarterly	3
		When existing limits are approached or exceeded	3
Monthly	11		
At customer's request	7	In response to changes in market planning	3
In response to agency rating changes	5		
In response to changes in financial condition	4	Total	126

TABLE 7.1. Circumstances and Timing of Credit Line Revisions in Participating Companies
Source: The Conference Board

[705]   **HOW TO USE CREDIT LIMITS.** There are two important factors that you must consider in order to use credit limits effectively.

[705.1]   **Credit Limits Are Guides.** Credit limits should be used as guides; that is, orders that exceed the credit limit should not be rejected automatically. Instead, the credit department should launch an investigation to determine whether the customer's condition warrants a higher limit or whether the sale can be made on some secured terms. When a customer exceeds his credit limit, this signals the credit department that contact with the customer should be made in the interests of working out a solution in everyone's best interests.

[705.2]   **Credit Limits Must Be Revised.** Credit limits, to be both useful and effective, must be revised regularly to take into account the changes that all businesses undergo. Most credit managers schedule this revision to coincide with the publication of financial statements or other regularly issued financial information. To this end, credit limits are set for a specified period of time, usually a year or six months. In addition, any special information received about a company—rating changes, changes in buying or paying habits, etc.—should signal the credit department that a new investigation of that customer and his credit limit might be necessary. See Table 7.1 for the results of a Conference Board study on this topic.

[706]   **FACTORS THAT INFLUENCE CREDIT LIMITS.**

[706.1]   **Financial Health of the Customer.** The financial health of your customer —his ability to pay his bills as evidenced by his financial statement, agency rating, etc.—can be the most important factor in your decision about his credit limit, though it is not always so.

[706.2]   **Customer Needs.** Next in importance to a customer's ability to pay his bills is the customer's credit needs. The credit limit should be commensurate with need.

[706.3]   **Company Credit Policy.** If your company has a conservative credit policy in regard to credit exposure, then lower credit limits would be the natural result. A liberal credit policy would suggest higher credit limits.

[706.4]   **Company Sales Policy.** If your company is trying to introduce your product into new stores or a new territory, it may mean that credit limits will be higher. If your company is trying to restrict distribution, credit limits could be lower.

[706.5]   **Competition.** What the competition is offering frequently has a great influence on the credit limits your company must allow. If, for example, a competitor is extending credit up to $20,000, your limits must be comparable or you risk losing the customer.

[706.6]   **Size of Your Company.** If yours is a large, well-financed company, you can afford more risk—and thus higher credit limits—for any one customer as you can assume greater credit exposure. If, on the other hand, your company is small and financially lean, then your credit limits might well be lower.

[706.7]   **Profit Margin.** If your profit margin is large, then you can afford a greater risk, hence higher credit limits. Contrariwise, if your profit margin is small, then your credit limits would tend to be lower as well.

[706.8]   **Length of Your Terms.** The longer your terms, the greater the credit risk. Therefore, your credit limit for any one customer would be proportionate to the length of time in which he is required to pay.

[706.9]   **Effectiveness of Your Collection Efforts.** If you know that your effectiveness in collecting past-due bills is high, you can risk larger credit limits than if you know your collection efforts are likely to be disappointing.

[706.10]   **Your Importance as a Supplier to the Customer.** If you are a principal supplier to a customer, then you may be obliged to set a higher credit limit than you would ordinarily assign if you were a minor supplier.

[707]   **CLASSIFICATION OF CREDIT LIMITS.** Credit limits can be devised to apply to any one of a number of methods used to record customer orders and payments. Note the following common classifications:

[707.1]   **Requirements Limit.** This implies that all orders in any amount will be shipped to a customer automatically. Obviously, such a limit must be reserved for a very few, top-flight customers only—such as the U.S. government or one of the corporate giants.

[707.2]   **Normal Requirements Limit.** Your very best customers who do not qualify for the "requirements limit" might well be assigned a "normal requirements limit." Normal requirements can be determined by your past experience with the customer or what is normal for similar customers in his field.

[707.3]   **Total Outstanding Balance.** Most credit limits are set on the total outstanding balance a customer is allowed to accumulate. Although this system does provide an effective means of control over a customer's purchases, you should be aware that it requires complete, up-to-date records at all shipping or credit outlets. If there are many, this can increase credit-department costs considerably.

[707.4]   **Size of Order.** You may choose to establish an order limit as a credit limit. This can easily be set up because in most instances the realistic short-run needs of a customer can be determined. An order limit of this type is particularly helpful if a customer is ordering from multiple points but it could create an exposure beyond the desired amount.

[707.5]   **Number of Orders.** Many credit managers have found that limits

Technique	Number of Mentions		
Agency ratings	82	Bank references	24
Financial statement analysis	27	Historical information	19
Over-all account analysis	26	Formula	13
Trade references	24		

TABLE 7.2. Sources of Credit Limits
Source: The Conference Board

should not be placed on small orders that are received in great quantity at many different credit or shipping points. These can be processed most efficiently without credit checks, but the credit manager should ensure that receivables are watched closely and be ready to take immediate collection action if necessary.

[708]   **METHODS OF SETTING CREDIT LIMITS.** Credit managers use several methods to set credit limits for their customers. To find out the popularity of the different methods according to a recent Conference Board study, refer to Table 7.2.

[708.1]   **Agency Ratings.** Most credit managers who use credit limits set them up on the basis of agency ratings. All customers with a Dun & Bradstreet rating of 5A1, for example, could receive a "requirements limit" while customers with a DD2 rating could receive a credit limit of $5,000 total outstanding balance. The advantages of using agency ratings as the basis for credit limits are many. First and foremost is the ease and speed with which limits can be assigned for all customers. Equally important is the fact that agency ratings reflect careful and thorough investigation of the customer. Dun & Bradstreet ratings, moreover, are divided into a capital rating and a composite credit rating. This means that a credit limit based on a D&B rating is at least partially a credit limit based on financial worth. See Figure 7.1 for a sample credit limit chart, based on ratings in D&B's *Apparel Trades Book*. A credit limit chart is also available based on ratings in the *Dun & Bradstreet Reference Book* (See Table 4.2).

[708.2]   **Financial-Statement Analysis.** Credit managers often assign credit limits on the basis of the results of financial-statement analysis. In simplified form, this could mean a credit limit of 5 percent, 10 percent or 15 percent—depending upon the line of business, economic conditions, etc.—of the customer's net worth (usually tangible net worth) as shown in his financial statement. (The percentage may slide according to the company's agency rating.) Some credit managers prefer to assign a credit limit equaling a given percentage of working capital as they think that working capital is a better reflection of a company's ability to pay its bills. In complex form, credit limits assigned on the basis of financial-statement analysis could mean that a thorough analysis of all elements of a financial statement is undertaken for each customer. See Chapter 9 for the methods of making such an investigation.

[708.3]   **Overall Account Analysis.** This is the most time-consuming—and there-

| | | | | | SLOW PAY | | INQUIRE |
	1A	1B	2A	2B	3A	3B	1C 2C 3C 4D
A	R E Q U I R E M E N T S				2,500	1,500	
B	5,000	3,000	1,500	1,500	INQUIRE		
C	10,000	7,500	5,000	5,000	2,500	1,500	
D	7,500	5,000	4,000	3,500	1,500	1,000	A
E	5,000	4,000	3,500	3,000	1,000	1,000	L
F	3,000	2,500	2,000	1,500	INQUIRE		L
G	4,000	3,000	2,500	2,000	1,000	750	N
H	3,000	2,500	2,000	1,500	750	500	O
J	1,500	1,000	1,000	1,000	350	INQUIRE	R
K	500	500	500	500	INQUIRE		E
L	1,000	800	800	800	INQUIRE		Q
M	800	500	500	500	INQUIRE		U
O	500	350	250	200	INQUIRE		I
R	150	100	100	100	INQUIRE		R
S	150	100	100	100	INQUIRE		E
T	I N Q U I R E O N A L L						

IMPORTANT NOTE:

The average lines indicated above are not intended to suggest limits, but are offered merely as a guide to help process orders. It is suggested inquiry be made on orders in excess of these amounts or when slowness or past due items exists.

Most credit executives consider it good business to inquire on all first orders.

The letters B, F, K, and S in the estimated Financial Strength column indicate in a general way what is considered relative in size. — Usually no figures — Not inclined to be automatically as liberal as figure cases.

$ . . . this sign preceding a rating indicates that an important part of the total net worth consists of real estate or other assets not usually considered working capital . . . therefore these guide lines do not hold true for ratings with this symbol.

FIGURE 7.1

Apparel Trades Book Suggested Credit Limit Chart for Processing Orders

fore the most costly—method of assigning a credit limit. It involves financial-statement analysis in its complex form, historical analysis, character analysis, plus coverage of all factors discussed in Chapter 5, "Credit Investigation." As a result, most credit managers reserve this method for their most difficult and complex accounts.

[708.4]   **Trade References.** Assigning a credit limit on the basis of trade references can be done in various ways.

[708.4.1]   HIGH CREDIT (HIGHEST). On the basis of ledger experience obtained from a D&B report or Interchange report, some credit managers assign a credit limit identical to the highest credit given by the customer's other suppliers.

[708.4.2]   HIGH CREDIT (LOWEST). If the company has a conservative credit policy, it might choose to assign a credit limit identical to the lowest high credit registered on the D&B or Interchange report.

[708.4.3]   AVERAGE CREDIT. More usual is the assignment of a credit limit that is the average of high credits shown on the D&B or Interchange report.

[708.5]   **Bank References.** Knowledge of the credit line established by your customer with his bank may be of some value in setting your credit limit. Since the bank is in a different posture from you—you are one of many trade creditors—the use of that information is limited. However, an unsecured line, for instance, can give you confidence in setting up a more generous limit.

[708.6]   **Historical Information.** Historical information refers to your own ledger experience with a customer. This information could be the basis of your decision in these ways:

[708.6.1]   ARBITRARY AMOUNT. You may choose to assign arbitrarily a certain amount as the credit limit for a short period of time. During this period you observe the customer's payment performance and adjust the credit limit up or down as necessary. Another alternative is to ship all orders up

		Estimated Financial Strength		Payments Appraisal				Composite Appraisal			
B	A	Over	$1,000,000	1	2	3	4	A	B	C	D
	.... (See Note[1])			1	2	3	4	A	B	C	D
	C	Over	500,000	1	2	3	4	A	B	C	D
F	D	Over	300,000	1	2	3	4	A	B	C	D
	E	Over	200,000	1	2	3	4	A	B	C	D
	.... (See Note[1])			1	2	3	4	A	B	C	D
	G	Over	100,000	1	2	3	4	A	B	C	D
K	H	Over	50,000	1	2	3	4	A	B	C	D
	J	Over	30,000	1	2	3	4	A	B	C	D
	.... (See Note[1])			1	2	3	4	A	B	C	D
	L	Over	20,000	1	2	3	4	A	B	C	D
	M	Over	10,000	1	2	3	4	A	B	C	D
S	O	Over	5,000	1	2	3	4	A	B	C	D
	R	Over	3,000	1	2	3	4	A	B	C	D
	.... (See Note[1])			1	2	3	4	A	B	C	D
	T	Up to	3,000	1	2	3	4	A	B	C	D

X .... Not Classified .... See Note [2]

FIGURE 7.2

Apparel Trades Book Key to Ratings

$ The dollar sign ($) preceding a rating indicates that an important part of the total worth consists of real estate or other assets not usually considered working capital.

Note[1] The letters B, F, K, and S in the Estimated Financial Strength column, indicate in a general way what is considered relative in size. To illustrate: the letter B indicates size comparable to concerns classified in the range A to C inclusive; the letter F, comparable to those from D to G inclusive; the letter K, comparable to those from H to M inclusive; and the letter S, comparable to those from O to T inclusive.

Note[2] The letter X is not to be construed as unfavorable but, in the column or columns in which used, signifies circumstances difficult to definitely classify within condensed rating symbols and should suggest to the subscriber the advisability of reading the detailed report.

to a predetermined amount without any investigation and with no plan to set a limit in the future.

[708.6.2]   NO LIMITS. Some credit managers will grant requirements as long as the customer pays promptly or discounts his bills. The first time slow payment is observed, an investigation is undertaken and a credit limit assigned.

[708.6.3]   AVERAGE PURCHASE. Probably the most common method of setting credit limits based on your own ledger experience with a customer is to calculate his average monthly purchases of the past, add (or deduct) his probable future increases (or reductions), and assign that figure as his monthly credit limit.

[708.7]   **Formulas.** There is a growing tendency to use formulas as the basis of assigning credit limits because they are easily adapted to computer use and can offer the best appraisal of a safe risk. The range of specific formulas is, of course, infinite but credit managers have identified these factors as being important to consider. In their order of importance, they are as follows:

[708.7.1]   IMPORTANT FORMULA CONSIDERATIONS.
1. Financial-statement ratios.
2. Dun & Bradstreet rating.
3. Bank reports.
4. Trade references.
5. Paying experience.
6. Personal visits—major accounts.
7. Customer's requirements.
8. Salesman's opinion.
9. Major supplier.
10. Profitability of product.
11. Competitive conditions.
12. Degree of need for customer's business.
13. Customer's reputation.
14. Character of management.
15. Years in business.
16. Growth potential of customer.
17. Source of disposing of off-specification material.
18. Seasonal factors.
19. Area and industry economic conditions.

[708.7.2]   EXAMPLES OF FORMULAS. By way of illustration, examples of formulas are given below.
1. Net worth (or working capital) divided by the number of the customer's suppliers.
2. Formula for new accounts, adapted from William J. Shultz and Hedwig Reinhardt in *Credit and Collection Management.*
    a. Calculate cost of goods sold from the customer's latest income statement.
    b. Adjust cost of goods sold upward or downward in anticipation of customer's purchasing needs according to your judgment of his inventory situation and general business developments in his field.

c. Estimate the share of these cost of goods sold which are the type of products your company sells.

d. Estimate the share of the above amount you could supply.

e. Assign that amount as the customer's yearly credit limit with possible differentiation for in- and off-season orders and more or less prompt paying habits of the new customer.

3. *Complex formula adaptable to computer use.* The early 1960's saw the introduction of truly successful formulas used to establish credit limits. With the advent of computer systems in the credit department, these formulas were adapted to computer use and produced even better results for credit management. Here are the basic procedures for one system described by CRF.

a. *Customer submits financial statement.* Each customer of the company is asked to submit a financial statement. The credit analyst then assigns numerical codes to the various statement entries. (These codes are used to identify the nature of the entry rather than the dollar amount.) Totals appearing in the statement are not identified by codes.

b. *The case is entered into the computer.* Next, the credit analyst prepares the case for entry into the computer system by filling out a data entry form, including:

   (1) Line of business.
   (2) Legal name of the customer.
   (3) Address.
   (4) Account number.
   (5) Date of financial statement.
   (6) Number of coded balance sheet entries.
   (7) Percent of total purchases supplied by the vendor.
   (8) Payment record.
   (9) Years current management has been in business.
   (10) Number of days sales contained in the profit and loss statement (calculated as months in the profit and loss period, times 30 days).
   (11) Dollar amounts for the following categories:
       (a) Net sales.
       (b) Cost of sales.
       (c) Pre-tax profit.
       (d) Income tax.
   (12) Net selling terms plus thirty.
   (13) Veracity codes.

c. *Analysis is undertaken.* For each of the categories listed below, the computer will assign a percentage of the company's net worth to the credit limit according to the value of that category in the company under consideration. In the entire system, percentages range from +15 percent to a −5 percent.

   (1) *Basic allowance—10 percent of net worth.* This is the basic amount of credit extended to any customer: 10 percent of net worth as shown on the customer's financial statement or 10 percent of his estimated financial

strength as shown by his Dun & Bradstreet rating. When a customer statement is not available, there is usually enough information from other sources to estimate his net worth. When intangibles, such as goodwill, are substantial, these should be deducted from net worth before applying the formula.

(2) *Requirements.* This is the amount (figured as a percentage) of the customer's requirements that the company will be asked to furnish. Contribution to the credit limit ranges from 0 (for under 25 percent) to +10 percent of net worth (for over 50 percent of requirements furnished by the company).

(3) *Payments.* This refers to the customer's paying habits with the company, with other trade suppliers or both. Contribution to the credit limit ranges from −5 percent of net worth (for a consistently late payment record) to a +10 percent of net worth (for a discount record).

(4) *Years in business.* This figure is the number of years current management has run the business. (Dun & Bradstreet records show that the likelihood of failures decreases as the business gets older.) Contribution to the credit limit ranges from 0 (for under three years) to +5 percent of net worth (for over ten years).

(5) *Profit margin.* "Profit margin" is defined as "net income before income taxes, divided by net sales." For each one percent of pre-tax profit (loss) margin, the customer receives 2/10 percent of net worth added to (or, if there were losses, subtracted from) his credit limit.

(6) *Current ratio.* The current ratio is found by dividing the current assets by the current liabilities. This indicates the available working capital in the business and the liquidity condition. The rule-of-thumb is that a business should have a two-to-one current ratio in order to pay suppliers' bills within terms. The ratio also shows the value current assets have to liquidate current debts and represents the margin of protection that current creditors have. Contribution to the credit limit ranges from −5 percent (for a current ratio of less than .75) to a +10 percent of net worth (for a current ratio of 2.00 or above).

(7) *Quick ratio.* The quick ratio is obtained by dividing cash plus receivables by current liabilities. This is the familiar acid-test ratio and is a qualitative measure of working capital and the extent to which current debt can be paid before relying on inventory. Contribution to the credit limit ranges from −5 percent of net worth (for a quick ratio of less than .50) to +15 percent of net worth (for a quick ratio of 2.00 and over).

(8) *Ratio of current liabilities to inventory.* This ratio indicates

the reliance on available inventory for payment of debt. Contribution to credit limit ranges from a −5 percent of net worth (for a ratio of 1.00 and over) to +10 percent of net worth (for a ratio of less than .65).

(9) *Ratio of inventory to net working capital.* Net working capital is defined as current assets less current liabilities. This ratio represents how much working capital is tied up in inventory. Contribution to the credit limit ranges from −5 percent of net worth (for a ratio of less than .25 or more than .99) to +5 percent of net worth (for a ratio of .50 to .99).

(10) *Ratio of net worth to debt.* This is a quantitative ratio showing the degree of control by management and the degree of dependency on borrowed capital and on other creditors. It measures the soundness of the total capital structure. Contribution to credit limit ranges from a −5 percent of net worth (for a ratio of less than 1.00) to +10 percent of net worth (for a ratio of 2.00 and above).

(11) *Quality of receivables.* The quality is determined by dividing the customer's net receivables by the average daily sales (D.S.O.). The result is then subtracted from the customer's net selling terms plus thirty. Contribution to the credit limit is plus or minus .10 percent of net worth for each day of deviation from the customer's selling terms plus thirty.

(12) *Inventory turnover.* This figure is determined by dividing inventory into the cost of sales. It measures manufacturing efficiency, inventory control, merchandising capacity, and quality of inventories. Contribution to the credit limit ranges from 0 (for a ratio of less than 5.00 or more than 30.00) to +10 percent of net worth (for a ratio of 10.00 to 30.00).

(13) *Judgment factors.* The computer supplies a subtotal but does not render a final figure, as the credit analyst may make a final modification based on factors not revealed by the standard entry form.

[709]   **DUNSCORE.** Dunscore, a commercial credit index, is a numerical score ranging from 0 to 100, which indicates the manner in which a particular company will most probably pay its trade bills. To be introduced nationally in 1975, it was developed and tested by Dun & Bradstreet— using advanced statistical techniques—to enable subscribers to predict payment patterns, to easily set up a credit-by-exception system, and to select accurately optimum cutoff points for their sales. You may purchase Dunscore information alone or you may use it together with D&B ratings to develop the Dunscore system described below.

[709.1]   **Dunscore Calculation.** The Dunscore is calculated by using a formula containing the most significant factors that determine credit worthiness

GROUP	DUNSCORE	PROBABLE PAYMENTS
I	75 - 100	Prompt or Better
II	65 - 74	Slow Up To 30 Days
III	55 - 64	Slow Up To 60 Days
IV	40 - 54	Slow Up To 90 Days
V	20 - 39	Slow Up To 180 Days
VI	0 - 19	Extreme Slowness Indicated

DUNSCORE CREDIT QUALITY CLASSIFICATION TABLE

TABLE 7.3. Dunscore Classification

DUNSCORE SYSTEM

DUNSCORE AND D&B RATING

ESTIMATED FINANCIAL STRENGTH $35,000-50,000	RATING DD	COMPOSITE CREDIT APPRAISAL			
		high 1	good 2	fair 3	limited 4
		CREDIT LIMIT			
DUNSCORE GROUP 75-100		$4,000	$2,500	$1,500	REF
65-74		1,500	1,000	500	REF
55-64		REF	500	300	REF
40-54		REF	REF	REF	REF
20-39		REF	REF	REF	REF
0-19		REF	REF	REF	REF

TABLE 7.4. Dunscore System

in terms of the likelihood of prompt payment. The particular values of these items for the company being evaluated are placed into the formula and its individual score is computed by D&B.

[709.2]   **Dunscore Classification.** Table 7.3 shows probable payments according to Dunscore group.

[709.3]   **Dunscore Limits.** A company's Dunscore plus its D&B rating provide a useful framework according to which you may assign credit limits. You may also consider additional variables—your own trade experience, your customer's requirements, etc.—when setting your limits. Table 7.4 gives an example of the credit limits that might be assigned to companies with an estimated financial strength rating of DD and varying composite credit appraisal ratings and Dunscore.

[709.4]   **Dunscore System.** The Dunscore system for establishing credit limits and processing orders that you choose will depend upon whether yours is an automated or manual credit operation.

[709.4.1]   DUNSCORE AUTOMATED SYSTEM. Here's how the automated system works:

1. As credit manager, you assign the credit limit to each rating by Dunscore and composite credit appraisal level. This information is computer-stored.
2. D&B sends initial Dunscores and ratings on your accounts with periodic update of changes.
3. The credit limit per Dunscore group and rating are compared with the D&B information.
4. With the output of the account's most recent Dunscore, rating,

and credit limit, a decision is made. The computer will automatically process those orders falling within the credit limits established for the company.

[709.4.2] DUNSCORE MANUAL SYSTEM. Here's how the manual system works:

1. As credit manager, you assign credit limits to each rating by Dunscore group and composite credit appraisal level. The information is filed.
2. D&B sends initial Dunscores and ratings on your accounts with periodic update of changes.
3. Manually filed credit limit per Dunscore group and rating is compared with D&B information.
4. Most recent Dunscore, rating, and credit limit are available for decision-making. You may automatically approve orders falling within the credit limit.

[709.4.3] DUNSCORE SYSTEM OUTPUT FORMATS. Depending upon whether your system is automated or manual, the Dunscore system provides you with the following output formats:

1. *Automated system.* D&B sends you magnetic tape or tabulating cards.
2. *Manual system.* D&B sends you tabular listings.

[709.4.4] DUNSCORE SYSTEM GOALS. The goals of the Dunscore system fall into three areas:

1. *Production.* The Dunscore system promotes efficient management of accounts receivable by using Dunscore, rating, and credit limit. It reduces paperwork and storage requirements as well as minimizing errors and inefficiencies. Finally, it provides for effective allocation of credit manpower resources.
2. *Communications.* The Dunscore system permits instantaneous forecasts of customers' payment patterns. It speeds up credit decisions.
3. *Economics.* The Dunscore system means cost savings from less clerical personnel and minimum storage and maintenance requirements. There is faster cash flow from accounts receivable.

[709.5] **Advanced Applications.** The Dunscore can also be used in more advanced situations, particularly in planning and in financial simulation. The examples below can give you an idea of how Dunscore can be applied to your own credit problems.

[709.5.1] DETERMINING THE OPTIMUM CUTOFF SCORE: THE CREDIT SCREEN. Table 7.5 illustrates the effect of a company's credit portfolio on profits. Poor receivables carry added costs that reduce and, in some instances, even eliminate profits. The situation shown in Table 7.5 assumes sale of a product with a unit selling price of $24 and a unit cost of $20. As you can see, losses on sales at lower scores are sustained until the level of 62, when a profit of $174 is realized. This represents the level of profit maximization as highlighted in the last column.

If sales are made to all credit applicants which score 62 or better, a profit of $1,979 will result. Selection of any score higher or lower will result in a lower profit figure. You would therefore designate 62 as the cutoff score, representing the lowest index score for which credit will be

Score	# Prompt at Each Level	# Slow at Each Level	Profit (Loss) Each Level*	Profit by Selection of Cutoff Score
0–10	0	1	$ (23)	$1,227
11–20	0	56	(464)	1,250
21–30	6	28	(141)	1,714
31–40	10	44	(92)	1,855
41–50	8	23	(16)	1,947
51–61	6	25	(16)	1,963
62	37	14	174	1,979
63–70	45	11	195	1,805
71–80	13	6	75	1,610
81–90	54	8	247	1,535
91–100	312	10	1,288	1,288

*Computation of profit or loss at each level results from subtracting from revenue total costs including bad-debt expense of a proportion of slow accounts that prove to be uncollectable plus interest cost of financing past-due receivables and pursuit costs for delinquent accounts.

TABLE 7.5

Determining Optimum Cutoff Score: The Credit Screen

granted in this particular example. A "credit screen" is formed, only permitting sales to customers who fall into this desired credit category.

[709.5.2]   IMPACT OF CHANGES IN PROFIT PER UNIT ON CUTOFF SCORE. This example (see Table 7.6) illustrates the use of the Dunscore to quickly permit change in the selection criteria of credit applicants when the profit per unit of a product changes. Here, while per-unit cost has remained constant at $20, an increase in demand for the company's product has caused the selling price to rise to $40, resulting in a substantial increase in profit per unit. What should your new credit policy be to maximize profits?

Given the same distribution of credit applicants as before, the Dunscore clearly indicates how profit can be increased in this situation by now selling to accounts that previously had been undesirable. As illustrated, the cutoff should now be lowered to 11 with the resulting profit of $11,390 representing the maximum. Conversely, a decline in per-unit profit would result in a tightening of credit selection with the cutoff score raised to a level higher than 62.

Score	Profit (Loss) Each Level	Profit By Selection of Cutoff Score
0–10	$ (23)	$ 11,367
11–20	124	11,390
21–30	243	11,266
31–40	596	11,023
41–50	400	10,427
51–61	400	10,027
62	974	9,627
63–70	1,075	8,653
71–80	259	7,578
81–90	1,079	7,319
91–100	6,240	6,240

TABLE 7.6

Impact of Changes in Profit per Unit on Cutoff Score

CHAPTER 8

SPECIFIC CREDIT SYSTEMS

[800]   **SPECIFIC CREDIT SYSTEMS.** In this chapter, you will find comprehensive descriptions of several specific credit systems. These range from a complex manual system capable of handling thousands of accounts to a very sophisticated computer system that represents the highest degree of credit-department efficiency. You will, of course, recognize that none of the systems described below will precisely fit your needs; nevertheless, they can be a guide to improvements in your currently existing system and they can suggest procedures you might choose to incorporate into your system in the process of computerization.

[801]   **MANUAL SYSTEM: A LARGE PHARMACEUTICAL COMPANY.** The following is a system used by the drug division of a large pharmaceutical (and allied lines) company. Although the accounts-receivable function is handled by computer, credit checking, clearing, and order approval are largely manual. The company operates on a prebilling system in which bills are generated before an order is shipped. There are multiple order, billing, and distribution points, but one central credit department serves the entire country.

[801.1]   **Personnel.** The credit department is staffed by the following people:

[801.1.1]   CREDIT MANAGER. A credit manager supervises the work of the department. He reports to the company treasurer.

[801.1.2]   ASSISTANT CREDIT MANAGER. There is an assistant credit manager who reports to the credit manager.

[801.1.3]   CREDIT SUPERVISORS. There are three credit supervisors responsible for all customers within the three regions into which the country has been divided. The credit supervisors report to the assistant credit manager.

[801.1.4]   CREDIT CORRESPONDENTS. Credit correspondents make initial credit investigations, recommend credit limits to the supervisor, review orders that exceed limits up to certain amounts. The credit correspondents report to a credit supervisor and are assigned work by region.

[801.1.5]   ORDER EDITORS. Order editors located at the various distribution centers and thus not under credit-department jurisdiction are given the responsibility of approving orders that do not exceed the credit limits or routing unapproved orders to the credit correspondents.

[801.2] **Handling the First Order.** The company receives orders by telephone or letter from retail pharmacies and drug wholesalers. When the new order is from a retail pharmacy, the salesmen is asked to complete a "pharmacy account application," which solicits the following information:

[801.2.1] SALESMAN'S PHARMACY ACCOUNT APPLICATION. The account application supplies:

1. Name and address of the pharmacy plus date started.
2. Type of business (proprietorship, partnership, or corporation).
3. Names of the officers or partners.
4. Three commercial references.
5. Bank reference.

[801.2.2] INITIAL SCREENING. When the order comes in, it is screened by the order editor to verify that it is coming from a new customer. If it is a new account, it is referred to a customer service representative who makes sure that the account meets the company's requirements for the sale of drugs, and then requests the salesman to take an application.

[801.2.3] D&B CHECK. The credit correspondent, to whom the new order is assigned, calls D&B for the latest credit information on the new customer. If the customer has a 1 or 2 composite credit appraisal rating and a satisfactory estimated financial strength rating, the order is approved up to $1,000 and a D&B report is ordered for the files. If the composite credit appraisal rating is 3 or 4 [fair or limited], if the rating is blank, if there is a discrepancy between the name on the order and the name reported by Dun & Bradstreet, or if the estimated financial strength rating is unsatisfactory, the order is held and the following steps are taken:

1. A D&B report is ordered.
2. Credit Interchange reports are ordered. (This company belongs to several associations that furnish trade clearances to members. These clearances represent the credit experiences of approximately 200 drug manufacturers or companies in allied lines.)
3. If necessary, up to three trade references are contacted.
4. If necessary, a bank check is made.
5. If necessary, an audited financial statement is requested.

Depending on the circumstances, these steps are taken in sequential order or simultaneously.

[801.2.4] CREDIT ANALYSIS. The information received is analyzed by the credit correspondent. His analysis could range from a detailed review of the company's financial situation to a more limited check of trade and bank references.

[801.2.5] ORDER APPROVAL. On the basis of his analysis, the credit correspondent will recommend to his supervisor approval or rejection of the order. This pharmaceutical company reports that applications must be disposed of within ten working days of their receipt or adequate compensating circumstances must exist and be identified. Applications are filed ten days ahead from the date of receipt to ensure that they are handled in time.

[801.2.6]   SETTING THE CREDIT LIMIT. This company uses order credit limits that are set by the credit correspondent according to the following criteria:

1. *Kind of business.* The company distinguishes between its retail pharmacy and wholesaling customers. Wholesalers are further classified as either large national wholesalers, or small regional ones. The company has found it economically feasible to establish a single upper limit for all retail pharmacy customers. Wholesaler limits range from requirements for large national firms to "referral."

2. *Customer needs.* The company considers the customer's needs in establishing its credit limit.

3. *Financial strength.* The credit correspondent's appraisal of the customer's ability to pay its bills is a key in setting the credit limit. Ten percent of net worth is a rule-of-thumb lower limit.

4. *Paying habits.* The company reviews the payment record of the customer when establishing the credit limit. Close watch is also kept on the customer's payments to this pharmaceutical company.

[801.2.7]   DISTRIBUTION COMMITTEE APPROVAL. Lines of credit extended to customers who handle narcotics and/or prescription drugs sold by the company must be approved by a distribution committee made up of representatives from the company's legal, credit, sales, data-processing, and distribution staffs.

[801.3]   **Handling Subsequent Orders.** Subsequent orders from customers are handled in the following way:

[801.3.1]   ORDER EDITOR SCREENING. The order editor checks the name and address on the order with that appearing on a Wheel-dex card for that firm to make sure that the order comes from a valid customer. The Wheel-dex card also lists the customer's credit limit in code.

[801.3.2]   PULLING THE HEADER CARD. Next, the order editor pulls the customer's "header card" on which appear his name, address, and customer profile. This includes the following information:

1. Accounts-receivable number.
2. Customer number.
3. Special instructions.
4. Terms.
5. Billing instructions.
6. Date when business came under present control.
7. Date of the last name change.
8. Credit limit.
9. Information required by drug-regulating agencies.

[801.3.3]   APPROVING THE ORDER. If the value of the order falls within the credit limit assigned to the customer, the order editor approves the order, pulls necessary product cards on which quantities corresponding to the customer's order are mark-sensed, and delivers the header and product cards to the data processing department where the bill will be produced by computer. The computer also calculates the discount and registers the terms on the statement. This pharmaceutical company reports that between 90 and 95 percent of its orders are approved by the order editors.

[801.3.4]   REJECTING THE ORDER If the order exceeds the credit limit assigned to the customer or if the customer is a special case of some sort, the order editor will refer it to the credit correspondent, who will review the individual case. The credit correspondent is authorized to approve an order that exceeds the credit limit by 50 percent as long as this does not go over a dollar limit set by the company. If it does, the order is referred to the credit supervisor, the credit manager, or the treasurer, depending upon the size of the order. If any order is held because it is over the limit or because there is an outstanding past-due balance, the distribution center is notified by Telex and the customer is informed by telephone or mail the same day of what is required to release the order.

[801.4]   **Updating Credit Information.** This company has no procedure for periodic updating of credit information. Instead, this is done on an exception basis when the following occurs:

[801.4.1]   CHANGE IN THE D&B RATING.

[801.4.2]   CHANGE IN BUYING HABITS.

[801.4.3]   CHANGE IN PAYING HABITS.

[801.4.4]   SPECIAL CIRCUMSTANCES such as a check returned for insufficient funds, natural disasters, etc.

[801.5]   **Collection Activities.** The drug division of this company experiences relatively few collection problems because of the nature of the product and because of strict adherence to terms that the company requires. Nevertheless, the company does use some statements and a series of form letters to collect its overdue accounts. All form letters are individually reviewed by the credit correspondent. The salesman is informed of the collection process as it progresses but he does not generally participate in collection efforts. If the collection-letter series has not produced results within seventy-five to eighty days from invoice date, the customer is contacted personally or by telephone.

[801.6]   **Credit Department Reports to Management.** The credit department furnishes these reports to the treasurer:

[801.6.1]   DAYS' SALES OUTSTANDING. The D.S.O. is calculated according to the formula recommended by the Credit Research Foundation and furnished on a monthly basis.

[801.6.2]   AGINGS. The credit department supplies monthly agings.

[801.6.3]   SPECIAL WRITE-UPS. The credit department describes the particular circumstances of all past-due accounts that represent more than a specific dollar value set by the company.

[801.6.4]   LITIGATION REPORTS. A quarterly litigation report describing the process of credit litigation is compiled.

[801.6.5]   YEAR-END REPORT. A year-end report is written in which the work of the department is summarized. Statistics are given for such activities as number of orders processed, number of customer contacts made, etc.

[801.6.6]   CASH FORECASTS. The credit manager draws a monthly cash forecast, which is directed to the treasurer.

[802]   **SEMI-AUTOMATED CREDIT OPERATION: A LARGE METALS COMPANY.** The following section describes a semi-automated credit operation currently

being used by one group (consisting of three divisions) of this large metals company. The company as a whole has a decentralized credit operation. Each division (or, as in the case to be described, each group of divisions) has its own credit personnel, approval, review, and records procedures. For this division, however, a computerized system has been designed and is scheduled to go into operation in the near future. Differences between the semi-automated and fully automated systems will be highlighted in Section 802.7.

[802.1]   **Personnel.** The credit operation for this group of divisions is served by the following personnel:

[802.1.1]   GENERAL CREDIT MANAGER. The credit operation for the entire company is supervised by the general credit manager, who reports to the company's assistant treasurer. The general credit manager has a staff function and his duties (described in the company position description, Figure 8.1) include establishing policy, developing reports to top management, and general coordination of credit operations throughout the company.

[802.1.2]   CREDIT MANAGER. The person responsible for handling credit operations for this particular group of three divisions is the credit

---

Job Title: General Credit Manager

Purpose: To protect the company's investment in receivables and to promote profitable sales by encouraging division credit personnel to grant credit so as to meet corporate goals.
   In order to accomplish the primary purpose of this job as stated above, the general credit manager must by example and persuasion prevail upon division credit people to convert marketing goals into targets for bad debts, days' sales outstanding, and marginal account exposure.

Duties: 1. The most important duty of the general credit manager is to compose a formal written credit policy that provides guidelines flexible enough to encompass varied businesses and the changes that time brings without being so flexible as to provide no direction. As a corollary, the general credit manager must obtain acceptance of the policy by division management either through management directive or persuasion or both.

Duties: 2. Inform management, both division and corporate, of all significant trends or developments.
   In order to so advise management, the general credit manager needs period reports from divisions that indicate the D.S.O. trend, agings by risk class, and major exposure accounts.

Duties: 3. Counsel division credit management based on a review of the reports received.

Duties: 4. Devise and procure better systems, reports, and analytical techniques for the optimum use of management by exception.

Duties: 5. Assist divisions in difficult credit and collection problems.

Duties: 6. Approve all credits for the corporation.

Duties: 7. Maintain consulting relationships on the executive level with other departments and divisions.

Duties: 8. Initiate and develop external relationships with customers, banks, credit organizations, attorneys, accountants, and competitors.

Duties: 9. Develop and maintain statistics reflecting each division's receivables investment in relation to the company and the industry.

Summary: The overall function of the general credit manager is to provide professional assistance to all levels of management in maintaining an optimum receivables investment. Such professional assistance is predicated on a wide knowledge of up-to-date practices and procedures in approving credits, obtaining collections, and reporting on both the quantity and quality of the investment in receivables.

FIGURE 8.1. Company Position Description

```
┌─────────────────────────────────────┐
│                                     │
│   To: CREDIT DEPARTMENT      DATE   │
│                                     │
│      Request for Credit Rating      │
│                                     │
│                                     │
│   Name of Company                   │
│                                     │
│   Address                           │
│                                     │
│   Requested by                      │
│                                     │
│   Commodity                         │
│                                     │
│   Contemplated order $              │
│                                     │
│   Contemplated terms                │
│                                     │
│   Remarks                           │
│                                     │
│                                     │
│                                     │
│                                     │
│                                     │
│                                     │
└─────────────────────────────────────┘
```

FIGURE 8.2

Request for Credit Rating

manager. He reports to the general credit manager (although other credit managers report to division officers in the financial area). The credit manager's duties include order approval, classification of accounts, review, and collection procedures.

[802.1.3]   STAFF ASSISTANT. A staff assistant is responsible for file maintenance, dunning letters, and the posting of cash remittances.

[802.2]   **Handling the First Order.** Company salesmen solicit orders, which are then handled in the following way:

[802.2.1]   SALESMAN TELEPHONES INFORMATION. The salesman calls the credit manager to inform him of a prospective order. The credit manager fills out a "request for credit rating" (shown in Figure 8.2) with information supplied by the salesman, including the name and address of the customer, the commodity required, the amount, and the anticipated terms. The credit department requires the above information, but the salesman may furnish at his discretion the customer's other suppliers and what percentage of the customer's needs are met by the company's competitors. The salesman also records the name of the person with whom he has dealt at the customer's company.

[802.2.2]   DUN & BRADSTREET CHECK. The credit manager checks the Dun & Bradstreet Reference Book to find out whether the customer is listed, his rating, and how long he has been in business.

[802.2.3]   ORDER APPROVAL. If the amount of the order does not exceed the credit limit the company has set up according to the D&B rating, the order is immediately approved without further checks. The credit manager telephones the approval to the salesman.

[802.2.4]   ORDER REVIEW. If the order exceeds the limit set up according to the D&B rating, the order is held and the following steps are taken:

1. A D&B Business Information Report is ordered.
2. A bank check may be made.
3. Suppliers may be contacted.
4. Financial statements may be requested.
5. Salesmen may be contacted to supply additional impressions of the customer.

On the basis of his analysis of the information collected, the credit manager will approve, reject, or modify the order.

[802.2.5] CLASSIFICATION OF THE CUSTOMER—ASSIGNING THE CREDIT LIMIT. The credit manager next must assign one of five classifications to the customer and, on the basis of his classification, assign a credit limit. The company uses the following five classifications:

1. *Prime.* A prime account represents one of the giants of industry. There is no doubt about his ability and willingness to pay his bills. This is a requirements limit.
2. *Good.* A good account represents a highly rated customer whose ability and willingness to pay are virtually unquestioned but whose account is followed more closely. It may be that he does not release financial information or that he is a giant in a smaller industry.
3. *Rating-Approval.* A "rating-approval" account is a customer whose credit limit is assigned according to his D&B rating. The limit is determined by taking a certain percentage (which slides according to the rating) of the company's estimated financial strength.
4. *Limited.* A limited account is one with a payment-record problem or otherwise questionable financial situation. It may be, too, that needed financial information is not available. His credit limit depends upon his requirements and the credit manager's analysis of the information available.
5. *Marginal.* A marginal account represents a definite risk. The company will accept marginal accounts as long as the losses resulting from them do not exceed profits made from them. A marginal account has a definite payments problem—often payments are extremely slow—usually coupled with a very poor financial situation.

[802.2.6] STORING CREDIT INFORMATION. The name of the customer, his classification, and his credit limit are recorded in a desk volume kept by the credit manager. A small card system, color-keyed according to classification, is also kept. On each card the following information is recorded:

1. Customer's name and address.
2. Account number.
3. Name of the product he buys.
4. Terms.
5. D&B credit rating.
6. Date of *Reference Book* from which the rating was taken.
7. Date the customer's file was last reviewed.
8. His credit limit.
9. Who made the review and approved the credit limit (either the credit manager or the general credit manager).

These cards are filed chronologically-alphabetically to ensure customer review according to the schedule established by the company (See below, Section 802.4.1). In addition, information accumulated about the customer is stored in a vertical file arranged alphabetically.

[802.3]   **Handling Subsequent Orders.** Orders from established customers are handled in the following way.

[802.3.1]   SALES REPORT. A report that a sale has been made—noting customer's name and address, commodity, amount, terms, etc.—comes into the credit department.

[802.3.2]   ORDER REVIEW. The credit manager reviews the order to make sure that it is within the credit limit and that there are not any outstanding past-due balances.

[802.3.3]   ORDER APPROVAL. If both of the above conditions are met, the order is approved. If they are not met, the credit manager must decide each case on its own merits. The order will be shipped automatically unless the credit manager stops it.

[802.4]   **Reviewing Credit Information and Classification.**

[802.4.1]   FREQUENCY OF REVIEW. The company reviews its accounts from the credit standpoint according to their classification on the following schedule:

1. Prime accounts are reviewed once a year.
2. Good accounts are reviewed every eight months.
3. Rating-approval accounts are reviewed once every eight months.
4. Limited accounts are reviewed once every six months.
5. Marginal accounts are reviewed every four months.

[802.4.2]   CONTENT OF REVIEW. The credit manager analyzes the information in the customer's folder to determine whether the proper classification and limit are assigned. This information includes:

1. Current Dun & Bradstreet Business Information Report (the company considers a report to be indate if written within six to seven months).
2. Current D&B rating (from the most recent *Reference Book*).
3. The company's own trade experience with the customer (which is obtained from a computer-generated "Customer Credit History" (See Figure 8.3).

If an urgent change in the customer's condition becomes apparent—through a D&B rating change or poor payment performance—a review is undertaken immediately and the sales department is informed. Otherwise, all reviews are handled in sequence.

[802.5]   **Collection Activities.** The credit department keeps track of open items and administers its collection activities according to the following system.

[802.5.1]   ACCOUNTS-RECEIVABLE–CREDIT-DEPARTMENT RELATION. The receivables clerk has all open invoices filed chronologically according to due date. He sends to the credit department a copy of the invoice three to four days before it is due.

[802.5.2]   CREDIT DEPARTMENT INVOICE FILES. The credit department files the invoices received chronologically-alphabetically in accordian files. These files are kept by the staff assistant.

[802.5.3]   PAYMENTS BEFORE DUNNING. If payments are made before dunning

```
DATE RUN 08/07/73                                                              PROGRAM NO C9041 PAGE NO   6

                                      CREDIT DEPARTMENT
                                   CUSTOMER CREDIT HISTORY
                                          07/31/73

CUSTOMER NAME                CUST NO    RISK CLASS         CREDIT LIMIT     HIGH CREDIT    HIGH CR DATE  LAST SALE
                                          PRIME            REQUIREMENTS    1,157,007.31      06/31/73     07/31/73

TOTAL OPEN INVOICES     CURRENT     1-30 DAYS OVERDUE  31 TO 60 DAYS OVERDUE  61 TO 90 DAYS OVERDUE  OVER 90 DAYS OVERDUE
     259,675.23      175,899.37         38,748.19                                                       25,027.67

                         ****12 MONTH PERIOD BEGINNING 07/31/72 AND ENDING 07/31/73****
 TOT # OF INV  TOT # OF INV PAID  TOTAL BILLING   TOTAL AMT PAID  PAID WITHIN TERMS  PAID AFTER DUE DATE  DAYS AFTER DUE DATE
     20               13          2,708,491.50     2,440,816.27    # 13   100.0%         #            %      LOW       HIGH

 TERMS     NO TERMS CODE     NET 30 DAYS

********************************

CUSTOMER NAME                CUST NO    RISK CLASS         CREDIT LIMIT     HIGH CREDIT    HIGH CR DATE  LAST SALE
                                          PRIME            REQUIREMENTS      788,116.68      10/03/72     07/31/73

TOTAL OPEN INVOICES     CURRENT     1-30 DAYS OVERDUE  31 TO 60 DAYS OVERDUE  61 TO 90 DAYS OVERDUE  OVER 90 DAYS OVERDUE
     359,498.88      310,523.04         48,975.84

                         ****12 MONTH PERIOD BEGINNING 07/31/72 AND ENDING 07/31/73****
 TOT # OF INV  TOT # OF INV PAID  TOTAL BILLING   TOTAL AMT PAID  PAID WITHIN TERMS  PAID AFTER DUE DATE  DAYS AFTER DUE DATE
    131              119          3,349,554.69     2,990,055.80    # 10     7.4%       #109       92.6%      LOW   1 HIGH 108

 TERMS    NET 10TH PROX     NO TERMS CODE     CASH DOCUMENTS     NET 30 DAYS

********************************

CUSTOMER NAME                CUST NO    RISK CLASS         CREDIT LIMIT     HIGH CREDIT    HIGH CR DATE  LAST SALE
                                          PRIME            REQUIREMENTS      198,434.96      07/28/73     07/26/73

TOTAL OPEN INVOICES     CURRENT     1-30 DAYS OVERDUE  31 TO 60 DAYS OVERDUE  61 TO 90 DAYS OVERDUE  OVER 90 DAYS OVERDUE
     124,909.80      121,183.41                                                                          3,726.39

                         ****12 MONTH PERIOD BEGINNING 07/31/72 AND ENDING 07/31/73****
 TOT # OF INV  TOT # OF INV PAID  TOTAL BILLING   TOTAL AMT PAID  PAID WITHIN TERMS  PAID AFTER DUE DATE  DAYS AFTER DUE DATE
     31               23            984,436.02       959,526.21    # 22    97.2%       #  1        2.8%      LOW   2 HIGH   2

 TERMS    NET 30 DAYS

********************************
```

FIGURE 8.3. Customer Credit History

begins, the receivables clerk informs the credit department of this fact and the invoice is removed from the credit department's files, and processed. If payments are made after dunning has begun, the invoice is removed and filed for a period of six months in case later disputes arise.

[802.5.4] DUNNING. The company follows the following steps to collect its accounts:

1. Five days after the due date, a duplicate invoice with a stamped reminder is mailed to the customer. Mailings are not made until 4:30 P.M. to ensure that payments made within the five-day grace period can be recorded.
2. Two weeks later the first collection letter goes out. It is a computer-produced form letter whose mailing must be approved by the credit manager. Before collection letters are mailed, a last-minute check with the accounts-receivable department is made to avoid unnecessary dunning.
3. Two weeks after the first letter, a second letter follows.
4. Two weeks after the second, a third letter, typewritten and signed by the credit manager, is sent.
5. Two weeks later, a fourth letter, also typewritten and especially designed for the case, is sent out.
6. A fifth letter is scheduled to follow in two weeks, but before this

FIGURE 8.4. Monthly D.S.O. Report

FIGURE 8.5. Monthly Credit Report

letter is mailed the customer is telephoned by the staff assistant or credit manager to solicit payment or promise of payment.

7. The fifth letter is to inform the customer that unless payment or promise of payment is immediately forthcoming, the account will be placed for collection.

8. If payment is not forthcoming, the account is placed for collection either with an agency or with the company's attorneys.

[802.6]   **Reports to Top Management.** The company issues the following monthly reports to top management.

[802.6.1]   D.S.O. The company uses D.S.O. as the major indicator of credit-department operations. An example of the D.S.O. report is shown in Figure 8.4.

[802.6.2]   MONTHLY CREDIT REPORT. The credit department also furnishes a monthly credit report (see Figure 8.5), which includes the following information:

1. Total billings.
2. Summary aging by terms.
3. Marginal-account summary aging by terms.
4. Notes receivable.
5. Bad debts (and bad-debt reserves).
6. Major exposure accounts (owing over $50,000).

[802.7]   **Conversion to Fully Automated System.** This company has designed a fully automated system to remedy defects in the current credit operation and to supply more and better credit information to the department on its own activities and results.

[802.7.1]   IMPROVEMENTS OVER CURRENT SYSTEM. One of the major improvements the new system will effect over the currently existing system is designed to achieve "credit by exception." Order entry will be built into the system so that each order can be checked against the credit limit and the outstanding balance automatically. This frees the credit manager to devote his attention to problem cases and other credit problems. Another defect that the new system will remedy is the end-of-month cash application. Before, there was a time lag during which payments could have been made but not recorded for credit-department use. The new system will provide for up-to-the-minute cash application that takes into consideration the five-day grace period allowed by the company.

Finally, the new system will enable the credit department to know the group's total credit exposure to any one company. This was not possible under the old system because of the different products sold and because sales were not reconciled: Sales and credit records were recorded according to account number (of which one company could have several for all of its shipping points). By adding a "headquarters" number to the system, according to which all appropriate account numbers can be grouped, the company will now be able to determine its total exposure to any one customer.

[802.7.2]   AUTOMATIC DUNNING. The new system will provide for computer-generated collection letters.

[802.7.3]   NEW AND REVISED REPORTS FOR THE CREDIT DEPARTMENT. The new computer system has been designed to provide more and better information to the credit department.

1. *Revised reports.*
   a. Open-invoice items report.
   b. Aged trial balances by risk.
   c. Aged trial balances by customer.
   d. Past-due receivables.
   e. Customer history credit report.
2. *New reports.*
   a. Customer monthly activity report.
   b. Customers exceeding credit limit report.
   c. Customer master listing.
   d. Headquarters listing by customer.
   e. Master customer number directory.

[803]   COMPUTERIZING THE CREDIT OPERATION: THE FULLY AUTOMATED SYSTEM OF A LARGE CLOTHING MANUFACTURER. With the advent of widespread computerization of the accounts-receivable function, many credit managers became aware of the enormous possibilities a computerized credit operation could offer for increased speed and efficiency of those functions credit departments had traditionally carried out manually. Some credit managers responded to this challenge and began to work closely with the data-processing personnel of their companies to develop sophisticated, useful credit systems. Unfortunately, others have been slow to respond and the results have been most serious. Computerized accounts-receivable systems have been set up that do not fulfill the

information requirements of the credit department, that do not generate reports to management the credit department wishes to produce, and that are staffed by a new breed of well-trained technicians and managers who speak a language the credit manager often finds difficult to understand. The lesson here is quite apparent: In order to develop a useful computerized credit system and thus maintain a position of importance and ever-growing responsibility in his company, the credit manager must work with data-processing personnel from the beginning to see that his requirements are met. This means that the credit manager must be knowledgeable about computer systems and how they can be put to work for his department. This section, divided into two parts as described below, is designed as your introduction to this field. The first part of the section will present a description of a sophisticated, computerized accounts-receivable system. Although there are many excellent systems in operation throughout the country, the system described below was chosen because it can be adapted to many different operating environments to fit a company's individual needs. Because the accounts-receivable system lies at the heart of the computerized credit function, it is important that you be familiar with at least one such system. The second part of the section is devoted to a description of the computerized credit operation of a large clothing manufacturer. This will describe an accounts-receivable system and how it has been utilized by the credit department.

[803.1]   **A Computerized Accounts-Receivable System.** The Multiple Business Entity–Accounts Receivable Management System (MBE–ARMS), developed by Fortex Data Corp., a Dun & Bradstreet company, provides accounts-receivable processing and supports related activities such as credit-collection and sales analysis for one or more separate and diverse business organizations. The flexibility of the system is such that it may be used for processing the accounts-receivable data of multiple related or unrelated business entities. Examples of such business entities are businesses within a conglomerate, separate divisions, groups, or other corporate organizational categories of a single entity, or separate businesses within a service-bureau environment. Applicable to manufacturing, service, and retail business environments, the system will support accounts-receivable processing for any combination and quantity of open-item balance forward (revolving), or installment, sales to a customer. These several diverse processing requirements are included in the MBE–ARMS system in one master file (data base). Activity for each customer account within the respective business entity is processed in a single access of the data base; the integrity of each entity for the activity, balances, controls, etc., is, of course, maintained.

Flexible and efficient control, operation, and reporting techniques allow each business to utilize only those portions of the system that are required for its processing and in a manner best suited to its individual requirements. Account management, delinquency, customer statement billing, and system input and control information is provided separately for each business as well as other levels such as location, region, or corporate division.

SUMMARY OF SYSTEM FEATURES. In addition to those normal functions associated with recording the amount due from a customer, reducing that amount by payments, etc., the MBE–ARMS system provides features that permit a more encompassing solution of problems or requirements found in the area of accounts-receivable processing.

1. *Automated surveillance of receivables processing and support activities.* The MBE–ARMS system provides an automated solution of problems such as credit authorization and past-due collection. For example, the following highlights identify the types of features provided.

   a. Posting of activity to customer accounts on a real-time or daily basis while simultaneously updating account delinquency status.

   b. Report of a change in basic customer account data can automatically cause the preparation of a report that will identify the updated fields to be used in responding to customer inquiries.

   c. Automatic preparation of a credit-collection worksheet, collection card, when an account enters a specified delinquent category. The specific delinquency category can be defined for each business.

   d. Automatic preparation of past-due notices for delinquent accounts in agreement with a procedure or multiple procedures that can be variable for each business.

   e. Deferral of aging, earning of service charge, preparation of past-due notices and statements and the maturing of installments for disputed accounts or where special arrangements have been made with the customer. The deferral capability can also be utilized for a specific invoice (obligation) within an account.

2. *Flexibility of design.* The system is designed to allow flexibility in processing for each business and its respective customer accounts. The options available can be unique for each business and group of customer accounts.

   a. Application of finance charge is variable for each account in both the method of calculation and rates to be applied. Further, where necessary, this flexibility can be utilized for a given obligation.

   b. Multiple-account-obligation types; e.g., installment, balance forward, open item and others can be combined in a single customer account. There are no limitations to the number of each type which can be active for a given account.

   c. Repayment terms and dunning policy are available at the customer account level according to the options specified for each business entity.

   d. Management reporting is based upon the individual requirements and specifications of each business entity.

   e. Auditing of account balances and payments is provided. Sales terms tables can be utilized to define the terms of sale and any related payment discount which may be required. Descriptive billing is supported separately for each business.

f. Small-balance write-off and discount policies are defined for each business.

g. Up to twenty-two separate billing cycles can be stipulated for each business entity.

h. Report-preparation facility based on data "extraction" techniques. Program design has included definition and identification of points for extraction of reports to be defined in the future.

3. *Control techniques.* Control over the system's operation is maintained for each business entity and for the complete system or data base. System-control reports of dollar and record status and activity are prepared in addition to extensive control and validation processing performed on system input. All control reports are automatically produced and must be printed each time the system is processed. Highlights of the features provided include:

a. Batch balancing and detail validation of all system input.

b. Control reporting by type of transaction of both record count and dollar amounts.

c. Dollar amount activity properly entered into the system but unable to post properly to an individual account is maintained in the system as "suspense" for subsequent redirection to the proper account or obligation. Processing of the system is under the control of a system control file.

SYSTEM DATA BASE

1. *Structure.* All customer account and business entity data is organized in a hierarchical structure for each separate business organization in the system. Business records contain all pertinent data unique to the business, such as name, address, repayment tables, sales terms, discounts, and descriptive billing and delinquent account dunning procedures. Each account is likewise organized with a customer account record followed by the detail account data for each customer account. The system may use most file-access methods: sequential, index sequential, direct, and IMS (an IBM data-access method). This facility is supported by removal of all input-output functions from the respective processing modules, i.e., the cash application module accesses the data base; therefore the respective structure is transparent.

Periodically, portions of the master file can be transferred to a second file of historical activity by account. A third systems file, the systems control file, a fixed-length indexed sequential file, contains no account or business data, but rather supports the dating, report-request, and processing-control features of the system. Elements common to all business entities on the system such as service charge rates, standard statement message board support, and standard descriptive billing identification of transaction codes are also maintained in this file. The file also functions as a communication region between programs and businesses.

2. *Business entity data base content.* The business segment of the data base provides all data required to support the individual processing, billing, and reporting of a business's accounts receivable. Separate name and address data, remittance addresses, sale transaction descriptions, multiple dunning and repayment methods, sales terms, and payment discount procedure are provided for each business. Separate accounts-receivable processing parameters such as limits for small-balance write-offs and applicable discount provisions are also provided for each business in the system.

3. *Customer account data base content.* The customer segments of the data base provide detailed identification of the customer, account balance and activity, delinquency, and sales history for the entire account as well as for each separate customer purchase "obligation." Summary account data is maintained in a customer record and is followed by detail account obligation records. Although a customer account could consist of a single-obligation type (for example, open-item, balance-forward, or installment) a business may, however, elect to combine obligation types in a single account. For example, a customer may have contracted to pay his account on an open-item basis for normal purchases and on installment terms for large-item purchases. Under MBE–ARMS, the business can elect to create separate accounts and provide separate billings for this customer or combine both "obligations" into a single account. Where combined, the two obligations are maintained separately with individual payment history, service charge application (where appropriate) and past-due reporting capability, but are combined for customer billing, total account balance, and delinquency determination.

Detail activity to each customer account is maintained to support customer account status inquiry, month-end processing of accounts, and statement preparation when desired. Customer sales, credit, and debit transactions during a month are compressed and retained on the data base as "occurs depending on" extensions to the basic customer account records. Upon completion of any required billing cycle and month-end requirements, the transactions are summarized and removed from the data base; the summarized records can be added to a separate history file so that a complete customer history may be prepared, as required, reflecting all transactions for each account.

SYSTEM REPORT CAPABILITIES

1. *Report extraction.* Report preparation extraction in the MBE–ARMS system is initiated by the processing of a report request transaction and automatically as a by-product of maintenance and cycle processing of the accounts. Individual records of data extracted from the data base are prepared and are processed (when necessary sorting is provided) by a standard print program

containing individual report modules for each report. Standard points of extraction such as a "business customer and obligation break" have been defined to allow access to the data base for reports other than those currently prepared.

2. *System reports and frequency.* The frequency of report preparation in the MBE–ARMS system is categorized by those reports that are standard during system processing, reports prepared as a result of system or account activity, and management and account summary reports that are processed on a request-only basis.

    a. Standard reports produced with each systems processing run:

        (1) System-control reports—reports of file activity and status and volume of processing completed.

        (2) Input-control reports—reports produced by the edit program for those input batches that are out of balance or contain errors and, therefore, require review and correction; reports of balanced, error-free batches are optional.

        (3) File maintenance and exception reports—reports of transaction activity that rejected or produced exception conditions during posting of the master file or system-control file; reference reports of such transactions that were not rejected and had no exceptions (that is, were posted) are optional.

        (4) Suspense reports—reports that are prepared during any dollar transaction posting activity to the customer segment of the data base where the respective transaction could not be completely applied.

    b. Reports prepared as a result of system or account activity.

        (1) Exceptions reports—reports of payments and sales to status accounts, such as delinquent or exceeded credit lines, to allow daily review by management and collection personnel.

        (2) Conversion-additions reports—account-identification reports that result from the addition of new accounts or changes in basic account data.

        (3) Billing-dunning reports—reports produced for the billing and dunning of customer accounts:

            (a) Statements—personalized or nonpersonalized for each business entity.

            (b) Past-due notices—personalized or nonpersonalized for each business entity.

            (c) Statement-exception report—statements that may require review or special handling prior to being sent to the customer.

            (d) Collection worksheet—an account summary of status and history prepared as a collection worksheet for delinquent accounts.

        (4) Accounting reports—reports produced that are normally requested by the accounting area of a business, such as trial balances, aging of account balances, etc.

```
                          FORTEX DATA CORPORATION
                             ACCOUNTS RECEIVABLE
                            NOTES RECEIVABLE STATUS

NCH  CHICAGO        IL       CENTER # 325                    PERIOD ENDING 10/10/73              PAGE    1

OUNT                    INVOICE  PERIOD    CURRENT    CUMULATIVE    BALANCE    AMOUNT    A M O U N T S   P A S T   D U E
BER  ACCOUNT NAME/CONTRACT #  AMOUNT EFF. TERM  PAYMENT   PAYMENTS      OF         IN       1-30     31-60    OVER 60
                                DATE DATE  MATURED    MATURED    CONTRACT   ARREARS    DAYS     DAYS     DAYS

5010  ABC COMPANY
             111111      1800 0374 0377    0.00       0.00        1800.00    0.00      0.00     0.00     0.00
      ACCOUNT    TOTAL    1800                0.00       0.00        1800.00    0.00      0.00     0.00     0.00
      % AGED TO BALANCE                                                        .0        .0       .0       .0
5020  SOUTHWEST INDUSTRIES
             320050       120 1073 1074    0.00       0.00         120.00    0.00      0.00     0.00     0.00
      ACCOUNT    TOTAL     120                0.00       0.00         120.00    0.00      0.00     0.00     0.00
      % AGED TO BALANCE                                                        .0        .0       .0       .0
5040  HIC SCREW COMPANY
             540011       180 1073 0475    0.00       0.00         180.00    0.00      0.00     0.00     0.00
      ACCOUNT    TOTAL     180                0.00       0.00         180.00    0.00      0.00     0.00     0.00
      % AGED TO BALANCE                                                        .0        .0       .0       .0
```

FIGURE 8.6. Sample Report Produced by the MBE-ARMS System

c. Request-only reports—reports prepared on a request basis for special review of an account or categories of accounts.

(1) Authorization report—report of all active or status accounts during a billing cycle to be used for credit-extension approval for retail receivable obligations.

(2) Customer data base inquiry—report of all information in a customer account or on file for a business entity. There are various types of inquiries designed to produce only the desired amount of data.

(3) Name-address list—listing of customer name, address, and account number within a business entity. (For an example of an MBE-ARMS report, see Figure 8.6.)

Each user of MBE-ARMS can specify the specific content and format of all reports in paragraphs "b" and "c" above. Changes to standard reports will require modification to the product.

[803.1.4]   SYSTEM INPUT.

1. *Input forms.* (See Figure 8.7, for an example of an input form). Input to the system is obtained from encoded entries of sales, credits, debits, adjustments, and file-maintenance documents or transactions to the system data base. When submitted, the transactions are batched by system-batch types for ease of control and to provide reports in a readable format in the event of out-of-balance batches or erroneous-invalid fields encountered during system validation. The system also utilizes batch controls for "line" (real-time) processing. The following batch types have been defined for the system:

a. Cash remittance.

b. Debit-credit adjustment transactions.

CUSTOMER NON-MONETARY ACTION TICKET
CPI 2503

BATCH	TRANS DATE	BUSINESS NO.	ACCOUNT NO.	TRANS FUNCTION

ADD CHGE CNVT
0 3 0 5 0 9
25 26

LEGEND
A FINANCE CHARGE RATE CODE
B FINANCE CHARGE METHOD
C REPAYMENT SCHEDULE CODE
D DUN PROCEDURE CODE
E DUN NOTICE DISPOSITION CODE
F STATEMENT DISPOSITION CODE
G REVOLVING BALANCE FORWARD ONLY
   NO CREDIT CARDS ISSUED

REQUIRED CUSTOMER DATA

TITLE	CUSTOMER NAME	STREET ADDRESS LINE NO. 1

H REVOLVING BALANCE FORWARD ONLY
   PAYMENT DUE DATE
I PAYMENT DISCOUNT QUALIFICATION CODE
J OBLIGATION MAY NOT MATURE
K CREDIT APPROVED BY
L CREDIT LINE
M CREDIT POINTS
N CUSTOMER INQUIRY CONTACT CODE

CITY	STAT.	ZIP CODE	DATED OPENED	FC RATE

B	C		D	E	F	G	H		I
FC METH	REPY SC	ACCT TYPE	DUN	DUN DISP.	STMT DISP.	CRDS	DUE	PRIMARY PHONE	DISC. CD
59	60	61 62 63		0 1 2 3 4 64	0 1 2 3 4 65	66 67	68 69 70		79 80

OPTIONAL CUSTOMER DATA

STREET ADDRESS LINE NO. 2	NON BILLABLE MONTHS (CALENDAR)	OPTIONAL CUST. DATA	SSN
	1 2 3 4 5 6 7 8 9 10 11 12		

K	L	M	N		
STREET ADDRESS LINE NO. 3	CR AUTH	CR LINE	CR PTS	BANK NO.	D D A NO.

DUNS NUMBER	SIC CODES	D&B RTE	D&B SCORE	D&B SALES VOLUME	D&B NET WORTH

PREPARED BY   DATE   APPROVED BY   DATE

FIGURE 8.7

Form Used for Entry of Data into the Computer System

c. Sales and monetary conversion activity.
d. File maintenance.
e. Convert–add–replace customer–business data.
f. System-control input.
g. Edit recycle maintenance.

2. *Input preparation.* Source-input forms are machine-readable media such as punched card, magnetic tape, or disc for entry to the system. Input to the system may also be in the format of a data file produced for another system. For example, a daily file of sales transactions that are produced by order entry system or cash remittances received from a bank lock box service.

[803.1.5] PROCESSING TECHNIQUES.

1. *System computer requirements.* The MBE–ARMS system is designed for operation on a medium to large-scale computer system. The system is written in ANS COBOL for operation on IBM 360 or 370 equipment under OS or DOS. Teleprocessing is supported through the use of IBM software products, CICS and IMS.

2. *Functional program design.* The MBE–ARMS basic system consists of but five computer programs (in addition to sort and on-line programs), each consisting of a number of functional program modules. (See Figure 8.8 for a flow-chart of this system as illustrated in a sequential batch processing mode). The system is also available with other types of data base structure and will support on-line real-time processing.

a. Edit program—provides all editing of system input and performs all file-maintenance functions to the systems control file.

b. Update program—performs all maintenance of business and customer account records from transaction input to the system. The update program also prepares data base extracts of selected reports for later report preparation by the print program.

c. Accrual program—performs all time-dependent functions such as those related to the cyclical or month-end processing of customer accounts. Included in this classification of processing is such activity as the earning of service charge, delinquency identification for balance forward obligation, maturing of installment payments, and small-balance write-offs. The accrual program has report extraction responsibility for all cyclical and month-end report requirements as well as other selected reports.

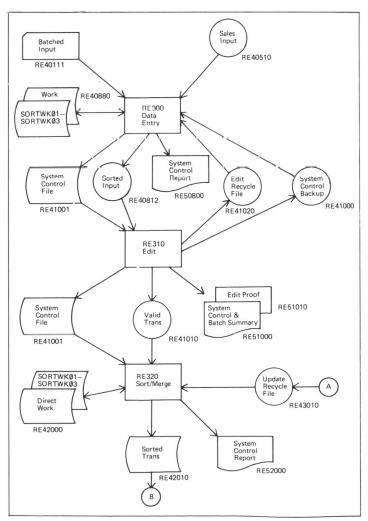

Figure 8.8
MBE-ARMS System Flow Chart

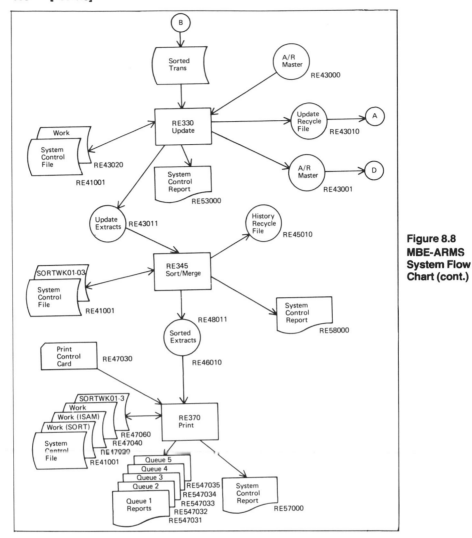

**Figure 8.8
MBE-ARMS
System Flow
Chart (cont.)**

d. History update program—accumulates summarized transacted activity for each business and account. The history update program can also prepare extracts of these accumulated transactions, on request, for later report preparation by the print program.

e. Print program—provides the detail formatting of system output reports prepared from the extracts produced by the update, accrual, and history update programs. Common report requirements are defined once by this program and detail report "modules" are prepared for the detail formatting of each report. Output media may be printed forms, punched cards, magnetic tapes, discs, microfilm, microfiche, etc.

3. *Modular operation.* The design of the individual programs in the system allows the running of only those programs required for the particular daily system processing. For example, the accrual

program of the system need not be run following each update and the history update need be run only when transactions are no longer desired on the current data base and are desired to be retained in the history data base.

4. On-line capability for entry of input transactions, cash and other dollar transaction applications, credit or account inquiry, and related functions is provided in MBE–ARMS

SYSTEM-CONTROL PROCEDURES.

1. *Input controls.* Prior to submission for data entry, all source documents to be input to the system are grouped and control totals are prepared for each group (batch). Upon entry to the system, the batch is balanced internally to ensure that all source documents have been correctly entered and are present. All out-of-balance batches are printed or displayed on the respective on-line terminal for review. Upon completion of the editing of all input data, a summary of all records input, rejected, or passed on for update processing is prepared for comparison against marginal input controls and subsequent update processing results. All rejected transactions are printed with an appropriate error message to allow reconciliation of the respective control reports.

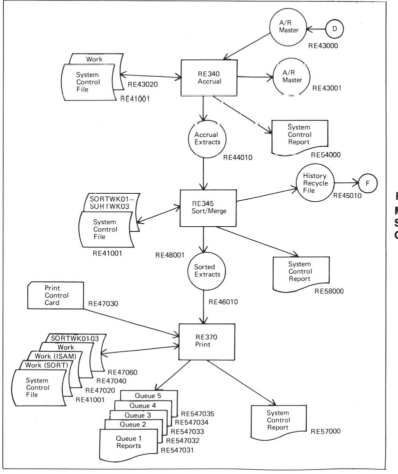

**Figure 8.8
MBE-ARMS
System Flow
Chart (cont.)**

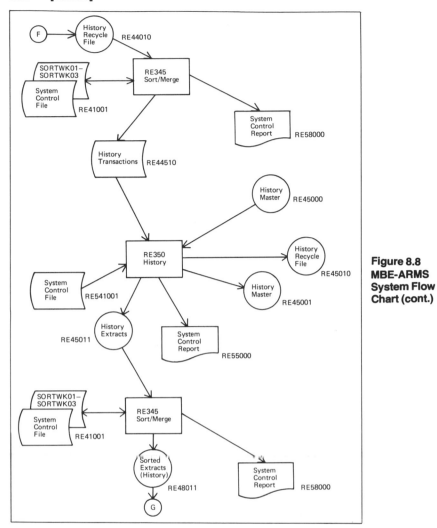

**Figure 8.8
MBE-ARMS
System Flow
Chart (cont.)**

2. *Account number check digit.* As an option to be exercised on each business entity to be processed, each account number in system input data can be verified for a check digit calculated on Modulus 10 or Modulus 11 (or no check digit verification, if preferred) to prevent keypunch or transposition errors in account numbers or input transactions.

3. *File record counts and dollar controls.* Detail record counts and a summary of account balances are prepared to protect against system or operation errors. In the event the respective detail does not agree with the summary trailer record maintained, an error condition is noted and, if desired, the system will terminate processing to allow identification of the error before it is compounded. All input files (other than sort inputs) are checked for sequence (each succeeding record key is equal to or greater than its predecessor) and, if desired, the system will terminate processing if an out-of-sequence condition exists.

4. *Suspense processing.* In a sequential processing environment, the dollar transactions entered into the system in the proper format (validation tests are satisfied) but which cannot be properly posted to an individual account or obligation (wrong account number, wrong invoice number) are retained in detail on the system in a suspense category for subsequent redirection to the proper account or obligation. The system will control transactions in suspense and will assist in "working" the suspense transactions through the preparation of the suspense report. This report is organized by transaction code within the business entity and displays each detail transaction and totals for items in suspense prior to a given update, items being applied, and a listing of new items suspending.

[803.1.7]   DUN & BRADSTREET—MBE–ARMS INTERFACE. The MBE–ARMS system recognizes that in order for the credit manager to render the best decision on any particular credit case, he must have access to two basic information areas. The first is the status of the customer's account with his own company; this is the information provided by the MBE–ARMS system just described. The second area of information is the credit history of his customer with other companies. MBE–ARMS therefore has implemented an interface with the extensive information resources of Dun & Bradstreet as the most efficient source of this second area of information. The method of interface is described below:

1. *Statement of interface objective:* To provide the efficient receipt and automatic update of data element changes and additions from the Dun & Bradstreet system and to prepare information of trade credit experience from the MBE–ARMS system for direct input to the D&B Business Information Center. The interface facility is

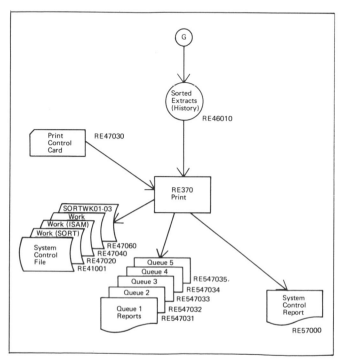

Figure 8.8
MBE-ARMS System Flow Chart (cont.)

based upon the existence of the D-U-N-S Number for each customer in both the D&B and Fortex business files. Where the D-U-N-S Number has not been previously assigned by the user of the MBE-ARMS system, a facility is provided to support assignment of the D-U-N-S Number.

2. *Definition of D-U-N-S.* The Data Universal Numbering System (D-U-N-S) is a business identification system administered by Dun & Bradstreet. In administering the system, D&B assigns random, nonindicative account numbers to commercial business establishments, notifies each establishment of the number assigned to it, explains how the number may be used to advantage, and keeps an up-to-date master file of all establishments for this service. Business "establishments" in this system include branches, factories, and purchasing points as well as headquarters. A large company, therefore, actually might have many different D-U-N-S Numbers, since each branch or establishment would have its own number. The Data Universal Numbering System— D-U-N-S—has gained wide acceptance by American industry and D-U-N-S Numbers have been assigned to nearly three million business establishments in the United States. These companies account for well over 95 percent of the flow of business documents (invoices, purchase orders, shipping tickets, credit memos, and the like) in this country. How are D-U-N-S Numbers assigned? In the Data Universal Numbering System, every establishment is identified by a nine-digit number. The numbers are assigned randomly and are nonindicative; that is, the number itself has no geographical or product significance. Each D-U-N-S Number ends with a special digit known as a Modulus ten, double-one-double-one check digit. This check digit makes it possible for a computer or other data-processing system to catch transcription errors. In D-U-N-S, the block of numbers from 00-000-000 through 00-099-999 plus the respective check digits of each will never be used. This block of numbers has been set aside as a Reserve Users Block. Users of the system may assign numbers from the "block" to any of their accounts that are not covered in D-U-N-S. For example, the system covers commercial establishments, but a user may also sell to or buy from a group of noncommercial enterprises to which D-U-N-S Numbers are not assigned. Numbers would be assigned for these accounts by the user himself from the Reserve Users Block.

   D-U-N-S has been set up to provide the widest possible coverage of business establishments consistent with the practical problems of maintaining accuracy. Numbers are assigned to headquarters locations and also to major branches and to certain remittance locations (e.g., lock boxes, P.O. boxes) even though the latter may not always qualify as "physical" locations.

3. *Narrative definition of MBE–ARMS system support.* A further description of the relationship of the Dun & Bradstreet and the MBE-ARMS information files is provided by the flow-chart

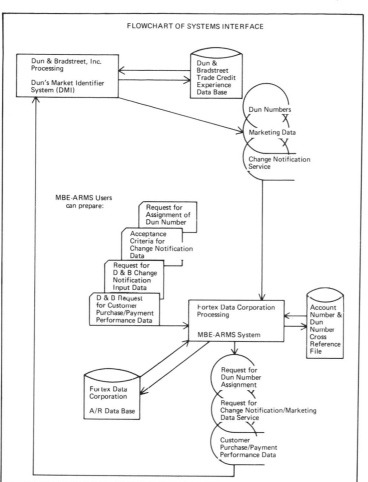

FIGURE 8.9

Dun & Bradstreet-MBE-ARMS Interface

description of system interface included in the write-up on this page (see Figure 8.9). The following paragraphs include an identification of the Dun & Bradstreet services that are available, the types of input transactions that can be prepared by the user of MBE–ARMS to secure Dun & Bradstreet service, and a description of the corresponding processing of these input transactions by Dun & Bradstreet and MBE–ARMS.

a. *User-prepared input transactions (action request) which are processed by MBE–ARMS.* A user of MBE–ARMS will be able to prepare any of the following action requests for any business entity utilizing the system. The specific format of the request is in agreement with the standard MBE–ARMS report requests. The number of requests that can be prepared for any business entity at one time is limited only by the operating environment of the respective user.

   (1) *Request for assignment of D-U-N-S Numbers.* A D-U-N-S Number is an optional data element that may be defined for each customer maintained in the MBE–ARMS data base. This transaction can be utilized to cause the prepara-

tion of a data file that would then be utilized by Dun & Bradstreet for the assignment of D-U-N-S Numbers and the subsequent reentry and updating of customer data of the respective business entity.

(2) *Request for customer purchase-payment performance data.* This request will result in the preparation of a data file containing credit performance data for all customers of the specified business entity. The file will be created by MBE–ARMS and will be delivered to Dun & Bradstreet for their analysis.

(3) *Request for Dun & Bradstreet Change Notification input data.* This request is prepared to cause an inquiry of the D&B information file for status of selected data elements for all customers of the specified business entity. Dun & Bradstreet will prepare the change record, which will subsequently be processed by MBE–ARMS to complete the updating of the respective data elements subject to the "acceptance criteria" defined in the following paragraph.

(4) *Acceptance criteria for Change Notification data.* This transaction will allow each user of MBE–ARMS to specify the data elements contained in the Dun & Bradstreet Change Notification record that will be utilized to update the corresponding data fields in the data base for the respective user of MBE–ARMS. This facility could be utilized, for example, to cause the automatic updating of the D&B rating while preventing the change to the customer address data element.

b. *MBE-ARMS-produced data files which are the result of processing a user transaction (section request).* The specific records (files) that are discussed in this section will be delivered to Dun & Bradstreet for their processing. As noted in the following paragraphs, Dun & Bradstreet will in certain situations return the data file to the MBE–ARMS user for subsequent processing against his data base.

(1) *Request for D-U-N-S Number assignments.* Dun & Bradstreet can utilize this data file to identify customers that require D-U-N-S Number assignment and where appropriate insert the D-U-N-S Number into the data field provided in the record. The updated file will be returned to the MBE–ARMS user by Dun & Bradstreet.

(2) *Request for Dun & Bradstreet Change Notification data.* This record will cause Dun & Bradstreet to prepare a Change Notification record for each customer of the MBE–ARMS user. The Change Notification records prepared by Dun & Bradstreet will be returned to the user of MBE–ARMS for updating.

(3) *Customer purchase-payment performance data.* MBE–ARMS will produce credit experience records for all customers of a specified business entity. These records will

be analyzed by Dun & Bradstreet and utilized to update their resources.

c. *Information which can be received from Dun & Bradstreet in response to an MBE–ARMS user request.* The following general types of information can be obtained from Dun & Bradstreet through an MBE–ARMS user request and can subsequently be processed by MBE–ARMS as input data.

   (1) *D-U-N-S Number Assignment.* MBE-ARMS will receive a record that includes the assigned D-U-N-S Number and create the appropriate update transaction.

   (2) *Change Notification Service.* The Change Notification record can be requested by an MBE–ARMS user. This record will be processed by MBE–ARMS and all specified updating of the user's data base will be completed.

   (3) *Marketing data.* Dun & Bradstreet maintains extensive data for other business organizations and provides access to this information through a variety of "indicators," such as SIC code, location, sales, etc.

   (4) *ECUS Data.* Exception Credit Update Service data may also be requested.

d. *D-U-N-S Number—the linkage between Dun & Bradstreet and MBE–ARMS.* The common method of customer identification in both systems is the D-U-N-S Number. Although access to either system will require the usage of the D-U-N-S Number, MBE–ARMS will not require that the D-U-N-S Number be used as the account identification number by users of the system. The alternative methods of system linkage are described in the following paragraphs.

   (1) *Indirect access.* This method will be utilized where the D-U-N-S Number is not the customer number; however, the D-U-N-S Number is maintained as a data element in the customer data base. To support this situation, a cross-reference file will be created and utilized by MBE–ARMS to identify the customer.

   (2) *Direct access.* In those cases where the MBE-ARMS user is utilizing the D-U-N-S Number to identify the customer accounts, i.e., the D-U-N-S Number is the customer number, all communication is direct.

e. *MBE–ARMS data base support to system.* When a user of MBE–ARMS desires to utilize the optimal extended credit and collection facilities offered through the Dun & Bradstreet interface, it will be necessary to identify those customers for whom the facility is desired. MBE–ARMS will create an additional record for each customer, which will be utilized to maintain data elements relating to the extended credit and collection facility.

[803.2]   **The Fully Automated System of a Large Clothing Manufacturer—Description.** The preceding sections described in some detail a computerized accounts-receivable system. This section will describe how a different computerized accounts-receivable system is being used by a large clothing manufacturer for credit-department functions. Although this company has many divisions and multiple shipping points throughout the country, all credit and collection activities are carried out from one centralized location. This is an on-line system using cathode-ray tubes and handles well in excess of 75,000 accounts.

[803.2.1] DEPARTMENT STRUCTURE AND PERSONNEL. The credit department is composed of eight units, seven of which are each responsible for a region (set up geographically according to dollar volume) and one that is responsible for special accounts (such as the military). There is a general credit manager who supervises operations and who reports to the comptroller. A typical regional unit is staffed as follows:

1. *Regional credit manager.* The regional credit manager supervises the work of his unit and approves all orders for all except "requirements" accounts. He reports to the general credit manager for operations and to the comptroller for credit and collection responsibilities.
2. *Collectors.* There are as many as five collectors responsible for administering collection activities.
3. *Order clerk.* An order clerk logs orders on the order card (see below).
4. *Credit and correspondence clerks.* There are two credit and correspondence clerks who handle special, detailed processing, research, records, and follow-up work not involving invoices.
5. *Office personnel.* The unit has a file clerk and a typist.

[803.2.2] ORDERS. Orders are written in the company's showrooms, at customers' locations, at shows, etc. Order form varies according to division, but generally contains the following information:

1. Customer's name and address.
2. Account number (assigned by the coding department according to shipping point).
3. Account number (a seven-digit number of which the first two are a state code and the other five are the account number itself).
4. Season.
5. Completion date.
6. Date order written.

There follows, of course, a description of the items ordered, pricing, etc.

[803.2.3] ORDER ENTRY. Orders are received by the accounts-receivable department in either one of two forms: (1) keypunched and batched according to division for entry into the computer, or (2) written out in longhand, in which case they must be keypunched in the accounts-receivable department itself. Orders are then batch-entered into the computer, which generates an "accounts-receivable register," containing the following data:

1. Account number.
2. Account name.
3. Division.
4. Invoice number.

5. Invoice date.
6. Dating code.
7. Entry code.
8. Number of pieces ordered.
9. Merchandise amount.
10. Freight charge.
11. Accounts-receivable amount.
12. Discount amount.
13. Net amount.

[803.2.4]   CREDIT PROCESSING: OLD ACCOUNT. The order is transmitted to the credit department where the following procedures are followed if the order is from an established account.

1. *Order logged on master order card.* The order clerk records the following information on the customer's master order card (cards are filed alphabetically by state).
   a. Date order was written.
   b. Divisional code.
   c. Number of pieces.
   d. Approximate dollar amount.
   e. Completion date.
2. *Automatic approval of requirements accounts.* The order clerk can identify, by means of a classification sheet, requirements accounts. These orders are automatically approved by the order clerk.
3. *Credit approval by regional credit manager.* Except for requirements accounts, all orders are attached to the master order card and transmitted to the regional credit manager. It is his responsibility to clear them. He follows this procedure.
4. *Retrieval, via cathode-ray tube (CRT), of credit information.* The regional credit manager has a CRT on his desk. By entering the account number, he retrieves the following credit information, which is instantaneously displayed on the screen before him. (see Figure 8.10).
   a. Customer's name and address.
   b. Account number.
   c. Dun & Bradstreet credit rating. (This information is supplied by Dun & Bradstreet on magnetic tape for direct entry into the computer system.)
   d. The credit limit.
   e. The high credit and the date when it was reached.
   f. The amount and date of the most recent payment check.
   g. An eighteen-month history of the account.
5. *Retrieval of open-items screen.* The regional credit manager may also retrieve, via the CRT, an open-items screen, which contains, in addition to identification data, the dollar amount of each singular transaction still open, a transaction code, and an aging.
6. *Credit decision.* Based on his judgment of the account—the status of monies owing, payment history, credit limit, customer requirements, etc.—the regional credit manager will give his decision on

	2346400		*D+B A14* 06/73	HIGH CR	LIMIT REQMTS $134,118 04/73	
DETROIT MICH	48226			LAST CHK 09/14/3	$15,954.00	
TOTAL A/R	CURRENT	-30-	-60-	-90-	-120-	-150-
03/72 50,686	45,659	2,863	524	345		1,295
04/72 46,435	43,135	398	1,443	202	42	1,215
05/72 66,248	61,362	1,751	290	1,500	202	1,143
06/72 97,494	95,066	654-	1,567	290	25-	1,250
07/72 82,656	77,855	3,397	700	5-	81	628
08/72 107,983	89,080	15,631	1,830	700	5-	747
09/72 82,816	75,766	4,313	545-	1,840	700	742
10/72 66,568	59,356	3,224	3,403	557-	718	424
11/72 93,632	87,565	1,269	810	3,403	557-	1,142
12/72 57,266	51,015	1,886	433-	810	3,403	585
01/73 62,111	51,667	5,848	217	287-	678	3,988
02/73 59,084	52,071	2,237	3,930	217	287-	916
03/73 127,382	123,809	813	1,168-	3,091	217	620
04/73 84,405	76,355	5,250	8	1,152-	3,130	814
05/73 58,296	52,085	64-	3,453	8	1,152-	3,966
06/73 76,610	74,764	408	2,982-	3,453	8	959
07/73 67,380	60,648	5,361	54-	31	178	1,216
08/73 96,685	93,025	2,937	170-	66-	31	928
ACTUAL 85,880	55,300	27,047	101	754		

FIGURE 8.10. Information Supplied via CRT

the order. If approved, he stamps his approval on the order, and notes this information on the master order card, which is returned to the files. If the order is not approved, he may request payment of past-due balances, may request payment in advance, or take other action deemed necessary to work out a solution satisfactory to the company and the customer.

[803.2.5]   CREDIT PROCESSING: NEW ACCOUNT. If an order received by the credit department is from a new account, the following procedures are followed:

1. *Master order card prepared.* A master order card is prepared for the customer.
2. *Dun & Bradstreet rating requested.* The order clerk telephones Dun & Bradstreet to obtain the latest rating.
3. *Dun & Bradstreet report obtained.* The telephoned request for the rating automatically triggers a report to be sent to this company, under the terms of its contract with D&B.
4. *Credit limit established.* A dollar credit limit is established for the account. This company uses a percentage of net worth as indicated by the D&B estimated financial strength rating plus the

composite credit appraisal rating to determine the credit limit. You should note that this company uses credit limits as guidelines. The company takes into account, moreover, the fact that the credit limits it uses represent a desirable credit limit for one of its customer's suppliers. If this company represents, in fact, several of one customer's suppliers (because the customer buys from several divisions of the company) the amount of credit actually extended may deviate substantially from the actual credit limit established.

5. *If a negative credit situation exists.* If no Dun & Bradstreet information is available for the new account, or if the account has a low estimated financial strength and/or composite credit appraisal rating, the order is held and the letter shown in Figure 8.11 is sent out, marked appropriately. Before canceling the order, the company will send out a second and final copy of this letter if the first one does not produce results.
6. *Order approved.* If the information sought is satisfactory (or the Dun & Bradstreet rating is satisfactory) and the order is in line, the regional credit manager will approve it.

[803.2.6] CASH APPLICATION. This clothing manufacturer uses a very effective cash-application system whose procedures are as follows:

1. *Cash transmittal.* All checks are sent directly to the accounts-receivable department; lock boxes are not used. The check is photocopied and then deposited. Photocopies of the checks are

ACCOUNT NO. [ ] DATE [ ]

Gentlemen:

Thank you for the following order(s), however, we are unable to release your order(s) for shipment because of the reason specified below.

ORDER DATE	DIVISION	QUANTITY	APPROX. AMOUNT	COMPLETION DATE

[ ] At the present time your account is past due, and merchandise cannot be shipped unless your account is current. Please return this letter with your check attached today, to my personal attention, so as not to delay delivery.

[ ] We have been unable to obtain credit information sufficient to grant our regular terms. Please submit a certified financial statement.

[ ] Our Credit Agencies are not recommending your account at the present time, therefore, we cannot ship this merchandise on our regular terms of sale and would appreciate a certified check in advance, mailed to my personal attention.

[ ] Although your account is not past due, it is over the credit line we have established for your account. Please return this letter with your check attached to be applied against open invoices now due, so as not to delay delivery.

Very truly yours,

CREDIT AND COLLECTION MANAGER

FIGURE 8.11

Letter Explaining Held Shipment

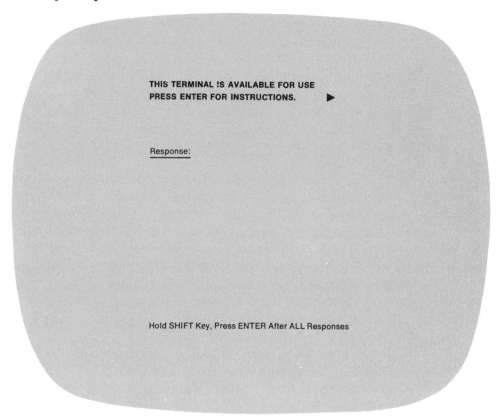

FIGURE 8.12. CRT Screen

sent to CRT operators for cash application, together with bank tapes (which list checks individually). The checks are batched and identified by state, cash date, and a batch number.

2. *Batch entry.* The CRT operator enters the batches in the steps listed below. Her instructions appear on the CRT screen as well as the results of her operations. Examples of the CRT screen readings (and responses) are presented in Figure 8.12.

   a. *Terminal availability.* The first "screen" indicates that the CRT terminal is available for use.

   b. *Option selection.* The CRT operator selects the operation she is going to perform, in this case "batch entry."

   c. *Batch entry.* The CRT operator then supplies this information:
      (1) Operator number.
      (2) State code.
      (3) Application (in this case cash).
      (4) Date.
      (5) Batch number.
      (6) Batch amount.

   d. *Check entry.* Next, the CRT operator enters the customer's check number and amount for each check of the batch.

   e. *Account identification.* Once all checks have been entered, the first will reappear on the screen for account identification. The account can be identified by

(Continued on page 215.)

```
B 101

SELECT OPTION:                                          FORMAT:
    1. BATCH RETRIEVAL
        OPERATOR NUMBER
        BATCH DATE (MM/DD/Y),
        BATCH NUMBER ..............................1AA, MM/DD/Y, NNN
    2. BATCH ENTRY .................................2
    3. CREDIT INQUIRIES
        OPERATOR NUMBER .........................3AA
    4. RECONCILIATIONS
        OPERATOR NUMBER
        BATCH DATE (MM/DD/Y),
        BATCH NUMBER ............................4AA, MM/DD/Y, NNN ▶


Responses:

101,09/23/0,001 (For VILLAGER Cash, Operator Code must begin with V)


2

301

401,09/23/0,001          (See note above)
```

```
BB01

        1. OPERATOR NUMBER,
        2. STATE CODE,
        3. APPLICATION
            CASH=CA    CREDIT MEMO=CR
        4. DATE (MO/DA/Y),
        5. BATCH NUMBER
        6. BATCH AMOUNT        NOT REQUIRED FOR RE OR SP

    ▶


Response:

10,33,CA,09/23/0,001,100.00
```

FIGURE 8.12. CRT Screen

NA-15

DATE: 09/23/0   BATCH: 1   STATE: NO. OF CHKS: 00   APPLIED: 00

CHECK NUMBER   CHECK AMOUNT $10.00
    ENTER: FORMAT:
        CHECK NO.   NNNNNN

▶

Response:

    000001

BB03

ENTER AMOUNTS FOR DATE 09/23/0   BATCH NO 01
▶ 10.00   20.00   30.00   40.00&!

Response:

    See above.

    END key (&) is used only after all check amounts have been entered.
    Enter only 1 line of amounts at a time, if there are more lines to enter, do not press END key.

FIGURE 8.12. CRT Screen

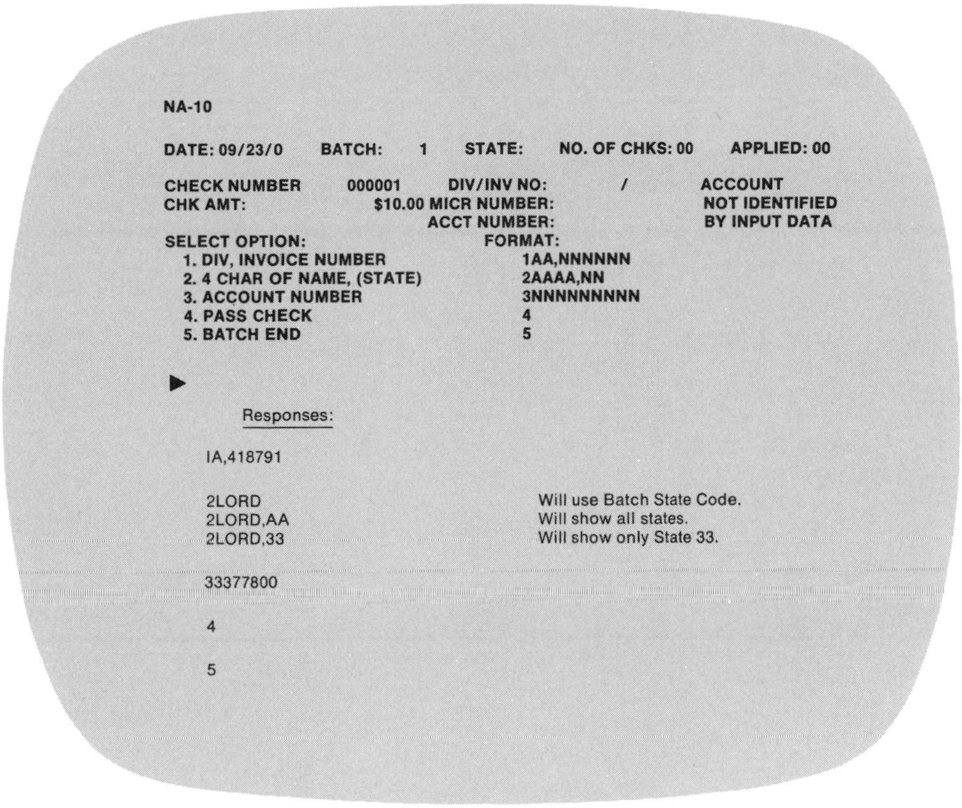

NA-10

DATE: 09/23/0   BATCH: 1   STATE: NO. OF CHKS: 00   APPLIED: 00

CHECK NUMBER   000001   DIV/INV NO: /   ACCOUNT
CHK AMT: $10.00 MICR NUMBER: NOT IDENTIFIED
                              ACCT NUMBER: BY INPUT DATA
SELECT OPTION: FORMAT:
  1. DIV, INVOICE NUMBER   1AA,NNNNNN
  2. 4 CHAR OF NAME, (STATE)   2AAAA,NN
  3. ACCOUNT NUMBER   3NNNNNNNNN
  4. PASS CHECK   4
  5. BATCH END   5

▶

         Responses:

    IA,418791

    2LORD   Will use Batch State Code.
    2LORD,AA   Will show all states.
    2LORD,33   Will show only State 33.

    33377800

    4

    5

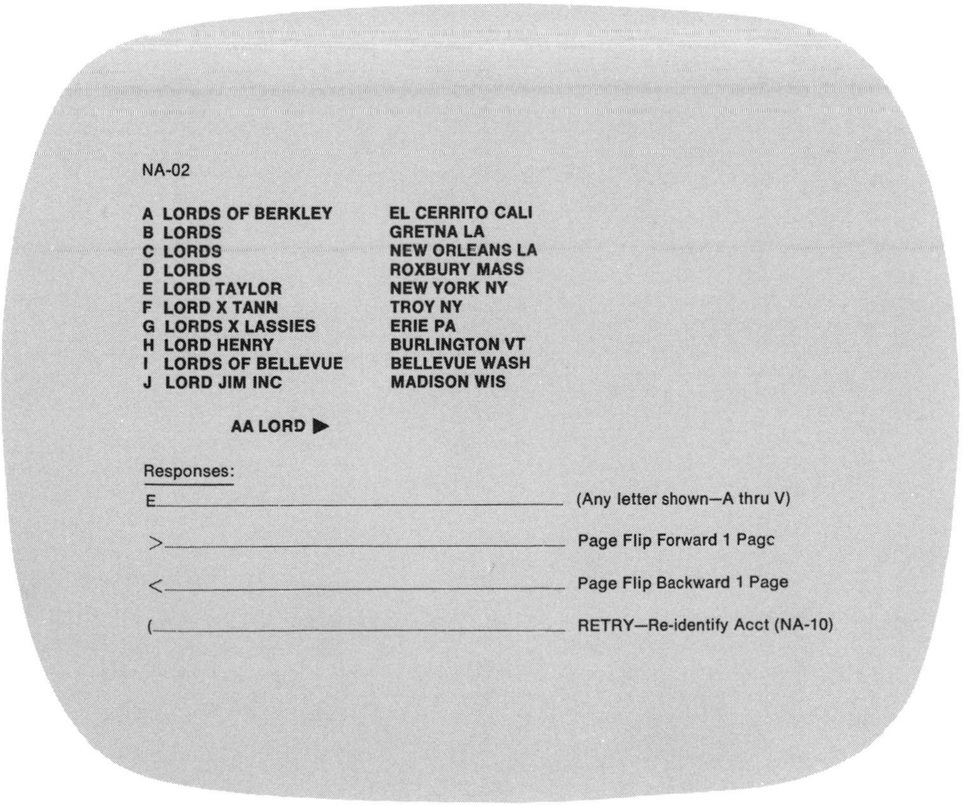

NA-02

A LORDS OF BERKLEY   EL CERRITO CALI
B LORDS   GRETNA LA
C LORDS   NEW ORLEANS LA
D LORDS   ROXBURY MASS
E LORD TAYLOR   NEW YORK NY
F LORD X TANN   TROY NY
G LORDS X LASSIES   ERIE PA
H LORD HENRY   BURLINGTON VT
I LORDS OF BELLEVUE   BELLEVUE WASH
J LORD JIM INC   MADISON WIS

         AA LORD ▶

Responses:
E_____ (Any letter shown—A thru V)

>_____ Page Flip Forward 1 Page

<_____ Page Flip Backward 1 Page

(_____ RETRY—Re-identify Acct (NA-10)

FIGURE 8.12. CRT Screen

NA-11

DATE: 09/23/0   BATCH: 001   STATE:
CHK NO: 000001
CHK AMT: $10.00

DIV/INV NO: /
MICR NUMBER:
ACCT NUMBER: 3377800

LORD TAYLOR
424 5TH AVE
NEW YORK NY

SELECT OPTION: FORMAT:
  1 (DIV) 1AA
  2 DIV, INV NO1, INV NO2, ...2AA, NNNNNN, NNNNNN
  4 PASS CHECK OR 5 BATCH END ....4 OR 5
  6 TRANSFER 6
  7 WORKSHEET REQUEST 7
  8 DIV, (ON ACCOUNT) 8AA
▶
Responses:

1_____   Select all Divisions
1@_____   Select all Divisions—Allow No Discount
1A_____   Select only Division A
1A@_____   Select only Division A—Allow No Discount
2A,055772,418791,003824,003826
4
5
6
7
8A

PI-01

A	055772	A	U	199.00	08	15.92	183.09
B	418791	A	A	14.75	08	1.18	13.57
C	003824	A	B	14.75	08	1.18	13.57
D	003826	A	B	184.04	08	14.72	169.32
▶				10.00—	14.54	1.16	3.38

Responses:

; _____	ACCEPT Key—Zero balances only.
: _____	Write off difference
:/x _____	Write off difference with Transaction Code.
:A/T or :A/T_____	Write off to Div with Transaction Code.
?B/200/M _____	Invoice Charge Back—Against Item B.

General Charge Backs. (All Paid Items Same Div)

?O _____	Entire difference
?O/B _____	Entire difference—Code B
?O/100.00/E _____	$100.00, Code E
?O/100.00?E/123456 ___	$100.00, Code E, With Claim No.
?O/100.00-/E/123456/050 ___	$100.00cr, Code E, With Claim No., 5% Disc.

General Charge Backs (Mixed Divisions Paid)

?O/B/A1_____	Entire Difference, Code B, Div A1
?O/25.00/C/A1_____	$25.00, Code C, Div A1
?O/25.00/C/A1/123456 ___	$25.00, Code C, Div A1, With Claim No.
?O/25.00/C/A1/123456/080 ___	$25.00, Code C, Div A1, With Claim No., 8% Disc.

$C _____	Delete Item C
+_____	On Acct Key
+B _____	On Acct Key—Div B
)_____	Resume Key—Go to OI-01
(_____	Retry Key—Eliminate all Key Offs
*_____	Cancel—Re-identify Acct (NA-10)
>_____	Page Flip Forward—1 Page
<_____	Page Flip Backward—1 Page

FIGURE 8.12. CRT Screen

(1) Division, invoice number.

(2) First four characters of the name, plus the state.

(3) Account number.

f. *Account identification by characters of name.* If the operator has chosen to identify the account by the first four characters of the name, all possibilities (and their states) are flashed on the screen. The operator then selects the proper account.

g. *Check application.* The check must be applied on account, against a divisional invoice or against open items. If the check is applied against the invoice number, the "paid items" screen will appear. This shows the invoice number, division code, entry code, the gross amount, the percentage of discount, the actual discount, and the net amount. This must coincide with the check total or the difference must be reconciled (through charge-backs or some other means).

[803.2.7]   COLLECTION ACTIVITIES. This company pursues collections vigorously according to the following procedures.

1. *Statements.* Monthly statements are generated by the computer and mailed to customers. This company has found that this is an effective incentive to payment.

2. *Weekly aged trial-balance.* A weekly aged trial balance is prepared and distributed to the collection clerks, who are responsible for knowing the status of the accounts assigned to them. By manually going through this trial balance, they will know the appropriate action to be taken for that date.

3. *Dunning letters.* This company has two dunning letters, one for accounts that are thirty days past due, the other for accounts more than thirty days past due. These are computer-generated.

4. *Telephone.* When an account becomes sixty days past due, collectors telephone to find out why and to solicit payment.

5. *Collection agencies.* If the account becomes ninety days past due, shipments are held. If the regional credit manager decides that an account is uncollectible by him, he passes it on to the comptroller, who will decide upon further action. This could mean that the account is placed for collection with a collection agency or attorneys.

[803.2.8]   CREDIT-DEPARTMENT REPORTS. The following reports are prepared for the use of the credit department.

1. Weekly aged trial balance.

2. Weekly order hold report.

3. Aged summary trial balance (week ending).

4. Aged summary trial balance (totals of invoices).

[803.2.9]   CREDIT REPORTS TO FINANCIAL MANAGEMENT. The following reports are used by financial management to evaluate the credit department's performance.

1. Summary aged trial balance.

2. Summary totals by type of transaction.

3. Summary totals by credit unit.

CHAPTER 9

FINANCIAL ANALYSIS

[900]   **FINANCIAL ANALYSIS.** Credit managers undertake an analysis of their customers' finances as part of their effort to determine whether customers will have enough money to pay their trade obligations when they fall due. Financial analysis, therefore, is a part of the larger investigation of a customer's ability to raise sufficient funds and includes an analysis of industry and general economic conditions, the legal composition of the business, and those other topics of investigation discussed in Chapter 5. Financial analysis, moreover, complements character analysis, which should reveal whether customers have the intention of paying their bills if they have the money.

     The idea of futurity is important in financial analysis. Credit managers deal with statements, profit-and-loss figures, and other records of a company's past performance. Yet it is the short-term future prospects that interest the trade creditor most. In dealing with this financial information, the credit manager must evaluate it only as it can indicate future payment ability. This chapter is designed to tell you how a set of figures from the past can help you predict future financial condition.

[901]   **INTERPRETATION OF STATEMENTS.** Credit managers most often deal with financial statements of companies, and by this we mean the balance sheet.

[901.1]   **Definition of a Financial Statement (Balance Sheet).** A balance sheet is an organized presentation of a company's financial position as represented by the disposition of its assets, liabilities, and net worth as of a certain date. For an example of a financial-statement (balance sheet) form used by Dun & Bradstreet see Figure 9.1.

[901.2]   **Date of Financial Statement.** The date when a financial statement is drawn is of considerable importance. Financial statements are usually drawn up on a yearly basis, with December 31 the most common closing

INFORMATION FURNISHED TO
Dun & Bradstreet, Inc.

STATEMENT FORM C
(Please use the reverse side of this form for submitting important supplementary details)

As a Basis for Credit, Insurance, Marketing and other business decisions by its customers

NOTE: Transmittal of financial statements on this particular form is optional. Financial statements on your own stationery or on that of your accountant will be equally useful. The full report of your accountant is preferred.

Business Name Used for Buying ....
Other Name or Style Used, if any ....
Street Address .... Mail Address ....
City .... State .... ZIP .... County ....
Line of Business .... Telephone (include Area Code) ....

FINANCIAL CONDITION AT .... 19... ☐ Fiscal ☐ Interim

ASSETS

CASH .... $
GOVERNMENT SECURITIES ....
MARKETABLE SECURITIES ....
NOTES RECEIVABLE (Customers) ....
ACCOUNTS RECEIVABLE (Customers)
  Not Due .... $
  Past Due ....
  Less Reserves ......
INVENTORY
  Finished Goods .... $
  In Process ....
  Raw Materials ....
OTHER CURRENT ASSETS
.... $
  TOTAL CURRENT ....
FIXED ASSETS
  Land .... $
  Buildings ....
  Machinery & Equipment..
  Furniture & Fixtures ..
  Less Depreciation ..
INVESTMENTS—RELATED CONCERNS
  Stocks & Bonds .... $
  Loans & Advances ......
  Accounts Receivable ....
INVESTMENTS—OTHER
.... $
MISCELLANEOUS RECEIVABLES
  Officers & Employees ... $
DEPOSITS ....
SUPPLIES ....
  TOTAL .... $

LIABILITIES

DUE BANKS
  Unsecured .... $
  Secured ....
NOTES PAYABLE–TRADE ACCEPTANCES
  Merchandise ....
  Machinery & Equipment..
ACCOUNTS PAYABLE
  Not Due .... $
  Past Due ....
ACCRUALS
  Salaries & Wages ...... $
TAXES (Except Federal income)
FEDERAL INCOME TAXES ....
DUE RELATED CONCERNS
  Loans & Advances ...... $
  Merchandise ....
LOANS & ADVANCES
  From Officers .... $
LONG TERM LIABILITIES—DUE WITHIN 1 YEAR
  Real Estate Mortgages ... $
  TOTAL CURRENT ....
LONG TERM LIABILITIES—DUE AFTER 1 YEAR
  Real Estate Mortgages ... $
PREFERRED STOCK
COMMON STOCK
CAPITAL—PAID IN SURPLUS ....
EARNED SURPLUS—RETAINED EARNINGS
NET WORTH (Proprietor or Partners) .....
  TOTAL .... $

BASIS OF INVENTORY VALUATION
RECEIVABLES PLEDGED OR DISCOUNTED .... YES ☐ .... NO ☐
CONTINGENT LIABILITIES $ .... (SEE OVER)

ABOVE FIGURES PREPARED BY .... Name .... Independent Accountant Yes ☐ No ☐

SUMMARY STATEMENT OF INCOME

NET SALES $ _____ FROM _____ TO _____
FINAL NET INCOME (LOSS) $ _____
DIVIDENDS OR WITHDRAWALS $ _____

BUSINESS NAME ....
SIGNED BY ....
TITLE .... DATE ....

SG-10172011S1

FIGURE 9.1

Financial Statement Form Used by Dun & Bradstreet, Inc.

STATEMENT OF INCOME

From _____ 19 ___ TO _____ 19 ____

NET SALES .... $
COST OF GOODS SOLD ....
GROSS PROFIT (LOSS) ON SALES
EXPENSES
  Selling .... $
  General ....
  Administrative ....
NET INCOME (LOSS) ON SALES..........
OTHER INCOME
....
OTHER EXPENSES
.... $
NET INCOME (LOSS) BEFORE TAXES
  Federal Income Tax ..... $
  Other Taxes on Income..
FINAL NET INCOME (LOSS) ....

SURPLUS OR NET WORTH RECONCILIATION

SURPLUS OR NET WORTH AT START..... $
ADDITIONS
....
DEDUCTIONS
  Final Net Loss .... $
  Dividends ....
  Withdrawals ....
SURPLUS OR NET WORTH AT END ...... $

When financial statements prepared or certified to by independent accountants are transcribed to this form, indicate whether the statements transcribed are identical with the accountant's statement(s) Yes ☐ No ☐. If No, please describe adjustments. Attach copy of accountant's certificate. ☐

THE FOREGOING STATEMENTS, IF CONSOLIDATED, INCLUDE THE FIGURES OF WHAT OTHER CONCERNS? ....

ANNUAL RENT $ .... LEASE EXPIRES .... 19 .... FIRE INSURANCE ON: Merchandise $ .... Machinery & Equipment $ .... Furniture & Fixtures $ .... Bldgs. $ .... IS EXTENDED COVERAGE CARRIED? ....
IS BUSINESS INTERRUPTION (Use & Occupancy) INSURANCE CARRIED? ..... ARE OFFICERS AND EMPLOYEES BONDED? .....
BASIS OF VALUATION OF: Fixed Assets .... Marketable Securities—Investments ....
ARE LIABILITIES SECURED IN ANY MANNER? Yes ☐ No ☐ If Yes, describe the security and the manner of payment ....
STATE AMOUNT OF EACH CONTINGENT LIABILITY: (Describe) ....

REAL ESTATE—LOCATION	Title—In Name Of	Value Mkt. ☐ Cost ☐	Mortgage	Due Date	Net Income—R. E.
....		$	$		$
....					
....					

NUMBER OF EMPLOYEES	FULL TIME	PART TIME	COMMISSION SALESMEN
HEADQUARTERS			
BRANCH AT			
BRANCH AT			

IF THERE ARE ADDITIONAL BRANCHES, PLEASE ATTACH LIST GIVING LOCATIONS AND NUMBER OF EMPLOYEES.

Full Names of all Officers, Directors, Partners or Proprietor. If Partners, state if General, Special or Limited FULL NAMES AND TITLES	% of Ownership	Year of Birth	Marital Status	Amount of Life Insurance Carried for the Benefit of the Business
A.				$
B.				
C.				
D.				
E.				

Printed in U.S.A

date. Statements are sometimes provided that are not for the fiscal closing. It may even be that a December 31 statement is an interim one. It is important to determine this since there may be significant fiscal adjustments that have not been made, in which case the net worth will be overstated. You must be aware of what seasonal period a customer is in when the statement is drawn up in order to understand correctly the figures. You should pay particular attention to the date of the statements when you are comparing more than one.

[901.3]   **Veracity of a Financial Statement.** Although they are supposed to represent the true financial picture of a firm, financial statements are subject to any sort of deliberate or accidental misrepresentation. Your analysis of financial-statement items will help you determine whether the financial statement is true, but there are other tools to assist you in verifying a financial statement.

[901.3.1]   AUDITED AND UNAUDITED FIGURES. Not every financial statement is a presentation of financial facts that has been prepared and checked by professional, independent accountants. Those statements audited by professional CPA's are more likely to be reliable than the figures prepared and checked by the company itself.

[901.3.2]   AUDITOR'S OPINION. Pay particular attention to the auditor's certificate when you have audited figures at your disposal. Not every audit is carried out with the same independence and with the same degree of thoroughness of verification. The auditor's or accountant's certificate will note any limitations—such as the auditor's inability to take a physical count of the inventory or a reliance upon the firm's unchecked book figures—imposed upon him when making the audit. You should determine how these limitations will affect the veracity and usefulness of the statement.

[901.3.3]   CHECKING THE FIGURES. Whether you are analyzing estimates, unaudited figures, or audited figures, you can follow these procedures to check the accuracy of the figures.

1. *Check the sales.* One of the best checks of the balance-sheet figures is the sales figure. Sales give a quick check against the reasonableness of certain assets and liabilities. Knowledge of industry norms for ratios will be useful in this regard.
2. *Check present values against the purchase price.* Sometimes a man who has just bought a business will say his fixtures are worth $8,000 and inventory $6,000. He shows no liabilities. You could remark that $14,000 was a high price for the store. The owner replies, "Not at all. I got a bargain. I paid only $9,000." Then the figures can be presented on the basis of the *actual* price paid for the fixtures and merchandise together with comments about the value of the assets.
3. *Check values against insurance.* If assets are reported at one figure and the insurance carried on them is shown at a very different figure, this could be your clue that the assets are inflated, or, conversely, that insurance coverage is inadequate.
4. *Check present net worth with starting capital.* Present net worth should be reasonably higher (or lower) than the starting capital

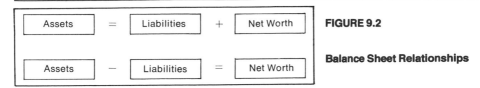

FIGURE 9.2

Balance Sheet Relationships

(or previous net worth). Changes should be explainable or accounted for.

5. *Check trade record against reported liabilities.* Find out if obligations as reported by the trade are reasonably close to those shown on the balance sheet.

6. *Check with outside sources.* Previous owners can confirm purchase price and amounts owing. Cash and even merchandise can be confirmed. Evidence of certain debts and secured borrowing arrangements appear as a matter of public record.

[901.4]   **Balance-Sheet Relationships.**

[901.4.1]   ASSETS AND LIABILITIES. In a balance sheet, all assets are listed on one side, and all liabilities are listed on the other. The total assets minus the total liabilities equals the net worth (see Figure 9.2). The total of the current assets minus the total of the current liabilities equals net working capital.

[901.4.2]   EXCHANGING EQUAL VALUES. The mere switching of one asset for another (cash for merchandise, for example) of the same value does not change the total values or the net worth. When an asset is added to one side (merchandise) and an equal liability is created (account payable), there is no change in net worth. This is the application of the rule that an equal amount added to each side of a scale does not change the worth.

[901.4.3]   CHANGING WORTH. When more is added to the assets than to the liabilities, worth goes up. When more is added to the liabilities than to the assets, worth goes down. It is usually the income and expense transactions reflected in the profit and loss statement that actually change net worth.

[901.5]   **Owners' Equities and Creditors' Rights.** From a credit standpoint, the important question the credit manager asks is, What "equities" do the owners have and what rights do the creditors have? For example, if a business has $10,000 of assets and creditors are owed $2,000, the creditors have an investment of $2,000 in assets, and the owners have an equity of $8,000. Reverse the picture to show what happens when the creditors have $8,000 in the business. Instead of $5 of assets for each dollar of creditors' money, the "coverage" has dropped to $1.25 (see Figure 9.3).

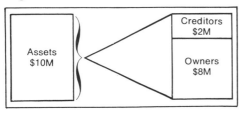
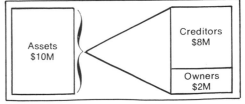

FIGURE 9.3. Composition of Assets

[902]   **ASSET ANALYSIS.** Credit managers analyze the assets of a company primarily to determine its liquidity—the amount of funds it has to pay its trade bills or the ease with which it can convert nonliquid assets to liquid form, voluntarily or by necessity in the case of bankruptcy. Assets appear on the balance sheet in order of descending liquidity; however, we shall discuss assets in this order:

1. Current assets.
2. Fixed Assets.
3. Long-term investments.
4. Intangible assets.
5. Deferred charges and prepaid expenses.
6. Miscellaneous or "other" assets.

[902.1]   **Current Assets.** Current assets are any items of economic value that can be converted to cash within one year or the normal operating cycle of the business. Current assets are frequently classified as "quick" or "liquid" current assets or "slow" current assets. Figure 9.4 shows a classification of assets and liabilities according to whether they are current or non-current (slow). Current assets include the following items:

[902.1.1]   CASH. Cash is money at hand or easily obtained. Cash includes:

1. Money in safes and in the bank.
2. Checks.
3. Money orders.
4. Any other instruments received as cash by a bank.

Cash does not include:

1. Postdated checks.
2. I.O.U.'s.

An abnormally large cash balance (especially if carried as cash on hand and not in the bank) may include I.O.U.'s and postdated checks and you should be alert for this possibility. In addition, you should make the distinction between the following:

1. *Foreign and domestic currency.* If a company carries part of its cash balance in a foreign currency, you must be aware of what the exchange rates are—or are likely to be—in order to properly evaluate this asset.
2. *Restricted and unrestricted cash.* Occasionally, a firm will carry as cash funds that have been earmarked or otherwise set aside for some special purpose. Such assets are not properly classified as cash but, whatever the classification, you should treat them as a slow or non-current asset.

[902.1.2]   MARKETABLE SECURITIES. Marketable securities can be classified according to their liquidity or their "nearness to cash" as follows:

1. *U.S. government securities* (including bonds, Treasury notes, etc.). Such government securities are considered just as liquid as cash by most credit analysts and are accepted as listed on financial statements. They often represent a wise investment of corporate excess funds.

ASSETS	CURRENT	NON-CURRENT	INTANGIBLE
Accounts Receivable			
Customers (Less Reserves)	X		
From Affiliate, if concern is in healthy shape and accounts are being paid on regular terms	X		
From Affiliate, if concern is in unhealthy shape, or accounts are not being paid on regular terms		X	
From Directors		X	
From Employees		X	
From Officers		X	
From Partners		X	
From Subsidiary, if concern is in healthy shape, and receivables are being paid on regular terms	X		
From Subsidiary, if concern is in unhealthy shape, or accounts are not being paid on regular terms		X	
Miscellaneous		X	
Other		X	
Advances			
For Merchandise	X		
For Mining Royalties		X	
For Traveling		X	
To Affiliate		X	
To Employees		X	
To Subsidiary		X	
Advertising			X
Assets, Miscellaneous		X	
Automobiles		X	
Bills Receivable (Same as Accounts Receivable)			
Blending Rights			X
Bond Discount			X
Bonds	X		
Bookplates			
At Cost			X
Metal Value		X	
Bottling Rights			X
Brands, Trade			X
Building and Loan Shares	X		
Buildings		X	
Canadian Government Securities	X		

LIABILITIES	CURRENT	NON-CURRENT	NET WORTH
Accounts Payable			
For Merchandise	X		
For Services	X		
To Directors	X		
To Employees	X		
To Officers	X		
To Partners	X		
To Related Concerns	X		
Sundry	X		
Accruals			
Commission	X		
Interest	X		
Other Expenses	X		
Pay Rolls	X		
Rent	X		
Salaries	X		
Taxes	X		
Wages	X		
Advances from Customers	X		
Bills Payable (Same as Notes Payable)			
Bonds			
Amount Maturing within One Year	X		
Amount Maturing after One Year		X	
No Definite Maturity Date	X		
Capital (If Partnership or Proprietorship)			X
Capital Stock			
A, B, or C Stock			X
Common Stock			X
Minority Interest		X	
Preferred or Preference Stock			X
Capital Surplus			X
Chattel Mortgage	X		
Common Stock			X
Conditional Bill of Sale	X		
Contingencies, Reserve for			
Contracts Payable	X		
Credit Balance	X		
Customers' Deposits	X		
Debentures			
Amount Maturing within One Year	X		
Amount Maturing after One Year		X	

FIGURE 9.4. Guide to Classification of Assets and Liabilities.
Source: *Practical Financial Statement Analysis* by Roy A. Foulke

ASSETS	CURRENT	NON-CURRENT	INTANGIBLE	LIABILITIES	CURRENT	NON-CURRENT	NET WORTH
Cash				Deferred Credit or Income		X	
In Bank	X			Deferred Taxes on Income		X	
In Closed Bank		X		Deferred Income		X	
In Sinking Fund		X		Deposits			
On Hand	X			From Customers	X		
Restricted		X		From Employees	X		
Cash Value of Life Insurance		X		From Officers	X		
Catalogues			X	From Salesmen	X		
Claims for Refunds under				Depreciation (Deduct from			
Carry-back Provisions of				Related Asset)			
Tax Law	X			Dividends Payable	X		
Coal Lands		X		Donated Surplus			X
Contracts			X	Due Factor	X		
Copyrights			X				
Debenture Discount			X	Earned Surplus			X
Debtors, Sundry		X		Earnings			
Deferred Charges (See also				Employed in Business			X
Prepaid items)		X		Reinvested			X
Deficit (Profit and Loss)			X	Retained			X
Delivery Equipment		X		Employees' Deposits	X		
Deposits							
With Factor	X						
With Mutual Insurance							
Company		X		Federal Income Taxes	X		
With Workmen's Compensation				Funded Debt			
Commission		X		Amount Maturing within			
Designs			X	One Year	X		
Development Expense			X	Amount Maturing after			
Dies			X	One Year		X	
Docks		X					
Drawings			X				
Emergency Plant Facilities		X		Income Deferred		X	
Equipment		X		Income Taxes	X		
Experimental Expense			X				
Exploration Expense			X				
Federal Government Securities				Loan from Factor	X		
(see United States Government				Loans Payable (Same as			
Securities).				Notes Payable)			
Financing Expense			X				
Fixed Assets		X					
Fixtures		X		Minority Interest		X	
Foreign Assets—Restricted		X		Mortgages			
Formulas			X	Amount Maturing within			
Franchises			X	One Year	X		
Furniture		X		Amount Maturing after			
Good Will			X	One Year		X	
Government Securities				No Definite Maturity Date	X		
(see United States Government				Net Worth (If Partnerhip			
Securities)				or Proprietorship)			X

FIGURE 9.4. Guide to Classification of Assets and Liabilities (cont.)

ASSETS	CURRENT	NON-CURRENT	INTANGIBLE	LIABILITIES	CURRENT	NON-CURRENT	NET WORTH
Improvements		X		Notes Payable			
Insurance Deposits		X		For Merchandise	X		
Insurance Premium, Prepaid		X		To Banks	X		
Interest Accrued		X		To Individuals	X		
Inventory				To Others	X		
Advances on Merchandise	X			To Partners	X		
Finished Goods	X			To Stockholders	X		
In Transit	X			Term Loans (Same as Bonds)			
On Consignment	X						
Raw Materials	X						
Supplies		X					
Work in Process	X	X		Officers' Deposits	X		
Investments		X					
Investments in and Advances to Subsidiaries and Affiliates		X					
				Paid-in Surplus			X
				Payrolls Accrued	X		
Land		X		Preferred or Preference Stock			
Lasts			X	Provision for Income Taxes	X		
Leasehold Improvements		X					
Leaseholds			X				
Licenses			X				
Life Insurance Cash Surrender Value	X	X		Reinvested Earnings			
Listed Securities	X			Rent, Unpaid	X		
Loan to Affiliate		X		Retained Earnings			
Loan to Subsidiary		X		Reserves			
				Bad Debts (Deduct from Accounts Receivable)			
Machinery		X		Contingencies			
Magazine Titles			X	Depletion (Deduct from Related Assets)			
Mailing Lists			X				
Maintenance Materials and Parts		X		Depreciation (Deduct from Related Assets)			
Marketable Securities	X						
Merchandise (see Inventory)				Discounts (Deduct from Accounts Receivable)			
Mineral Land		X					
Mines		X		Inventory Adjustments (Deduct from Related Assets)			
Miscellaneous Assets		X					
Miscellaneous Receivables		X		Obsolescence (Deduct from Related Asset)			
Models			X				
Mortgages Receivable		X		Retirement Capital Stock	X		
Municipal Bonds	X			Self-insurance		X	
Municipal Bonds in Default		X		Taxes	X		
				Unexpired Subscriptions		X	
Notes Receivable (Same as Accounts Receivable)				Unrealized Profits		X	
Organization Expense			X	Salaries	X		
Packaging and Shipping Items		X					
Patents			X				
Patterns			X				
Pension Funds		X					

FIGURE 9.4. Guide to Classification of Assets and Liabilities (cont.)

ASSETS	CURRENT	NON-CURRENT	INTANGIBLE	LIABILITIES	CURRENT	NON-CURRENT	NET WORTH
Plant		X		Salesmen's Deposits	X		
Prepaid Items				Sales Lien	X		
Insurance		X		Separation Allowances	X		
Rent		X		Shareholders' Equity			X
Royalties		X		Social Security Taxes	X		
Supplies		X		Stock			X
Taxes		X		Stock Subscriptions	X		
Processes			X	Stockholders' Equity			X
Profit and Loss (Deficit)			X	Subordinated Debentures			
Property		X		(Same as Debentures)			
				Sundry Accounts Payable	X		
Quarries		X		Surplus Account			
				Capital Surplus			X
Real Estate		X		Deficit (Deduct)			X
Refundable Federal Taxes				Donated			X
on Income	X			Earned			X
Research Expense			X	Paid-In			X
Revenue Stamps	X			Profit and Loss—If Red (Deduct)			X
Rights, Publishing			X	Surplus			X
Royalty, Prepaid		X		Surplus from Appreciation			X
				Undivided Profits			X
Savings and Loan Shares	X						
Securities		X					
Ships		X		Taxes, Unpaid	X		
Sight Drafts Outstanding	X			Withheld at Source	X		
Sinking Fund		X		Term Loans (Same as Bonds)			
State Bonds	X			Trade Acceptances Payable	X		
Stocks and Bonds		X					
Stock Subscriptions			X				
Subscription Lists			X	Unearned Income		X	
Sundry Debtors			X				
Surplus (Deficit)			X				
				Wages, Unpaid	X		
Timber (Standing or Uncut)		X					
Tools		X					
Tracings			X				
Trade Acceptances	X						
Trade Brand			X				
Trade-marks			X				
Trade Name			X				
Treasury Bonds		X					
Treasury Stock			X				
Trucks		X					
Unamortized Mortgage or Bond Expense			X				
United States Government Securities	X						
Agencies of the Federal Government	X						
Unlisted Securities		X					
Vessels		X					

FIGURE 9.4. Guide to Classification of Assets and Liabilities (cont.)

2. *State and municipal securities.* These securities, which take the form of bonds, are next in liquidity to U.S. obligations. Because defaults have been known in the past, however, credit analysts generally do not consider them as liquid as cash.

3. *Corporate securities.* Corporate securities can be the source of additional profits for the company under investigation—or a source of considerable loss. Although investments in corporate securities are usually carried on balance sheets at their cost, you must determine the market value to properly evaluate this asset. Conservative credit analysts carry corporate securities at the lower of cost or market. If a company's investment of excess funds in corporate securities in any one company is larger than the norm, you should be alert that this may represent an eventual attempt to take over that company or at least to control its activities. In such a case, the subject concern would be even more reluctant to sell its investment in order to pay off trade debt promptly. Abnormally large investment in corporate securities—no matter how distributed, should be the cause of additional investigation on your part.

[902.1.3]   ACCOUNTS RECEIVABLE. Accounts receivable should be classified and analyzed as follows:

1. *Trade accounts receivable.* This item represents amounts of money due from customers as a result of the sale of a company's goods or services. It should be the largest entry under accounts receivable and generally represents one of the largest asset entries. When examining trade accounts receivable, you should be alert to the following:

   a. *That they are not pledged.* Companies may pledge their trade accounts receivable to secure their bank or other debts. If this is the case, your protection as a creditor may be small.

   b. *That trade accounts receivable are listed after a reasonable deduction has been made for bad debts and for anticipated discounts.* Credit Research Foundation publishes studies of the bad-debt reserve ratios in major American industries. The ratio is derived by dividing the reserve for doubtful accounts by the domestic trade receivables balance. If the company you are investigating has not made sufficient provision, you must revise the figures before evaluating its financial position.

   c. *That the remaining receivables are good.* An aging of accounts receivable is helpful in making this determination. If you know the selling terms of your customer, you can calculate how many of his receivables are overdue and by how much. In addition, you should be aware of any adverse conditions existing within the industry or region of your customer's clients that could affect collections.

   d. *That only those installment receivables due within one year are included in the current accounts-receivable item.*

2. *Trade acceptances.* If it is the custom of the industry to require trade acceptances, then this item represents a very liquid asset. If, however, industry practice is to sell goods on open-account terms, then trade acceptances generally represent the effort of a company to ensure payment from a doubtful risk. In this case, the value of the asset is in doubt.

3. *Accounts receivable from subsidiaries or affiliated companies.* If these receivables are in fact current assets, they must represent amounts owing from the sale of merchandise and the amounts must be collected within (or approaching) the usual selling terms of the company. Otherwise, this item could represent advances, loans, or goods delivered on consignment and should not be considered current.

4. *Notes for merchandise sold.* Notes for merchandise sold are generally used in installment sales, in which case only those falling due within a year should be considered current assets; but they may be used to ensure payment from a past-due account. In this case, the value of the entry is questionable and should be investigated thoroughly before considering it as listed.

[902.1.4]   MERCHANDISE. Merchandise presents many problems for the credit analyst who is attempting to evaluate it accurately. He must attempt to appraise not only the reliability of the count, the inventory's condition, and value, but he must also determine whether the amount of inventory shown is normal for the season and the industry. Nevertheless, this work must be done well because of the importance that merchandise has on the determination of net profit and creditor protection.

1. *Classification of inventory.* Inventory consists of different items according to whether the company is a manufacturer or a wholesaler or retailer. If a wholesaler or retailer, the inventory consists of all the goods that can be sold without further processing plus supplies used in shipping. If the subject of your investigation is a manufacturer, his inventory is made up of three different kinds of goods (plus shipping supplies), each of which has a different value from the credit point of view. These are:

   a. *Raw materials.* Raw materials are traditionally considered the most valuable item in inventory because they can usually be sold easily at their evaluated price in the event of liquidation.

   b. *Works-in-progress.* These are considered to be the least valuable item in merchandise because additional labor must be performed and a sales effort made before these goods can be converted to cash. For this reason, credit analysts often evaluate this item lower than it is carried in the financial statement.

   c. *Finished goods.* The value of the finished goods varies greatly according to many different circumstances. If the goods are popular products in good condition that can be easily and readily sold, then the credit analyst might be justified in according them the value indicated in the financial statement.

If, on the other hand, the goods are of questionable salability or are in less than perfect condition, then they may be carried at too high a value in the financial statement.

It is up to you, as the credit analyst, to determine the true value of each inventory item. Your valuation of inventory should take into consideration the cost of selling this inventory, should that be necessary. Remember, too, that the final sale price of even finished goods in excellent condition may be considerably lower in a forced sale than if they had been sold regularly through normal channels.

2. *Inventory counts.* When examining the merchandise figure, be sure to take into account how the inventory was taken. Actual physical counts carried out by respected auditors are the most reliable and are definitely preferable to perpetual inventory systems. Estimates presented by the company may be of little value. Accountants' estimates may be a true reflection of inventory but even these should be considered most conservatively by credit analysts. It goes without saying that merchandise on consignment should not be included in the inventory figure as this is not an asset of the company.

3. *Valuation of inventory.* The valuation of the inventory is, of course, the most critical consideration of the credit analyst. From his point of view, the inventory should be valued at the *lower of cost or market.* This is especially true when the FIFO method of inventory valuation (described below) is used. Nevertheless, there are many different ways of evaluating the cost of inventory on hand that determine whether the cost value is likely to be higher or lower than the market value. You must be aware of which method has been used in the preparation of the financial statement and how the final figure compares with your appraisal of the value of the inventory in the current market. The most common methods of inventory valuation are described below:

a. *First-In-First-Out (FIFO).* Under this method, the accountant assumes that inventory items bought first are those that are sold first. As a result, the entire inventory is valued at the cost of the most recent purchases. When prices rise, the result is that the value of the inventory increases. Profit calculated under this system is higher because the cost of goods sold is lower. The opposite, of course, is true when prices are falling.

b. *Last-In-First-Out (LIFO).* Here the accountant prepares the figures on the assumption that the last articles bought are the first ones sold (or used). Depending on how recent the figures are, this could mean that the inventory is valued at the current value. Because there is a base inventory whose valuation is not affected by recent purchases, however, in periods of rising prices, the inventory valuation tends to be low. Because recent history shows nothing but rising prices, this method of inventory valuation tends to be the most conservative and is thus preferred by credit analysts. In periods of falling prices, however, remember that the inventory valuation may be high.

c. *Base-stock.* This method resembles LIFO in that there is a quantity of inventory that is always carried at the same price regardless of the valuation of later purchases.

d. *Averages.* Some accountants use an average cost of inventory (which can be weighted) to calculate merchandise on hand.

e. *Retail method.* Retailers often use a different method entirely to arrive at the inventory figure. The procedure is as follows: The merchant enters the cost of the merchandise and the selling price of each article of merchandise. At the end of the accounting period, the difference between the sums of these two figures gives the markup or gross profit. After deductions (for discounts, returns, etc.) are made, this percentage is then subtracted from the remaining inventory to arrive at the valuation.

[902.1.5]   TAX REFUNDS. When justified, claims for tax refunds represent a potential current asset. Claims arise, under present law, when a company suffers a loss and claims a tax refund based on taxes paid in the previous three years. Although refunds are generally paid within ninety days after filing the return, disputes can mean delay. As the credit analyst, you must determine whether the claim is justified, or, if it has been disputed, how long the delay might last.

[902.2]   **Fixed Assets.** Fixed assets are tangible materials, goods or services, or land that are used in the production of a company's goods. Land, buildings, or equipment owned by a company but not used in the production of its goods or services should not be listed as fixed assets but as investments. Although fixed assets can have considerable value, they are not ordinarily converted into cash for the payment of trade obligations except in bankruptcies or other cases of financial embarrassment. Fixed assets can add appreciably to the credit risk a company represents but you must evaluate them carefully. Consider the following information:

[902.2.1]   CLASSIFICATION OF FIXED ASSETS. Fixed assets are usually broken down as follows:

1. Real estate.
2. Buildings.
3. Plant equipment.
4. Furniture and fixtures.
5. Other equipment.

[902.2.2]   VALUATION OF FIXED ASSETS. Fixed assets are usually carried on the books at the cost price when purchased. With the exception of land, fixed assets should be regularly and systematically depreciated (see below). You should be aware that historic cost—even depreciated—can be very different from the replacement value in the market. Land, especially, which is not depreciated, can have a value very much larger than what is shown on the financial statement. Factories, on the other hand, may be of no use to anyone if the original owner ceases operation. As a result, proper evaluation of fixed assets is extremely difficult. Sometimes, fixed assets are reappraised upward during an accounting period. This may be the result of careful study by a qualified independent appraiser and, if so, produces a better picture of the assets of a company. Frequently, however, fixed assets may be revalued upward merely to improve the balance sheet of a firm. As a credit analyst, investigate carefully the upward reappraisal of fixed assets. You should be sure, of course, that fixed assets do not have liens upon them or are otherwise pledged and out of reach of general creditors.

[902.2.3]   DEPRECIATION. All fixed assets except land should be systematically depreciated, and depreciation can greatly distort the value of fixed assets. Machinery can be depreciated over a long period of time when its usefulness is much shorter. On the other hand, machinery that is completely depreciated can still be in fine condition for many more years. The rate of depreciation varies according to management philosophy but you would do well to find out what it is.

[902.3]   **Investments.** Investments represent the placement of a company's cash assets in other assets of a permanent nature, or whose yield will occur later than a year from the date of the financial statement.

[902.3.1]   CLASSIFICATION OF INVESTMENTS. Investments include the following items:

1. Investments in subsidiaries or affiliates.
2. Investments in stocks or bonds maturing later than one year from the date of the financial statement.
3. Cash surrender value of life insurance policies.
4. Cash and securities placed in special funds.
5. Fixed assets not used by the business in the production of its goods or services.

[902.3.2]   VALUATION OF INVESTMENTS. The valuation of investments presents certain pitfalls that you should recognize. According to the investment, they are as follows:

1. Investments in subsidiaries can be shown at the cost of acquiring the subsidiary or at its net worth if wholly owned. Cost price is preferred by credit analysts as net worth could be composed of advances from the subject concern itself. Remember that the value of a subsidiary of a company in liquidation can be great but slowly realizable.
2. The cash surrender value of a life insurance policy on a principal of the business is a very liquid asset but one that will not often become available to creditors except in the case of financial embarrassment. Often, moreover, this asset has been pledged as security for a loan.
3. Cash or securities set aside in special funds will generally become available to creditors only in the case of financial difficulty.

[902.4]   **Intangible Assets.**

[902.4.1]   CLASSIFICATION OF INTANGIBLE ASSETS. Intangible assets include the following items:

1. Goodwill.
2. Copyrights and Trademarks.
3. Development costs.

    4. Patents.

    5. Mailing lists and Catalogs.

    6. Treasury Stock.

    7. Formulas and Processes.

    8. Organization Expense.

[902.4.2]   VALUATION OF INTANGIBLE ASSETS. Intangible assets are character-ized by their great value to ongoing concerns and their limited value to firms in bankruptcy. Today, most companies carry intangible assets at an arbitrary dollar amount; whatever the figure, credit analysts should always value them conservatively.

[902.5]   **Prepaid Expenses and Deferred Charges.**

[902.5.1]   CLASSIFICATION OF PREPAID EXPENSES AND DEFERRED CHARGES. Prepaid expenses are business expenses that have been paid in one accounting period but are applicable to a subsequent period. Deferred charges is simply another term for the same thing.

    These assets include:

    1. Prepaid insurance.

    2. Prepaid taxes.

    3. Prepaid rent.

    4. Prepaid interest.

    5. Research-and-development expense (intangible).

[902.5.2]   VALUATION OF PREPAID EXPENSES AND DEFERRED CHARGES. While many accountants classify these assets as current, conservative analysts still regard them as non-current because they have no value to creditors since they cannot generally be converted to cash to pay trade bills. They can influence a company's future operations.

[902.6]   **Miscellaneous Assets.** Miscellaneous assets are those which cannot be placed under any of the preceding headings. Various entries that may be considered miscellaneous assets, together with valuation considerations, are given below.

[902.6.1]   ADVANCES TO AND RECEIVABLES FROM SUBSIDIARIES. These are classi-fied as miscellaneous assets because their collection within one year or the operating cycle of the business may be doubtful. Many advances are made on a more or less permanent basis and receivables are often not collected within normal selling terms.

[902.6.2]   RECEIVABLES FROM OFFICERS AND EMPLOYEES. Although you will occasionally see receivables from employees listed under current assets on the theory that an employee's salary can always be attached in case of default, such receivables are more properly classified as miscellaneous. Receivables from officers (or other key figures such as directors or stockholders) are of doubtful value from the credit point of view because most companies are reluctant to press important personnel for payment. If this figure is abnormally large, a most thorough and careful investiga-tion on your part is merited.

[903]   **APPRAISAL OF LIABILITIES.** There is a close relationship between the credit worthiness of an account and the amount that is already owing—its current liabilities. If a man already owes so much that he can't pay all of his obligations, his state of solvency is such that there's little likelihood that granting him additional credit will help him out of his situation. If a man has a good equity in the business, there is a degree of stability that encourages the granting of credit. Before the vital comparison of total debt to net worth can be made, however, the liabilities listed on the balance sheet must be examined to determine their accuracy and significance.

[903.1] **Current Liabilities.** Current liabilities are all the obligations of a company that must be paid within one year of the date of the financial statement. If you have any doubt about when an obligation will become due, it is of course safer to consider it a current liability. Current liabilities are payable, generally, in cash at a specific date. Current liabilities include the following:

[903.1.1] ACCOUNTS PAYABLE. Accounts payable are debts resulting from the purchase of merchandise on open-account terms. No other type of obligation should be included under this entry. In addition to the amount of this item, you should consider to how many creditors it is owing, whether any discounts will be taken, whether any of it is past due, and whether it is normal for the season when the statement was drawn. All of these factors shed light on the importance of this item to the company under investigation.

[903.1.2] NOTES PAYABLE. Notes payable should be broken down and analyzed as follows:

1. *Notes payable to banks.* Many companies use short-term financing provided by banks (and, occasionally, other financial institutions). Usually, credit managers regard a healthy bank-borrowing relationship as a favorable credit sign. You should be aware, however, of too large an amount of notes payable to banks because this could be an indication that the loans have been secured by some asset. Too small bank borrowings in relation to requirements, on the other hand, could indicate that bank financing was not available—a negative credit factor. Specifically, you should investigate carefully these areas of company-bank relationships.

   a. *Line of credit.* If a company has a line of bank credit, this is an indication that the bank regards it as a good credit risk. Attempt to determine the amount of this line to judge more precisely the bank's evaluation of that company.

   b. *Secured loans.* You should be aware of whether bank loans are secured by any asset of the firm or otherwise endorsed or guaranteed by any principal, director, officer, or other person. The Uniform Commercial Code requires filing of records that such guarantees exist. Credit analysts usually regard secured or guaranteed bank financing as a signal that the bank views the subject concern as a less favorable credit risk.

   c. *Unsecured loans.* Unsecured loans are a sign of the bank's confidence in the company. As a creditor, moreover, you will be interested in knowing that loans are unsecured because that means that the bank will have no advantage over you regarding its claims in the case of financial embarrassment.

d. *Rate and amount of bank borrowing.* The rate of bank borrowing is an indication of a company's credit worthiness. Loans should be cleaned up periodically, but you should be alert to the possibility that loans have been reduced just before the statement date to improve a company's financial picture. Bank borrowing should be in relation to the company's season.

2. *Notes payable to individuals or companies other than banks.* Companies may borrow from individuals or concerns other than banks for convenience or because the bank financing required was not available. You should find out which is the case. In any event determine whether such loans have been secured by any assets and when they will fall due. Often notes given to individuals are backed by private, oral agreement that the debt will be retired first if financial embarrassment threatens. If the amounts involved are large, you may wish to request a general or specific subordination agreement. A general subordination agreement recognizes the preference of the claims of all other creditors while a specific subordination agreement recognizes the preferred status of the claims of a named creditor in the case of financial embarrassment. Usually only banks and large suppliers can obtain subordination agreements.

3. *Trade acceptances.* Unless it is the practice of the industry to require trade acceptances, the appearance of this item on the balance sheet—especially if it is large—is an indication that other suppliers consider this company a doubtful risk. You should investigate the reasons for trade acceptances.

4. *Other notes.* Other notes payable could include purchase money notes, merchandise advances, etc.

[903.1.3] ACCRUED EXPENSES. Accrued expenses are those which will belong to the period covered by the financial statement but which are not yet due. They include accrued:
1. Wages.
2. Taxes.
3. Insurance.
4. Rent.
5. Interest.

[903.1.4] ADVANCE PAYMENTS. Advance payments, particularly common in industries manufacturing products with long completion times or for the government, should always be shown as a current liability. Because these obligations are not payable in cash, but in merchandise as it is produced, they are not viewed negatively by credit analysts even when they are large.

[903.1.5] CURRENT PAYMENTS DUE ON DEFERRED DEBT. Those amounts of deferred debt payable within one year of the statement date should be listed as current liabilities. These include payments on long-term or installment notes, bonds, and mortgages.

[903.2] **Long-term Liabilities (Deferred Debt).** Long-term liabilities (sometimes called deferred debt) are all obligations of a company that will fall due later than one year from the date of the statement. Long-term liabilities include the following:

[903.2.1] MORTGAGES. Mortgages (which, before the adoption of the Uniform Commercial Code, were divided into real-estate mortgages on land and buildings, and chattel mortgages on other fixtures and equipment) represent long-term secured financing. As a credit analyst, you should find out the following information about mortgages:

1. What is the security?
2. What is the rate of payment?
3. What is the interest rate?
4. Who is the secured party?
5. What is the final maturity date?

Real-estate mortgages are generally viewed favorably by credit analysts because they free capital for more profitable use. Mortgages placed on other assets could mean that general creditors have little protection in the case of financial embarrassment.

[903.2.2] BONDS. Bonds represent a company's agreement to repay borrowed money on a certain date at a specific rate of interest. As a credit analyst, find out this information about bond issues:

1. Are the bonds secured by any asset of the company?
2. Do the provisions of the issue give preferred status to bondholders in the event of financial embarrassment?
3. Do the provisions of the issue call for immediate payment of the outstanding balance on the default of any one payment?
4. What was the purpose of the issue?
5. What is the rate of repayment?
6. What is the interest rate?
7. What is the method of retirement?
8. Do bondholders have any rights in the management of the business?
9. What is the final maturity date?

[903.2.3] LONG-TERM NOTES PAYABLE (INSTALLMENT NOTES). Long-term obligations represent any commitments of a company to pay money later than one year after the date of the financial statement.

As in the case of mortgages and bonds, you should endeavor to find out:

1. Are these obligations secured and, if so, by what assets?
2. What is the rate of payment?
3. What is the interest rate?
4. What is the final maturity date?
5. To whom is the money owing?

[903.3] **Net Worth.** Net worth is the owners' share in the assets of the business. It is listed on the liabilities side of the balance sheet because it is the amount "owing" to the owners of the firm after all other debts have been paid.

[903.3.1] CALCULATION OF NET WORTH. Net worth is calculated as follows:

$$\text{assets} - \text{liabilities} = \text{net worth}$$

[903.3.2]   TANGIBLE NET WORTH. Many credit analysts place more emphasis on the tangible net worth of a company than on its net worth. Tangible net worth is calculated as follows:

$$\text{net worth} - \text{intangible assets} = \text{tangible net worth}$$

[903.3.3]   COMPOSITION OF NET WORTH. For proprietorships and partnerships, net worth is generally just one figure, the difference between the assets and the liabilities. For a corporation, the net worth is most often broken down as follows:

1. *Capital stock.* Capital stock is the total of the transferable interests of the owners of the corporation. Capital stock may be issued or unissued and it may be divided into common and preferred classes. Credit analysts should determine the features of preferred shares to see how they will affect payment of trade obligations in the case of financial embarrassment, how they can affect the management of the company, and how dividend rates required will affect liquidity. Treasury stock or issued stock that has been reacquired by the corporation may be listed but you should be certain to deduct it when calculating tangible net worth.
2. *Paid-in or capital surplus.* This represents money or the value of other assets contributed to the firm but for which no stock or owners' rights have been issued.
3. *Earned surplus.* Earned surplus is the amount of earnings retained in the company and not disbursed in dividends.
4. *Appraisal surplus.* The listing of an appraisal surplus is the correct way to indicate the upward reappraisal of an asset.

[903.3.4]   SIGNIFICANCE OF NET WORTH. The net worth of a company is its book value. The actual worth of the company if it were on the market could be considerably higher or lower. Credit analysts are interested in the net worth of companies because it leads to effective ways to obtain information about them (Dun & Bradstreet, for example, publishes directories of businesses classified according to net worth) and to compare them. In addition, the composition of the net worth, especially the value of the surplus accounts, reveals much about management philosophy, operating results, and the margin of protection available to creditors.

[903.4]   **Reserves.** Reserves are funds currently in the possession of the company and which have been set aside for special purposes. Reserves appear everywhere on the balance sheet except that they are never listed as an asset. There are three major types of reserves.

[903.4.1]   VALUATION RESERVES. Valuation reserves are provided to reduce the values of related assets to amounts considered indicative of their present-day or realizable values. Valuation reserves should be deducted from the gross values of the assets to which they apply. The major valuation reserves are those applied to:

1. Depreciation.
2. Bad debts.
3. Depletion.
4. Discounts.
5. Reductions to lower of cost or market.

6. Amortization of intangible assets.

[903.4.2]   LIABILITY RESERVES. Liability reserves are provided to meet known or predictable liabilities. Such reserves should be classified as current liabilities when it is clearly evident that within twelve months of the date of the balance sheet, part of the working capital will be required to meet the obligations for which the reserves were created. Major liability reserves include those for:

1. Income taxes.
2. Renegotiation charges (on government contracts).
3. Subscriptions or other forms of advance payment.

[903.4.3]   SURPLUS RESERVES. Surplus reserves are those set up to restrict the use of surplus funds to specific programs or indefinite contingencies. As they do not represent actual liabilities, they may be considered part of a company's net worth though many credit analysts deduct them to be on the safe side. Surplus reserves can include those for:

1. Contingencies.
2. Insurance.
3. Decline in asset values.
4. Expansion.

[903.5]   **Contingent Liabilities.** Contingent liabilities are a company's possible future obligations whose occurrence depends on future events. Contingent liabilities include, for example, the following:

[903.5.1]   CLASSIFICATION OF CONTINGENT LIABILITIES.

1. Lawsuits.
2. Discounted accounts or notes receivable.
3. Returns and cancellations.
4. Guarantees or endorsements.
5. Contracts and other possible commitments.

[903.5.2]   EVIDENCE OF CONTINGENT LIABILITIES. Even when such liabilities are not shown on the balance sheet, you should endeavor to determine their existence. On the balance sheet, however, look for these indications of contingent liabilities:

1. Footnotes.
2. Offsets to contingent assets.
3. Special reserves.
4. Net values after deductions.

[904]   PROFIT-AND-LOSS ANALYSIS—THE INCOME (OR PROFIT-AND-LOSS) STATEMENT. The income statement is a listing of the total revenues for a given period, from which expenses and costs are deducted to give the resulting profit or loss. Whereas the balance sheet is a statement of the financial position as of one moment, the income statement shows the progress, the movement (or lack of it) of a company from one date to another. The balance sheet corresponds to a snapshot. A still picture of a train, for example, neither shows how fast the train is moving nor its direction. The income statement, a moving picture of the train, shows both speed and direction. For this reason, the income statement—the basis for profit-

From ___JAN 1_____, 19 — TO ___DEC 31___, 19 —

NET SALES .... $	686894	
COST OF GOODS SOLD........................	496292	
GROSS PROFIT (LOSS) ON SALES...............	190601	
EXPENSES		
Selling ....$ 33249		
General 13866		
Administrative 68343		
OFFICERS' SALARIES 45000		
....		
....		
....................$	160459	
NET INCOME ON SALES......................	30142	
OTHER INCOME		
....*INTEREST*....$ 1209		
....*RENT.-LOT*.... 2400		
....*M.I.SC:*........ 1425	5038	
OTHER EXPENSES		
....*BAD. DEBTS*..$ 6539		
....*DEPREC.*...... 4887		
....*CHARITY*..... 553		
...*OTHER.*........ 2487	14468	
NET INCOME (LOSS) BEFORE TAXES	20711	
Federal Income Tax ....$ 5888		
Other Taxes on Income.. $ 1083		
....	6971	
FINAL NET INCOME (LOSS)....................$	13739	

FIGURE 9.5

Statement of Income

and-loss analysis—is an essential tool in the financial evaluation of your customers.

[904.1] **Explanation of Income Statement Items.** The explanation of income statement items that follows relates to Figure 9.5.

[904.1.1] SALES. The primary source of income is gross sales, both cash and credit. Gross means before any deductions are made. Net sales is the amount left after returns, allowances, and discounts are deducted from gross sales. Deductions can be important. In a department store, for example, the returns can run over 10 percent of gross sales. Net sales is a significant figure. It is used for all comparative purposes and percentage calculations.

[904.1.2] COST OF GOODS SOLD. Cost of goods sold is the amount in dollars that went to acquire or produce goods that were sold during the period. The calculation used is this:

inventory at beginning + value of goods purchased or made − inventory at end = cost of goods sold

In the factory operation, the cost of goods sold will include three elements:

1. The cost of raw materials.
2. Manufacturing labor expense.
3. Manufacturing expense.

For a complete description of the cost of goods sold schedule, see Figure 9.6.

[904.1.3] GROSS PROFIT. Gross profit on sales is the amount left over after deducting the cost of goods sold from net sales. Merchants can widen the margin (in terms of gross profit per dollar of sales) by careful buying on the one hand and "getting good prices" for their merchandise on the

Finished Goods Inventory. Jan. 1, 19—		$ 33,000
Work in Process Inventory, Jan. 1, 19—		$ 25,000
Raw Material Costs		
Raw Material Inventory, Jan. 1, 19—		$ 72,000
Purchased Raw Materials	$ 63,800	
Less Purchase Discounts	1,800	
Net Purchases		62,000
Freight In		1,400
Cost of Raw Materials Available for Use During Year		135,400
Less Raw Material Inventory Dec. 31st, 19—		68,000
Raw Material Cost for Year		67,400
Direct Labor Costs		31.100
Factory Overhead Costs:		
Indirect Factory Labor (foremen, etc.)		9,000
Heat, Light & Power		2,496
Factory Supplies		1,504
Depreciation on Machinery & Equipment		3,677
Total Factory Overhead Costs for Year		16,677
Total Cost of Goods Available for Completion		140,177
Less Work in Process Dec. 31, 19—		23,000
Cost of Finished Goods Completed During Year		117,177
Cost of Finished Goods Available for Sale		150,177
Less Finished Goods Inventory Dec. 31, 19—		35,000
Cost of Goods Sold for Year Ended Dec. 31, 19—		115,177

FIGURE 9.6

Cost of Goods Sold Schedule and Explanation

Inventory, Jan. 1, 19—		The inventory we had on hand at the beginning of the year.
Finished Goods	$ 33,000	
Work in Process	25,000	
Raw Material	72,000	
Total	130,000	
Purchases for Year Net	63,400	Cost of acquiring inventory for use during the year.
Direct Labor Costs for Year	31,100	The wages paid to production workers during the year. This expense is added to the value of inventories and is not shown as an expense to the company until a sale from inventories is made. The expense, in other words, is capitalized into the asset inventories.
Factory Overhead Costs for Year	16,677	This represents such charges as foremen's salaries, depreciation on factory and machinery, power costs in running factory, etc. As with direct labor, factory overhead is added to the value of inventories.
Cost of Inventory Available for use	241,177	This is the total value of inventory we had on hand at the beginning of the year plus the cost of the inventory we produced during the year. The total amount represents the cost of inventories we had, or produced, which is available for use or sale.
Less Inventory at Dec. 31, 19—		This represents the physical count and valuation we make of our inventories at the end of the year. Since we know the total costs of the goods available for use and sale, by deducting the costs of the goods not used or sold, we can get the cost of goods sold.
Finished Goods	35,000	
Work in Process	23,000	
Raw Material	68,000	
Total	126,000	
Cost of Goods Sold for Year	115,177	

other. This is one of the significant figures that determine how the business goes. The gross profit is the amount the concern has available to pay all its numerous overhead expenses.

$$\text{net sales} - \text{cost of goods sold} = \text{gross profit}$$

[904.1.4]   NET INCOME (LOSS) ON SALES. This is the amount earned after all expenses directly applicable to operations are deducted from gross profit. It measures the operating success of the enterprise before taking into account any income received or expense incurred outside the ordinary conduct of the business. In many small concerns this is the final net profit or loss for the accounting period.

[904.1.5]   OTHER INCOME. Here is recorded income other than normal operating income. Examples include:
1. Net profit after expenses from the rental of a piece of real estate owned but not used in the business.
2. Profit from the sale of stocks or bonds.
3. Interest on securities owned.

[904.1.6]   OTHER EXPENSES. These are of three broad types:
1. Items not connected with the normal operations, including fire losses, losses in cancellations of leases.
2. Operating expenses of prior years that come to light during the current period.
3. Extraordinary items of operating expense during the period due to unusual and generally nonrecurring conditions.

[904.1.7]   TAXES. This is the amount of taxes management has estimated will be assessed for the period covered by the income statement. It does not mean that this is the amount now owing, for periodic payments have been made during the year on a pay-as-you-go basis.

[904.2]   **Surplus or Net Worth Reconciliation.** The reconciliation of net worth or surplus is a part of the balance sheet itself. (See Figure 9.7). You can consider it the bridge between the two (the balance sheet and the income statement) because it can show income obtained or disbursed by the

SURPLUS OR NET WORTH AT START.......$		22,674
ADDITIONS		
Final Net Income ....$	14,512	
PURCH+RETIREMENT		
5000 SHS. CORP. STK.		
COST OF 4000	1,000	15,512
DEDUCTIONS		
Final Net Loss ....$		
Dividends	12,000	
Withdrawals		
....		
....		
....		12,000
SURPLUS OR NET WORTH AT END ....$		26,186

FIGURE 9.7

Surplus or Net Worth Reconciliation

Additions to Net Worth	Deductions from Net Worth
*1. Profits (retained earnings).	†1. Losses, cash dividends, or withdrawals.
2. Sale or exchange of capital stock for cash or other assets.	2. Retirement of capital stock, by paying out cash or creating debt.
3. Credits to surplus not reflected in the profit-and-loss statement. Particularly prior years' tax refunds.	3. Debits to surplus not reflected in the profit-and-loss statement. Particularly, additional assessments on prior years' taxes.
4. Surplus arising from upward revaluation of assets.	4. Write-off of asset values.
5. Retirement of debt at less than its value, including compromise or composition settlement of debt.	5. Retirement of debt at more than its actual value, such as paying a premium to obtain bonds for sinking-fund purposes.
6. Decrease in surplus reserves if not considered part of net worth.	6. Increase in surplus reserves if not considered part of net worth.
*Example:	†Example:

$150,000 previous net worth (12/31/—)
  25,000 profit retained
$175,000 new net worth 12/31/—(closing)
	$150,000 previous net worth (12/31/—)
	  25,000 loss sustained
	$125,000 new net worth—12/31/— (closing)

FIGURE 9.8. Changes in Net Worth

company that does not appear in the income statement but is reflected in the balance sheet. A net worth reconciliation is therefore needed in order that the credit analyst may understand why and how net worth changed from one period to the next. Net worth changes for these reasons (see also Figure 9.8):

[904.2.1]   NET WORTH GOES UP.

1. *When earnings are retained.* This is the most common source of increases in net worth and the largest single source of funds used by industrial concerns to meet their requirements. It is also the source of increase in net worth most favored by credit granters because it represents healthy operations and sound management philosophy.
2. *When assets are written up.* An upward reevaluation of assets should always be carried as a surplus account on the balance sheet as well as appearing in the net worth reconciliation. Most credit analysts recognize that such upward valuations can be thoroughly warranted, but are equally aware that it is an easy method to improve falsely a company's financial picture.
3. *When new capital is added.* New capital can be added by the sale of capital stock or the contribution of funds or other assets for which no stock is issued. Credit analysts view favorably the addition of new capital to the firm.
4. *When liabilities are written down.*

[904.2.2]   NET WORTH GOES DOWN.

1. *When losses are sustained.*
2. *When assets are written down.*
3. *When capital is withdrawn.*
4. *When liabilities are written up.*

[904.3]   **Interpretation of Profit-and-Loss Figures.**

[904.3.1]   USE OF NET WORTH RECONCILIATION. In addition to the information indicative of the credit risk a company represents presented above, understanding changes in net worth is a necessity in your analysis of working capital (see Section 907).

[904.3.2]   USE OF THE SALES FIGURE.   The sales figure is a most helpful reference in many ways. In the first place, it may show the credit manager the reasonable requirements of the customer and then help him to determine the probable purchases in his own line. This is done by examining sales together with a breakdown of products the customer uses. The sales figures also help the credit analyst to test certain assets in the balance sheet. For example, an item of inventory seems very precise when it is given as "$18,367." But when the analyst finds that sales are $25,000 for a whole year, it is apparent that further inquiry should be made. It may be that in the inventory there is a lot of merchandise that is going or has gone stale and is no longer salable at a regular markup. But again there may be reason for what seems to be a very heavy stock of merchandise. Knowledge of the sales figure together with knowledge of the percentages of sales various income items generally represent can provide the following information.

1. The number of months' supply of raw material.
2. The number of months' income needed to pay the liabilities.
3. The number of months' supply of goods-in-progress.
4. The number of months' supply of finished goods.
5. The collection period of receivables in months.

[904.3.3]   USE OF THE COST OF DOING BUSINESS FIGURES.   Where the credit man or woman has found an account slipping or is trying to get the account on a discount basis, the gross profit earned and the expenses paid out may provide the key, particularly if there are standards or yardsticks with which to make comparisons. Dun & Bradstreet provides these yardsticks in the form of their Cost of Doing Business Studies prepared for 185 lines of business from Internal Revenue Service Line of Business statistics. D&B prepares these figures on corporations, partnerships, and proprietorships. They are available free from your local D&B office.

[904.3.4]   DETERMINATION OF ABILITY TO PAY PROMPTLY.   A profit-and-loss statement, when combined with a balance sheet, gives a picture of whether a business can or cannot pay promptly. Here are the steps:

1. Look at monthly income from sales and add it to the cash on hand.
2. Deduct amounts that must be paid out for rent, utilities, salaries, etc. This gives the amount available to pay creditors.
3. Compare this with the amount owing.

[905]   RATIO ANALYSIS.

[905.1]   Definition of Ratios.   Ratios are numbers or percentages that show the relationship of one figure (representing one idea or thing) to another figure (representing another idea or thing). It is a convenient device to illustrate relationships. It is impossible to look at any financial figures without thinking in terms of relationships or comparisons.

[905.2]   Use of Ratios.   Ratios may be used in two major ways as follows:

[905.2.1]   INTERNAL ANALYSIS. Ratios form the basis of internal analysis, or the analysis of the items in one balance sheet, their relation to each other, and what that means for the financial health of the company. A quick glance at the current ratio, for example, may be all the financial analysis a credit person needs before approving an account.

[905.2.2]   COMPARATIVE ANALYSIS. Rarely will you examine an account without comparing it to one of three other entities listed below. More rarely still is the comparison made on any other basis than ratios. You will, therefore, probably compare selected ratios of your customer with one or more of the following:

1. Ratios of the same customer as calculated at a different time. In this way you will get the trend of the ratios.
2. Ratios of other companies in the field. (Dun & Bradstreet's Key Business Ratios provide the mechanism for this comparison, see Figure 9.9).
3. Ideal ratios, which result from theoretical considerations or your own experience of what would be best.

[905.3]   **Standard Business Ratios.** The ratios and their interpretations that follow are those used most often by credit analysts to evaluate the financial health of their customers.

[905.3.1]   CURRENT ASSETS TO CURRENT DEBT. This ratio is obtained by dividing the total of current assets by total current debt. Current assets are the sum of cash, notes, and accounts receivable (less reserves for bad debt), advances on merchandise, merchandise inventories, and listed federal, state, and municipal securities not in excess of market value. Current debt is the total of all liabilities falling due within one year. Years ago, this ratio was regarded as the one true test of solvency, the general feeling being that any concern whose "current ratio" was better than "two for one" was, per se, in good condition, while any business whose showing fell below that relationship was likely to find itself in difficulty. Time has since shown that no single ratio is a true criterion of financial condition.

[905.3.2]   NET PROFITS ON NET SALES. This is obtained by dividing the net earnings of the business, after taxes, by the net sales (the dollar volume is less returns, allowances, and cash discounts). This is an important yardstick in measuring profitability, but it should be related to the ratio that follows. Based upon the historical trend in many industries surveyed by Dun & Bradstreet, it is encouraging to note that starting in 1961, after a long period of declining rates, there has been an upswing in profit margins in most lines of business.

[905.3.3]   NET PROFITS ON TANGIBLE NET WORTH. The ratio is obtained by dividing net profits after taxes by tangible net worth. Tangible net worth represents the equity of owners, partners, or stockholders in the business, as reflected by the figure that results from subtracting total liabilities from total assets, and then deducting such intangibles as goodwill, trademarks, patents, copyrights, leaseholds, mailing lists, treasury stock, organization expenses and underwriting discount and expense. The modern tendency is to look more and more to this ratio, rather than to profits-to-sales margins, as a final criterion of profitability. Generally, a profits-to-worth relationship of at least 10 percent is regarded as a necessary objective for providing dividends plus funds for future growth.

[905.3.4]   NET PROFITS ON NET WORKING CAPITAL. The ratio of net profits on net working capital is obtained by dividing net profits, after taxes, by net working capital. Net working capital represents the excess of current assets over current debt and is obtained by subtracting total current debt from total current assets. This margin represents the cushion available to the business for carrying inventories and receivables, and for financing day-to-day operations. To illustrate how net working capital is computed: If a concern has current assets of $1 million and a current debt of $400,000, its net working capital is $600,000. This particular ratio is useful in measuring profitability of concerns whose operating funds are provided in large part by long-term borrowings, and whose permanent capital is therefore abnormally small in relation to the volume of sales.

[905.3.5]   NET SALES TO TANGIBLE NET WORTH. This is obtained by dividing net sales by tangible net worth. The result gives a measure of the relative turnover of capital. If capital is turned over too rapidly, liabilities build up excessively, especially when amounts owed to creditors become a substitute for permanent capital. And if capital is turned too slowly,

Line of Business (and number of concerns reporting)	Current assets to current debt (Times)	Net profits on net sales (Per cent)	Net profits on tangible net worth (Per cent)	Net profits on net working capital (Per cent)	Net sales to tangible net worth (Times)	Net sales to net working capital (Times)	Collection period (Days)	Net sales to inventory (Times)	Fixed assets to tangible net worth (Per cent)	Current debt to tangible net worth (Per cent)	Total debt to tangible net worth (Per cent)	Inventory to net working capital (Per cent)	Current debt to inventory (Per cent)	Funded debts to net working capital (Per cent)
5641 Children's & Infants' Wear Stores (44)	5.37	4.00	10.50	10.90	0.00	0.10	**	6.0	6.0	24.6	69.4	73.0	31.3	20.1
	2.81	2.49	10.00	10.83	3.85	4.29	**	4.5	17.6	47.8	107.5	102.5	60.9	31.0
	1.72	0.71	3.45	4.26	2.75	3.21	**	3.6	42.0	97.5	198.0	159.6	84.0	62.2
5611 Clothing & Furnishings, Men's & Boy's (190)	4.56	4.62	13.71	17.01	4.54	5.35	**	6.1	5.3	24.3	57.7	63.4	36.6	12.1
	2.98	2.79	8.16	10.39	3.22	3.80	**	4.3	12.1	46.0	98.2	89.3	61.7	25.1
	1.97	1.07	3.57	4.17	2.23	2.70	**	3.1	24.2	85.0	174.2	127.9	95.1	46.8
5311 Department Stores (179)	4.44	3.31	10.19	13.08	4.69	5.72	**	7.0	13.1	24.7	55.1	59.0	42.9	19.0
	2.90	2.07	6.76	8.81	3.26	4.26	**	5.5	32.5	43.7	90.7	77.5	69.2	40.2
	2.09	0.96	2.90	4.04	2.65	3.32	**	4.4	62.4	70.0	131.1	108.7	103.0	70.0
Discount Stores (187)	2.65	3.11	16.06	22.17	8.18	11.22	**	6.9	14.6	48.2	86.0	108.4	52.3	20.4
	2.09	1.61	11.36	12.50	5.72	6.88	**	4.9	32.3	77.5	129.7	139.8	67.2	39.2
	1.55	0.75	5.14	6.40	4.17	4.68	**	4.0	56.5	124.4	204.3	195.2	97.7	76.7
Discount Stores, Leased Departments (44)	2.97	4.27	16.06	21.28	8.19	8.98	**	5.4	11.8	43.0	76.8	80.9	49.1	20.4
	2.21	2.16	11.63	12.75	5.17	5.62	**	4.4	26.7	80.1	141.8	122.8	68.3	37.0
	1.63	0.63	4.42	5.65	3.66	3.96	**	3.4	40.1	128.9	246.7	160.2	113.6	61.9
5651 Family Clothing Stores (94)	4.84	4.29	12.74	14.85	4.95	5.59	**	7.0	5.5	20.3	58.2	50.7	37.1	22.5
	2.93	2.28	7.27	9.03	3.21	3.67	**	4.8	12.1	43.6	103.8	87.1	58.4	35.4
	2.13	1.01	4.13	4.60	2.19	2.74	**	3.6	26.5	76.5	158.7	123.7	89.3	54.9
5252 Farm Equipment Dealers (89)	2.88	3.85	14.37	21.66	7.26	10.28	24	5.9	9.5	43.0	100.5	80.1	60.2	11.0
	1.60	1.80	7.98	10.23	5.00	5.68	37	4.0	17.5	146.4	198.5	145.9	86.5	26.8
	1.35	0.99	4.54	6.23	3.02	3.34	59	2.6	39.7	213.7	257.4	239.1	113.9	48.0
5969 Farm & Garden Supply Stores (73)	3.30	6.13	23.26	41.67	5.23	9.23	**	14.6	18.6	25.0	61.8	40.0	72.6	24.1
	1.97	2.99	12.71	20.01	3.13	5.94	**	8.8	39.7	46.1	78.6	79.5	115.4	57.7
	1.41	1.85	6.32	12.50	2.33	4.07	**	5.7	65.7	89.0	128.0	138.9	212.7	118.7
5712 Furniture Stores (177)	5.61	4.78	13.70	13.98	4.78	6.28	37	6.9	4.9	21.3	45.9	32.2	55.7	9.1
	2.76	2.75	8.16	8.18	2.78	2.95	97	4.8	11.9	55.7	96.9	66.4	91.2	21.7
	1.74	1.07	3.69	3.78	1.61	1.64	191	3.5	26.3	117.2	192.9	118.5	139.5	40.2
5541 Gasoline Service Stations (69)	3.75	4.93	15.24	42.17	4.87	14.54	**	28.4	27.6	18.1	29.7	34.1	83.3	20.0
	2.18	2.52	9.08	21.44	3.19	7.33	**	10.9	49.6	30.2	66.5	70.3	129.9	74.8
	1.49	1.05	5.05	7.82	2.05	4.89	**	7.6	77.6	69.9	113.8	112.7	238.4	172.7
5411 Grocery Stores (134)	2.50	1.63	15.39	32.59	14.24	31.36	**	23.1	49.1	37.8	64.7	79.2	67.9	26.6
	1.81	0.91	9.41	18.20	10.30	21.10	**	16.1	72.1	60.8	100.4	130.7	91.8	64.6
	1.38	0.53	5.06	9.67	6.60	12.55	**	11.9	99.9	93.6	169.1	204.4	129.3	148.5

** Not computed. Necessary information as to the division between cash sales was available in too few cases to obtain an average collection period usable as a broad guide.

FIGURE 9.9. Dun & Bradstreet, Inc., Key Business Ratios: Retailing

funds become stagnant, and profitability suffers.

[905.3.6] NET SALES TO NET WORKING CAPITAL. This is similar to the concept above, except that the net sales are divided by the net working capital. If the ratio is too high, the tendency of the business often is to owe too much as a consequence of depending upon credit granted by suppliers, the bank, and others as a substitute for an adequate margin of operating funds.

[905.3.7] COLLECTION PERIOD. This is obtained by dividing the annual net sales made on credit terms by 365 days to obtain the average daily credit sales, then dividing the average daily credit sales into notes and accounts receivable, including any discounted. Example: A concern makes annual sales of $365,000 on open-account terms. Average daily credit sales are therefore $1,000. If the total notes and accounts receivable of this concern are $32,000, the collection period is thirty-two days.

The ratio is helpful in analyzing the collectibility of receivables. Generally, it is felt the collection period should not exceed the net maturity indicated by selling terms by more than ten to fifteen days. When comparing the collection period of one concern with that of another, allowances should be made for possible variations in selling terms.

Line of Business (and number of concerns reporting)	Current assets to current debt	Net profits on net sales	Net profits on tangible net worth	Net profits on net working capital	Net sales to tangible net worth	Net sales to net working capital	Collec-tion period	Net sales to inventory	Fixed assets to tangible net worth	Current debt to tangible net worth	Total debt to tangible net worth	Inventory to net working capital	Current debt to inventory	Funded debts to net working capital
	Times	Per cent	Per cent	Per cent	Times	Times	Days	Times	Per cent	Per cent	Per cent	Per cent	Per cent	Per cent
5251 Hardware Stores (90)	6.00	4.81	14.20	20.34	4.52	5.49	**	5.7	4.9	17.4	41.0	64.1	24.9	8.1
	3.23	2.81	8.75	10.14	3.20	3.68	**	4.0	14.5	36.9	100.0	86.5	49.0	28.8
	2.09	0.99	2.72	4.04	1.96	2.38	**	3.2	26.1	79.7	174.2	122.0	82.1	54.2
5722 Household Appliance Stores (82)	1.62	2.03	9.20	17.30	3.03	6.17	41	6.4	17.4	101.3	203.8	148.3	102.4	27.8
	1.38	0.88	5.79	7.13	2.81	3.81	79	4.2	39.5	194.1	313.4	198.3	170.1	50.9
5971 Jewelry Stores (76)	4.83	6.75	13.49	14.60	2.98	3.22	**	3.9	3.6	25.1	48.7	61.9	39.5	9.4
	3.17	3.61	8.44	9.12	2.02	2.37	**	2.7	9.6	44.2	89.4	84.5	63.2	19.7
	2.10	1.92	4.14	4.22	1.64	1.83	**	2.4	21.6	83.3	139.8	120.0	94.8	38.2
5211 Lumber & Other Bldg. Mtls. Dealers (170)	4.57	3.60	13.72	17.54	5.25	6.93	33	8.7	11.2	20.9	56.8	51.4	46.5	11.2
	2.62	2.37	9.05	10.89	3.43	4.57	53	6.0	22.1	45.6	90.1	74.2	78.0	37.2
	1.85	1.53	4.59	6.22	2.42	3.06	71	4.2	43.4	81.2	141.5	102.4	132.4	60.9
5399 Miscellaneous General Mdse. Stores (74)	5.82	3.80	13.79	15.99	5.80	6.07	**	6.6	7.6	19.0	57.9	59.5	26.0	13.8
	3.62	2.15	8.21	8.94	3.34	3.80	**	4.3	16.9	37.1	121.8	96.6	52.9	43.9
	1.89	1.03	2.58	3.08	1.94	2.31	**	3.1	34.7	81.4	177.3	142.6	80.0	80.7
5511 Motor Vehicle Dealers (101)	2.43	2.42	21.74	30.43	11.86	18.49	**	10.2	7.8	54.0	80.0	100.5	73.3	13.8
	1.69	1.65	12.93	22.30	8.80	12.40	**	8.2	18.7	98.1	156.4	153.9	89.2	44.1
	1.35	0.86	7.58	11.98	6.36	7.96	**	6.6	50.6	165.9	246.6	221.5	112.7	114.6
5231 Paint, Glass & Wallpaper Stores (42)	5.75	5.00	13.83	26.53	4.07	6.32	**	8.6	9.0	16.3	27.1	39.0	29.3	7.7
	3.52	3.20	9.90	14.82	2.73	4.20	**	6.4	20.1	27.0	44.3	76.4	55.1	19.7
	2.54	1.64	4.55	8.82	2.15	3.00	**	4.5	36.3	47.6	76.7	110.7	100.0	27.8
5661 Shoe Stores (86)	5.09	3.09	10.54	13.42	4.74	5.70	**	4.9	6.2	21.4	54.6	79.3	34.8	4.8
	2.76	1.68	6.32	6.97	3.65	4.55	**	3.8	12.5	45.4	92.9	106.0	50.0	19.0
	2.07	0.59	2.17	2.30	2.81	3.09	**	3.1	25.6	86.8	153.1	154.0	66.5	49.6
5531 Tire, Battery & Accessory Stores (55)	4.36	5.00	15.22	20.45	5.21	7.54	**	8.2	6.6	23.5	56.0	59.1	31.8	19.7
	2.21	2.03	9.62	12.32	3.50	4.80	**	5.3	16.3	52.3	76.3	90.2	91.4	30.1
	1.71	0.99	3.85	5.13	2.62	3.38	**	3.9	35.4	116.8	181.8	129.7	149.4	63.7
5331 Variety Stores (64)	4.75	3.87	15.27	19.15	5.48	7.22	**	5.1	14.1	19.6	50.5	90.9	31.1	15.2
	3.00	2.11	8.81	11.39	3.55	4.61	**	4.1	24.4	39.3	73.5	124.3	42.9	43.0
	2.06	1.07	3.72	4.62	2.59	3.37	**	3.0	51.4	66.9	105.4	156.4	69.2	66.1
5621 Women's Ready-to-Wear Stores (167)	4.32	4.52	15.78	21.30	5.95	7.45	**	10.0	7.0	27.3	69.2	46.0	53.8	15.0
	2.81	2.30	8.53	10.96	3.96	4.92	**	6.7	18.2	49.2	100.1	72.3	87.2	33.2
	1.82	0.98	4.26	5.14	2.67	3.27	**	5.0	37.8	92.4	163.1	114.8	129.7	56.0

** Not computed. Necessary information as to the division between cash sales was available in too few cases to obtain an average collection period usable as a broad guide.

FIGURE 9.9. Dun & Bradstreet, Inc., Key Business Ratios: Retailing (cont.)

[905.3.8]

NET SALES TO INVENTORY. This is obtained by dividing annual net sales by merchandise inventory as carried on the balance sheet. This quotient does not yield an actual physical turnover. It only provides a yardstick for comparing stock-to-sales ratios of one concern with another or with those for the industry. When the ratio of net sales to inventory is too high, it may expose a chronically understocked condition in which sales are being lost because of lack of adequate inventories in stock and failure to offer proper depth of selections to customers. If the ratio is too low, compared with figures that are more or less typical of those for the industry, it may be that inventories are top-heavy, stagnant, or obsolete.

[905.3.9]

FIXED ASSETS TO TANGIBLE NET WORTH. Fixed assets represent depreciated book values of building leasehold improvements, machinery, furniture, fixtures, tools and other physical equipment, plus land, if any, and valued at cost or appraised market value. The ratio is obtained by dividing fixed assets by tangible net worth. Ordinarily, the relationship

Line of Business (and number of concerns reporting)	Current assets to current debt (Times)	Net profits on net sales (Per cent)	Net profits on tangible net worth (Per cent)	Net profits on net working capital (Per cent)	Net sales to tangible net worth (Times)	Net sales to net working capital (Times)	Collection period (Days)	Net sales to inventory (Times)	Fixed assets to tangible net worth (Per cent)	Current debt to tangible net worth (Per cent)	Total debt to tangible net worth (Per cent)	Inventory to net working capital (Per cent)	Current debt to inventory (Per cent)	Funded debts to net working capital (Per cent)
5077 Air Condtg. & Refrigtn. Equipt. & Sup. (53)	5.17	4.06	17.14	17.44	7.09	7.48	39	11.9	7.1	21.6	72.2	53.1	39.9	8.7
	2.35	2.48	10.00	11.58	4.66	5.24	54	6.8	13.9	67.4	115.5	71.7	91.3	20.9
	1.73	2.06	5.38	5.60	3.00	3.69	72	4.7	30.9	116.2	226.9	102.1	145.9	37.9
5013 Automotive Equipment (159)	4.19	4.09	16.26	20.39	5.77	6.69	28	7.5	7.4	26.3	48.9	69.8	41.5	8.1
	2.88	2.70	10.89	11.92	4.04	4.45	36	5.0	15.5	44.4	73.0	89.0	62.1	25.3
	1.95	1.39	5.72	7.03	2.78	3.52	46	3.9	29.4	90.0	128.8	112.9	96.7	45.0
5095 Beer, Wine & Alcholic Beverages (93)	2.77	2.05	16.34	23.97	13.50	18.85	10	14.0	9.1	34.6	94.4	84.3	68.7	13.9
	1.79	1.06	8.56	12.10	8.28	12.55	20	9.0	24.9	86.7	163.0	111.1	99.2	37.7
	1.39	0.34	3.55	4.50	5.86	8.01	37	6.6	42.9	173.3	284.4	207.2	146.5	70.6
5029 Chemicals & Allied Products (46)	3.57	4.09	17.58	27.97	9.63	15.74	36	15.7	16.9	25.9	89.8	38.3	94.7	21.9
	1.90	1.64	10.71	14.68	6.25	8.19	43	11.4	28.1	88.1	186.7	89.0	126.8	54.9
	1.40	0.80	6.27	9.04	3.00	4.13	58	7.9	65.1	153.9	335.9	121.0	217.1	100.0
5037 Clothing & Accessories, Women's & Children's (68)	4.64	2.43	11.21	17.78	8.62	10.94	27	21.9	2.5	23.0	70.5	33.0	74.2	4.9
	2.23	1.20	5.69	8.70	5.22	6.16	43	9.2	5.0	73.8	104.3	63.3	125.7	28.8
	1.72	0.44	2.10	2.42	3.27	3.82	58	6.1	16.4	121.6	160.8	101.8	200.0	55.5
5036 Clothing & Furnishings, Men's & Boys' (53)	3.48	2.70	11.92	12.15	6.74	8.44	26	8.6	2.9	36.0	68.6	63.2	54.9	5.5
	2.29	1.12	5.81	7.86	4.97	5.42	41	4.9	9.4	71.4	124.6	86.6	76.3	14.8
	1.71	0.48	2.08	2.31	2.76	2.86	71	4.1	24.1	128.4	148.1	127.0	109.6	38.1
5081 Commercial Machines & Equipment (56)	4.61	3.09	14.43	15.63	6.18	7.85	46	10.9	4.6	26.0	58.5	41.8	66.7	12.6
	2.22	1.45	6.56	7.25	4.34	4.96	61	8.0	9.7	67.5	106.9	61.5	117.4	21.7
	1.65	0.75	2.28	3.08	2.83	3.12	79	5.0	23.1	133.9	225.4	98.4	186.7	52.4
5045 Confectionery (33)	3.49	1.71	16.05	20.13	16.17	19.02	11	21.7	3.5	37.3	107.6	74.2	46.3	26.0
	2.15	1.06	9.27	9.52	10.50	11.38	20	14.0	10.3	72.5	161.1	89.8	79.4	32.3
	1.69	0.48	5.78	6.52	6.16	8.11	25	7.5	32.5	125.3	263.9	120.7	144.5	65.0
5043 Dairy Products (51)	2.55	2.20	17.72	37.54	13.97	29.87	20	60.9	20.4	38.3	87.7	26.5	125.5	19.7
	1.58	0.83	8.02	12.22	9.51	14.17	29	30.2	43.9	67.8	135.8	46.2	223.5	33.3
	1.14	0.23	2.19	3.04	5.40	9.43	34	16.9	67.4	156.0	284.6	123.4	492.9	207.2
5022 Drugs & Druggists' Sundries (101)	3.12	2.15	15.53	18.23	8.87	9.45	28	8.0	9.3	39.1	76.2	74.6	57.8	16.3
	2.07	1.37	8.75	9.37	5.97	6.20	36	6.7	22.9	71.9	126.6	110.3	83.5	31.4
	1.64	0.77	5.28	5.35	4.31	4.82	48	5.3	39.4	134.8	211.1	138.9	122.6	55.4
5064 Electrical Appliances, TV & Radio Sets (98)	2.35	2.39	14.28	15.48	8.27	9.66	31	8.0	3.5	62.1	119.6	75.3	78.6	13.3
	1.90	1.42	9.13	10.77	6.15	6.91	45	6.2	7.9	105.2	159.2	118.2	102.0	27.9
	1.55	0.77	4.99	5.67	4.41	5.15	56	4.4	20.7	158.3	272.0	162.0	137.7	49.7
5063 Electrical Apparatus & Equipment (140)	2.80	3.05	16.78	18.30	7.55	8.12	39	10.3	6.2	45.3	71.0	69.1	69.0	8.1
	2.17	1.63	10.26	11.96	5.48	6.00	46	7.4	15.5	73.6	114.7	83.3	102.0	18.9
	1.77	0.90	6.01	6.45	3.80	4.74	57	5.9	30.1	122.8	173.1	105.5	156.4	40.1
5065 Electronic Parts & Equipment (52)	3.09	3.50	15.59	17.66	5.94	6.08	34	5.2	9.1	45.1	78.3	86.0	54.8	10.7
	2.29	2.13	10.94	11.26	4.29	4.71	45	4.2	19.0	82.0	144.2	105.7	77.0	35.7
	1.77	1.10	5.80	6.29	2.93	3.33	57	3.1	30.8	112.5	213.0	128.0	99.0	61.6
5083 Farm Machinery & Equipment (61)	4.63	3.09	15.66	20.45	6.31	7.20	32	10.0	4.2	19.0	53.9	47.5	55.1	6.4
	2.21	1.78	8.47	10.85	4.56	5.48	44	5.3	11.1	64.6	94.3	80.8	93.1	15.7
	1.64	1.17	4.85	6.78	2.55	3.15	67	3.6	24.7	137.4	191.1	124.0	145.5	39.5
5039 Footwear (64)	2.87	3.51	13.07	13.67	6.99	7.37	37	11.3	1.7	43.2	55.4	48.0	65.5	16.0
	2.25	2.29	8.74	9.26	4.10	4.90	58	6.6	3.2	73.1	144.4	72.5	113.6	34.2
	1.68	1.04	3.96	4.86	2.42	2.87	78	3.6	15.8	143.4	184.3	127.2	200.0	72.3
5048 Fresh Fruits & Vegetables (67)	3.32	2.60	18.64	40.35	12.73	24.38	14	98.5	24.8	28.8	61.3	11.2	89.5	17.6
	2.05	1.31	11.92	23.26	8.59	13.63	20	37.9	41.0	53.9	102.5	54.4	171.7	39.4
	1.13	0.75	6.30	12.65	5.29	8.79	32	12.8	83.1	100.6	163.9	105.0	463.4	138.6

FIGURE 9.9. Dun & Bradstreet, Inc., Key Business Ratios: Wholesaling

between fixed assets and tangible net worth should not exceed 100 percent for a manufacturer, and 75 percent for a wholesaler or retailer. Beyond these limits, so disproportionate an amount of capital is frozen into machinery or "bricks and mortar" that the necessary margin of operating funds for carrying receivables, inventories, and day-to-day cash outlays, as well as maturing obligations, becomes too narrow. This not only exposes the business to the hazards of unexpected developments, such as sudden change in the business climate, but creates possible drains on income in the form of heavy carrying and maintenance charges should a serious portion of fixed assets lie idle for any length of time.

[905.3.10]   CURRENT DEBT TO TANGIBLE NET WORTH. This is obtained by dividing current debt by tangible net worth. Ordinarily, a business begins to pile up trouble when the relationship between current debt and tangible net worth exceeds 80 percent.

[905.3.11]   TOTAL DEBT TO TANGIBLE NET WORTH. This is obtained by dividing

Line of Business (and number of concerns reporting)	Current assets to current debt	Net profits on net sales	Net profits on tangible net worth	Net profits on net working capital	Net sales to tangible net worth	Net sales to net working capital	Collection period	Net sales to inventory	Fixed assets to tangible net worth	Current debt to tangible net worth	Total debt to tangible net worth	Inventory to net working capital	Current debt to inventory	Funded debts to net working capital
	Times	Per cent	Per cent	Per cent	Times	Times	Days	Times	Per cent	Per cent	Per cent	Per cent	Per cent	Per cent
5097 Furniture & Home Furnishings (81)	2.98	3.40	14.42	20.14	6.85	7.82	40	9.5	6.8	42.3	74.1	58.0	66.6	16.0
	2.10	1.56	8.42	10.09	4.83	5.50	49	6.8	13.5	75.4	140.2	88.1	108.7	31.7
	1.67	0.94	4.17	5.94	3.24	4.33	70	4.6	30.7	138.3	198.4	117.8	138.3	43.9
5041 Groceries, General Line (196)	3.15	1.21	13.86	16.81	20.27	25.58	8	18.0	11.7	39.7	83.1	86.8	49.7	20.9
	2.00	0.57	7.77	9.79	12.43	15.08	12	12.5	32.3	80.2	138.1	123.8	76.6	37.4
	1.51	0.23	3.49	4.30	7.69	9.45	17	8.7	67.7	139.7	224.8	172.8	108.6	83.2
5072 Hardware (174)	4.08	2.62	10.81	13.08	5.71	7.20	32	6.6	6.3	26.3	55.5	75.2	38.4	6.5
	2.62	1.76	7.02	8.34	3.80	4.61	43	4.9	13.6	50.9	98.7	97.1	67.0	19.0
	1.81	0.80	3.64	4.07	2.73	3.31	52	3.7	25.1	98.2	152.9	130.0	100.6	36.2
5084 Industrial Machinery & Equipment (97)	3.27	3.78	17.24	23.65	7.90	8.80	34	11.2	8.4	35.5	79.6	62.5	65.4	13.5
	2.12	2.03	8.50	11.03	4.73	5.50	43	6.6	18.8	69.5	134.0	92.1	103.0	41.7
	1.59	0.75	4.17	4.76	3.24	4.04	59	4.0	46.6	139.7	216.8	125.1	150.3	67.9
5098 Lumber & Construction Materials (146)	3.60	3.05	16.67	23.17	8.64	11.36	36	11.3	8.8	32.5	75.3	52.5	60.3	14.0
	2.20	1.85	11.00	13.02	5.73	6.18	47	8.0	21.9	68.5	125.6	83.7	104.4	33.0
	1.64	0.94	6.18	7.00	3.38	4.01	64	5.8	39.5	124.6	247.4	118.4	173.2	64.7
5047 Meats & Meat Products (48)	2.93	1.33	21.62	22.58	25.38	29.41	15	76.4	9.6	37.2	65.9	33.5	133.5	12.8
	2.03	0.74	12.13	13.76	16.04	20.44	22	42.0	29.0	79.2	114.5	60.3	197.1	30.7
	1.45	0.23	3.54	4.72	9.36	14.67	30	24.2	50.0	175.3	256.6	104.1	378.0	71.3
5091 Metals & Minerals (76)	4.03	3.54	14.13	21.01	6.34	7.46	39	7.9	11.2	28.9	54.1	57.8	54.1	11.5
	2.36	2.07	8.44	10.51	4.04	4.96	47	5.3	22.2	66.2	110.5	93.3	85.9	27.3
	1.51	1.21	5.11	6.57	2.38	3.45	60	3.7	43.5	134.7	172.7	141.1	130.5	59.4
5028 Paints & Varnishes (38)	6.13	3.56	12.92	19.35	4.74	6.29	33	8.0	6.1	17.7	33.8	45.0	42.4	7.0
	3.50	2.55	5.52	8.09	3.29	4.26	41	6.4	16.1	25.6	68.1	69.4	60.4	16.1
	2.00	1.13	3.10	4.76	2.52	3.27	48	5.4	27.7	70.9	93.7	93.0	99.9	40.3
5096 Paper & Its Products (121)	3.88	2.33	11.31	14.92	8.06	10.73	31	11.8	7.8	30.4	67.6	57.1	57.5	12.2
	2.34	1.23	7.00	8.79	5.39	6.66	40	8.1	14.5	59.8	107.4	83.2	95.9	23.1
	1.70	0.60	3.43	4.26	3.63	4.61	51	6.1	35.7	104.2	177.6	102.2	146.6	53.8
5092 Petroleum & Petroleum Products (86)	3.45	3.21	14.52	37.55	7.70	15.38	25	35.4	26.6	20.7	42.3	23.1	112.7	18.9
	2.07	1.31	9.09	16.02	4.80	9.40	34	24.2	48.5	38.8	90.3	47.9	174.0	62.3
	1.50	0.69	3.53	8.79	3.08	5.59	52	13.7	86.7	86.5	189.1	84.3	287.5	130.0
5033 Piece Goods (128)	3.17	2.39	11.04	13.84	8.13	8.91	29	9.1	2.1	43.9	61.1	62.5	59.4	8.7
	2.10	1.36	6.35	7.22	4.74	5.96	47	6.1	5.0	84.1	122.2	91.2	100.0	17.4
	1.64	0.67	3.68	3.89	3.25	3.51	68	4.6	15.2	132.8	176.8	124.3	146.5	41.2
5074 Plumbing & Heating Equipment & Supplies (179)	3.66	3.13	13.04	16.30	6.58	7.62	36	8.4	6.8	31.4	59.8	65.4	53.0	9.8
	2.63	1.77	7.76	9.72	4.50	5.24	45	6.0	13.2	53.3	97.9	82.5	79.9	20.4
	1.94	0.99	4.28	5.39	3.32	3.70	58	4.8	28.4	99.2	158.6	106.1	120.0	44.1
5044 Poultry & Poultry Products (45)	3.39	2.21	15.79	31.97	14.44	25.90	14	66.7	12.1	27.1	61.0	24.7	111.9	19.4
	2.09	0.83	8.11	10.77	10.52	16.16	21	31.1	26.5	59.3	104.2	49.4	157.8	95.4
	1.39	0.26	2.55	3.50	6.47	8.17	31	15.0	80.8	108.7	263.0	100.0	248.2	187.0
5093 Scrap & Waste Materials (61)	4.10	3.37	12.11	24.18	7.32	10.61	20	30.0	19.3	21.3	36.3	28.5	59.1	15.9
	2.41	1.59	6.95	12.57	3.74	7.51	36	11.5	36.0	37.2	103.1	63.8	127.3	47.5
	1.54	0.80	4.72	8.09	2.67	4.39	48	7.1	59.4	88.3	182.8	103.6	229.5	107.7
5014 Tires & Tubes (44)	2.58	3.09	14.15	17.50	6.11	8.26	32	9.7	13.8	50.1	101.2	60.7	84.6	8.9
	1.93	1.80	7.69	10.00	4.51	5.87	42	6.0	24.9	87.3	122.3	94.8	116.7	30.4
	1.58	0.93	3.67	6.21	3.43	4.33	63	4.4	45.1	125.7	251.6	137.0	150.0	66.7
5094 Tobacco & Its Products (97)	2.71	1.04	13.94	23.78	21.35	27.49	13	25.6	9.4	46.2	81.0	60.7	81.2	8.8
	1.97	0.73	9.65	13.12	12.40	17.28	16	18.5	17.3	82.5	118.2	93.0	114.1	20.9
	1.43	0.40	5.40	7.02	7.48	10.42	24	12.3	31.9	152.0	170.1	141.5	164.0	40.9

FIGURE 9.9. Dun & Bradstreet, Inc., Key Business Ratios: Wholesaling (cont.)

total debts by tangible net worth. When this relationship exceeds 100 percent, the creditors' rights in the assets of the business exceed the equity of the owners. The management of top-heavy liabilities entails strains and hazards that can become a threat to business survival—they cloud business judgment and often create anxieties that sap management energies. More than this, they expose the business to the risks of unexpected contingencies, such as sudden downturns in sales, changes in style or consumer preference, rapid rises in business costs, strikes, fires, floods, and a host of other factors that can upset the operation of a modern enterprise. A concern that is carrying a large short- or long-term debt load under such circumstances faces rough going.

[905.3.12]   INVENTORY TO NET WORKING CAPITAL. This is obtained by dividing the merchandise inventory by net working capital. This becomes an additional measure of inventory balance, for if an excessive percentage

Line of Business (and number of concerns reporting)	Current assets to current debt	Net profits on net sales	Net profits on tangible net worth	Net profits on net working capital	Net sales to tangible net worth	Net sales to net working capital	Collection period	Net sales to inventory	Fixed assets to tangible net worth	Current debt to tangible net worth	Total debt to tangible net worth	Inventory to net working capital	Current debt to inventory	Funded debts to net working capital
	Times	Per cent	Per cent	Per cent	Times	Times	Days	Times	Per cent	Per cent	Per cent	Per cent	Per cent	Per cent
2871–72–79	3.37	4.21	11.09	26.87	4.75	7.17	33	17.0	21.5	25.0	58.3	32.1	109.2	11.1
Agricultural Chemicals	1.92	2.51	6.77	15.08	2.96	4.50	52	9.5	41.8	56.4	151.1	49.2	139.9	39.2
(43)	1.34	1.66	4.48	8.39	2.14	3.25	97	5.7	74.3	124.7	260.8	121.5	223.2	85.9
3722–23–29	3.54	5.38	12.69	17.00	3.78	5.17	43	7.0	36.5	26.2	60.3	51.1	61.3	32.8
Airplane Parts &	2.32	2.51	8.09	10.65	2.76	3.90	60	5.0	53.9	55.1	113.1	82.4	88.0	60.1
Accessories (70)	1.73	0.75	1.42	2.87	1.95	2.56	73	3.5	81.6	98.1	177.4	116.8	131.9	96.6
2051–52	3.31	3.22	14.30	38.38	6.85	20.49	16	38.8	52.8	19.4	38.6	37.2	118.0	21.7
Bakery Products	1.96	1.56	6.51	21.68	4.34	11.58	23	28.9	77.7	36.7	53.6	53.8	200.0	68.4
(62)	1.41	0.46	2.37	5.08	3.50	7.33	32	15.5	105.0	60.3	107.4	84.6	284.0	147.9
3312–13–15–16–17	3.21	4.31	11.89	24.57	3.29	6.95	37	6.9	60.1	25.4	56.4	74.9	60.1	35.0
Blast Furnaces, Steel Wks	2.24	3.21	6.77	15.28	2.29	4.78	45	5.4	78.3	38.5	73.2	87.2	86.3	79.3
& Rolling Mills (69)	1.68	1.66	3.92	8.59	1.73	3.58	51	4.5	107.8	57.5	114.5	112.1	123.0	125.0
2331	1.98	2.19	23.19	30.41	14.68	17.47	30	20.0	5.9	90.9	99.5	62.6	136.9	8.1
Blouses & Waists, Wom-	1.50	1.23	12.60	14.90	9.98	11.39	46	11.2	11.7	141.8	194.7	98.6	211.7	46.4
en's & Misses' (53)	1.28	0.49	3.73	4.35	6.49	7.38	61	7.2	25.3	314.9	383.7	222.6	296.6	81.5
2731–32	3.55	7.18	14.11	23.63	2.85	5.23	45	9.0	14.8	24.1	37.7	46.8	52.5	6.3
Books: Publishing, Pub-	2.36	3.77	9.44	12.61	2.05	3.04	64	4.4	36.3	42.5	90.0	62.0	100.0	33.6
lishing & Printing (58)	1.92	2.08	5.47	7.16	1.60	2.21	82	3.2	50.7	93.9	151.8	84.2	155.2	77.0
2211	6.64	3.32	8.27	14.93	2.77	4.63	48	7.9	39.3	10.9	37.5	44.6	45.0	32.2
Broad Woven Fabrics,	3.78	2.50	5.24	9.38	2.05	3.26	61	5.9	56.0	20.1	80.4	60.3	58.5	52.1
Cotton (45)	2.52	1.33	3.48	4.24	1.69	2.83	70	4.2	68.9	32.1	147.8	84.7	102.5	73.5
2031–32–33–34–35–36–	2.70	4.22	14.06	26.56	5.60	11.02	16	6.5	45.0	32.4	59.0	96.5	61.2	19.5
37 Canned & Preserved	1.79	2.58	10.32	16.65	3.61	6.19	25	4.5	56.7	70.9	123.0	126.5	85.4	47.8
Frts, Vegs & Sea Fds (80)	1.37	0.99	5.54	8.78	2.48	4.54	36	3.2	89.5	133.4	223.4	241.0	122.0	83.6
2751	3.13	5.55	14.13	33.97	4.22	9.69	36	**	42.8	26.2	53.6	25.0	89.9	16.5
Commercial Printing	2.09	2.38	8.11	19.75	3.21	5.68	47	**	58.1	45.2	71.6	55.3	180.3	48.9
except Lithographic (80)	1.49	1.08	3.51	6.22	2.21	4.34	62	**	92.3	75.3	134.4	87.9	264.0	114.9
3661–62	3.66	6.01	16.45	22.02	3.73	4.86	54	5.9	25.0	31.5	47.1	52.1	70.1	13.4
Communication Equip-	2.40	4.01	9.79	12.52	2.64	3.26	69	4.5	42.2	57.0	89.8	74.4	96.9	43.1
ment (75)	1.83	1.50	3.57	4.43	2.05	2.60	87	3.5	65.4	78.5	163.7	106.6	128.3	80.7
3271–72–73–74–75	3.34	6.36	15.07	38.92	3.46	9.01	40	26.3	49.7	19.5	56.9	29.6	85.2	33.2
Concrete, Gypsum & Plas-	2.45	3.80	9.26	23.25	2.47	5.95	50	10.9	70.8	31.6	83.6	53.9	155.0	85.0
ter Products (84)	1.77	1.82	3.14	8.25	1.74	3.96	68	6.1	95.5	55.4	147.9	76.8	329.9	133.3
2071–72–73	3.73	6.79	18.32	29.17	5.09	8.19	14	10.6	35.0	15.9	37.0	63.4	45.4	20.2
Confectionery & Related	2.58	3.53	8.75	17.45	3.85	6.46	21	7.4	55.3	30.7	56.3	94.4	61.8	40.9
Products (49)	2.08	0.98	4.33	8.88	2.40	4.74	33	5.1	83.0	63.7	128.1	121.0	92.9	88.0
3531–32–33–34–35–36–	4.39	6.91	13.80	17.46	3.53	4.70	39	6.4	25.0	20.9	51.8	54.5	41.9	20.2
37 Const., Min. & Hdg.	2.99	3.30	9.96	12.70	2.28	3.23	57	4.1	36.0	39.6	86.8	77.9	62.0	45.6
Machy. & Equipt. (87)	2.39	1.67	5.10	5.61	1.92	2.38	75	2.9	57.2	72.0	159.7	94.7	102.6	64.4
2641–42–43–44–45–46–	3.91	4.38	12.67	21.68	4.26	7.41	36	11.4	25.9	22.1	53.3	45.3	58.3	26.3
47–49 Converted Paper &	2.74	2.85	8.34	13.57	3.10	4.88	45	7.9	51.6	33.0	73.9	66.9	95.8	46.2
Paperboard Prods. (75)	1.89	1.23	4.39	8.24	2.30	3.74	61	5.7	78.7	56.5	113.7	91.0	159.5	81.3
3421–23–25–29	4.53	6.58	15.95	22.50	3.57	4.57	36	6.6	22.1	17.8	36.6	57.3	45.4	8.5
Cutlery, Hand Tools &	3.49	4.73	10.62	15.04	2.50	3.56	47	4.9	36.7	30.9	65.1	71.2	57.8	42.6
General Hardware (92)	2.42	2.14	6.49	8.47	1.83	2.81	55	3.4	56.8	55.4	122.3	97.4	94.4	62.9
2021–22–23–24–26	2.29	2.76	14.87	58.30	9.07	32.29	18	47.4	47.3	33.8	60.6	34.8	135.7	29.0
Dairy Products	1.54	1.36	8.51	26.34	5.98	16.21	27	28.5	66.7	55.1	92.7	73.7	261.5	68.7
(119)	1.23	0.57	4.15	10.56	3.80	9.71	33	14.2	93.8	89.3	149.7	122.6	433.0	132.0
2335	2.66	2.04	12.89	13.81	10.36	12.61	33	17.1	3.4	49.2	104.7	50.8	112.8	15.8
Dresses: Women's,	1.74	0.77	4.77	7.17	7.36	8.90	52	9.9	10.9	119.0	188.5	81.3	160.3	33.2
Misses' & Junior's (108)	1.44	0.15	1.48	1.64	4.44	5.09	61	7.3	21.5	198.6	266.1	125.8	239.0	67.1
2831–33–34	3.49	9.31	20.54	28.97	3.06	4.33	45	7.3	31.8	23.4	41.7	49.8	66.4	9.8
Drugs	2.78	6.10	12.76	18.14	2.01	3.19	60	5.3	47.8	35.7	66.3	62.9	95.8	30.9
(67)	2.16	2.48	4.46	8.97	1.59	2.56	71	4.2	63.8	61.3	127.0	79.9	132.4	82.5

** Not computed. Printers carry only current supplies such as paper, ink, and binding materials rather than merchandise inventories for re-sale. Building Trades contractors have no inventories in the credit sense of the term. As a general rule, such contractors have no customary selling terms, each contract being a special job for which individual terms are arranged.

FIGURE 9.9. Dun & Bradstreet, Inc., Key Business Ratios: Manufacturing & Construction

of net working capital is reflected by unsold inventory, difficulty may be experienced in meeting currently maturing obligations. Ordinarily, the relationship of inventory to net working capital should not exceed 80 percent.

[905.3.13] CURRENT DEBT TO INVENTORY. Dividing the current debt by inventory yields yet another indication of the extent to which the business relies on funds from disposal of unsold inventories to meet its debts.

[905.3.14] FUNDED DEBTS TO NET WORKING CAPITAL. Funded debts are all long-term obligations, as represented by mortgages, bonds, debentures, term loans, serial notes, and other types of liabilities maturing more than one year from statement date. The funds for paying funded debts at maturity normally arise from three sources, namely: refunding (i.e., borrowing new money to repay the old), or raising new capital, or accumulating earnings into working capital over a period of time. Since the likelihood of obtaining new equity capital or refunding at maturity date can be

Line of Business (and number of concerns reporting)	Current assets to current debt	Net profits on net sales	Net profits on tangible net worth	Net profits on net working capital	Net sales to tangible net worth	Net sales to net working capital	Collection period	Net sales to inventory	Fixed assets to tangible net worth	Current debt to tangible net worth	Total debt to tangible net worth	Inventory to net working capital	Current debt to inventory	Funded debts to net working capital
	Times	Per cent	Per cent	Per cent	Times	Times	Days	Times	Per cent	Per cent	Per cent	Per cent	Per cent	Per cent
3641–42–43–44 Electric Lighting & Wiring Equipment (57)	4.14	5.74	15.13	21.56	3.85	6.04	41	7.8	18.8	23.2	42.2	49.7	53.9	13.6
	3.17	3.60	9.37	12.84	2.78	3.66	54	5.5	41.4	37.9	71.1	71.8	73.6	40.9
	2.05	1.41	3.98	4.82	1.89	2.83	66	4.0	59.9	54.3	128.1	96.1	101.1	80.6
3611–12–13 Electric Transmission & Distribution Equipment (66)	3.45	5.76	13.61	17.01	4.14	4.66	54	5.1	28.0	31.5	43.2	69.7	55.0	13.5
	2.78	3.30	8.78	11.01	2.76	3.29	68	4.0	41.1	46.6	89.3	82.6	73.7	37.8
	2.05	1.15	3.25	3.99	1.96	2.64	82	3.1	56.9	87.2	126.2	102.8	101.7	59.3
3621–22–23–24–29 Electrical Industrial Apparatus (55)	4.57	4.74	12.57	18.56	3.45	4.79	49	6.8	28.9	21.7	42.8	58.3	59.2	15.5
	2.84	3.91	10.42	12.87	2.76	3.64	61	4.9	42.3	38.1	83.9	74.5	74.4	39.5
	2.15	1.66	5.14	6.80	2.26	2.81	79	4.3	58.3	63.5	115.4	85.7	100.7	56.3
1731 Electrical Work (134)	3.91	3.93	21.18	27.15	8.42	10.88	**	**	11.1	25.9	65.4	**	**	5.7
	2.14	1.81	8.90	12.50	4.51	6.60	**	**	20.5	57.3	126.7	**	**	19.0
	1.60	0.46	1.74	2.13	3.14	4.14	**	**	43.1	125.5	228.1	**	**	44.2
3671–72–73–74–79 Electronic Components & Accessories (95)	3.33	5.35	15.44	19.72	3.73	4.77	53	6.2	30.4	32.6	58.1	55.2	70.0	21.7
	2.52	3.44	8.93	12.15	2.66	3.35	66	4.8	49.6	51.0	86.2	73.2	90.0	48.4
	2.02	1.04	3.70	4.93	2.03	2.60	79	3.5	72.5	68.1	146.6	95.5	125.8	79.2
3811 Engineering, Laboratory & Scientific Instruments (41)	4.51	6.02	13.44	17.42	2.98	3.84	51	6.6	20.9	22.0	44.6	57.3	51.1	13.5
	2.91	3.69	6.02	9.55	2.22	2.69	67	4.1	38.7	36.6	60.2	71.8	73.5	35.1
	2.28	1.21	2.61	3.69	1.67	2.29	84	3.6	46.6	55.9	123.8	85.6	104.6	68.9
3441–42–43–44–46–49 Fabricated Structural Metal Products (136)	3.74	4.72	14.66	20.91	5.03	8.03	38	10.5	23.9	28.4	57.0	54.0	63.9	18.3
	2.28	2.72	9.07	13.46	3.37	5.13	53	6.4	41.8	49.2	104.0	81.0	100.0	47.8
	1.70	1.08	4.54	7.15	2.34	3.53	67	5.1	72.7	88.5	184.3	110.2	162.8	93.6
3522 Farm Machinery & Equipment (81)	4.63	5.02	13.92	18.91	4.07	5.73	32	5.6	23.6	21.3	54.6	68.6	43.9	15.2
	2.79	3.08	9.06	11.81	2.87	3.82	50	4.2	39.6	45.0	89.4	84.5	67.9	34.8
	1.75	1.08	3.68	4.55	2.03	2.66	73	3.1	56.6	87.0	143.2	109.9	106.4	66.2
3141 Footwear (99)	3.40	3.80	13.17	16.00	5.41	7.65	38	8.8	12.7	32.9	54.7	64.1	57.9	11.0
	2.20	1.80	8.82	11.15	4.03	4.65	52	5.5	22.8	65.1	111.4	92.8	96.9	25.7
	1.62	0.75	2.64	3.66	2.91	3.42	73	3.9	38.5	125.1	179.6	116.3	138.3	49.2
2371 Fur Goods (21)	6.70	1.78	11.29	12.21	7.76	8.18	41	12.5	1.0	13.5	**	43.9	35.2	**
	2.33	0.82	2.31	4.49	5.34	6.33	50	7.2	2.4	62.9	**	69.4	139.8	**
	1.53	0.26	0.67	0.78	2.82	3.30	72	5.0	5.7	147.1	**	102.9	176.9	**
1511 General Building Contractors (187)	2.13	3.14	20.48	31.92	12.49	19.93	**	**	11.5	60.9	89.5	**	**	17.9
	1.54	1.82	12.41	18.23	7.60	11.73	**	**	24.3	122.5	198.9	**	**	42.4
	1.18	0.72	5.93	7.49	3.85	6.58	**	**	43.6	255.6	372.3	**	**	90.7
3561–62–64–65–66–67–69 General Industrial Machinery & Equip. (113)	3.67	5.81	13.02	19.74	3.70	5.03	46	7.9	26.4	21.8	48.9	56.1	55.5	13.6
	2.74	3.40	9.23	12.49	2.60	3.66	62	4.9	45.0	42.0	78.8	76.4	73.7	34.7
	2.14	1.22	3.08	4.67	1.84	2.75	79	3.6	57.2	65.1	118.2	87.4	122.7	60.5
2041–42–43–44–45–46 Grain Mill Products (76)	3.13	4.19	14.64	30.74	6.12	11.08	21	16.9	30.2	23.3	66.8	50.0	76.7	22.0
	2.15	2.20	9.58	18.92	4.59	8.99	32	10.1	58.2	52.3	97.6	78.7	103.2	63.1
	1.67	0.84	3.42	7.23	3.51	5.71	45	7.2	80.7	80.4	144.5	110.9	160.4	101.5
3431–32–33 Heating Apparatus & Plumbing Fixtures (45)	3.74	4.35	12.51	17.83	4.53	5.42	34	6.9	22.0	23.9	54.7	67.2	45.6	23.9
	3.09	2.93	8.35	11.23	3.00	4.11	51	5.0	42.4	39.6	82.6	85.3	83.8	37.9
	1.97	1.38	5.12	5.86	2.39	3.07	65	4.0	57.5	78.0	134.7	101.1	122.6	45.0
1621 Heavy Construction, except Highway & Street (109)	3.11	4.52	15.83	33.39	5.96	13.97	**	**	28.7	28.1	56.5	**	**	18.1
	1.91	2.26	7.86	16.39	3.84	7.30	**	**	57.8	53.7	95.5	**	**	41.6
	1.34	0.25	0.99	2.14	2.05	3.59	**	**	76.1	105.6	191.5	**	**	75.9
2251–52 Hosiery (43)	5.05	4.09	12.58	23.73	4.38	7.76	30	9.7	28.9	18.3	38.0	55.1	42.3	22.2
	2.64	1.92	6.56	7.90	3.03	4.98	50	5.6	46.4	46.3	69.9	78.7	82.3	43.9
	1.60	(0.89)	(2.27)	(2.82)	2.24	3.41	66	4.5	66.1	83.1	129.7	133.3	133.4	84.7
3631–32–33–34–35–36–39 Household Appliances (44)	3.38	6.01	17.13	26.76	4.08	6.01	49	6.0	19.4	31.5	53.3	67.3	57.7	22.8
	2.55	4.68	13.10	17.40	3.08	4.09	57	4.6	34.8	51.2	89.6	86.5	77.5	36.8
	1.66	2.56	8.42	13.59	2.58	3.03	68	3.7	52.5	100.5	138.3	108.1	105.6	56.1
2812–13–15–16–18–19 Industrial Chemicals (68)	3.25	6.29	14.39	26.29	3.37	6.37	48	8.7	48.1	25.0	51.3	53.0	77.8	47.4
	2.59	3.82	9.71	16.66	2.24	4.34	61	6.5	73.8	38.3	82.1	73.9	101.0	73.2
	1.82	1.91	5.35	8.00	1.70	3.18	68	4.7	102.3	66.1	136.7	95.7	164.9	112.9

( ) Indicates Loss

** Not computed. Printers carry only current supplies such as paper, ink, and binding materials rather than merchandise inventories for re-sale. Building Trades contractors have no inventories in the credit sense of the term. As a general rule, such contractors have no customary selling terms, each contract being a special job for which individual terms are arranged.

FIGURE 9.9. Dun & Bradstreet, Inc., Key Business Ratios: Manufacturing & Construction (cont.)

affected by a number of variables—such as the prevailing business conditions, or the financial condition of the business—analysts tend to compare funded debts with net working capital in determining whether or not long-term debts are in proper proportion. Ordinarily, this relationship should not exceed 100 percent.

[906]   **COMPARATIVE ANALYSIS.** As indicated previously, credit analysts virtually always compare the company they are investigating with the same company as of a different date, with other similar companies in the field, or with a hypothetical, "ideal" company. Comparative financial analysis refers, however, to the first of those three possibilities.

[906.1]   **Preliminary Considerations.** Before beginning a discussion of comparative analysis of financial-statement items, you should be aware of certain preliminary considerations.

Line of Business (and number of concerns reporting)	Current assets to current debt	Net profits on net sales	Net profits on tangible net worth	Net profits on net working capital	Net sales to tangible net worth	Net sales to net working capital	Collection period	Net sales to inventory	Fixed assets to tangible net worth	Current debt to tangible net worth	Total debt to tangible net worth	Inventory to net working capital	Current debt to inventory	Funded debts to net working capital
	Times	Per cent	Per cent	Per cent	Times	Times	Days	Times	Per cent	Per cent	Per cent	Per cent	Per cent	Per cent
3821–22 Instruments, Measuring & Controlling (53)	4.32	5.71	15.30	18.03	3.14	3.81	51	5.8	28.4	21.3	47.5	56.1	45.6	23.7
	2.83	4.00	9.28	11.80	2.29	3.05	64	4.1	40.4	44.3	90.3	74.1	69.6	38.1
	2.28	1.41	3.29	4.80	1.71	2.17	83	3.1	57.9	71.6	130.4	89.4	97.9	64.5
3321–22–23 Iron & Steel Foundries (56)	3.45	4.86	15.92	33.38	3.59	8.13	40	21.6	47.9	22.6	33.1	31.5	77.3	16.8
	2.37	3.19	9.39	15.40	2.71	5.30	48	10.3	63.4	30.7	58.8	63.1	115.4	39.2
	2.02	2.07	5.55	12.08	2.09	3.72	60	5.9	79.0	53.8	80.5	89.1	177.6	75.1
2253 Knit Outerwear Mills (56)	2.94	3.91	19.97	27.82	6.46	8.73	30	9.9	13.2	35.8	58.4	58.3	80.0	12.8
	2.01	2.87	11.71	16.33	4.04	6.40	49	6.9	28.4	60.6	89.0	96.8	114.9	33.8
	1.55	1.35	5.77	9.18	2.84	4.18	68	4.7	54.8	126.9	163.1	147.2	154.9	61.7
2082 Malt Liquors (30)	2.92	5.08	9.84	32.80	4.16	12.75	11	18.3	53.7	17.8	40.0	34.1	129.5	39.8
	2.31	1.65	4.97	12.64	2.49	8.95	16	15.1	70.7	24.9	58.2	55.6	137.4	94.4
	1.74	(0.55)	(1.61)	(6.23)	2.07	5.69	25	11.6	103.8	44.0	91.4	77.9	210.0	138.8
2515 Mattresses & Bedsprings (46)	3.06	3.00	10.01	16.36	6.06	9.19	41	11.7	14.4	24.6	55.6	66.8	66.9	13.0
	2.58	1.36	5.12	9.18	3.76	5.70	50	7.7	29.1	46.2	95.2	76.7	101.1	30.9
	1.69	0.55	3.39	4.17	2.36	4.00	61	6.4	50.0	92.3	131.8	103.9	140.8	76.5
2011 Meat Packing Plants (92)	3.70	1.33	14.79	25.89	19.05	34.13	12	55.1	42.9	23.9	58.2	34.1	87.3	16.5
	2.00	0.67	8.57	17.96	10.45	19.79	15	30.1	63.2	52.7	95.9	69.0	143.3	47.6
	1.47	0.20	2.59	5.73	7.00	12.57	20	21.2	90.0	100.6	184.5	111.4	227.7	88.4
3461 Metal Stampings (104)	4.35	4.90	12.16	21.75	4.39	8.16	34	11.1	30.9	17.4	44.0	44.4	64.5	26.4
	2.55	2.84	7.93	13.33	3.11	5.06	43	7.3	54.1	34.6	71.6	71.6	105.7	59.2
	1.67	0.72	2.59	6.72	1.94	3.48	58	5.2	82.2	72.0	153.5	102.4	162.4	85.6
3541–42–44–45–48 Metalworking Machinery & Equipment (124)	4.36	5.93	12.76	20.02	3.23	5.54	46	13.4	34.8	18.9	38.8	36.2	56.4	15.0
	2.83	3.06	6.94	11.21	2.13	3.46	61	5.9	48.3	29.6	71.4	66.2	91.1	43.1
	1.96	0.62	0.93	1.75	1.49	2.29	76	3.2	69.6	62.0	114.8	92.5	161.0	76.8
2431 Millwork (55)	4.14	4.25	21.08	29.04	6.25	8.56	34	10.9	23.7	26.0	58.9	52.6	72.0	17.1
	2.27	2.61	10.08	16.83	4.10	5.74	48	8.1	39.0	51.3	106.0	73.9	94.5	44.7
	1.75	1.37	5.40	6.08	2.92	4.09	59	5.5	61.8	87.8	204.9	118.2	144.6	77.7
3599 Miscellaneous Machinery, except Electrical (90)	4.45	5.75	14.65	31.54	4.03	7.14	33	23.8	32.7	19.0	29.7	22.5	61.8	7.9
	2.71	3.20	6.87	12.70	2.76	4.67	46	9.4	51.1	32.8	59.1	54.2	103.1	27.5
	1.84	1.23	3.89	7.49	1.83	3.44	61	5.0	70.8	65.4	113.3	87.3	194.7	70.1
3714 Motor Vehicle Parts & Accessories (89)	3.70	5.72	16.23	26.74	3.60	5.91	35	9.0	27.2	25.6	55.2	55.2	54.8	27.8
	2.77	4.26	11.53	19.20	2.68	3.93	44	5.8	37.1	37.1	78.4	73.3	80.3	47.4
	2.19	2.96	8.22	11.21	2.16	2.87	54	4.1	62.5	55.4	117.9	96.0	116.7	73.1
3361–62–69 Nonferrous Foundries (47)	4.03	5.65	14.63	29.96	4.05	8.71	42	18.9	33.3	18.6	34.2	27.6	74.2	12.9
	2.75	2.74	8.63	17.46	3.01	5.28	47	13.4	54.5	29.1	84.9	44.5	130.4	30.0
	1.59	1.08	1.41	5.79	2.15	4.00	53	6.7	77.8	73.6	175.3	83.7	260.4	122.5
2541–42 Office & Store Fixtures (60)	3.54	5.66	16.00	26.81	4.80	9.50	36	12.2	20.2	30.8	79.2	45.1	74.6	25.4
	2.22	2.45	8.58	12.85	3.52	4.86	58	7.2	42.6	55.8	114.3	75.8	116.4	46.9
	1.59	0.48	2.21	2.34	2.23	3.32	70	4.5	70.6	91.2	155.5	123.7	174.4	109.0
2361–63–69 Outerwear, Children's & Infants' (58)	2.70	2.46	15.29	18.50	8.83	12.11	30	12.9	6.8	46.9	55.7	51.1	81.1	7.4
	1.89	1.40	8.31	10.16	5.88	7.84	42	7.5	11.2	92.1	116.9	89.9	126.8	18.7
	1.46	0.49	2.54	2.72	3.69	4.50	60	5.9	24.2	175.5	315.8	146.5	208.7	37.5
2851 Paints, Varnishes, Lacquers & Enamels (112)	3.81	3.96	12.91	20.55	4.60	6.80	35	8.7	25.4	23.3	44.4	58.1	53.3	15.6
	2.92	2.61	8.87	13.50	3.40	4.85	46	6.4	40.8	40.1	72.6	73.3	81.3	33.1
	2.13	1.50	5.39	6.87	2.51	3.43	59	5.0	55.4	64.2	106.8	89.3	109.7	56.1
2621 Paper Mills, except Building Paper (55)	3.52	4.91	10.01	28.19	2.56	6.22	34	11.4	67.8	19.0	50.5	45.1	68.0	39.9
	2.82	3.28	6.27	14.02	1.97	4.30	43	7.8	87.4	22.1	75.4	60.6	98.0	117.4
	2.17	1.56	3.27	6.85	1.67	3.78	54	6.2	117.5	40.5	121.4	82.7	172.3	156.7
2651–52–53–54–55 Paperboard Containers & Boxes (61)	4.17	3.87	19.66	30.20	4.37	10.80	33	11.7	46.7	17.1	59.1	54.3	64.4	40.3
	2.22	2.63	7.38	14.20	3.06	6.45	36	8.0	70.5	38.5	75.2	80.0	92.8	67.5
	1.64	1.35	4.28	7.95	2.06	4.76	44	6.2	101.2	64.1	129.1	140.9	162.7	124.5
3712–13 Passenger Car, Truck & Bus Bodies (46)	3.54	3.14	14.02	19.64	6.78	7.67	29	9.0	18.5	25.6	47.6	59.4	64.1	17.3
	2.07	1.82	8.48	10.11	4.21	5.35	41	6.1	30.5	69.2	116.0	88.6	90.8	31.9
	1.49	1.16	4.21	6.14	2.46	3.92	56	4.3	66.3	128.5	218.6	141.1	151.9	48.1

( ) Indicates Loss

FIGURE 9.9. Dun & Bradstreet, Inc., Key Business Ratios: Manufacturing & Construction (cont.)

[906.1.1] DATE OF STATEMENTS. Make sure that the statements you are comparing are of the same day—or close to it—in successive years. This will reduce the possibility of distortions resulting from statements taken at different seasons or periods of operating activity.

[906.1.2] ACCOUNTING METHODS. The accounting procedures used to obtain certain balance-sheet figures—especially the inventory figures—should remain the same for the statements you are comparing. If procedures change, you should find out why and what the results will be on your analysis. Classification of balance-sheet items should likewise be consistent.

[906.2] **Comparative Analysis Forms.** It is helpful to design and use comparative analysis forms, often called "spread sheets," to facilitate classification and posting of balance-sheet items. Examples of forms used for comparing balance sheets, profit-and-loss statements, net worth reconciliation, and business ratios are found in Figures 9.10 and 9.11.

Line of Business (and number of concerns reporting)	Current assets to current debt (Times)	Net profits on net sales (Per cent)	Net profits on tangible net worth (Per cent)	Net profits on net working capital (Per cent)	Net sales to tangible net worth (Times)	Net sales to net working capital (Times)	Collection period (Days)	Net sales to inventory (Times)	Fixed assets to tangible net worth (Per cent)	Current debt to tangible net worth (Per cent)	Total debt to tangible net worth (Per cent)	Inventory to net working capital (Per cent)	Current debt to inventory (Per cent)	Funded debts to net working capital (Per cent)
2911 Petroleum Refining (51)	2.08	6.89	12.68	54.90	3.66	11.12	44	15.0	81.5	26.5	55.6	52.6	156.6	88.3
	1.68	5.03	9.86	31.24	1.91	8.16	55	11.5	103.9	39.1	71.0	73.3	224.7	152.2
	1.44	2.63	5.76	20.49	1.45	5.54	81	8.9	124.4	55.1	128.7	100.1	293.1	210.7
2821–22–23–24 Plastics Materials & Synthetics (39)	3.05	6.40	18.17	32.81	4.22	7.96	47	12.3	32.0	27.1	42.9	42.8	84.3	24.4
	2.28	4.14	11.30	20.61	2.84	5.21	58	8.7	63.6	44.8	70.5	65.5	132.9	62.6
	1.73	2.54	6.36	10.85	1.99	4.22	65	5.9	89.9	67.5	151.2	95.6	226.5	103.7
1711 Plumbing, Heating & Air Conditioning (100)	2.82	2.96	17.95	23.78	9.56	12.60	**	**	9.5	44.5	90.8	**	**	10.7
	1.87	1.45	10.65	13.23	6.25	8.43	**	**	19.4	99.1	148.4	**	**	24.2
	1.44	0.51	4.17	7.09	4.55	5.32	**	**	38.4	170.9	232.8	**	**	61.3
2421 Sawmills & Planing Mills (89)	3.67	9.45	21.88	69.22	4.82	10.52	19	13.3	31.8	17.0	28.3	45.7	65.3	13.3
	2.22	4.96	14.19	39.12	2.70	6.10	30	9.3	54.9	27.9	80.5	68.2	116.1	76.8
	1.51	2.89	9.23	17.45	1.55	3.98	37	5.9	86.4	68.1	195.3	117.3	183.3	178.4
3451–52 Screw Machine Products (75)	3.92	5.06	10.56	23.64	3.69	7.93	34	9.4	34.3	17.2	56.8	59.3	61.5	15.9
	2.66	2.88	6.52	11.68	2.36	4.75	42	6.5	53.8	33.3	68.3	87.4	79.0	48.6
	1.68	0.57	2.67	5.76	1.61	3.06	53	3.9	77.9	59.8	128.0	119.0	140.5	81.3
2321–22 Shirts, Underwear & Nightwear, Men's & Boys' (57)	2.62	4.04	17.80	23.10	6.28	7.67	29	6.7	5.1	56.0	85.5	77.2	70.4	6.8
	1.95	2.27	9.99	10.20	4.59	5.63	54	4.9	12.9	91.3	106.3	109.3	102.9	21.1
	1.49	1.00	3.92	4.53	4.06	4.18	65	3.5	29.3	169.1	141.9	165.3	131.5	44.0
2841–42–43–44 Soap, Detergents, Perfumes & Cosmetics (65)	4.22	6.26	17.96	26.60	4.41	6.74	30	9.8	20.8	23.9	42.7	44.8	73.5	10.4
	2.59	4.20	13.04	17.77	3.11	4.47	47	7.7	36.6	39.9	84.4	55.1	100.3	19.4
	2.13	1.38	4.00	7.04	2.24	2.97	64	5.7	53.9	72.0	120.5	75.0	137.7	46.9
2086 Soft Drinks, Bottled & Canned (75)	3.03	5.71	14.83	69.60	4.91	18.58	17	23.2	56.8	17.6	33.5	41.6	93.2	20.3
	1.97	3.87	11.93	40.28	3.30	10.15	21	16.3	75.6	33.2	49.8	62.1	178.2	64.4
	1.33	2.75	7.52	27.71	2.24	6.80	27	13.4	104.9	54.0	121.9	109.4	251.2	196.7
3551–52–53–54–55–59 Special Industry Machinery (95)	4.50	5.35	13.93	19.86	3.17	5.61	44	7.1	22.5	17.5	50.0	43.5	58.0	13.3
	2.81	3.04	7.00	10.32	2.09	3.14	68	4.7	33.8	36.4	86.1	69.6	82.3	31.0
	2.17	1.01	1.66	3.04	1.55	2.15	83	3.5	51.0	62.9	123.5	88.1	123.3	65.2
2337 Suits & Coats, Women's & Misses' (76)	2.91	2.96	13.07	16.56	9.14	10.74	32	20.9	2.5	46.6	98.7	36.8	107.7	11.0
	1.97	1.36	8.04	9.16	6.61	7.96	45	10.6	6.4	84.4	121.3	71.9	142.3	23.1
	1.60	0.40	3.23	3.35	4.43	4.82	57	6.0	12.1	148.8	216.9	106.3	200.5	68.9
2311 Suits, Coats & Overcoats, Men's & Boys' (95)	3.44	3.22	15.06	17.30	6.44	7.08	23	9.5	3.6	37.7	69.4	58.0	66.6	9.5
	2.23	1.81	8.09	8.92	4.21	4.48	49	8.5	7.0	70.3	109.3	82.2	90.5	20.4
	1.85	0.85	3.22	3.47	2.89	3.19	78	3.8	22.3	113.4	171.5	123.8	126.2	36.0
3841–42–43 Surgical, Medical & Dental Instruments (60)	5.81	9.83	16.59	23.90	2.97	4.36	45	7.1	17.1	16.5	34.6	43.4	45.0	13.9
	3.66	5.78	11.05	16.72	2.07	2.99	62	4.9	26.3	27.3	58.9	63.2	68.7	26.1
	2.55	2.48	5.89	8.66	1.64	2.07	78	3.9	40.9	42.0	75.3	85.9	94.1	39.5
3941–42–43–49 Toys, Amusement & Sporting Goods (63)	3.57	6.81	19.63	29.46	4.79	6.20	39	6.8	17.5	29.4	74.8	64.2	89.6	22.8
	2.26	3.60	13.19	16.06	3.27	4.38	56	5.6	34.0	57.1	106.6	79.7	89.6	34.4
	1.66	2.10	7.43	8.64	2.34	2.91	84	3.9	59.1	112.9	192.8	118.6	127.7	70.4
2327 Trousers, Men's & Boys' (50)	3.20	2.86	15.95	19.81	9.13	9.90	39	9.8	3.5	42.9	97.9	48.4	70.5	13.0
	2.09	1.56	7.32	8.12	5.06	5.90	52	6.4	8.0	92.5	122.8	76.0	110.2	35.7
	1.65	0.35	1.84	1.92	3.83	4.07	79	4.4	29.0	142.6	163.6	147.4	203.5	45.8
2341 Underwear & Nightwear, Women's & Children's (66)	3.13	3.06	13.19	15.64	7.06	7.91	34	9.6	4.5	37.6	56.3	62.5	65.1	10.2
	2.22	1.73	9.11	9.88	5.03	5.97	46	6.4	9.0	73.8	94.5	87.8	96.4	28.2
	1.61	0.92	4.35	4.44	3.39	3.96	72	4.2	26.0	118.7	149.4	134.4	174.0	51.3
2511–12 Wood Household Furniture & Upholstered (126)	4.56	5.32	16.25	27.06	4.67	7.43	33	9.0	22.2	20.9	43.1	50.3	65.0	17.0
	2.70	3.25	10.62	16.80	3.10	4.94	45	6.5	38.5	35.8	67.1	77.1	76.5	29.6
	1.84	1.50	5.41	7.22	2.31	3.24	55	4.8	56.2	83.5	131.5	120.7	105.9	56.6
2328 Work Clothing, Men's & Boys' (36)	5.77	5.15	17.33	18.43	5.15	6.30	34	5.9	5.8	17.4	45.1	55.8	46.7	5.1
	3.18	2.68	9.51	10.51	3.55	3.68	50	4.5	15.8	45.0	93.0	79.8	66.3	19.1
	1.96	1.14	3.63	4.02	2.68	2.82	67	3.6	31.9	104.2	134.4	108.0	104.1	32.4

( ) Indicates Loss

** Not computed. Printers carry only current supplies such as paper, ink, and binding materials rather than merchandise inventories for re-sale. Building Trades contractors have no inventories in the credit sense of the term. As a general rule, such contractors have no customary selling terms, each contract being a special job for which individual terms are arranged.

FIGURE 9.9. Dun & Bradstreet, Inc., Key Business Ratios: Manufacturing & Construction (cont.)

STATEMENT DATE					
Cash					
Notes Receivable					
Accounts Receivable					
Inventory					
TOTAL CURRENT ASSETS					
Land					
Fixtures, Equipment					
Other Fixed Assets					
TOTAL ASSETS					
Due Banks					
Accounts Payable					
Federal Income Taxes					
TOTAL CURRENT LIABILITIES					
PREFERRED STOCK					
COMMON STOCK					
PAID IN SURPLUS					
EARNED SURPLUS					
NET WORTH (Proprietor or Partners)					
TOTAL LIABILITIES AND CAPITAL					
NET WORKING CAPITAL					
TANGIBLE NET WORTH					
NET SALES					
NET PROFIT					
Dividends or Withdrawals					
Res. for Depreciation					
Res. for Bad Debts					

FIGURE 9.10. Balance Sheet—Five-Year Comparison of a Financial Statement

[906.3] **Methods of Comparative Analysis.** There are various methods that you can use to set up your balance-sheet and profit-and-loss figures to highlight changes and trends. They include the following:

[906.3.1] COMMON-SIZE STATEMENTS. Instead of just listing dollar amounts and dollar changes, you may choose to assign all assets the value of 100 percent (and all liabilities the value of 100 percent) and then calculate the percentage of this that each asset or liability item represents. Although you will not be able to make direct comparison of the dollar size of balance-sheet items from year to year, the changing percentages can often be more revealing.

[906.3.2] PROGRESS FROM BASE YEAR. Some credit analysts measure each succeeding year's progress—or lack of it—in relation to one base year. This can be done with percentages or dollar amounts or both.

[906.3.3] SUCCEEDING YEAR PROGRESS. You may also choose to calculate percentage change in relation to what had been accomplished in the previous year.

[906.4] **Orderly Statement Analysis.** The consistent employment of a systematic method for statement analysis, with only moderate practice, saves time, for the analyst, always undertaking the task in the same fashion, spares himself confusion; saves space in a written analysis, since clearly flowing thoughts can be expressed concisely; makes certain that no essential details are overlooked; and yields a report that is coherent and conclusive. The following method aims to discover in what direction a concern is going, how rapidly it is traveling, and whether there remains enough fuel to complete the trip. The six steps that follow are to be expanded and refined, or curtailed as the circumstances warrant, but they should always be taken in the same order.

[906.4.1]   USE OF THE PROFIT-AND-LOSS STATEMENT AND BALANCE SHEET.

1. Observe the amount of earnings for the year, the dividends paid; from the balance sheet, changes in capital stock; and from the surplus reconciliation, adjustments charged or credited directly

STATEMENT DATE																
		% of Net Sales 100%	Typical % for Line 100%		% of Net Sales 100%	Typical % for Line 100%		% of Net Sales 100%	Typical % for Line 100%		% of Net Sales 100%	Typical % for Line 100%		% of Net Sales 100%	Typical % for Line 100%	
NET SALES																
COST OF GOODS SOLD																
GROSS PROFIT (LOSS) ON SALES																
EXPENSES Owners' Compensation																
Employees' Wages																
Occupancy Expense																
Advertising																
Bad Debt Loss																
Buying Expense																
Depreciation, Fixtures																
All Other Expense																
NET INCOME (LOSS) ON SALES																
OTHER INCOME																
OTHER EXPENSES																
NET INCOME (LOSS) BEFORE TAXES																
Federal Income Taxes																
Other Taxes on Income																
NET INCOME (LOSS) AFTER TAXES																
Adjustments—Add																
Adjustments—Deduct																
NET INCOME (LOSS) AS ADJUSTED																
SURPLUS OR NET WORTH AT START																
ADDITIONS Adjusted Net Income																
DEDUCTIONS Adjusted Net Loss																
Dividends—Withdrawals																
SURPLUS OR NET WORTH AT END																

	My Business	Typical	My Business	Typical	My Business	Typical	My Business	Typical	My Business	Typical
Current Assets to Current Debt	Times	Times	Times	Times	Times	Times	Times	Times	Times	Times
Net Profit on Net Sales	%	%	%	%	%	%	%	%	%	%
Net Profit on Tangible Net Worth	%	%	%	%	%	%	%	%	%	%
Net Sales to Tangible Net Worth	Times	Times	Times	Times	Times	Times	Times	Times	Times	Times
Net Sales to Net Working Capital	Times	Times	Times	Times	Times	Times	Times	Times	Times	Times
Collection Period	Days	Days	Days	Days	Days	Days	Days	Days	Days	Days
Inventory Turnover	Times	Times	Times	Times	Times	Times	Times	Times	Times	Times
Current Debt to Tangible Net Worth	%	%	%	%	%	%	%	%	%	%

FIGURE 9.11. Income Statement—Net Worth Reconciliation—Financial Ratios

to surplus. Earnings minus dividends plus or minus surplus adjustments plus proceeds of capital stock issued minus capital stock retired equals net worth increase.

2. Study the earning record for the past several years to ascertain the trend of profits, and compare with the industry standards.

3. If the year was unprofitable, follow a similar procedure: Loss plus dividends plus or minus surplus adjustments plus capital stock retired minus capital stock issued equals net worth reductions.

4. If profit-and-loss details are lacking, draw conclusions from the change in earned surplus, capital stock, and provision for income taxes.

[906.4.2]   EFFECTS OF CHANGES IN NET WORTH ON BALANCE SHEET. Determine what parts of the balance sheet suffered from the net worth decline or benefited from the net worth increase.

1. How much of the gain or loss is reflected in working capital?

2. In fixed assets?

3. In reduction or increase in non-current liabilities?

[906.4.3]   BALANCE SHEET CHANGES AND FINANCIAL POSITION. Have the foregoing changes strengthened or weakened the general financial position?

1. Rate of working capital turnover.

2. Rate of inventory turnover.

3. Rate of receivables turnover.

4. Relation of inventory to working capital.

5. Relation of debt to net worth and working capital.

6. Relation of fixed assets to net worth.

The trend of these relationships is especially significant.

[906.4.4]   CAUSES OF IMPORTANT UNFAVORABLE CHANGES. You should determine the following:

1. If the trend of sales is contrary to the industry, why?

2. Do losses lie in sales, production, or merchandising practices?

3. If inventory is appreciably heavier in relation to sales, why?

4. Are collections slowing up? Why?

5. Has fixed asset expansion been justified by larger sales and earnings?

The extent to which answers to the foregoing questions should be ferreted out will be determined by the degree of credit risk and the size of losses or other changes.

[906.4.5]   DETERMINE PROPOSED REMEDIES. Having ascertained the causes of significant unfavorable changes, inquire what is being done to overcome the difficulty when it is a borderline risk.

An inquiry that clearly reveals the analyst's grasp and understanding of the problem is far more likely to command a satisfactory response or to expose the management's own ignorance or ineptness.

[906.4.6]   FORMULATE CONCLUSIONS. Formulate the conclusion by considering the rate of profit or loss in conjunction with the adequacy or inadequacy of the working capital and the remedial measures being taken by the company where such measures are necessary.

[907] **WORKING-CAPITAL ANALYSIS.** Net working capital—the excess of current assets over current liabilities—is that capital which is used to finance the current operations of a business. As such, it is a vital element in any company's financial health and one of the key factors that can influence the credit decision. How much working capital a company has—and in what balance-sheet items it exists—relates directly to its ability to pay its bills to you, the trade creditor. Operations with insufficient working capital—called overtrading—are one of the significant causes of business failure. To arrive at the correct credit decision, therefore, you should undertake an analysis of an important or risky customer's working capital.

[907.1] **Information Derived from Working-Capital Analysis.** Working-capital analysis, by showing what funds are available to a company and how they are used, can help you answer these questions:

[907.1.1] DIVIDEND POLICY. Has a company's dividend policy depleted the working funds of the company or has it permitted a healthy increase in net worth?

[907.1.2] FIXED ASSETS. Does the company have too large an investment in fixed assets for its operation?

[907.1.3] EARNINGS. Are sufficient profits being made and earnings retained to provide for the healthy expansion of the business?

[907.1.4] LONG-TERM LIABILITIES. Are the current maturities on long-term liabilities within easy payment reach of the company without claiming too large a portion of its working capital?

[907.2] **Changes in Working Capital.** These changes would appear on a statement of sources and applications of funds, discussed later in this chapter. Because working capital is the excess of current assets over current liabilities, it can only be changed—increased or decreased—by changes in the following:

[907.2.1] CHANGES IN NET WORTH. Increases in net worth represent contributions to working capital; decreases in net worth represent deductions from working capital. (See Figure 9.12 for a summary of the ways in which working capital can be changed.) Increases and decreases in net worth are the major source of important changes in working capital.

[907.2.2] CHANGES IN LONG-TERM LIABILITIES. An increase in long-term liabilities (deferred debt) represents contributions to working capital because it means that funds are coming into the firm. A decrease in long-term liabilities represents deductions from working capital because it indicates that funds have been used to retire debt. Credit analysts do not look very favorably upon this method of increasing working capital—especially when compared to retaining earnings in the firm—for the following reasons:

1. Long-term debt often limits sources of short-time financing.
2. Long-term debt is often secured by some assets that are no longer available to trade creditors.
3. Future earnings are committed to the repayment of these long-term obligations. In certain lines long-term debt is normal

INCREASES in WORKING CAPITAL	DECREASES in WORKING CAPITAL
1. Increase in Net Worth.	1. Decrease in Net Worth.
2. Creation or increase in deferred debt.	2. Reduction or retirement of deferred debt.
3. Decrease in slow assets. a. Net decrease in fixed assets. b. Net decrease in other slow assets.	3. Increase in slow assets. a. Net increase in fixed assets. b. Net increase in other slow assets.

Window of Working Capital:

Current Assets	$100,000	Current Liabilities	$ 50,000
Working Capital =		$50,000	
Fixed Assets	10,000	Long Term Debts	5,000
Other Assets	10,000	Net Worth	65,000
TOTAL ASSETS	$120,000	TOTAL LIABILITIES & NET WORTH	$120,000

FIGURE 9.12. Sources of Increases and Decreases in Working Capital Funds

practice and its existence should be looked at in the light of all the circumstances.

[907.2.3]   CHANGES IN NON-CURRENT ASSETS. Any increase in non-current assets represents a deduction in working capital; any decrease in non-current assets represents a contribution to working capital. Increases in fixed assets, the most common application of funds to non-current assets, are often the cause of financial difficulty and you should be particularly alert for overextension in this area. Depreciation of fixed assets is thought by some analysts to be a common source of funds from non-current assets that can contribute to working capital. (See Section 909.5.)

[907.3]   **Changes in the Composition of Working Capital.** Often more significant than the net increases and decreases in working capital themselves are the changes in the composition of working capital. You will readily see how, from the creditor's standpoint, a major shift from cash assets to assets represented by goods-in-progress can change the credit risk that a company represents. Not only must you determine the changes in working capital, therefore, you must determine and analyze the significance of changes in the composition of working capital. Remember, too, that the significance of the changes is often your primary concern rather than the dollar amount of change.

[908]   **BREAK-EVEN ANALYSIS.** The term "break-even" refers, of course, to that point in a business' operation at which income on the one hand equals all operating and administrative expenses on the other—as a result, that company has neither profits nor losses for the period. It breaks even. As a credit manager, it will be useful for you to be able to calculate the break-

even point for your own company and for the companies who seek credit from your firm. In the case of your own company, you will find that changes in credit policy can affect costs and sales—and thus your own break-even point. Knowledge of other companies' break-even points enables you better to judge their economic stability: Companies whose income hovers near their expense figure are more subject to large variations in their profits and losses as cost-income variables change. In addition, knowledge of break-even points—where available—can help you forecast trends as you determine whether sales and costs are rising or falling.

[908.1]   **Break-Even Charts.** The easiest way to calculate the break-even point is to use a break-even chart, such as the one illustrated in Chart 9.1. Note that the chart is set up so that volume (in units) is recorded along the horizontal axis and total income and total costs are set up along the vertical axis.

[908.2]   **Determining Break-Even Chart Variables.** In order to plot the break-even chart, you must determine (or estimate) the following information:

[908.2.1]   TOTAL COSTS. Total costs must be determined (or estimated) and set up according to the following classifications:

1. *Fixed costs.* Fixed costs are those which will be incurred no matter how many units are produced. These could be certain salaries, machinery, and operating expenses.

CHART 9.1. Break-Even Chart

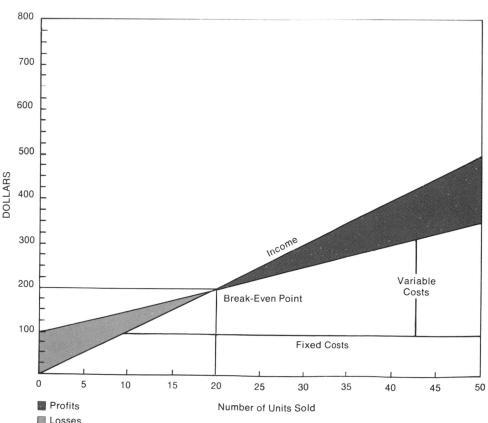

2. *Variable costs.* Variable costs are those which will increase or decrease according to the volume of merchandise produced. The largest variable cost is generally raw materials used in production.

[908.2.2]   SELLING PRICE.   In order to be able to project total income, you must establish a selling price for your product.

[908.3]   **Plotting the Break-Even Chart.** Once you have established the variables listed above, you are ready to plot the information to determine the break-even point. Here is the procedure.

[908.3.1]   FIXED COSTS. Go up the vertical axis until you reach the number corresponding to your fixed costs. Rule a horizontal line. In the example used in Chart 9.1, fixed costs are $100.

[908.3.2]   VARIABLE COSTS. Variable costs—which should be expressed in the form "X number of dollars per unit produced"—will be plotted next. Variable costs start at zero but are plotted starting at the level of fixed cost and, in this example, increase at the rate of $5 per unit produced.

[908.3.3]   TOTAL COSTS. When variable costs are plotted starting at level of fixed costs (in the example, at $100), the resulting line is that of total costs.

[908.3.4]   INCOME. Income, the product of the number of units multiplied by the selling price, is plotted last. In our example, income is based on a selling price of $10 per unit.

[908.3.5]   BREAK-EVEN POINT.   The break-even point appears where the income

CHART 9.2. Break-Even Chart

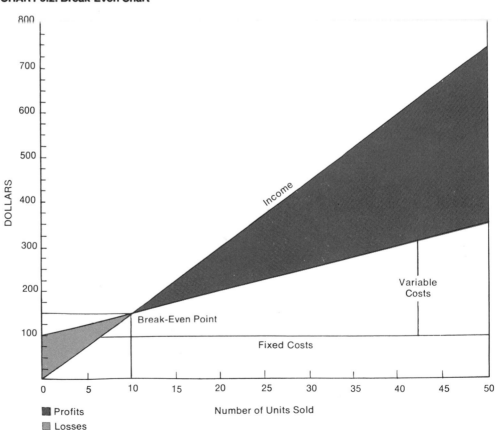

and the variable-cost lines intersect. (Remember, however, that the variable-cost line is built upon fixed costs as well.) In our example, the break-even point occurs when 200 units are produced, and sold.

[908.4]   **Break-Even Chart Analysis.** Beyond telling you what the break-even point is, your analysis of the break-even chart will provide insight into important financial phenomena. The first thing you will notice is that profits are increasing as volume increases, once the break-even point is reached. You will note, too, that the fewer the units sold before the break-even point is reached, the greater the losses. What is not quite so obvious is that the percentages of increased profit (or loss) per additional unit sold are not uniform. For example, if you have reached the break-even point and then sell 5 additional units, you will have profits of $25 ($100 of fixed costs have been paid; income of $50 [5 units @ $10] minus variable costs of $25 [5 units @ $5] equals $25). Your percentage increase is infinite. If you raise your volume to 55 units (an increase over your previous sales of 30), your profits will rise to $175, an increase of $150. The percentage increase over the previous level is 600 percent!

If instead you increase sales by 15 units to 150, your *increase* in profits is only $75 or 13 percent. The same principle, in reverse, of course, holds true for losses as well.

[908.5]   **Changing Break-Even Chart Variables.** Perhaps the greatest service the use of break-even charts can provide is to help you see the changing

CHART 9.3. Break-Even Chart

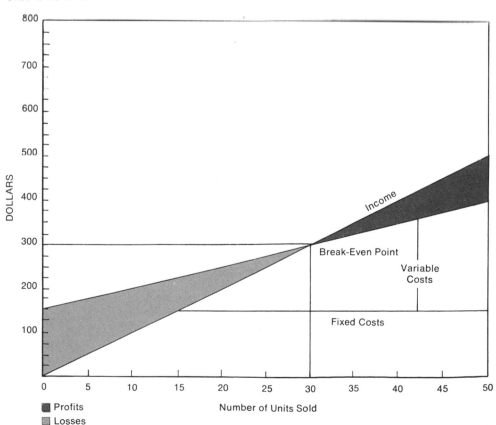

profit picture when variables in business operations are changed. In other words, a break-even chart will let you see immediately how changed selling price, changed fixed costs, or changed variable costs will affect your profits. Charts 9.2, 9.3, and 9.4 show what happens when these changes occur.

[908.5.1]   INCREASED SELLING PRICE. If we continue to use our original example, examine what happens when selling price is increased $5 to $15. The break-even point drops to 10 units and profits increase dramatically. (Of course, these examples are extreme to illustrate principles involved.)

[908.5.2]   INCREASED FIXED COSTS. If the selling price remains at the original $10 and fixed costs increase by $50 to $150, look at the result. The break-even point advances to 30 and profits are harder to come by.

[908.5.3]   INCREASED VARIABLE COSTS. If, continuing to use the original example, we increase variable costs by $2 a unit to $7, these are the results: The break-even point is advanced to approximately 33 units and profits increase at a much slower rate.

[909]   **CHANGES IN FINANCIAL POSITION.** The balance sheet and the income statement (profit and loss statement) have been with us a long time. You as a credit analyst can detect changes in the financial position of the business you are analyzing by making comparisons of these statements

CHART 9.4. Break-Even Chart

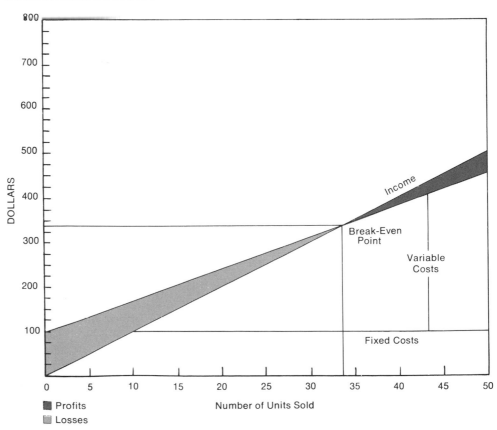

with those of the same company for the previous year. Some accountants have provided a third statement frequently called a statement of the sources and application of funds and sometimes referred to as a where-got where-gone statement. In 1971 the Accounting Principles Board of the American Institute of Certified Public Accountants issued opinion number 19 which stated the objectives and purposes of reporting the changes that had taken place from one year to the next in the financial position of a company. This had the effect of elevating the statement of changes in financial position to a status equal to that of the balance sheet and income statement.

Objective. The statement takes one of several forms and may be given one of many different names, but the objectives are:

1. To reflect the funds generated from operations during the period.
2. To summarize the financing and investing activities during the period.
3. To show the complete disclosure of changes in the financial picture during the period.

Disclosure. The 1971 opinion allows leeway as to format but the disclosure requirements call for a presentation that must prominently disclose:

1. Cash or working capital that has been provided from or used in the operations.
2. Separate reporting of the effects of extraordinary items.
3. Individual disclosure of the effects of other financing and investing activities.
4. Separate identification of the purchase of long-term assets such as investments, land and building, and intangibles.
5. Proceeds from the sale of long-term assets, with separate identification of those items.
6. Any conversion to common stock of long-term debt or preferred stock.
7. Long-term debt issuance, assumption, redemption, or repayment.
8. Any issuance, redemption, or purchase of capital stock either for cash or by the use of other assets.
9. Dividends, whether in cash or in kind, or any other distribution.

[909.1]   **Terminology.** There has been some confusion over terminology particularly as to such terms as cash flow, flow of funds, funds provided, funds used, working capital provided, working capital used, sources, uses, flow-through, and add-back. Unfortunately, even accountants use different terms for the same thing; there is ambiguity primarily caused by the fact that "funds" has meant different things over the years. "Resources provided" and "resources used" are now utilized by some accountants. Perhaps someday these terms or some others will be adopted uniformly. In the meantime the analyst will simply have to make certain that the terms being used are understood for what they mean.

Perhaps the major distinction to be understood is the contrast between the cash and working-capital approaches.

	THIS YEAR	PREVIOUS YEAR
OPERATIONS		
Net income	23,000	21,000
Add (deduct) items not involving the use of working capital		
Equity in earnings of related companies	(3,000)	(2,000)
Depreciation	9,000	8,000
Depletion	4,000	4,000
Deferred income tax	3,000	2,000
Working capital provided by operations	36,000	33,000

TABLE 9.1

Working Capital Provided by Operations (Working-Capital Approach) Add-Back Format

[909.2]   **Presentations.** While the accountant's presentation may take many forms, there are two basic approaches in measuring and reflecting the flow from operations. They are the working-capital approach and the cash approach. The net flow provided by operations can be computed by either a flow-through approach or by adding back such items as depreciation or depletion.

[909.2.1]   WORKING-CAPITAL APPROACH. This is the traditional approach and stresses the liquidity concept. This method evolved from the effort to fulfill the needs of financial institutions and trade creditors. Since it presupposes an understanding of the term "working capital," it is for the sophisticated analyst and not the investing public.

You will see in Table 9.1 that additions and deductions have been made to net income to arrive at the working capital provided by operations. It is not easy to visualize what has actually happened.

[909.2.2]   CASH-FLOW-THROUGH APPROACH. This approach, not used by many accountants, segregates the separate but related inflows and outflows from operations. It can be used in either the working-capital or the cash approach. You can see from Table 9.2 that sales are a source of working capital (or cash) and expenses are a use of working capital (or cash). The adjustments for those items that do not affect working capital are presented in a clear manner. It is easier to grasp the concept as to why such items as depreciation and depletion are not included in the expenses which require working capital (or cash) than it is to see why depreciation is added to net income in Table 9.1.

This presentation parallels the normal operating cycle. Cash is expended for materials and services and these are converted into a product that is sold usually for credit. Collections are made, returning cash. A comparison of the approaches shows that the add-back technique is actually a shortcut in the computation of the operational flows and is not as clear or as informative as the flow-through approach.

[909.3]   **A Third Major Financial Statement.** The recognition by the accounting profession of the need for a third major financial statement is a step forward. However, there are wide differences in the way accounting guidelines are being followed.

OPERATIONS				
		This Year		Previous Year
Revenues:		650,000		610,000
Less: Revenues not resulting in an increase in working capital Equity in earning of unconsolidated companies		3,000		2,000
			647,000	608,000
Expenses:		627,000		589,000
Less: Expenses not requiring current outflow of working capital				
Depreciation	9,000		8,000	
Depletion	4,000		4,000	
Deferred income taxes	3,000		2,000	
Total		16,000		14,000
			611,000	575,000
Working Capital provided by operations			36,000	33,000

TABLE 9.2. Working Capital Provided by Operations (Flow-Through Approach)

[909.4]   **Statement of Source and Application of Funds.** Some accountants still use the Statement of Application of Funds illustrated by Table 9.3. This is simply the taking of the individual balance sheet items, calculating the net change in each either upward or downward from one year to the next, and sorting the items by whether they are sources or uses of funds.

[909.4.1]   SOURCES OF FUNDS. There are three sources of funds, or three means by which cash can be made available to the corporation to pay trade bills or use in some other way. The three are a decrease in assets, an increase in liabilities, or an increase in net worth.

[909.4.2]   USES OF FUNDS. There are three ways that funds may be used or applied. They are through increases in assets, decreases in liabilities, or decreases in net worth.

Source of Funds	
Increase in trade accounts payable	$20,000
Increase in notes payable—banks	10,000
Increase in deferred income taxes	5,000
Increase in common stock	10,000
Increase in earned surplus	5,000
Total sources	$50,000
Use of Funds	
Increase in cash	$5,000
Increase in accounts receivable	7,000
Increase in marketable securities	5,000
Increase in inventories	8,000
Increase in prepaid expenses	2,000
Increase in land and building (net)	5,000
Increase in equipment (net)	3,000
Decrease in preferred stock	5,000
Decrease in long-term debt	10,000
Total uses	$50,000

TABLE 9.3

Statement of Application of Funds (Where-got, Where-gone Statement)

This statement has limited value. It is true that significant changes may be turned up by a review of this statement but it is also true that the expert analyst probably would turn up the same things through a review of two or more balance sheets on the company.

[909.5]   **Statement of Changes in Financial Condition.** While the individual accountant may regard the Statement of Application of Funds, a similar Uses and Sources approach, or the Working Capital Provided by Operations approach as meeting the requirements for the third major financial statement, the most useful approach may be one which combines the cash flow-through format with a Statement of Changes in Financial Position as illustrated by Tables 9.4 and 9.5. You can see that the changes in current assets and current liabilities is the proper relationship to operations and investing and financing activities. Additionally, the cash-flow approach more clearly reflects all of the basic flows. One illustration of the kind of distortion resulting from the working capital approach with the add-back presentation is the common belief that depreciation is a source of funds. The presentation in Table 9.1 creates that illusion. The presentation in Tables 9.2 and 9.4 clearly shows that it is more correctly stated that depreciation does not require a cash outflow. Perhaps even more important, the working-capital approach mixes the operational inflows and outflows from financing and investing activities. Significant short-term financing and investing activity is shown only as a net change in the analysis of the working-capital items. To illustrate the problem, short-

Schedule 1		
Analysis of Revenue Flows:		
Operating revenue (from income statement)		$350,000
Less: Increase in accounts and notes receivable that have no effect on cash flow		12,000
Net cash flow from operations		$338,000
Analysis of Expense Flows:		
Operating expenses (from income statement)		315,000
Plus: Increase in inventory which caused an increase in cash outflow		14,000
		329,000
Less: Changes in items that have no effect on cash outflow		
Depreciation	$8,000	
Depletion	5,000	
Amortization of goodwill	8,000	
Increase in accounts payable	7,000	
Increase in income tax	5,000	
Increase in accrued liabilities	3,000	
Increase in deferred income taxes	7,000	
Net changes not requiring cash outflow		43,000
Net cash outflow from operations		286,000
Net cash flow from operations		$ 52,000

TABLE 9.4. Cash Flow from Operations for the Year Ended December 31, 197-

Resource provided:	
Net cash flow from operations (Schedule 1)	$52,000
Sale of investments	5,000
Sale of real estate	30,000
Increase in current position of long-term debt	3,000
Increase in long-term debt	18,000
Total resources provided	$108,000
Resource applied:	
Plant & Equipment (additions)	60,000
Payment of short term bank loans	8,000
Payment of long-term debt	10,000
Treasury stock acquired	5,000
Dividends paid	15,000
Increase in cash	10,000
Total resources applied	$108,000

TABLE 9.5

Statement of Changes in Financial Position for the Year Ended December 31, 197–.

term borrowing to finance a seasonal inventory bulge may be essential to profitable operations. The net changes at year-end will not truly reflect the financing requirements. A look at Table 9.5 provides illustrations of this point in regard to sale of real estate and the purchase of plant and equipment and also the payment of long-term debt and taking on of new long-term debt.

[909.6]

Use of Flow Information. The business owner, the credit executive and, for that matter, the investment analyst look at the historical cash flow to help in determining the future ability of the company to:

1. Meet debt retirement requirements.
2. Finance replacement and expansion costs.
3. Maintain regular dividends to the owners.

In the small business this can be done simply by looking at the operating statement to see the past income from sales and other sources, if any, and then looking at the balance sheet to find outgo items such as accounts payable and payments on loans, and returning to the operating statement for outgo items in the form of expenses. Assumptions must be made as to whether there will be any increase in requirements for such assets as accounts receivable, inventory, or fixed investment. By adding the cash to average monthly sales, you can see on a rough basis whether there is likely to be enough flow of cash to meet debts as they become due.

The statements that reflect changes in financial position are basically historical. However, they do provide some insight into the basic health of the business and, with supporting information, can be used to help evaluate the likelihood that the business will be able to meet its obligations as they become due. Obviously, there is a need for information regarding significant expected changes in sales, working-capital requirements, and capital equipment. The net cash flow from operations reflected in Table 9.4 can be useful. For instance, if the requirements for working capital and the fixed investment are growing at a rate significantly greater than increase in the net cash flow from operations, the business has a problem.

It is entirely possible that the problem could be discovered in another way. For instance, a heavy buildup in inventory could have this effect and could be seen by looking at the inventory figure in balance sheets for two consecutive years. The primary utility of this statement is in the opportunity to see the detail of the changes occurring and how the funds are flowing. In looking at Tables 9.4 and 9.5 you could assume that the investment in plant and equipment was financed largely through the sale of real estate and the taking on of long-term debt, hence there was no strain placed on the current position of the business.

While the Statement of Changes in Financial Position may be used more frequently by the investment analyst than the credit analyst, it behooves the latter to have familiarity with it, as it not only provides valuable information but gives him a better opportunity to ask the right questions of management when the credit exposure is large and the financial condition is in question.

[910]   **THE CREDIT IMPORTANCE OF DEBT FINANCING.** Every business has two sources for financing—its creditors and its owners. Depending on the form selected, it may be either debt or equity financing.

[910.1]   **Equity Financing.** Equity financing results from funds obtained as permanent investment from business owners who, depending on the type of organization, may be proprietors, partners, or stockholders. Equity financing increases net worth.

[910.2]   **Debt Financing.** Debt financing results from funds obtained through borrowing on notes, bonds, mortgages, debentures, open accounts, or other evidences of indebtedness. Debt financing increases total liabilities. Debt financing dates back to the time when the first businessman solved his need for new funds by obtaining a loan. Now every business, from the corner grocery to the large manufacturer, employs debt financing to some extent but its credit significance varies considerably from case to case.

When debt financing is moderate in amount, and confined to routine matters such as the acquisition of merchandise, services and supplies on credit, the purchase of equipment on installment terms, or seasonal borrowing from banks, it presents nothing unusual from a credit standpoint. As debt financing grows in size, its significance increases, and during recent years, the number of instances has risen where total debt financing is substantial in relation to total equity financing.

[910.2.1]   FACTORS THAT FAVOR INCREASED USE OF DEBT FINANCING. Growth of debt financing in recent years reflects the influence on the thinking of businessmen of a variety of considerations, including:

1. Tax savings on interest compared with dividends.
2. Increased volume of funds available from insurance companies and others on term loans.
3. Flexibility of debt financing in providing funds for a changing volume of government contracts.
4. Ease and low cost for arranging debt financing.
5. No dilution of equity and preservation of control with debt financing.

6. Avoidance of public disclosure of information.

7. Increased leverage in earnings when debt financing is used.

IDENTIFYING INSTANCES WHERE DEBT FINANCING IS SIGNIFICANT. Debt financing grows in credit significance as it increases in size. To identify situations where debt financing has risen to a point where it needs special considerations, a few guides can be helpful. Mr. Roy A. Foulke in his *Practical Financial Statement Analysis* points out that debt relationships need particularly careful review whenever:

1. Current liabilities become larger than three-quarters of tangible net worth.

2. Funded debt becomes larger than net working capital.

3. Total debt becomes larger than tangible net worth.

INVESTIGATING CASES WHERE DEBT FINANCING IS SIGNIFICANT. After a case has been identified as one where debt financing is significant because one or more of the above balance-sheet relationships has exceeded the limits shown, the case should receive special credit management attention. Answers to the following questions should be obtained:

1. Is the management factor superior, average, or below average?

2. Considering the manner in which the business operates, what degree of risk is incurred in relation to (a) maintenance of sales, (b) collection of receivables, (c) inventories, (d) facilities, (e) types of financing?

3. How does the financial condition and operating results of this business compare with those typical of its line?

4. Are the reasons given by management for selecting debt rather than equity financing understandable and reasonable?

5. Who provides the debt financing and how are repayments scheduled?

6. Are any items of indebtedness subordinated, guaranteed, or secured, and, if so, do you have full particulars?

7. Does available operating information, including cash projections, indicate that the business in the future will be able to meet without strain its regular expenses, interest on its debt financing, and scheduled debt retirements?

8. How do banks and suppliers view the substantial debt financing used by the business?

ANALYZING CONCERNS WITH SIZABLE DEBT FINANCING. There is no simple set of financial and operating relationships for general use as analytical tools when working with instances of debt financing. Each case must be appraised on its own merits. A careful weighing of all significant credit factors is the only way to decide whether a particular business should receive the credit line it requests. Nevertheless, here are some points that may be helpful in reaching your credit decisions:

1. Sizable debt financing by itself must be interpreted as signifying that the financial condition of a business is critical and that limited credit should be extended.

2. Substantial debt financing is customary and normal for certain lines. For example, dealers in commodities who "hedge" their

inventories often owe as much as five times tangible net worth. Therefore, the financial condition of a particular business should be considered in the light of what is typical of its line.

3. Your credit decision must reflect the strength of other credit factors that might offset the existence of heavy debt.

4. The significance of the same dollar amount of debt financing varies from company to company and even between two with the same net worth, because of differences in the (a) form of the various classes of debt (for example, open account debt, notes, debentures, or mortgages), (b) maturity dates and repayment provisions for the various debt items, (c) nature of security for debt items, (d) special debt provisions such as subordinations, restrictions on dividend payment, requirements for the maintenance of working capital, or right to convert to capital stock, (e) identity, character, and financial strength of the holders of the various classes of debt.

5. The existence of an effective subordination of an important liability substantially strengthens the credit worthiness of a business. Proper support for a large line of credit for a business with sizable debt usually is absent unless important items of indebtedness have been subordinated. This is particularly true in instances where debt is owed to individuals, such as the officials of a closely held corporation.

CHAPTER 10

ORGANIZATIONS RELATED TO THE CREDIT FIELD

[1000]   **ORGANIZATIONS RELATED TO THE CREDIT FIELD.** Every credit manager should be aware of those organizations which exist to provide special services, assistance, and information that will enable him to do his job better. These range from the National Association of Credit Management, a nonprofit trade association acting in the interests of all credit men, to credit-insurance companies that can cover the risks for which credit managers are responsible. Whatever your specific needs, there is some organization waiting to serve. The most important are discussed below.

[1000.1]   **National Association of Credit Management (NACM).** The National Association of Credit Management, located in New York City, is the largest organization in the credit field. It has more than 37,000 members in cities throughout the United States. The NACM is a nonprofit trade association that provides these services for the credit industry:

[1000.1.1]   ACTION ON LEGISLATION. NACM is active in the public policy area. The organization has worked in the past for the passage of such fundamental trade legislation as the Federal Reserve Act and the National Bankruptcy Act. The NACM's 100 local affiliated associations work to improve the legal structure of trade in their own areas, with assistance from the NACM National Legislation Department.

[1000.1.2]   CREDIT INTERCHANGE. Credit Interchange Bureaus of the NACM are the network through which valuable ledger experience is communicated throughout the country. The Credit Interchange process is described more fully in Section 1000.1.5. Over 900 NACM industry credit groups extend the service and functions of Credit Interchange into specific industries.

[1000.1.3]   ADJUSTMENT BUREAUS. The NACM's adjustment bureaus, also described in more detail in Section 1208, are an important means to arrive at an orderly and non-costly liquidation of a business, or a compromise settlement to ensure a troubled business' survival.

[1000.1.4]   COLLECTION SERVICES. Available for your use are more than seventy local NACM-affiliated collection bureaus. These bureaus use aggressive but tactful collection techniques, and because NACM is a nonprofit organization, the commissions collected are used to improve the NACM's credit services to you. NACM supplements the work of its affiliated collection bureaus with a National Collection Service, which operates on the national and regional levels.

[1000.1.5]   CREDIT INTERCHANGE BUREAUS. These are local Credit Interchange Bureaus organized in a system supervised by the Credit Interchange Board of Governors of the National Association of Credit Management. Although contact is less personal than in NACM industry credit groups, the information supplied by participation in a local bureau is extensive, accurate, and up-to-date. Moreover, NACM Credit Interchange is one of the least expensive methods to obtain factual ledger experiences of suppliers from broad geographic areas. The system works as follows:

1. You furnish your local bureau with information on the customers you are selling.
2. When you want information on a customer, you send a request to your local interchange bureau.
3. The interchange bureau sends you a copy of any report it has on file.
4. Your request is circulated through the system to produce responses from all of the subject's suppliers.
5. These responses are tabulated and distributed in a new report that is then placed on file.

[1000.1.6]   FRAUD DETECTION AND PREVENTION. With the cooperation of its nationwide local bureaus, the FBI, postal inspectors, and district attorneys, NACM assists in the detection of commercial frauds and their prevention through an intelligence file alerting members to fraud situations. In the past, the NACM has been active in the prosecution and punishment of fraudulent traders.

[1000.1.7]   FOREIGN SERVICES. Through the FCIB–NACM Corporation (formerly the Foreign Credit Interchange Bureau) NACM provides the trade record of foreign buyers to American producers. In addition, FCIB–NACM works with industry and government to solve trade complexities and difficulties. Weekly FCIB bulletins keep members up-to-date on the latest developments on the international trade front.

[1000.1.8]   PUBLICATIONS. The NACM is responsible for several publications that are of vital importance to you as a credit executive. These include:

1. *Credit Manual of Commercial Laws.* Published yearly, the *Credit Manual of Commercial Laws* contains information about new and previously existing laws related to trade and credit at federal and state levels—including the texts of important laws, regulations, and codes.
2. *Credit Management Handbook.* Last published in 1965, the *Credit Management Handbook* is indispensable to you for information on credit and collection processes and techniques. Written by more than a hundred contributors and editors, this *Handbook* covers such significant topics as Credit Policy, The Credit Man as Business Advisor, Credit Reporting Agencies, Foreign Credit, and many others.
3. *Credit and Financial Management.* This is the monthly magazine of

the NACM and as such offers up-to-date articles and commentary on matters important to credit and financial executives.

[1000.1.9] EDUCATION SERVICES. NACM, through its educational affiliate, the Credit Research Foundation of the National Institute of Credit, offers credit-management education opportunities for beginners to executives. For more detail, see the discussion of the CRF that follows.

[1000.2] **Credit Research Foundation (CRF).** The Credit Research Foundation, Inc., located in Lake Success, New York, is the education and research affiliate of the National Association of Credit Management. It was chartered in 1949 under Delaware laws as a nonprofit corporation and has its own membership, board of trustees, and committee structure.

[1000.2.1] PURPOSE. The foundation is concerned directly with research and education in credit and financial management, and its funds are used solely for that purpose. Its applied research projects are aimed toward developing more effective credit practices and techniques. On a broader basis, its inquiries and basic research seek to identify and quantify the impact of business credit upon a company's financial structure and upon the national economy.

[1000.2.2] MEMBERSHIP. Members of the CRF are business firms and financial institutions.

[1000.2.3] EDUCATION. In the field of education, the foundation conducts its own continuing education programs. These are:

1. *Mid-Career Program,* which is designed for middle-management personnel in the field of credit and financial management.
2. *Credit-management workshops and seminars,* which bring executives together for intensive discussion sessions on specific and timely topics.

[1000.2.4] AFFILIATION WITH NACM. In addition to the above projects, the foundation administers the education activities for the National Association of Credit Management. These include the Graduate School of Credit and Financial Management, which is an executive-development program conducted at Dartmouth College, Stanford University, Williams College, and the London Graduate School of Business Studies (see Chapter 3); and the National Institute of Credit, which offers training in the basic skills of credit management through local institute chapters in affiliation with local colleges and universities. Correspondence courses are also offered.

[1000.2.5] PUBLICATIONS. The results of research studies carried out by the foundation are published in booklet form. Titles range from "Compensation of Credit Executives" to "Electronic Funds Transfer System for Business Payments."

[1000.3] **Robert Morris Associates.** Robert Morris Associates (RMA) is a national association for commercial banks and their commercial loan and credit officers. It was established in 1914 and named after the American patriot who is recognized as the "financier of the Revolutionary War."

[1000.3.1] MEMBERSHIP. Almost 5,500 commercial loan and credit officers representing over 1,400 commercial banks in all fifty states, Puerto Rico, and the U.S. Virgin Islands, Canada, and Panama, actively participate in RMA. Membership in RMA is selective—it is for banks that are able to serve the commercial lending needs of their areas. Presently, its member banks represent a little more than 87 percent of all banking resources in the United States. Many RMA publications and services, moreover, are of interest to all credit managers.

[1000.3.2]   ORGANIZATION. Structurally, RMA is set up in two areas as follows:

1. *National administration.* The national leadership of Robert Morris Associates is provided by three elected officers and a rotating board of directors—all of whom are elected by the membership. A group of professional association executives and experienced bankers form the national staff, which conducts the daily association activities in RMA's headquarters in Philadelphia. Led by an executive manager, the staff includes a director of administration and member services, a director of public relations, a director of professional services, several assistants to these executives, and the necessary secretarial and clerical personnel to fulfill the many responsibilities. The national office is charged with many tasks including the publications and services discussed below.

2. *Local chapters.* RMA member banks are divided into chapters. Some of the chapters cover a major city and its immediately surrounding area; others cover larger territories. Each chapter elects its own leaders and plans its own regular meeting programs, committee activities, and special projects. All work at the chapter level is conducted on a voluntary basis by the individuals who represent their banks in RMA at the chapter and national levels.

[1000.3.3]   PUBLICATIONS. RMA publications include the following:

1. *The Journal of Commercial Bank Lending.* This monthly professional journal is a forum for the expression of ideas, concepts, and techniques of specific interest to bank loan and credit officers. RMA members receive it automatically, and nonmembers may receive it by subscription.

2. *Annual Statement Studies.* This is an annual book of composite balance sheets, income statements, and eleven widely used ratios based on the financial statements of borrowing customers of RMA's member banks. A recent edition was compiled from over 35,000 statements and covered some 300 industries. The statistical information forms an industrywide reference point for commercial loan and credit officers, accountants, management consultants, and other credit executives and financial analysts.

3. *Loan Officer Development Seminar.* Developed jointly with the American Institute of Banking, this thirty-six-hour middle-management seminar is designed to teach practical lending skills to newly appointed lending officers. It covers six major subject areas and utilizes a variety of training techniques. Sessions include:
   a. The Initial Loan Interview.
   b. Administration Decisions and Techniques.
   c. Documentation for the Credit File.
   d. Problem Loans.

e. Conveying Unpleasant Information.

f. Managing Loan Portfolios.

4. *Official forms.* Over the years, RMA has developed and continuously updated various financial-statement forms, spread sheets, and questionnaires—both general purpose and specialized. Some of the forms are for internal bank use, while others are designed to be completed by potential borrowers. Sample copies and prices are available from the RMA national office at no charge.

[1000.3.4]   LOAN MANAGEMENT SEMINAR. The RMA Loan Management Seminar is an annual one-week seminar conducted by RMA in cooperation with the Graduate School of Business at Indiana University for the loan officer already at or destined for the senior-management level. The seminar is a rigorous exercise in the exploration of ideas and concepts of benefit to the loan officer concerned with management of the loan function for profitability, safety, and liquidity.

[1000.3.5]   WORKSHOPS. RMA special workshops are conducted regularly in various parts of the country. Their purpose is to expose participants from member banks to in-depth treatment of various commercial loan and credit subjects.

[1000.3.6]   CODES. RMA promotes adherence to high standards of ethics in the banking and credit fields by the following:

1. *Code of Ethics for the Exchange of Credit Information.* This code was created by RMA in 1916 and has been updated in keeping with changing needs. RMA members subscribe to the code and find it mutually helpful in the proper conduct of their business.

2. *Statement of Principles in the Exchange of Credit Information Between Banks and Mercantile Concerns.* This statement (See Figure 6.1) has been jointly adopted by RMA and the National Association of Credit Management (NACM) to further encourage the improvement of credit standards.

[1000.3.7]   RESEARCH PROJECTS. Special research projects are undertaken by RMA whenever the need is foreseen. For example, in 1970 RMA published a study that projected commercial bank balance sheets and manpower requirements in 1975 and 1980. It has conducted research in conjunction with the Bank Administration Institute on EDP and the commercial lending function. From time to time, RMA also publishes in-depth treatments of lending subjects, which are published as "occasional papers."

[1000.3.8]   LEGAL AND LEGISLATIVE INTERESTS. RMA has taken active positions regarding national legislation of importance to commercial lenders. Contacts have been established with federal regulatory authorities for more effective cooperation on behalf of the commercial loan and credit officer.

[1000.4]   **Commercial Credit Insurance Companies.** Commercial credit insurance protects manufacturers, jobbers, wholesalers, and certain service industries (e.g., advertising agencies) against large, damaging credit losses. It also provides credit guidance and collection assistance. The service is geared to help companies achieve sound sales growth and, at the same time, control credit loss within a reasonable range. Credit insurance is provided by two companies—American Credit Indemnity (a subsidiary of Commercial Credit Company) and The London Guarantee and Accident Company. Both of these companies serve clients in the United States and Canada. In order to decide whether your company should have commercial credit insurance, review the following sections covering (1) some of the key policy features, (2) major conditions of a credit insurance policy, and (3) uses of a policy.

[1000.4.1] KEY POLICY FEATURES. A credit insurance policy provides protection against credit losses due to both insolvency and nonpayment of debtors located in the United States, Canada, and Puerto Rico. Although there are several different types of policies to meet client needs, the fundamental components of each policy are similar. Some of the key policy features are:

1. *Policy amount.* Each policy has a level of maximum liability that can range from thousands of dollars to millions of dollars. It is the maximum amount that can be paid by the insurer for credit losses occurring during the policy year. The policy amount is based on the policyholder's sales volume and the size of the individual debtor exposures. It is usually recommended that the policy amount be at least 5 percent of annual sales volume.

2. *Deductible.* A deductible or primary loss is also established for each policy. The insurance company pays all losses over the deductible amount up to the policy amount. Important to remember is that the deductible is subtracted from the aggregate credit loss and not from each individual bad debt.

   In setting a deductible amount, consideration is given to the insured's sales volume, bad-debt experience, the nature of the debtor risks, and the general risk environment of the industry. The deductible can be increased by the insured to reduce the premium charge.

   The deductible is stated as a minimum amount and as a percentage of the projected annual sales volume. For an example, assume that the deductible on a sales volume of $5 million is $15,000—or $^3/_{10}$ of 1 percent. If the sales volume for the policy term turns out to be $6 million, then the deductible is $^3/_{10}$ of $6 million, or $18,000. Should the actual sales volume for the policy be $4 million, then the deductible is the minimum of $15,000. The deductible is, in effect, a ceiling at which an insured attempts to control potential bad debts in much the same manner as he attempts to control any operating expense.

3. *Types of coverage.* There are three types of coverage under a credit insurance policy:

   a. *Regular coverage.* Regular coverage is provided on debtors that have favorable capital-credit ratings assigned by a mercantile reporting agency. The most widely used agency is Dun & Bradstreet, Inc. Table 10.1 shows an example of agency ratings and coverage limits. When an insured receives an order for $40,000 from an account rated CB1, he consults the table in his policy for the amount of coverage. If the maximum

| COLUMN ONE | | COLUMN TWO | |
Rating	Gross Amount Covered	Rating	Gross Amount Covered
5A, 4A or 3A 1	$ 100,000.	5A, 4A or 3A 2	$ 25,000.
2A 1	$ 50,000.	2A 2	$ 25,000.
1A 1	$ 50,000.	1A 2	$ 25,000.
BA 1	$ 50,000.	BA 2	$ 25,000.
BB 1	$ 50,000.	BB 2	$ 25,000.
CB 1	$ 50,000.	CB 2	$ 25,000.
(Blank) 1	$ 50,000.	(Blank) 2	$ 15,000.
CC 1	$ 30,000.	CC 2	$ 15,000.
DC 1	$ 25,000.	DC 2	$ 12,500.
DD 1	$ 20,000.	DD 2	$ 10,000.
EE 1	$ 10,000.	EE 2	$ 5,000.
FF 1	$ 5,000.	FF 2	$ 3,000.
GG 1	$ 2,500.	GG 2	$ 1,500.
HH 1	$ 1,500.	HH 2	$ 750.

TABLE 10.1. Table of Ratings and Coverage

of $50,000 is listed, then the $40,000 order is automatically covered. The insured does not have to submit the account to the credit insurance company for approval. When an insured requires more than the automatic limit on the table, then the debtor's name must be submitted to the insurer. A credit line is established and the account is specifically named in the policy. This named coverage can be canceled by the insurer as to future shipments if the financial condition of the debtor deteriorates seriously. It can also be canceled by the insured when need for it ceases to exist.

b. *Extraordinary coverage.* Debtors that are not covered by the table of ratings (i.e., debtors with lower capital-credit ratings or no rating) are subject to the insurer's approval. A credit limit is established for each account in this category and all accounts are named in the policy. This coverage can also be canceled by either the insurer or the insured.

c. *Blanket coverage.* A discretionary limit of protection can be established on smaller accounts not covered in the other sections of the policy. Small accounts covered in this manner do not have to be submitted to the insurer for approval. Liability or protection is limited by an aggregate amount.

4. *Optional features.* The credit insurance policy is flexible and can be tailored to meet specific client needs. Some optional features are:

a. *Coinsurance.* With coinsurance, the insured bears 10 percent of regular losses and 20 percent of extraordinary and blanket-coverage losses. This feature reduces the insurer's risk and the premium charge.

b. *Collection service.* This is available to the insured on all accounts, much of it without charge.

c. *Monthly reporting.* In some cases, the insured reports certain outstanding receivables monthly and pays a premium based on the reported amounts. This is usually more economical where there are wide swings in amounts of receivables.

d. *Work-in-progress.* Specially purchased and processed materials can be covered by special endorsement in the event of insolvency of the debtor.

e. *Interim adjustment.* This endorsement provides for up to three claims settlements during the policy term, which is one year.

f. *Insured's option to handle claims again insolvent accounts.* This endorsement recognizes that it may be advisable for the insured to pursue claims against insolvent accounts rather than have the insurer proceed.

g. *Bank endorsement.* A special bank endorsement is often used to provide the insured's bank with additional collateral on loans. The bank enjoys the same rights and privileges under the policy as those offered the insured and is the beneficiary in the event of a loss payment.

5. *Cost.* The cost or premium for a credit insurance policy will vary for each insured based on sales volume, risk, optional features, etc. It is generally a fraction of one percent of the sales volume.

[1000.4.2]   POLICY CONDITIONS. A sample policy is shown in Figure 10.1. The major sections are the following:

1. *Condition 1.* This condition defines the parameters for determining the amount of coverage in force at the date of shipment. It is important to understand that an insured's customer can lose its rating after shipment was made and the coverage remains intact.

2. *Condition 2.* This condition is optional and permits the insured to file an account within three months of the due date. With a special endorsement called "Substitution of Condition No. 2," the filing period can be extended to twelve months from date of shipment. The filing condition enables the insured to legally create a claim by filing an account with the insurer.

3. *Condition 3.* The eighteen forms of insolvency that are recognized as claims against the policy are defined in this section.

4. *Condition 4.* Instructions are included in this section for the insured to file an insolvent account with the insurer within ten days after acquiring knowledge of that insolvency.

5. *Condition 5.* This part of the policy spells out the function of the insurer's collection department. It indicates which services are without cost and specifies collection fees for other services.

6. *Conditions 6, 7 and 8.* These sections relate to claim settlements with the insured and subsequent actions.

[1000.4.3]   POLICY USE AND CLAIM SETTLEMENT. To obtain maximum benefit from a credit insurance policy, you must use it in the day-to-day credit operation. Coverages or credit lines must be kept current. When you, as a policyholder, get a new customer account, the policy must be checked to ensure the account can be covered automatically based on the ratings specified in the policy or under the blanket-coverage feature. If not, you should submit the account to the insurer and request that the desired credit line be established. At times, you and the insurer must work closely to obtain necessary financial information on a debtor account to assist in establishing a credit line.

AMERICAN CREDIT INDEMNITY COMPANY

OF NEW YORK

ESTABLISHED 1893

EXECUTIVE OFFICE   BALTIMORE, MD.   21202

(HEREINAFTER CALLED THE COMPANY)

1. 1   IN CONSIDERATION of the warranties and representations made
1. 2 in the application for this Policy of Credit Insurance, and of the payment
1. 3 of the premium as hereinafter provided, and subject to the other conditions
1. 4 hereinafter set forth and to the provisions of the Policy Declaration all of
1. 5 which are hereby made a part of this Policy, hereby guarantees the Insured
1. 6 named in the Policy Declaration against loss due to insolvency, as herein-
1. 7 after defined, of debtors, provided such insolvency occurs within the
1. 8 Insolvency Period. Such loss shall consist of the unpaid invoice price of
1. 9 bona fide sales of the Insured, shipped during the Shipment Period and
1.10 actually delivered in the usual course of business to individuals, firms,
1.11 copartnerships or corporations located in the United States of America
1.12 or Canada, and shall have been covered, filed and proved as hereinafter
1.13 provided. From the aggregate amount of net covered losses, ascertained
1.14 as hereinafter provided, there shall be deducted a Primary Loss, established
1.15 by the Primary Loss Percentage of total gross sales so made during the
1.16 Shipment Period, less all allowances actually made on said sales during
1.17 the Shipment Period, and less the invoice price of any of said sales returned
1.18 and accepted by the Insured during the Shipment Period. Such Primary
1.19 Loss, however, shall in no event be less than the Minimum Primary Loss.
1.20 The remainder, not exceeding the Policy Amount, less any amount owing
1.21 the Company, shall be the amount payable to the Insured by the Company.
1.22   This Policy shall not cover any loss occurring prior to the payment
1.23 of the premium, although the Policy may have been delivered; nor any
1.24 loss that is not a valid and legally sustainable indebtedness or has not been
1.25 allowed against the debtor or the debtor's estate.

1

FIGURE 10.1. Sample Credit Insurance Policy

CONDITIONS

1—GOVERNING RATING AND COVERAGE

2. 1   The governing rating is defined and agreed
2. 2 to be the rating of a debtor at date of shipment
2. 3 by the Governing Mercantile Agency, herein-
2. 4 after called Agency.
2. 5   The latest published rating book of the
2. 6 Agency shall be used to determine a debtor's
2. 7 governing rating for coverage on shipments
2. 8 made from the first day of the month named by
2. 9 that book through the last day of the month
2.10 preceding the month named by the next subse-
2.11 quent book, but if the Agency shall have
2.12 changed a rating by written report, compiled
2.13 during the currency of the latest published book
2.14 or within 4 months prior to the date thereof,
2.15 that report, of which the Insured shall have
2.16 received a copy from the Agency, or written
2.17 notice thereof from the Company, shall be used
2.18 to determine the debtor's governing rating for
2.19 coverage on shipments made after receipt by
2.20 the Insured of that written report from the
2.21 Agency, or written notice thereof from the
2.22 Company. If the Agency issues supplements
2.23 to the rating book, then, every issued supple-
2.24 ment shall be treated the same as a written re-
2.25 port received by the Insured from the Agency, so
2.26 that a change in rating in any such supple-
2.27 ment shall govern the same as a change in
2.28 rating by written report received by the Insured.
2.29 Every issued supplement shall be construed to
2.30 have been received by the Insured within 5 days
2.31 from the issuance date shown in the supplement.
2.32   Coverage on any loss under this Policy
2.33 shall be limited to that portion of the indebted-
2.34 ness of a debtor to the Insured which consists
2.35 of the unpaid invoice price of shipments made
2.36 within the Shipment Period, in the name of
2.37 the Insured or under any name authorized by
2.38 endorsement; provided, the debtor to whom
2.39 the goods were shipped and delivered shall
2.40 have had, at the date of shipment, a governing
2.41 rating for which coverage is specified in the
2.42 Table of Ratings and Coverage, as set forth on
2.43 the reverse side of the Policy Declaration.
2.44 Coverage shall be limited also to that portion

2.45 of the indebtedness on which Notification of
2.46 Claim has been filed as required in Condition 4.
2.47   The gross amount covered on the total
2.48 indebtedness of any one debtor shall neither
2.49 exceed the total amount owing to the Insured
2.50 by that debtor at date of insolvency, nor exceed
2.51 the amount set opposite the governing rating
2.52 of that debtor in the Table of Ratings and
2.53 Coverage.
2.54   If the indebtedness of a debtor at the date
2.55 of insolvency be for shipments made under
2.56 different governing ratings, the gross amount
2.57 covered on the total of such indebtedness shall
2.58 not exceed the largest amount set opposite any
2.59 one of that debtor's governing ratings in the
2.60 Table of Ratings and Coverage. Should a
2.61 change of rating reduce the limit of coverage
2.62 applicable to a debtor, shipments made there-
2.63 after shall not be covered unless and until the
2.64 covered prior indebtedness be less than the
2.65 amount set opposite the latest rating, in which
2.66 event the gross amount covered on the total of
2.67 such indebtedness shall not exceed the amount
2.68 set opposite said latest rating.
2.69   Irrespective of the foregoing paragraph, the
2.70 amount of coverage afforded on a debtor by
2.71 rating under the Table of Ratings and Coverage
2.72 at the beginning date of the Shipment Period
2.73 as set forth in the Policy Declaration or there-
2.74 after, shall not be reduced as to subsequent
2.75 shipments made the debtor while assigned a
2.76 rating as high or higher as to capital accom-
2.77 panied by as high or higher credit rating as set
2.78 forth in the Table of Ratings and Coverage.
2.79   Merchandise placed with a debtor on con-
2.80 signment for the debtor's own use or for resale
2.81 shall be covered to the extent used or resold,
2.82 and the date of withdrawal for use or resale
2.83 shall be construed as the date of shipment within
2.84 the meaning of this Policy.
2.85   Every prepayment made by the Insured for
2.86 freight on any shipment covered by this Policy,
2.87 and for which the debtor is legally liable, shall,
2.88 for all the purposes of this Policy, be treated as

2

FIGURE 10.1. Sample Credit Insurance Policy (cont.)

3. 1 part of the invoice price payable by the debtor
3. 2 to the Insured for the merchandise, and shall
3. 3 accordingly be so treated both in the calculation
3. 4 of the gross sales of the Insured and of the gross
3. 5 losses of the Insured.
3. 6   A debtor's name as listed in the agreed
3. 7 books of the Agency, or the name under which
3. 8 a report is issued on a debtor by the Agency,
3. 9 shall for the purposes of this Policy be construed
3.10 as the legal name of the debtor. If a debtor
3.11 should use a Division, Style or Trade name in
3.12 the conduct of his business, shipments made
3.13 to the debtor under such other names shall be
3.14 construed as having been made to the debtor
3.15 under the debtor's legal name. Shipments made
3.16 to a Branch location of a debtor shall be con-
3.17 strued as having been made to the debtor at the
3.18 location maintained as headquarters of the
3.19 debtor.
3.20   If, at the date of shipment to a debtor, the
3.21 Insured should hold an absolute guaranty of a
3.22 third party, in writing, securing payment of
3.23 the indebtedness, and such guaranty be valid
3.24 and legally binding at all times, then, as to a
3.25 loss on such debtor, the coverage applicable
3.26 to the guarantor at the date of shipment, if
3.27 higher than the coverage applicable to the
3.28 debtor, may, at the option of the Insured, be

3.29 used to govern coverage on the loss, but not
3.30 to exceed the amount guaranteed if that amount
3.31 be less than the amount of coverage applicable
3.32 to the guarantor. If more than one debtor's
3.33 account due the Insured shall have been secured
3.34 by written guaranty of the same guarantor,
3.35 and the Insured elects to have a loss on more
3.36 than one debtor governed by the coverage
3.37 applicable to the guarantor, as aforesaid, or
3.38 if the Insured also sustains a loss on sales, ship-
3.39 ments and deliveries made directly to the
3.40 guarantor, the limit of coverage applicable to
3.41 such combined obligation of the guarantor
3.42 shall not exceed the limit of coverage that would
3.43 have been applicable had the loss on such
3.44 combined . obligation resulted entirely from
3.45 sales, shipments and deliveries made directly
3.46 to the guarantor.
3.47   If the Insured, without the consent of the
3.48 Company in writing, shall make any agreement
3.49 with respect to the account of a debtor which
3.50 would, at the date of filing with the Company
3.51 or subsequent thereto, prevent or delay any
3.52 action thereon, or which would interfere with
3.53 the exercise of the Company's judgment on
3.54 any proposal made by the debtor to his creditors,
3.55 coverage on such account under this Policy shall
3.56 terminate and cease.

2—OPTIONAL FILING OF PAST DUE ACCOUNTS

3.57   The Insured, during the Insolvency Period
3.58 of this Policy, shall be permitted to file with
3.59 the Company for collection an account against
3.60 a debtor not insolvent as defined in Condition
3.61 3 at the time the account was so filed, and
3.62 so much of such account that was due and
3.63 payable at the date of filing, but not more
3.64 than 3 months past due under the original
3.65 terms of sale, shall be treated in any Claim

3.66 Settlement under this Policy as though the
3.67 debtor had become insolvent. The date of
3.68 filing of the account by the Insured shall be
3.69 the date postmarked or the date otherwise
3.70 delivered to the Company. Every such account
3.71 so filed shall include all indebtedness then due
3.72 and payable and shall be accompanied with a
3.73 Notification of Claim as described in Condition 4.

3—INSOLVENCY DEFINED

3.74   Insolvency for the purposes of this Policy
3.75 shall be determined to have occurred only when:
3.76   (1) a general meeting of unsecured credi-
3.77   tors shall be called by the debtor or on
3.78   behalf of the debtor and the date of
3.79   notice of such meeting shall be, for the

3.80   purpose of this Policy, the date of
3.81   insolvency;
3.82   (2) a voluntary or involuntary proceedings
3.83   shall have been instituted in a United
3.84   States Bankruptcy Court to adjudge a
3.85   debtor bankrupt;

3

FIGURE 10.1. Sample Credit Insurance Policy (cont.)

<table>
<tr><td>4. 1</td><td>(3) a petition shall have been filed in a</td></tr>
<tr><td>4. 2</td><td>United States Bankruptcy Court for</td></tr>
<tr><td>4. 3</td><td>the corporate reorganization of a</td></tr>
<tr><td>4. 4</td><td>debtor (Chapter X) or for the arrange-</td></tr>
<tr><td>4. 5</td><td>ment of the debts of a debtor (Chapter</td></tr>
<tr><td>4. 6</td><td>XI);</td></tr>
</table>

4. 1   (3) a petition shall have been filed in a
4. 2   United States Bankruptcy Court for
4. 3   the corporate reorganization of a
4. 4   debtor (Chapter X) or for the arrange-
4. 5   ment of the debts of a debtor (Chapter
4. 6   XI);
4. 7   (4) a receiver is appointed of the whole or
4. 8   any part of the property of a debtor;
4. 9   (5) a debtor, or a third party on behalf
4.10   of a debtor, shall have made a general
4.11   offer of compromise, in writing, to his
4.12   creditors for less than his indebtedness;
4.13   (6) possession shall have been taken of a
4.14   debtor's assets under an Assignment or
4.15   Deed of Trust executed by the debtor
4.16   for the benefit of his creditors;
4.17   (7) a creditors' committee shall have been
4.18   formed for the sole purpose of liquida-
4.19   tion;
4.20   (8) possession shall have been taken of a
4.21   debtor's business assets under a chattel
4.22   mortgage given thereon;
4.23   (9) a sale in bulk is made of a debtor's
4.24   property and the date of the actual sale
4.25   shall constitute the date of insolvency;
4.26   (10) a debtor's assets shall have been sold
4.27   under a writ of execution or attach-

4.28   ment, or a writ of execution shall have
4.29   been returned unsatisfied;
4.30   (11) a sole debtor shall have died;
4.31   (12) a sole debtor shall have been adjudged
4.32   mentally incompetent;
4.33   (13) a debtor shall have absconded;
4.34   (14) a debtor's assets shall have been sold
4.35   under a distraint or levy by any Taxing
4.36   Authority, or by a landlord;
4.37   (15) a debtor shall file an Assignment or
4.38   make a Proposal to creditors, under
4.39   the Canadian Bankruptcy Act, and the
4.40   date on which the Assignment is filed,
4.41   or the date on which the Proposal is
4.42   filed with the court, shall constitute
4.43   the date of insolvency;
4.44   (16) a Receiving Order is made against a
4.45   debtor under the Canadian Bankruptcy
4.46   Act and the date of the Receiving
4.47   Order shall constitute the date of
4.48   insolvency;
4.49   (17) a debtor's assets shall have been sold
4.50   under the Canadian Bank Act; or
4.51   (18) a Winding-Up Order under the
4.52   Dominion Winding-Up Act (Canada)
4.53   is made against a debtor.

4—NOTIFICATION AND FILING OF CLAIMS

4.54   When a debtor, within the Insolvency
4.55 Period of this Policy, becomes insolvent as
4.56 defined in Condition 3, the Insured, within
4.57 10 days after acquiring knowledge thereof
4.58 and during the Insolvency Period, shall file
4.59 Notification of Claim with the Company on
4.60 a form furnished by the Company and place
4.61 the entire account with the Company for
4.62 attention and collection. If knowledge of a
4.63 debtor's insolvency as defined in Condition 3
4.64 be received too late to file the claim with the
4.65 Company during the Insolvency Period, then a
4.66 grace period of 20 days shall be permitted for
4.67 the filing of such claim.
4.68   Every Notification of Claim filed shall be
4.69 accompanied with an itemized statement in
4.70 triplicate, showing fully the dates of shipment,
4.71 terms of sale, and the condition of the account,
4.72 together with all notes and other papers evi-
4.73 dencing the same, and all guarantees, securities,

4.74 or other documents relating thereto; and the
4.75 Insured shall, upon request, promptly furnish
4.76 all proofs, or any information and assistance
4.77 necessary for the proper handling of any account
4.78 in any proceeding.
4.79   All Notifications of Claim must be received
4.80 by the Company within the time above speci-
4.81 fied, in the office designated in the Policy
4.82 Declaration, and shall be handled upon the
4.83 terms and subject to all the conditions of this
4.84 Policy. The date of receipt of the Notification
4.85 of Claim shall be the date postmarked or other-
4.86 wise delivered to the Company.
4.87   The filing of any Notification of Claim by
4.88 the Insured under this Policy shall constitute
4.89 authority for the Company to place the account
4.90 represented thereby for collection with any
4.91 attorney selected by the Company.
4.92   Any claim withdrawn by the Insured may
4.93 not be refiled under this or any other Policy

4

FIGURE 10.1. Sample Credit Insurance Policy (cont.)

5. 1 issued by the Company.
5. 2   The receipt, retention or handling by the
5. 3 Company of any claim filed by the Insured shall
5. 4 not constitute a waiver of any of the terms or

5. 5 conditions of this Policy, nor shall it be an
5. 6 acceptance of such claim as covered by this or
5. 7 any other Policy.

5—COLLECTION OF ACCOUNTS AND SCHEDULE OF CHARGES

5. 8   The Company assumes responsibility for all
5. 9 money collected by its employees and by
5.10 attorneys of its selection, and will promptly
5.11 account for collections due the Insured, subject
5.12 to the following conditions:

5.13   Free Service:

5.14 No Charge shall be made on any collection
5.15 effected within 10 days after demand has
5.16 been made by the Company; neither shall
5.17 any Charge be made on any collection
5.18 effected on any undisputed or unlitigated
5.19 account, insofar as covered, after the debtor
5.20 shall have become insolvent as defined in
5.21 Condition 3.

5.22 If any balance remain unpaid at the ex-
5.23 piration of the 10 Day Free Service period,
5.24 the account shall remain with the Company
5.25 for handling. On every collection effected
5.26 otherwise than as hereinbefore limited and
5.27 defined, the following Charges shall be
5.28 paid by the Insured:

5.29   On Collections Effected Without Forwarding Service:

5.30 20% on the first $2,000.00
5.31 15% on the next $3,000.00
5.32 10% on the excess of $5,000.00.

5.33 Minimum charge of $20.00, except on col-
5.34 lections of $40.00 or less, charge to be 50%.

5.35   Forwarding Service:

5.36 Attorney Minimum Commissions:

5.37 20% on the first $300.00 collected
5.38 18% on the next $1,700.00 collected
5.39 13% on the excess of $2,000.00 collected.
5.40 Minimum commission—$25.00. On collec-
5.41 tions of $75.00 or less—33-1/3%. In localities
5.42 where charges are established by law, or by
5.43 Bar Associations, or where the above rates
5.44 are not recognized and higher rates are
5.45 demanded, such rates shall govern.

5.46 Company Service Charges:

5.47 In addition to the Commission charges of
5.48 attorneys, the Company will charge the
5.49 following rates:
5.50 5% on amounts collected, subject to
5.51 a minimum charge of $7.50, except on
5.52 collections of $45.00 or less, charge to
5.53 be 16-2/3%.

5.54   The invoice price of merchandise returned
5.55 or any amount paid direct to the Insured, on
5.56 any account filed with the Company, or the bal-
5.57 ance of an account withdrawn by the Insured,
5.58 shall be subject to the above Charges in effect at
5.59 date of notice to the Company.
5.60   If an account be disputed, in whole or in
5.61 part, or if the Company consider it necessary,
5.62 for the purpose of enforcing collection from the
5.63 debtor, guarantor, surety or endorser, or to
5.64 participate in any proceeding involving the

5.65 estate of the debtor, guarantor, surety or en-
5.66 dorser, the Insured shall authorize suit or other
5.67 proceeding and shall pay expenses required in
5.68 connection therewith, promptly advancing court
5.69 costs and legal fees when requested; failure to
5.70 do so shall be construed as a withdrawal of the
5.71 account by the Insured.
5.72   When litigation or any proceeding shall have
5.73 been authorized by the Insured, the amount
5.74 charged by the attorney as a non-contingent
5.75 legal fee shall be paid by the Insured; in addition

5

FIGURE 10.1. Sample Credit Insurance Policy (cont.)

6. 1 thereto, the Insured shall pay the stipulated
6. 2 Charge on collections effected, but such stipu-
6. 3 lated Charge shall be limited to the amount
6. 4 that the non-contingent legal fee is less than
6. 5 50% of the amount collected.
6. 6   The Company shall have authority, in the
6. 7 handling of an account under this Policy, to en-
6. 8 dorse notes, checks or drafts on behalf and in
6. 9 the name of the Insured, and to deposit them,
6.10 or the proceeds of collection thereof, in the ac-
6.11 count or to the credit of the Company, in any
6.12 of its depository banks.
6.13   The remittance to the Insured, with or
6.14 without charge, of any amount collected on any
6.15 account filed, and acceptance thereof by the
6.16 Insured, shall not be construed as a determina-
6.17 tion of coverage, nor as a waiver either by the
6.18 Company or the Insured of any of the terms or
6.19 conditions of this Policy.

6—FINAL STATEMENT OF CLAIM

6.20   When a claim for loss be made under this
6.21 Policy, the Insured shall complete a Final State-
6.22 ment of Claim form, which will be furnished by
6.23 the Company upon request. The completed form
6.24 must be received by the Company at its Execu-
6.25 tive Office, Baltimore, Maryland 21202, within
6.26 one month after the expiration of the Insol-
6.27 vency Period.

7—CLAIM SETTLEMENT

6.28   Settlement shall be made within 2 months
6.29 after receipt by the Company of a Final State-
6.30 ment of Claim, and the amount then ascertained
6.31 to be due the Insured shall be paid.
6.32   To ascertain the net loss in any settlement,
6.33 there shall be deducted from each gross loss
6.34 covered, filed and proved hereunder:
6.35   (1) all amounts collected from the debtor
6.36   or obtained from any other source;
6.37   (2) the invoice price of merchandise re-
6.38   turned, reclaimed or replevined, when
6.39   such merchandise is in the undisputed
6.40   possession of the Insured;
6.41   (3) any discount to which the debtor
6.42   would be entitled at time of settle-
6.43   ment, and
6.44   (4) any legally sustainable set-off that the
6.45   debtor may have against the Insured.
6.46   If at the date of insolvency of a debtor the
6.47 entire indebtedness of the debtor to the Insured
6.48 be in excess of the gross amount covered by this
6.49 Policy, then the above deductions shall be made
6.50 pro rata, in the ratio which the gross amount
6.51 covered bears to the whole of the indebtedness.
6.52 Having made the foregoing deductions from
6.53 each gross loss covered, filed and proved under
6.54 this Policy, the result shall be the net loss.
6.55   From the aggregate amount of net losses
6.56 there shall be deducted the amount of Primary
6.57 Loss; the remainder, not exceeding the amount
6.58 of this Policy, less any amount owing to the
6.59 Company, shall be the amount payable to the
6.60 Insured.
6.61   If any covered claim of the Insured against
6.62 a debtor be disputed, in whole or in part, the
6.63 same shall not be allowed in any settlement
6.64 under this Policy until such disputed claim shall
6.65 have been finally determined to be a valid and
6.66 legally sustainable indebtedness against the
6.67 debtor or the debtor's estate, at which time that
6.68 claim, so far as covered under this Policy, shall
6.69 be settled and the amount due the Insured
6.70 shall be paid.
6.71   The Insured shall assign to the Company,
6.72 on forms furnished and in the manner prescribed
6.73 by the Company, absolute title to all claims
6.74 allowed in settlement, together with all securi-
6.75 ties and guarantees relating thereto, and shall
6.76 warrant the legal validity of the indebtedness
6.77 for the amount of such claims, and that there
6.78 are no known defenses, off-sets or counter-
6.79 claims. The Company is entitled to deal with
6.80 claims assigned to them as it may see fit, includ-
6.81 ing but not limited to full power and authority
6.82 to take all proceedings for the collection or
6.83 compromise, and to give all receipts and
6.84 acquittances therefor. The Insured shall upon
6.85 demand reimburse the Company for any amount

6

FIGURE 10.1. Sample Credit Insurance Policy (cont.)

7. 1 paid by the Company to the Insured on any
7. 2 indebtedness which, in whole or in part, is
7. 3 disputed, or which after assignment is disputed,
7. 4 or which had not been allowed, or may after
7. 5 assignment be rejected or not established as a
7. 6 claim against the debtor or the debtor's estate,
7. 7 together with all expenses of any legal action
7. 8 thereon. Any claims assigned to the Company
7. 9 which shall not have been covered in full by
7.10 this Policy shall be handled by the Company
7.11 for the joint benefit of the Insured and the
7.12 Company as their interests appear.

8—DISPOSAL OF ASSIGNED CLAIMS

7.13   On claims assigned to it in Claim Settle-
7.14 ment, the Company will promptly remit to the
7.15 Insured, after deduction of all charges and
7.16 expenses, their pro rata interest, if any, in the
7.17 amount realized on any Claim.
7.18   The Insured, on each claim assigned shall
7.19 forward to the Company each payment received,
7.20 and shall remit the Company's share of any
7.21 credit allowed, and the charges applicable to the
7.22 Insured's share of the credit.
7.23   In the event the Company considers it neces-
7.24 sary for the purpose of enforcing collection from
7.25 the debtor, guarantor, surety or endorser, or to
7.26 participate in any proceeding involving the
7.27 estate of the debtor, guarantor, surety or
7.28 endorser, the Company and the Insured shall
7.29 share the expenses required in connection there-
7.30 with as their interests appear.
7.31   Any interest of the Insured in any security
7.32 acquired by the Company in relation to any
7.33 claim assigned to it will be evidenced, whenever
7.34 possible, by a separate instrument and delivered

7.35 to the Insured. If not so evidenced and any
7.36 amount be realized in connection with such
7.37 security, remittance will be made, less all
7.38 charges and expenses, to the Insured in pro-
7.39 portion to its interest in the proceeds.
7.40   If, after the deductions and remittances, the
7.41 remaining net amounts realized by the Company
7.42 should, in the aggregate, exceed the total
7.43 amount paid to the Insured in Claim Settlement,
7.44 the Company will remit to the Insured the excess
7.45 and all net amounts thereafter realized, less:
7.46   (1) the Company's share of interest paid
7.47   upon an assigned account;
7.48   (2) the Company's share of interest and
7.49   dividends paid on securities, and
7.50   (3) any amount owing to the Com-
7.51   pany.
7.52 The Company will then, upon the written
7.53 request of the Insured, reassign all claims
7.54 assigned to the Company in such Claim Settle-
7.55 ment.

9—COLLATERAL BENEFITS

7.56   This Policy shall not be assignable but,
7.57 upon written request of the Insured, the Com-
7.58 pany may provide that any loss, ascertained to
7.59 be payable as provided in Condition 7, shall be
7.60 paid to a Bank, Trust Company or other payee
7.61 designated by, and for the account of, the Insured.

10—TERMINATION

7.62   If, during the Shipment Period, the Insured,
7.63 or any included entity guaranteed by this Policy,
7.64 should become insolvent as defined in any of the
7.65 subdivisions of Condition 3, or should cease to
7.66 continue the business described in the Policy
7.67 Declaration, as heretofore carried on, or should
7.68 go into liquidation, or being a partnership
7.69 should be dissolved, then this Policy shall
7.70 thereupon terminate as to coverage on ship-
7.71 ments made thereafter. Temporary interruption
7.72 of the business, or the death, withdrawal or
7.73 admission of a member of a partnership com-
7.74 posed of more than two members, shall not so
7.75 terminate this Policy.

7

FIGURE 10.1. Sample Credit Insurance Policy (cont.)

11—WAR RISK EXCLUSION

8.1 Coverage under this Policy shall not apply
8.2 to any claim, if the direct cause of the past due
8.3 status of the account under Condition 2, or of the
8.4 insolvency under Condition 3, be due to an
8.5 enemy attack by a Foreign Government or
8.6 Sovereign Power or any action taken by the
8.7 United States of America, Canada, or other
8.8 Ally in resisting such attack.

12—GENERAL PROVISIONS

8.9 The premium for this Policy shall be paid by
8.10 check to the order of American Credit Indemnity
8.11 Company of New York and shall accompany the
8.12 application. The Company may at its option
8.13 accept premium notes or premium agreements.
8.14 If premium notes or premium agreements so ac-
8.15 cepted be paid at or before maturity, the premi-
8.16 um for this Policy shall be construed as having
8.17 been paid as of the date of such instruments. If
8.18 any note or agreement be in default, then at the
8.19 option of the Company, to be exercised within
8.20 60 days after any such default, by written notice
8.21 to the Insured by any Officer or Assistant Officer,
8.22 this Policy may be cancelled from its inception,
8.23 with full refund of any portion of the premium
8.24 paid. Should the Company not exercise its
8.25 privilege of cancellation as herein provided, the
8.26 Policy shall remain in effect, but no coverage
8.27 shall attach to any loss occurring prior to the
8.28 payment of any premium instrument in default.
8.29 The Company will acknowledge the receipt
8.30 of all Notifications of Claim and the Final State-
8.31 ment of Claim, but neither the acknowledgment
8.32 nor the retention thereof by the Company, nor
8.33 its failure to acknowledge receipt thereof, shall
8.34 be an admission of liability or a waiver by the
8.35 Company of any of the terms or conditions of
8.36 this Policy.
8.37 The warranties and representations made in
8.38 the application for this Policy of Credit Insur-
8.39 ance are the basis for this Policy and a part there-
8.40 of and are conclusively presumed to be material
8.41 to the risk assumed by the Company under this
8.42 Policy. False warranty, misrepresentation, con-
8.43 cealment or fraud in obtaining this Policy, or
8.44 in any Notification of Claim or Final Statement
8.45 of Claim filed under this Policy, or in the proof
8.46 or settlement of any claim for loss under this
8.47 Policy, shall void this Policy from its beginning
8.48 and the premium paid shall be forfeited to the
8.49 Company. The Insured shall permit the Com-
8.50 pany at any reasonable time to examine and take
8.51 extracts from the books, securities and papers of
8.52 the Insured bearing upon any matter involved in
8.53 any Notification of Claim or Final Statement of
8.54 Claim filed under this Policy, or in any Claim
8.55 Settlement under this Policy, or in any warranty
8.56 or representation made in the application for this
8.57 Policy, or in any claim made either by the
8.58 Insured or by the Company under this Policy,
8.59 and in that connection the Insured shall give
8.60 such assistance and information as the Company
8.61 shall require, but no such examination, in-
8.62 vestigation or proceeding shall be an admission
8.63 of liability or waiver of any of the terms or con-
8.64 ditions of this Policy. If, by the law of the State
8.65 or Province of Canada named in the Policy
8.66 Declaration as the address of the Insured, war-
8.67 ranties are prohibited or not recognized in the
8.68 application for a Policy, then in conformity
8.69 therewith, statements of the Insured in the
8.70 application for this Policy shall be accepted as
8.71 representations.
8.72 The rendering of any estimate or statement,
8.73 or the making of any settlement, shall not bar
8.74 the examination herein provided for, nor the
8.75 Company's right to unpaid Charges, nor the
8.76 Company's right to a refund of any amount
8.77 overpaid the Insured by the Company, nor bar
8.78 the right of the Insured to a refund of any
8.79 amount overpaid the Company.
8.80 This Policy shall be a valid and binding
8.81 obligation of the Company only if both it and
8.82 the Policy Declaration issued in connection
8.83 therewith be authenticated, as indicated there-
8.84 on, by the manual signature of an Officer or
8.85 Assistant Officer of the Company. It shall con-
8.86 sist of this printed form of Policy, Policy Appli-
8.87 cation, any endorsements thereto presently or
8.88 hereafter issued by the Company, and the Policy
8.89 Declaration. No notice to or knowledge of any
8.90 Agent or other person shall effect a waiver of

8

FIGURE 10.1. Sample Credit Insurance Policy (cont.)

9. 1 any provision thereof. No Agent shall be
9. 2 authorized to make any alteration therein or
9. 3 addition thereto, either verbally or in writing,
9. 4 or to waive any such provision, and no addition,
9. 5 alteration or waiver shall be valid unless ex-
9. 6 pressed in writing over the signature or facsimile
9. 7 signature of the President of the Company.
9. 8   No suit or action on this Policy shall be
9. 9 brought or be sustainable until after the full
9.10 compliance by the Insured with its terms and
9.11 conditions, nor unless commenced within 12
9.12 months after its termination. If the said limita-
9.13 tion of time for the commencement of suit be
9.14 prohibited by any specific statutory provision in
9.15 relation thereto, in force in the State or Province

9.16 of Canada named in the Policy Declaration as
9.17 the address of the Insured, the said limitation is
9.18 hereby amended to conform to the minimum
9.19 period of limitation permitted by said statutory
9.20 provision.
9.21   Any provision of this Policy which, on its
9.22 effective date, is in conflict with the statutes of
9.23 the State or Province of Canada named in the
9.24 Policy Declaration as the address of the Insured,
9.25 is hereby amended to conform to the minimum
9.26 requirements of such statutes.
9.27   All terms and conditions of this Policy shall
9.28 be conditions precedent to any claim by the
9.29 Insured.

13—POLICY ACCEPTANCE

9.30   This Policy and the Policy Declaration as
9.31 issued by the Company, upon acceptance by the

9.32 Insured, shall be considered to have been issued
9.33 on terms mutually agreed upon.

IN WITNESS WHEREOF the AMERICAN CREDIT INDEMNITY COMPANY OF NEW YORK

has caused this Policy to be signed by the signature or facsimile signature of its President at Baltimore, Maryland.

Senior Vice President

AUTHENTICATED:

. . . .
Assistant Secretary

Ed Weidman
President

THIS IS NOT A VALID CONTRACT WITHOUT AN ACCOMPANYING POLICY DECLARATION BEAR-ING THE SAME POLICY NUMBER AS IS ASSIGNED TO THIS POLICY, PROPERLY EXECUTED AND MANUALLY AUTHENTICATED.

9

FIGURE 10.1. Sample Credit Insurance Policy (cont.)

When an insolvency occurs, it should be filed promptly (the policy specifies within ten days from the time you acquire knowledge of it). Also, you can regularly file slow-paying accounts to improve the liquidity of your receivables.

Within thirty days of the expiration of the policy, you, as the insured, file a final statement of claim form on which all accounts filed during the term of the policy are listed. On this form, you also report actual sales volume for the term of the policy and other pertinent information. If your covered losses are $100,000 and your deductible is $20,000, your recovery is:

Covered losses	$100,000
Deductible (primary loss)	20,000
Loss payment	$80,000

If the policy carries coinsurance with $50,000 losses having 10 percent and $50,000 losses 20 percent and a deductible of $20,000, your recovery is:

Covered losses	$50,000	
Coinsurance 10 percent	5,000	$45,000
Covered losses	50,000	
Coinsurance 20 percent	10,000	40,000
		85,000
Deductible		20,000
Loss payment		$65,000

Shortly after the statement of claims is filed, an adjuster meets with you in your office to review the case. You receive a draft for the amount of the loss payment from the adjuster and the accounts included in the claims settlement are assigned to the insurer. Collections obtained thereafter are shared on a pro-rata basis between you and the insurer as both interests dictate.

[1000.5]   **Factors.** Factors are companies that purchase accounts receivable from other companies and take on the responsibility of credit decision-making and collection activity. They charge a fee for this service and also charge interest on funds advanced on accounts receivable before they come due. If the accounts receivable are purchased without recourse, this means that the factor must absorb all bad-debt losses resulting from those receivables. As a credit manager, you would not suffer bad-debt losses from factored accounts but you also lose the power to grant credit as that function is also taken over by the factor. Depending on your agreement with the factor, your customers may or may not be notified that a factor has entered the picture and payments should be made directly to him.

[1000.6]   **Information Industry Association (IIA).** Although not directly related to the credit field, the Information Industry Association (IIA) is of interest to credit managers because of the work it does to develop and make known information sources, as well as to protect these sources from government interference in their activities. Should you have information needs, the IIA, located in Bethesda, Maryland, stands ready to assist you in fulfilling them.

CHAPTER 11

FAIR CREDIT REPORTING ACT

[1100] **FAIR CREDIT REPORTING ACT.** Because the Fair Credit Reporting Act applies only to the reporting of *consumer* credit information, you may be surprised at the appearance of this chapter in a handbook devoted to *business* credits and collections. Since it became effective on April 25, 1971, however, the Fair Credit Reporting Act has caused widespread misunderstanding among business, bank, and credit executives who were unsure of its intent and application. As a credit manager, you may still have some unresolved questions about this act. The information that follows is designed to clarify the issues.

[1101] **PURPOSE OF THE LAW** The Fair Credit Reporting Act is, in fact, Title VI of the Consumer Credit Protection Act. As such, it is designed—like the Consumer Credit Protection Act itself—to protect *consumers* from unfair treatment when applying for consumer credit, when buying on consumer credit, and from having consumer credit information incorrectly stated or improperly distributed. The act does not apply to the application for, or granting of, *commercial* credit, nor to the distribution of commercial credit information. Specifically, as stated in Section 602(b) of the Fair Credit Reporting Act:

(b) It is the purpose of this title to require that consumer reporting agencies adopt reasonable procedures for meeting the needs of commerce for consumer credit, personnel, insurance and other information, in a manner which is fair and equitable to the consumer, with regard to the confidentiality, accuracy, relevancy and proper utilization of such information in accordance with the requirements of this title.

[1102] **DEFINITIONS—CONSUMER REPORTS VERSUS BUSINESS REPORTS.** Section 603 of the act (reprinted in Figure 11.1) refers to *consumer* reports, and the

---

" 603. Definitions and rules and construction

"(a) Definitions and rules of construction set forth in this section are applicable for the purposes of this title.

"(b) The term 'person' means any individual, partnership, corporation, trust, estate, cooperative, association, government or governmental subdivision or agency, or other entity.

"(c) The term 'consumer' means an individual.

"(d) The term 'consumer report' means any written, oral, or other communication of any information by a consumer reporting agency bearing on a consumer's credit worthiness, credit standing, credit capacity, character, general reputation, personal characteristics, or mode of living which is used or expected to be used or collected in whole or in part for the purpose of serving as a factor in establishing the consumer's eligibility for (1) credit or insurance to be used primarily for personal, family, or household purposes, or (2) employment purposes, or (3) other purposes authorized under section 604. The term does not include (A) any report containing information solely as to transactions or experiences between the consumer and the person making the report; (b) any authorization or approval of a specific extension of credit directly or indirectly by the issuer of a credit card or similar device; or (C) any report in which a person who has been requested by a third party to make a specific extension of credit directly or indirectly to a consumer conveys his decision with respect to such request, if the third party advises the consumer of the name and address of the person to whom the request was made and such person makes the disclosures to the consumer required under section 615.

"(e) The term 'investigative consumer report' means a consumer report or portion thereof in which information on a consumer's character, general reputation, personal characteristics, or mode of living is obtained through personal interviews with neighbors, friends, or associates of the consumer reported on or with others with whom he is acquainted or who may have knowledge concerning any such items of information. However, such information shall not include specific factual information on a consumer's credit record obtained directly from a creditor of the consumer or from a consumer reporting agency when such information was obtained directly from a creditor of the consumer or from the consumer.

"(f) The term 'consumer reporting agency' means any person which, for monetary fees, dues, or on a cooperative nonprofit basis, regularly engages in whole or in part in the practice of assembling or evaluating consumer credit information or other information on consumers for the purpose of furnishing consumer reports to third parties, and which uses any means or facility of interstate commerce for the purpose of preparing or furnishing consumer reports.

"(g) The term 'file,' when used in connection with information on any consumer, means all of the information on that consumer recorded and retained by a consumer reporting agency regardless of how the information is stored.

"(h) The term 'employment purposes' when used in connection with a consumer report means a report used for the purpose of evaluating a consumer for employment, promotion, reassignment or retention as an employee.

"(i) The term 'medical information' means information or records obtained, with the consent of the individual to whom it relates, from licensed physicians or medical practitioners, hospitals, clinics, or other medical or medically related facilities.

Figure 11.1. The Fair Credit Reporting Act (Public Law 91–508)

language of the law clearly refers to consumer reports and the reporting of consumer credit information throughout. It does not refer to and, therefore, does not apply to business reports such as the Dun & Bradstreet Business Information Report. In addition, there is an ample body of legislative history should this clear language need reinforcement. In answer to a direct question from a representative of the National Association of Credit Management at the hearings in May, 1969, Senator William Proxmire said the law, then in bill form, did not cover reports on businesses. The report of the Committee on Banking and Currency of the United States Senate which accompanied S. 823 (Fair Credit Reporting Act) stated: "The bill covers reports on consumers when used for obtaining credit, insurance or employment. However, the bill does not cover business credit reports or business insurance reports."

Perhaps the clearest statements of legislative intent were the remarks appearing in the *Congressional Record* made by Senator Proxmire and Representative Leonor K. Sullivan, who was one of the prime movers of this legislation in the House. Senator Proxmire, in proceedings from the Senate floor on October 9, 1970, said: "The act covers all reporting on consumers, whether it be for the purpose of obtaining credit, insurance or employment. However, credit reports or other reports on business firms are excluded." The proceedings in the House on October 13, 1970, started with a reference to the Senate report previously quoted and a question to Mrs. Sullivan: "Does the gentlewoman agree that we do exclude from this bill business reports from its coverage?" To which Mrs. Sullivan replied: "I am happy to inform the gentlemen that that is exactly my understanding of the bill. Business reports are not included."

[1102.1]   **Federal Trade Commission Guidelines.** The Division of Special Projects, Bureau of Consumer Protection of the Federal Trade Commission, has issued guidelines that remove any doubt on the question of the inapplicability of the law to business reports. Here is the question posed and the FTC's response:

> QUESTION: Is a report on an individual obtained in connection with the extension of business credit or writing of business insurance a "Consumer Report"?
>
> ANSWER: No. While Section 604(e) of the Act makes a report obtained by a person who has a legitimate business need for information on a consumer in connection with a business transaction involving the consumer, a "consumer report," other sections of the Act and its legislative history clearly indicate that only reports obtained in connection with employment, credit or insurance for personal, family or household purposes were intended to be covered. Accordingly, if a report is obtained on an individual for the purpose of determining his eligibility for business credit or insurance, it is not a "consumer report."

[1102.2]   **Purpose to Which Information Is Put Is the Criterion In Defining a Consumer Report.** As indicated by the FTC's comments and Sections 603 and 604 of the act, the purpose to which information is put is a criterion in defining a consumer report. To illustrate, if John Doe, the sole proprietor of a hardware store, is seeking credit to be used to add a new line of merchandise or to refurbish his store fixtures, the credit Mr. Doe is seeking is for business purposes. To use the words of the law, it is not being sought for personal, family, or household purposes. A report used to help determine Mr. Doe's credit worthiness in this instance would not be a consumer report and would not be covered by the act. However, if the same Mr. Doe is seeking credit to buy a color TV for his home use, he is seeking credit for personal, family, or household purposes and any report that is used to determine his credit worthiness for this transaction is a consumer report. In the context of the first illustration, he is acting in his business capacity; in the latter case, he is acting in his consumer capacity.

[1103]   **CONSUMER RIGHTS UNDER THE FAIR CREDIT REPORTING ACT.** The provisions of the Fair Credit Reporting Act have been summarized below. The Fair Credit Reporting Act gives consumers certain rights. As a consumer, in fact, you would have these rights, outlined by the Federal Trade Commission in its "The Fair Credit Reporting Act":

[1103.1] **Name and Address of Consumer Reporting Agency.** The right to be told the name and address of the consumer reporting agency responsible for preparing a consumer report that was used to deny you credit, insurance, or employment or to increase the cost of credit or insurance.

[1103.2] **Nature, Substance, and Sources of Information.** The right—at any time and for any reason—to be told the nature, substance, and sources (except investigative-type sources) of the information (except medical) collected about you by a consumer reporting agency.

[1103.3] **Person to Accompany You.** The right to take anyone of your choosing with you when you visit the consumer reporting agency.

[1103.4] **Information Free.** The right to obtain this information free of charge when you have been denied credit, insurance, or employment within thirty days of your interview. Otherwise, the reporting agency is permitted to charge a reasonable fee for making the disclosure.

[1103.5] **Recipients.** The right to be told who has received a consumer report on you within the preceding six months (or within the preceding two years if the report was furnished for employment purposes).

[1103.6] **Reinvestigation.** The right, in most instances, to have incomplete or incorrect information reinvestigated and, if the information is found to be inaccurate or cannot be verified, to have such information removed from the file.

[1103.7] **Notification.** The right to have the agency notify those you name (at no cost to you) who have previously received the incorrect or incomplete information that the information has been deleted.

[1103.8] **Your Version Recorded.** The right, when a dispute between you and the reporting agency cannot be resolved, to have your version of the dispute placed in the file and included in subsequent consumer reports.

[1103.9] **Your Version Sent.** The right to request the agency to send your version of the dispute to certain businesses for a reasonable fee.

[1103.10] **Reports Withheld.** The right to have a consumer report withheld from anyone who under the law does not have a legitimate business need for the consumer information.

[1103.11] **Damage Suit.** The right to sue a company for damages if it willfully or negligently violates the law and, if successful, to collect attorney's fees and court costs.

[1103.12] **Deletion of Adverse Information.** The right not to have most adverse information reported after seven years. One major exception is bankruptcy, which may be reported for fourteen years.

[1103.13] **Notification.** The right to be notified of the fact that a company is seeking information that would constitute an "investigative consumer report."

[1103.14] **Further Information.** The right to request from a company that ordered an investigative report, further information as to the nature and scope of the investigation.

[1103.15] **Nature and Substance.** The right to discover the nature and substance (but not the sources) of the information that was collected for an "investigative consumer report."

[1104]   **CONSUMER RIGHTS NOT PROVIDED BY THE FAIR CREDIT REPORTING ACT.** As a consumer, you would *not* have the following rights under the law:

[1104.1]   **Reports on Yourself.** The right to request a report on yourself from the consumer reporting agency.

[1104.2]   **Receipt of Copies.** The right, when you visit the agency, to receive a copy of its report or to physically handle your file.

[1104.3]   **Compelling Business.** The right to compel anyone to do business with you.

[1104.4]   **Federal Agency Intervention.** The right to have federal agencies intervene on your behalf.

[1104.5]   **Commercial Credit Protection.** The right to be protected by the act when you apply for *commercial* (as distinguished from consumer) credit or business insurance.

[1105]   **DUN & BRADSTREET REPORTS AND THE FAIR CREDIT REPORTING ACT.**   Because the Fair Credit Reporting Act applies only to consumer reports, the law does not affect Dun & Bradstreet Business Information Reports when they are used as a basis for business credit, insurance, marketing, or other business decisions. Since the terms of the contract under which Dun & Bradstreet issues reports to its subscribers specify that the reports are to be used for the business purposes just stated, D&B Business Information Reports are not affected by the law and subscribers are not required to notify customers that they have requested or are using D&B (or any other) commercial credit agency reports.

D&B has instituted internal procedures to avoid an inadvertent consumer use of their Business Information Reports. These procedures have had the added effect of providing their subscribers with an additional checkpoint to prevent their unknowing violation of the law. This refers specifically to the instance where an inquiry on an individual is received and that individual is not, to D&B's knowledge, engaged in business. D&B now informs the subscriber that his inquiry appears to be for a consumer report, which cannot be serviced on a business inquiry.

[1106]   **BANKS AND THE FAIR CREDIT REPORTING ACT.**

[1106.1]   **Bank Information and the Act.** For a time after the law took effect, some bankers informed Dun & Bradstreet that because of the Fair Credit Reporting Act, they could no longer provide information to credit agencies about their accounts. This was due to an incorrect understanding of the law on the part of those bankers, as has been pointed out by Howard W. Rathburn, president of Robert Morris Associates. Writing in the July 12, 1971, issue of *Eastern Banker,* Rathburn observes that the act "may compel disclosure of source or nature of information only when used to deny credit for personal, family or household use. The act does not require such disclosure where loans strictly for business or commercial purposes are involved. . . . In situations involving either consumers or commercial enterprises," Rathburn further pointed out, "the Act still allows a bank to reveal its own experiences to the inquirer without thereby issuing a 'consumer report' as defined in the Act." As these comments point out, there is nothing in the language and intent of the act that should cause banks to be reluctant to provide information to credit agencies on their accounts. The law does not cover business reports and, aside from that, it provides in Section 603(d) that "any report containing information solely as to transactions or experiences between the consumer and the person making the report" is not a consumer report. The legislators have made it clear that it was not their intent to bring banks under the act when they are reporting their own experiences with one of their customers, even though that customer is a consumer.

The Associated Credit Bureaus, Inc., recorded interviews with legislators, their aides, and other government officials and in one portion of that tape recording a question on this very subject was posed to Senator Proxmire. Here is the question and his response:

> QUESTION: What is the intent of the law with regard to a bank which supplies third-party information on a consumer to another bank?
>
> SENATOR PROXMIRE: The clear intent of the law is to cover a bank or other creditor as a credit reporting agency if the bank supplies third party information on a consumer. In other words, where the bank is acting as a credit agency, then it is covered by the Act as any other credit reporting agency is.
>
> *Creditors are, of course, free to communicate information on their own first-hand experience with the customers.* [Emphasis added] However, should they communicate third party information, it would be behaving as a credit reporting agency and, therefore, be regulated as a credit reporting agency is; so in this way we treat banks and credit reporting agencies exactly the same.

Senator Proxmire's comments have been reinforced by the Federal Reserve Board guidelines issued in May, 1971, entitled: "Financial Institutions and The Fair Credit Reporting Act." Question 18 and the response follow:

> QUESTION: What information may a financial institution give to third parties in response to inquiries about a consumer, without becoming a consumer reporting agency?
>
> RESPONSE: The financial institution may relate information solely as to its transactions or experiences with the consumer. For example, the financial institution may disclose that the consumer had a history of delinquency, or was current, and could give other information as to the status of any loans or deposits with it. To assure that it does not become a consumer reporting agency, it should not regularly give out information contained in credit applications bearing on the consumer's credit worthiness, credit standing, credit capacity, character, general reputation, personal characteristics or mode of living. In addition, it should not regularly give out information obtained in reports from consumer reporting agencies, or any other information obtained from third parties. For example, a financial institution which obtained information as a "user" may become a consumer reporting agency if it subsequently conveys the information to another financial institution.

The language of the law, the intent of the legislators, and the comments of the Federal Reserve Board make it clear that a bank does not come under the law merely by providing its own experience with a given account to a reporting agency.

[1106.2]   **Possible Pitfalls for Banks.** There is one possible area where banks should be very careful—an area where the dissemination by a bank of even information concerning businesses might place that bank in the position of a consumer reporting agency. That would be the case where the information passed on is (1) third-party information *and* (2) it is used by the recipient for a consumer purpose. (This situation is directly analogous to the earlier example of a D&B Business Information Report on Mr. Doe's corporation being used to determine the credit worthiness of Doe himself in seeking credit to buy a color TV for his home and the possibility that this might turn the D&B Business Information Report into a consumer report.) The key to this is for both banks and D&B to look consciously to the *use* to which the information is to be put. The ascertainment of the use or purpose of each inquiry is a procedure that would be in keeping not only with the act itself but also the Robert Morris Associates Code of Ethics for the Exchange of Credit Information and the Statement of Principles in the Exchange of Credit Information Between Banks and Mercantile Concerns. As far as D&B Business Information Reports are concerned, for the bank to disseminate them (as third-party information) to some other person has always been prohibited by D&B's contract terms with subscribers, which provide that all information furnished is for the subscriber's exclusive use. This could be particularly dangerous if the D&B Business Information Report did in fact contain obsolete information and was improperly used for consumer credit purposes.

CHAPTER 12

COLLECTION OF TRADE RECEIVABLES

[1200] **COLLECTION OF TRADE RECEIVABLES.** *"Sales is the lifeblood of any business, but accounts receivable is its heart which must pump steadily to nurture profits and growth."* This concept, basic to credit analysis, is sometimes overlooked by executives eager to get new accounts and increase business with existing customers. The results can be costly. Take the case of Fred Henton, president of Henton Container Corporation. It was a small corporation started by Fred and his brother Jeff. Fred, before starting the business, was a crackerjack salesman for a large corrugated box company. Jeff, gifted in his knowledge of machinery, had worked as a foreman and production manager in the paper industry. They were the ideal team and, with combined savings of $25,000, started the business. A reliable woman with a strong bookkeeping background was hired to manage the office. Things went well. The products manufactured were competitive, both in quality and in price, and sales, under Fred's direction, showed substantial gains. The customers were small- to moderate-size manufacturers and wholesalers. They were sold on 1–10-net-30-day terms. The major portion of the profits, and a long-term bank loan, were invested in additional machinery to keep up with production demands. The net worth increased over a five-year period from the initial investment of $25,000, to $140,000.

Fred had had a particularly successful week on the road. Advance orders were at an all-time high and conservative projections showed that sales at the end of the first quarter would be 20 percent ahead of a similar period the year before. So, Fred's surprise was understandable when George Smith, the loan officer at the Bennington National Bank, called.

"Say, Fred, what's happened to that straight-discount payment record you used to brag about?" George was also a personal friend and Fred's first impression was that he was kidding. "I'm serious," George continued. "One of the credit agencies just completed a trade survey and over half your suppliers say you're paying your bills ten to fifteen days slow."

Fred was stunned by the news. "I don't understand," he said, "business has never been better."

"Look," George suggested, "your accountant has sent us your year-end statement; suppose we discuss the figures over lunch next week?" Fred agreed, and after the call he approached the office manager.

"Mrs. Atkins, why aren't we discounting our bills?"

"I can't pay our suppliers until customers pay us," she explained. "The cash has been very slow."

"Well, we've worked hard building goodwill and there are certain customers you have to carry," Fred reasoned. "They are slow but good."

"Perhaps they are, Mr. Henton, but they owe us more money than ever before and they are now running sixty days past-due instead of the 'normal' thirty days late."

"Surely there are enough excellent payers among all the new accounts we've opened to offset the chronically slow people?"

"We have a number of fine customers," Mrs. Atkins agreed, "but we have also written off quite a bit of money in bad debts this year."

"You have to take some risks," said Fred the salesman, "otherwise competition will get the account."

"In some cases we would be better off," she retorted, getting in the last word.

Several days later Fred and George discussed the situation. The latest balance sheet on Henton Container Corporation looked like this:

December 31, 19–

Cash in bank	$8,124		Owing bank		$5,000
On hand	95		A/C payable		52,564
		8,219	Taxes		9,643
A/C rec.	108,021		Accruals		4,021
Less reserves	2,120				
		105,901			
Inventories					
Raw materials	31,374				
Finished goods	18,119				
		49,493			
Total Current Assets		$163,613	**Total Current Liabilities**		$71,228
Machinery and equipment	62,280		Owing bank		15,000
Less depreciation	6,308		Capital stock		25,000
		55,972	Surplus		115,000
Other fixed assets		6,643			
Total Assets		$226,228			
			Total liabilities Capital, surplus		$226,228

The statement of income, profit, and loss showed:

Net sales	$575,400
Cost of goods sold	420,042
Gross profit	155,358
Operating expenses	142,124
Net profit	$13,234

Among the operating expenses were bad-debt losses of $11,908.

In order to evaluate properly these figures, George computed the following ratios and compared them to those for the paperboard container industry as compiled by the Industry Studies Department of D&B.

Current assets to current debt	2.3:1
Working capital	$92,385
Quick ratio	1.6:1
Net profit on net sales	2.3%
Net profits on tangible net worth	9.4%
Net profits on net working capital	14.3%
Net sales to tangible net worth	4.1 times
Net sales to net working capital	6.2 times
Collection period	67.2 days
Net sales to inventory	11.6 times
Fixed assets to tangible net worth	44.7%
Current debt to tangible net worth	50.9%
Total debt to tangible net worth	61.6%
Inventory to net working capital	53.6%
Current debt to inventory	144.0%

"Your net sales were 4.1 times tangible net worth," George analyzed. "That puts you in the upper 25 percent of paperboard container manufacturers, according to Dun & Bradstreet's *Key Business Ratios*. Your inventory levels are favorable in relation to sales and we can eliminate 'stockpiling' as a cause of your trade slowness. But look at this, Fred"—George pointed to the operating figures—"your net profit compared with net sales comes to only 2.3 percent. That's low for the line; in fact, in the lowest 25 percent. This year your earnings were well below the $20,000 you have averaged during the first five years. You're making less money on substantially more sales."

"Well," Fred interjected, "raw materials went up last year and in order to stay competitive we would only increase our prices slightly."

"The percentage of cost of goods sold to sales showed a small increase over last year," George acknowledged, "which is hardly a significant reason for your present problem. But, you have written off almost $12,000 in bad debts. That's almost as much as your total profit. I don't have an aging of your accounts receivable but they appear to be in bad shape. As a rule of thumb, a company's collecton period shouldn't be more than one-third greater than their net selling terms. In your case no more than 40 days. Your collection period is 67.2 days, which is much more than the lowest quarter for your line.

"Fred, I'm sure you've heard the maxim, 'A sale is not complete until the money is collected'?"

"Many times," Fred answered wistfully.

"I'd like to carry that phrase one dramatic step further," George went on, "and show you what it means in terms of additional sales if the money is *not* collected."

He put a chart like Table 12.1 on the table:

"Specifically, the Henton Container Corporation would have to sell an *additional* $21,700 for *each* $500 in bad debts." Fred did some quick arithmetic and looked at George in disbelief. "That's right, Fred, in order

If you have an Actual Loss of:	And your net profit is:				
	2%	**3%**	**4%**	**5%**	**6%**
	You will require this amount of additional sales to offset the loss:				
$ 50.	$ 2,500.	$ 1,666.	$ 1,250.	$ 1,000.	$ 833.
100.	5,000.	3,333.	2,500.	2,000.	1,666.
200.	10,000.	6,666.	5,000.	4,000.	3,333.
250.	12,500.	8,333.	6,250.	5,000.	4,166.
300.	15,000.	10,000.	7,500.	6,000.	5,000.
350.	17,500.	11,666.	8,750.	7,000.	5,833.
400.	20,000.	13,333.	10,000.	8,000.	6,666.
450.	22,500.	15,000.	11,250.	9,000.	7,500.
500.	25,000.	16,666.	12,500.	10,000.	8,333.

TABLE 12.1. Additional Sales Necessary to Offset Losses

to make up that $11,900 you wrote off last year you would have to sell another $517,700, which would mean almost doubling your business."

It was obvious. The overextension of credit and neglect of the accounts receivable had caused a significant dent in the firm's profit and growth picture. As soon as Fred returned to the office he carefully reviewed the aging of the receivables, which showed the following:

Aging at December 31, 19–   Collections from January 1 15, 19

December	—	$34,369	$15,809
November	—	22,334	8,021
October	—	16,588	4,084
September	—	11,058	2,963
August	—	13,335	1,742
July	—	6,281	182
June	—	1,298	85
May	—	1,233	
April	—	1,096	
March	—	780	
February	—	49	
		$108,421	

Fred and Mrs. Atkins reviewed the duplicate statements and the past-due accounts. Some of the outstanding money was brought in by letters and phone calls. Other accounts were placed with a collection agency with varying results. Some, after careful evaluation, were charged off as bad debts. While Fred continued to establish overall policy, Mrs. Atkins was given the responsibility for credit and collections. She quickly developed her skills in these areas by taking courses, observation of other firms' techniques, and through the best teacher of all, experience.

Although the "Henton Case" is fictitious, what Mrs. Atkins would have learned reflects an actual situation.

[1201] COLLECTION POLICY. The key to an efficient collection operation lies in a knowledgeable, workable collection policy. A seller seeking a mass market and shipping goods on credit to accounts representing a variety of risks must expect a certain number of his accounts to run past-due. Even the best customers can suffer reverses that may affect their ability to pay within terms.

The primary job of the credit manager is to increase sales with a minimum of "calculated" risk. Second, he should administer a firm, well-defined collection policy.

[1201.1] **Reasons for a Well-Defined Collection Policy.**

[1201.1.1] DIFFICULTIES OF AGE. The chances of a receivable becoming a bad debt increase with its age. An account over ninety days past due is very hard to collect indeed. Age is relative to the "normal" terms of a particular industry.

[1201.1.2] FURTHER SALES. Slow collections inhibit further sales to the slow-paying customer. If careful, the customer will not want to go further in debt; and a practical credit manager will not encourage him to do so.

[1201.1.3] RESPECT. A firm, courteous collection policy builds respect for the seller.

[1201.1.4] CUSTOMER DELINQUENCY PREVENTION. A reputation for efficient and alert collection efforts will, in itself, act as a brake on customers who might otherwise allow an account to become past due.

[1201.1.5] PREVENTION OF DEBTOR OVEREXTENSION. When a creditor lets a debtor pay slowly and continues to sell him, the debtor may overextend himself, particularly the desperate debtor willing to use the creditor's money for his working capital.

[1201.1.6] DISCOUNT TERMS. Working capital that is "muscle-bound" with past-due receivables prevents a seller from taking advantage of discount terms offered by his own suppliers. If the seller's credit rating is affected by the slow retirement of his bills, he can lose the solicitation of prime suppliers.

[1201.1.7] MARGINAL ACCOUNT BUSINESS. Close control of receivables can allow a growing firm to maintain a liberal credit policy and sell "marginal" accounts that might ordinarily be bypassed.

[1201.1.8] INTERNAL FINANCE. A good flow of receivables cash allows a seller to internally finance payment of his maturing bills. If bank loans are used they can be directed to seasonal inventory requirements and plant improvements.

[1201.2] **Components of Collection Policy.** In order for the collection policy to help prevent the receivables problems described above, it should provide guidelines for the following areas:

[1201.2.1] COLLECTION RESPONSIBILITY. In most companies, the person who made the decision to extend credit is the one who is responsible for collecting the money. This makes sense because that person is most familiar with the case, the problems that might arise, and the solution best suited to the situation. Who this person is, of course, depends upon the company. In a single proprietorship, it is naturally the proprietor who will handle credit extensions and collections. As the size of the company increases, the bookkeeper, office manager, collection manager, or credit manager will take over this responsibility.

[1201.2.2]   USE OF NON-CREDIT DEPARTMENT PERSONNEL IN THE COLLECTION EFFORT. Credit policy should also set up guidelines for the use of non–credit department personnel in the collection effort. These others might include:

1. *Salesmen,* who could be called upon to make a personal appeal to the slow-paying customer or supply pertinent information. Although selling time is costly and use of salesmen for collection activities should be limited, most credit managers have found it wise to keep salesmen informed of any collection difficulties so the sales effort can be guided accordingly.

2. *Treasurer.* Often the treasurer, if he has not been involved in the collection effort from the beginning, is asked to step in on a difficult case. The use of his signature is often what is needed to jar the past-due customer into action. He can also make personal or telephone calls.

3. *Company president and other officers.* A letter from the company president—particularly the president of small- or medium-size companies—is an action that the credit manager could consider taking if warranted by the circumstances.

[1201.2.3]   WHEN TO START COLLECTION EFFORTS AND WHICH INTERNAL TOOLS TO USE. Collection policy should establish the amount of time allowed to pass before the first internal collection step is taken. Each situation should be examined to determine which collection tool should be used as an initial step and a projection should be made of the next action if the debtor does not respond.

[1201.2.4]   HOW FAST TO PROCEED. Collection policy should establish the intervals between each stage of the collection process. Limits should be set between the initial steps and the time the account is placed with an agency or an attorney. The credit manager may choose to vary his timing now and again for a change of pace or a special situation, but definite policy avoids letting an account get out of control.

[1201.2.5]   WHEN TO USE A COLLECTION AGENCY AND WHAT KIND TO CHOOSE. Collection policy should provide guidelines for the use of collection agencies. Since different agencies vary in the techniques they employ and the scope of their efforts, policy should let you know which kind to choose in different situations.

The astute credit manager develops an almost instinctive sense as to when to turn past-due accounts over to a collection agency. He knows the varying points of saturation for internal collection tools and is knowledgeable about the collection program of his agency.

Collection agencies should *not* be a "last-resort" method of getting money. They should be used as a logical and intelligent continuation of a company's internal collection procedures.

[1201.2.6]   WHEN AND HOW TO USE AN ATTORNEY. Collection agencies, if their own efforts are unsuccessful, usually forward an account to an attorney in behalf of their claimant. Collection policy should establish whether this facility of the agency should be used. Generally, attorneys do not vary greatly in their techniques and the policies of most collection attorneys are in accordance with the Commercial Law League of America.

[1201.2.7] TERMS OF SALE. Collection policy should reflect or state a philosophy about the use of terms of sale. Is your company using particularly competitive ones so that past-due accounts would represent more hazardous risks than otherwise? Or are your terms so conservative that it is unreasonable to expect a good proportion of your customers to discount their bills? Undoubtedly, your terms lie somewhere between these two extremes, but collection policy should be established in relation to your terms.

[1201.2.8] BAD-DEBT RESERVES. Part of the credit manager's duty is to establish the bad-debt reserve. At the moment, precise mathematical tools are not available for the credit manager to use to determine what his bad-debt reserve should be. He must rely, therefore, on his own judgment, past experience, industry norms, and credit and collection policy.

[1201.2.9] SPECIAL PROBLEMS. Collection policy should start credit personnel on the right road toward solving common collection problems such as unearned discounts, checks returned for insufficient funds, unhonored drafts, disputed accounts, and new orders from companies with past-due balances.

[1201.2.10] REPORTS TO TOP MANAGEMENT. Collection policy often suggests the methods and frequency of reporting collection efforts to top management. Most companies have found that the size of their receivables warrants a monthly aging as a minimum appraisal of the collection operation.

[1202] THE COLLECTION SYSTEM. There are four major aspects to a collection system. These are: (1) classification of the debtor; (2) collection tools; (3) following the collection effort; and (4) evaluating the collection effort.

[1202.1] **Classification of the Debtor.** Once an account has become past due, the person responsible for the collection effort should determine the category in which the debtor falls. This can be done by reviewing all information about the customer that has accumulated in his file, by conferring with salesmen who have recently called on the customer, by discussing his situation with other creditors at an interchange meeting, by obtaining the latest credit report on the client, or, often most effective, by calling on the client yourself. The accurate classification of the debtor can determine what collection tool to use. Whatever method or combination of methods you choose, the end result should be your classification of the debtor in one of these categories pinpointed in the *Executive's Credit and Collection Guide:*

[1202.1.1] NEGLIGENT. This is the debtor who has the money and the intention to pay, but needs reminding that his bill is past due. Such accounts do not represent very difficult collection problems.

[1202.1.2] HONEST BUT CONFUSED. Such a customer would have paid if he had correctly understood the terms. Credit-department personnel should be courteous in explaining what he does not understand—and be on the look-out that this excuse is not presented again.

[1202.1.3] TOO BUSY FOR SMALL BALANCES. This type of debtor often represents a serious hazard to some credit departments. He presents the justification for his slowness as "too much to do to be bothered with a little amount." He'll add it on to his next bill—and does. But as credit manager, you know that these small amounts can build up. Explain this to your slow-paying, busy customer and let him know that *all* bills must be paid promptly.

[1202.1.4] SEASONAL DELINQUENT. When the slow season arrives, the seasonal delinquent falls behind in his payments. Often, there is little the credit department can do but bear with this customer until his activity picks up again. Make sure, however, that this customer is not favoring other companies with prompt payments at your expense. This can sometimes be avoided by shipping quantities within the customer's seasonal needs.

[1202.1.5] NOT-AT-FAULT DEBTOR. When disasters strike—fires, floods, sickness—or when other unavoidable difficulties such as material shortages or labor troubles interrupt business operation temporarily, you should do everything you can to assist the debtor to get back on his feet. This isn't the time to intensify your collection effort; instead, write a letter of condolence in which you express your confidence that all will be well soon and your readiness—indeed desire—to suspend the credit obligation while the trouble lasts.

[1202.1.6] CHRONICALLY SLOW. There are two types of chronically slow debtors. One is the customer who has the ability to pay but makes all his creditors wait as a matter of policy. He figures he can always go to a competitive supplier if anyone complains—and often he is right. The credit department should act in accordance with its own company's policy. The other chronically slow payer is undercapitalized and depends on trade credit instead of additional financing to furnish working capital. In cases where the bank has denied this debtor an unsecured loan, it may be wise for you to review your credit exposure.

[1202.1.7] DEBTORS WHO CANNOT PAY. Some companies will say that they are temporarily overextended when, in fact, they are dangerously close to financial embarrassment. The best thing to do in such a case is to press for immediate full or partial payment. If efforts are unsuccessful, consideration must be given to the possibility that creditor aid would rescue the business permanently and if it would, attempts must be made to bring the creditors together to work out a solution. If the danger of insolvency is imminent or if the account is in virtual bankruptcy, then you must evaluate the circumstances and be prepared to take logical legal steps to collect what you can.

[1202.1.8] OUTRIGHT FRAUDS. The best protection against outright frauds is more thorough investigation before granting credit. If you are unlucky enough to be doing business with a criminal, then your only solution is to inform the trade and the appropriate law-enforcement agency.

[1202.2] **Collection Tools.** Let the circumstances and your imagination be your guide when it comes to the collection tools you choose to bring in payments from delinquent debtors. Every collection or credit manager has his favorite collection letter. Each can recall the most satisfying technique he has used in the past. As credit manager, however, your responsibility is to continue to develop the tools that will be effective for your company. Although you can rely upon well-known collection principles, you must creatively apply these principles in each collection effort. The tools described below, therefore, serve only as a reminder of where your ingenuity can start to work.

[1202.2.1]   INVOICE. It is hard to think of the invoice as a collection tool but few companies pay bills without receiving them. An original invoice should be sent as soon as merchandise is shipped. A duplicate invoice can be sent as a reminder about a week before the due date.

[1202.2.2]   STATEMENTS. Monthly statements should be sent including all amounts owing, both current and past due. Other efforts on past-due items can simultaneously continue. In cases where it is not economical to send statements to all accounts they can be used as a first collection tool.

[1202.2.3]   REMINDER NOTICE. This is usually sent after a grace period of ten days following the payment due date. The best reminder is impersonal in tone but always cordial at this initial phase of the collection cycle. Because there is always the possibility of an oversight, procedural difficulties, or a dispute about a shipment, it is better to give the customer the benefit of the doubt. If there is no response in ten to fifteen days, a second reminder, escalating in firmness of tone, should be sent. Gummed reminders should be eye-catching and vary in color. Or the reminder may be a simple duplicate of the original statement or invoice with a rubber stamp indicating the payment is past due. Reminder notices could also be a printed card.

[1202.2.4]   COLLECTION LETTERS. Collection letters are a widely used form of soliciting payment from delinquent customers. Because they are so widely used, however, originality pays substantial dividends. Your customers are more likely to begin payment when they receive well-thought-out letters. (For examples of credit and collection letters two large companies use, see Figures 12.1 through 12.17.) Remember these principles of all good collection procedures:

1. In your collection letters, for the purpose of clear reference, always include debtor's name and address, the date of the letter, the amount due, a description of merchandise or service bought, and a self-addressed return envelope.

2. Type collection letters individually and avoid a form letter wherever possible. The salutation should be to a particular individual. The more the letter talks about the debtor's individual situation, the more effective it will be. Like so many forms of persuasion, the collection of debts is most effective when done on a person-to-person basis.

3. Many concerns ship on the basis of telephone orders or various types of verbal reorders. Omit this in a letter unless the debtor denies ordering the merchandise. Motivate the debtor to pay by appealing to his sense of honesty and fair play, his valued

```
(date)

(buyer
customer
address)


Re:  Purchase Order (number)


(salutation):

We are pleased that you have ordered from        . For your convenience,
credit accommodations have been established.

At the time your order is shipped, an invoice will be sent to you.  Your re-
mittance is not expected until the due date on the invoice.  Correct posting
of your account will be accomplished and we can avoid contacting you need-
lessly, if you will refer to our complete invoice number on your check or
return a copy of the invoice with your payment.

Lasting value of the equipment you have ordered and selection of other
             products can be obtained through services available from
Field Engineering offices.  In addition, future orders requiring terms of sale
for special circumstances can be arranged.

It will be our pleasure to again serve you.

Sincerely,



Market Financial Services

dm    (customer account number)
```

FIGURE 12.1

Customer Welcome Letter

```
(date)

(individual
customer
address)


Re:  Scheduled Payment


(salutation:)

We can certainly appreciate the mutual advantages of your periodically
scheduling the payment of our invoices.  We accept the plan you suggest.
It seems to substantially comply with our standard terms of sale.

We should mention, however, that we too have a system.  Invoices overdue
ten days can result in an inquiry about payment.  Should you be contacted
about payment, please do not think it inconsistent with our understanding.
An exception isn't economical because of our automated methods and, on
occasion, lost or overlooked invoices will be brought to your attention
by our letter.

Thank you for this opportunity to be of service.

Sincerely,



(individual)
(title)
dm    (customer account number)
```

FIGURE 12.2

Accepting Scheduled Payment Terms

```
(date)

(buyer
customer
address)


Re:  Your Purchase Order (number)


(salutation):

Thank you for your recent order.  We appreciate this opportunity to
serve you and have entered your order under our reference (number.)

We have completed our routine credit inquiry.  However, (insert balance
of sentence as appropriate:)

(1)  one important aspect requiring consideration is lacking, your
     financial circumstances).

(2)  two important aspects requiring consideration are lacking, your
     financial circumstances and trade relations).

To guide us in providing you with credit accommodations, we ask your
help in completing the enclosed Account Review.  Your response, in the
envelope provided, will be retained in confidence.

Possibly your reply will be delayed beyond your requirements for this
equipment.  If so, may we suggest either an advance payment or, if you
wish, collect-on-delivery terms for this particular order.  You may then
return the completed Account Review at your convenience.

May we hear from you soon?

Thank you,


(individual)
(title)

ff   (customer account number)
Enclosure
```

FIGURE 12.3

Request for Account Review from New Customer

```
(buyer
customer
address)


Re:  Your Purchase Order (number)

(Salutation):

Thank you for this opportunity to again serve you.  We have entered your
order under our reference (number).

While we have previously provided credit terms for your convenience, the
amount of credit you have required recently has not been as substantial
as will be needed for your present order.

To guide us in providing you with expanded credit accommodations, we ask
your help in completing the enclosed Account Review.  Your response, in
the envelope provided, will be retained in confidence.

Possibly your reply will be delayed beyond your requirements for this
equipment.  If so, may we suggest either an advance payment or, if you
wish, collect-on-delivery terms for this particular order.  You may then
return the completed Account Review at your convenience.

May we hear from you soon?

Thank you,


(individual)
(title)

dm   (customer number)
Enclosure
```

FIGURE 12.4

Request for Account Review to Increase Credit

(date)

(individual
customer
address)

Re: Cash Discount Terms

(Salutation)

We have considered your suggestion that   offer a cash discount
for exceptionally prompt payment. This question is not a new one to us,
as some years ago we did provide discount terms.

We have found that such a discount is not to the mutual advantage of our
customers or ourselves. True, it does improve cash flow, but not significantly. The real liability in such discounts, from our experience, is the
friction generated with customers who misunderstand the conditions that
qualify the discount.

Perhaps more important from the customer's viewpoint is the lack of any
economic justification for a cash discount. Obtaining this accelerated
cash flow carries a price tag equivalent to (1-factor)% interest for a (2-factor)%
discount. Accordingly, you as our customer, would have to support this
concession in the increased price of our product.

Therefore, in declining your request for a cash discount, we do so
believing it is in the best interests of
and   that we continue our policy of net terms of sale.

Sincerely,

(individual)
(title)

ff   (customer account number)

FIGURE 12.5

Refusing Cash Discount Terms

(date)

(individual
customer
address)

Re: Scheduled Payment

(salutation):

We can certainly appreciate the mutual advantages of your periodically
scheduling the payment of our invoices. However, we are unable to accept
your proposal for scheduling payments to   .

The plan you suggest requires a significant variation from our standard
terms of sale. As we understand your proposal, our terms to you would
have to vary from net (number) to (number) days, taking into consideration the
mailing time for your remittance.

On the other hand, if it is more convenient for you to purchase on extended terms, net 60 to 120 days are available. There is a charge made
for this additional service. Your   Field Engineer will be happy
to discuss these terms at your request.

While we highly value the opportunity to serve you, and desire to provide
your firm with every reasonable technical and administrative service, we
feel obligated to offer terms fairly and uniformly to you and all other
          customers.

We will appreciate your planning payment so that it reaches us by the
due date specified on our invoices.

Thank you,

(individual)
(customer)

ff   (customer account number)

FIGURE 12.6

Refusing Scheduled Payment Terms

```
(date)

(Customer)
(address)


ATTN:  ACCOUNTS PAYABLE MANAGER

GENTLEMEN:

FRANKLY, WE ARE AT A LOSS TO KNOW HOW TO SUCCESSFULLY ASK FOR THIS SMALL
PAST DUE BALANCE.

REFERENCE              INVOICE              AMOUNT      DATE DUE

(number)               (number)             (amount)    (date)

                                BALANCE      (balance)

PLEASE . . . . . . .

SINCERELY,


(individual)
(title)

DP   (customer account number)
```

FIGURE 12.7

Small Balance Letter

```
(date)

(customer
address)


ATTENTION:  ACCOUNTS PAYABLE MANAGER

GENTLEMEN:

IS THERE A REASON WHY YOUR REMITTANCE IS DELAYED?

REFERENCE              INVOICE              AMOUNT      DUE DATE

(number)               (number)             (amount)    (date)

                                BALANCE DUE  (balance)

IF SO, PLEASE TELL US HOW WE MAY ASSIST YOU.

SHOULD YOUR CHECK ALREADY BE ON ITS WAY, THANK YOU.

SINCERELY,


(individual)
(title)

DP   (customer account number)
```

FIGURE 12.8

Inquiry Letter—First Week

```
(date)

(customer)
(address)

ATTN:  ACCOUNTS PAYABLE MANAGER

GENTLEMEN:

WE KNOW OF NO REASON WHY PAYMENT OF THIS OVERDUE BALANCE IS DELAYED.

REFERENCE              INVOICE           AMOUNT      DUE DATE

(number)               (Number)          (amount)    (date)

                       BALANCE DUE        (balance)

IF ADDITIONAL SERVICES ARE NEEDED, PLEASE EXPLAIN YOUR REQUIREMENTS SO
THAT WE MAY HELP.

SINCERELY,


(individual)
(title)

DP   (customer account number)
```

FIGURE 12.9

Reminder Letter—First Week

```
(date)

(customer)
(address)

ATTN:  ACCOUNTS PAYABLE MANAGER

GENTLEMEN:

YOUR PAYMENT OF THIS PAST DUE BALANCE WILL BE APPRECIATED.

REFERENCE              INVOICE           AMOUNT      DUE DATE

(number)               (number)          (amount)    (date)

                       BALANCE DUE        (balance)

PLEASE SEND US YOUR REMITTANCE BY RETURN MAIL.

THANK YOU,


(individual)
(title)

DP   (customer account number)
```

FIGURE 12.10

Request Letter—First Week

DATE (date)

(individual)
(customer)
(address)

FIGURE 12.11

Request Wire

PAYMENT OF THIS DELINQUENCY TODAY WILL BE APPRECIATED.

REFERENCE   INVOICE   AMOUNT

(number)   (number)   (amount)

(individual)

COPY TO: (city)

GENESCO

Genesco Park · Nashville, Tennessee, U.S.A. 37202

Credit Department

Re: _____
         (Division or Divisions)

FIGURE 12.12

Company Number 2: Collection Series

Gentlemen:

Your account with us IS NEW.

You owe us $_____.

You have not responded to any of our previous
requests for payment. You must admit this is
a poor way to begin a business relationship.

In our mutual best interest our terms must be
respected.

We shall expect a check in 10 days.

                    Yours very truly,

                    GENESCO, Inc.

                    Credit Department
                    Footwear Marketing

CC: Sales Manager
     Salesman

3A

GENESCO
Genesco Park · Nashville, Tennessee, U.S.A. 37202

Credit Department

$ _____

Gentlemen:

Several reminders have been sent to you since
your account matured but we have not received
a check or an explanation.

This condition is not satisfactory. You realize
that we must come to some understanding about
payment.

Why not take the necessary few minutes today
and either write us a check or tell us when we
can depend on receiving it?

Thank you.

                    Yours very truly,

                    GENESCO, Inc.

                    Credit Department
                    Footwear Marketing

3B

FIGURE 12.13

**Company Number 2:
Collection Series**

GENESCO
Genesco Park · Nashville, Tennessee, U.S.A. 37202

Credit Department

$ _____

Gentlemen:

Your account remains past due and we are at a
loss to understand why?

This fact has been brought to your attention in
previous letters, and we find that not only have
you not paid your account, you have not given us
the courtesy of a reply.

Perhaps you have a very good reason for not paying
us, but we do not know this unless we hear from
you.

Please give your past due balance the attention
it deserves and send us your check today, in the
enclosed envelope.

Thank you.

                    Yours very truly,

                    GENESCO, Inc.

                    Credit Department
                    Footwear Marketing

3C

FIGURE 12.14

**Company Number 2:
Collection Series**

GENESCO

Genesco Park · Nashville, Tennessee, U.S.A. 37202

Credit Department

Gentlemen:

We have given you ample opportunity to pay your past due balance of $ _____.

You have not done so, and we must advise you that we cannot continue the present condition.

Please send your check today, so that other action will not be necessary.

Thank you.

                    Yours very truly,

                    GENESCO, Inc.

                    Credit Department
                    Footwear Marketing

3F

FIGURE 12.15

Company Number 2: Collection Series

GENESCO

Genesco Park · Nashville, Tennessee, U.S.A. 37202

Credit Department

Dear Customer:

Our idea of a good collection letter is that it should be brief, friendly and successful.

This letter is brief - friendly - and it's success depends upon you.

The amount due is $ _____.   Thank you.

                    Cordially,

                    GENESCO, Inc.

                    Credit Department
                    Footwear Marketing

1D Please send check to Post Office Box shown on invoices.

FIGURE 12.16

Company Number 2: Collection Series

FIGURE 12.17

Company Number 2: Collection Series

reputation, his natural desire to avoid unnecessary disputes and to maintain excellent relations with his suppliers. Each of these appeals—in the order presented—often forms the basis for a single letter in a series. In all letters, communicate your confidence in your debtor's willingness and ability to pay.

Always allow the debtor to save face; do not imply he deliberately does not want to pay. Use a phrase such as, "You may have inadvertently overlooked this invoice" or "Perhaps my earlier letters were not referred to you."

5. Create a sense of urgency about the collection while maintaining a businesslike, courteous tone in your letter. Letters mailed in fairly rapid succession, say, one a week, can accomplish this. Remember that the wheel that squeaks the loudest or most insistently is usually the first one to be greased.

6. Retain your debtor's attention by using different letters, different shapes, sizes, and colors, different formats, interspersed perhaps with a telegram or telephone call (see sections 1202.2.5 and 1202.2.6). You might also send letters out over the signature of increasingly important people—the credit manager, the treasurer, or even the president of the company himself. Do not let sameness defeat the effect of urgency you want to create. At the same time, however, avoid gimmicks that are "too catchy" or violate businesslike tone and manner.

7. Send at least some items of the collection-letter series by registered mail, return receipt requested. The chances are better the debtor will read such a letter personally and this increases the chance for a response.

8. Try to get your debtor to at least explain the delay by writing something similar to: "Perhaps you have a perfectly understandable reason for not paying this bill. Won't you please let us know what the problem is?"

9. Attempt to get the debtor to make some kind of response so that he puts himself into a person-to-person situation. Give him precise directions as to a course of action:
   a. Suggest that he call or write to tell you about his problem.
   b. Suggest that he make a partial payment and develop a schedule to meet the balance.
   c. Get him to promise payment by a certain date.

   Even a tentative promise of payment obligates him psychologically. It is also a nice tool to have for future collection efforts. Once your debtor acknowledges that he will (or should) pay, he no longer has any excuses about disputed shipments, etc., on which he can fall back.

10. Have "address correction requested" printed on the outer envelope of collection letters just in case the debtor has moved. This imprint obligates the post office, at a modest fee per letter returned, to inform the sender the letter has not been delivered to the addressee, and to supply a forwarding address if known.

TELEGRAMS. Telegrams can be effective collection tools because they demand the recipient's attention. Telegram language, moreover, can be blunt without offending as people expect short, clipped phrases and sentences. For this reason, telegrams are more often used when the collection effort has reached the serious-urgent phase and prompt action is desired. Many credit managers have found, however, that the use of a telegram early in the collection cycle often prompts the action they want. Western Union has preprinted forms that make the use of telegrams even easier. You might also consider using Mailgrams, for which preprinted forms are also available (see Figure 12.18). These are letters transmitted by Western Union wire to a main post office, then delivered by mail carriers to the addressee in special envelopes. There are three types of Mailgram input available:

1. *Terminal originated.* Recommended for the sender who has less than 250 messages to deliver at any one time, or a single address message, these Mailgrams are sent from a leased terminal such as a Telex or TWX. An operator prepares a tape, then dials the Western Union computer on the machines. After transmittal of the message, the computer acknowledges receipt and switches it electronically to a servicing post office nearest the addressee. From the post office, a mail carrier delivers the Mailgram with the regular mail the next day.

2. *Computer originated.* Suggested for those requiring simultaneous delivery of messages in excess of 250, these Mailgrams are sent via

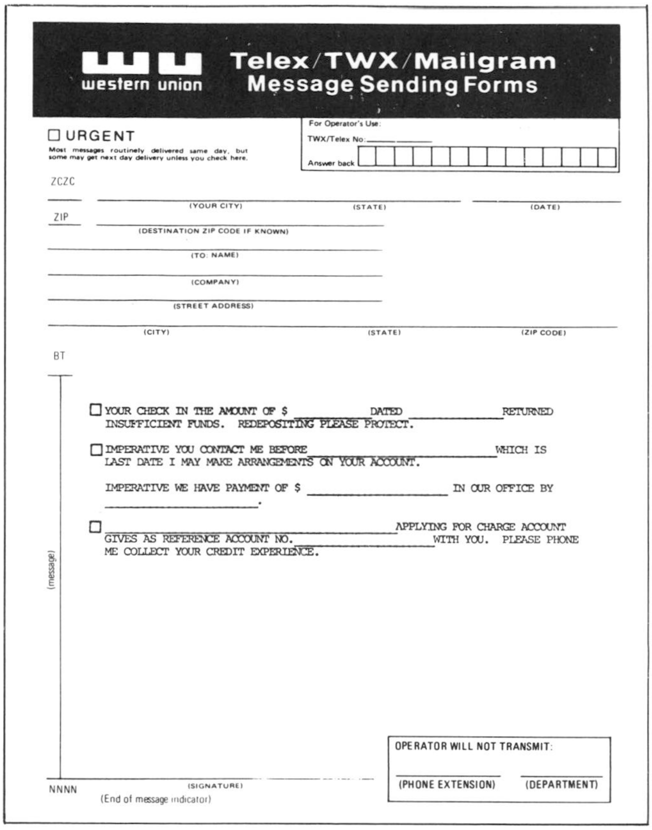

western union Telex/TWX/Mailgram Message Sending Forms

☐ URGENT
Most messages routinely delivered same day, but some may get next day delivery unless you check here.

For Operator's Use:
TWX/Telex No:
Answer back

ZCZC

(YOUR CITY) (STATE) (DATE)

ZIP (DESTINATION ZIP CODE IF KNOWN)

(TO: NAME)

(COMPANY)

(STREET ADDRESS)

(CITY) (STATE) (ZIP CODE)

BT

☐ YOUR CHECK IN THE AMOUNT OF $ ________ DATED ________ RETURNED INSUFFICIENT FUNDS. REDEPOSITING PLEASE PROTECT.

☐ IMPERATIVE YOU CONTACT ME BEFORE ________ WHICH IS LAST DATE I MAY MAKE ARRANGEMENTS ON YOUR ACCOUNT.

IMPERATIVE WE HAVE PAYMENT OF $ ________ IN OUR OFFICE BY ________.

☐ ________ APPLYING FOR CHARGE ACCOUNT GIVES AS REFERENCE ACCOUNT NO. ________ WITH YOU. PLEASE PHONE ME COLLECT YOUR CREDIT EXPERIENCE.

(message)

OPERATOR WILL NOT TRANSMIT:
(PHONE EXTENSION) (DEPARTMENT)

NNNN (SIGNATURE)
(End of message indicator)

FIGURE 12.18

Western Union Mailgram

a magnetic tape to one of Western Union's computer centers around the country. From there, the message is checked for accuracy and then computer-switched directly to the servicing post office, which sorts, ties, envelopes, and delivers the Mailgrams with the regular mail. The magnetic tape containing the Mailgram messages may be prepared by a data-processing department or a certified service bureau authorized by Western Union.

3. *Voice originated.* The most universal method of sending a Mailgram is via a toll-free call to one of Western Union's centralized telephone bureaus, or from a public message center. At a central telephone bureau, the call will be answered within three rings, any hour of the day or night. An operator types the message as it is dictated into a cathode-ray tube. Corrections are made electronically. The message is then transmitted to a central computer by push-button control. The computer then automatically switches the message to the appropriate post office for physical delivery the next day.

[1202.2.6] TELEPHONE CALLS. Once used only rarely because of cost, the telephone has now become the most common and effective collection tool for serious collection problems. In addition to speed, telephone calls offer special advantages listed below. Remember to confirm the point made in your telephone conversation with a letter written immediately after.

1. When you telephone, you can be sure you are directing your collection effort to the right person.
2. On the telephone, you can vary your approach to suit the individual situation and to fit the personality and mood of your debtor.
3. A telephone call enables you to find out the debtor's problem if your previous attempts have resulted in silence.
4. You can demand specific action on the telephone and find out why the customer will not respond to your requests.
5. If you still want to retain your customer's goodwill, a pleasant note injected into the conversation at the end might soothe his feelings.

[1202.2.7]   NOTES. If you can get your delinquent customer to sign a promissory note, you very definitely improve your chances for ultimate collection of the debt. First, the customer has acknowledged his debt. This can be most useful in the event that legal action must be taken. Second, he has given you assurance that he will pay the debt by a certain date. This is a psychological weapon that you, as credit manager, can employ if he fails to live up to his agreement. Third, the existence of a note is a stronger motivation for the debtor to pay your bill sooner than other overdue bills he might have outstanding. You will recognize, of course, that the suggestion to sign a note could bring on adverse feelings toward your company and should be reserved for serious collection problems. Taking a note also has disadvantages. In the event the debtor's financial condition is deteriorating, you cannot press for payment until the note matures. A defaulted note cannot be put back into the bank but must be replaced by the customer with a check, money order, or a new note with a future date.

[1202.2.8]   DRAFTS. Drafts, which are drawn up by the creditor and presented to the debtor through the debtor's bank, can be very effective collection tools. The draft is only good when the debtor signifies his willingness to pay the amount involved by writing "accepted" across the draft and signing his name. Because they will damage your customer's credit standing in the eyes of the bank—and ultimately in the eyes of other trade creditors as the information that drafts have been presented is communicated in agency reports and interchange meetings—you should resort to drafts only when your collection effort has reached a very urgent stage. You will find that they do produce action, however, as the debtor attempts to remain in good standing with his bank and the trade.

[1202.2.9]   POSTDATED CHECKS. One method that is frequently used by credit managers as a means of collecting past-due accounts by partial payment is a series of postdated checks. Postdated checks are promises to pay. The bad-check laws do not generally apply to postdated checks. They provide a special incentive for your customer to pay because if he does not, he will lose his credit standing with his bank.

[1202.2.10]   PERSONAL COLLECTORS. Personal collectors—and this could refer to the credit manager or his staff—should be reserved for very serious or large collection problems because the cost of a personal visit is high. When warranted, however, the personal effort is sure to speed the collection effort in one direction or another: either toward bringing in the payment in an amicable fashion or toward the decision to place the account with an agency or an attorney. The personal call offers all the advantages of the telephone call and more because the demand is on a face-to-face basis. The credit manager, should he make the call, can see for himself the kind of operation his customer is running. He can more easily judge the kind of man or woman with whom he is dealing. He can bring all the assets of his own personality to bear on the collection problem. A personal visit is often the most successful way to avoid legal proceedings as the final collection step.

[1202.2.11]   SALESMEN. Each company must decide whether salesmen should collect delinquent accounts in their territories. There are arguments for and against. Many concerns that have used salesmen in this manner sell to small retail stores and sometimes all payments are made to a salesman on his regular call. He becomes a mobile credit department. He decides on the spot to take a postdated check or to add another order to an account that has not yet paid for the previous shipment. In such cases, the salesman logically assumes the responsibility for past-due accounts.

If a policy decision has been made against using a salesman as a collector because it cuts into valuable selling time, a salesman can still be of great help to you by reporting any reason he knows of for slow payments. The salesman has a stake in the settlement because it clears the way for additional sales.

[1202.2.12]   COLLECTION AGENCIES. *Accounts are usually placed with collection agencies when the progression of internal steps has not brought results.* The last letter or phone call should notify the delinquent debtor that you are going to take this step if no remittance is received within a specified period of time, which should not exceed ten days.

1. *Value of a collection agency.* Although a collection agency can do nothing an individual credit manager cannot do, the efforts of a collection agency historically have produced results when your efforts at collection have failed. A debtor usually does not want a collection agency, and possibly other creditors, to know he pays his accounts slowly. If at all able, he usually prefers to avoid this reputation by paying in full or by discussing a mutually agreeable way of settlement. The collection agency can also supply, particularly to smaller businesses, experience and technical know-how. An account placed for collection has the attention of experts in the collection business. Such handling relieves the credit manager of the burden of collecting certain past-due accounts that could easily take up too much of his time. These accounts often present problems that an impartial collection agency, drawing on its experience with a wide variety of difficult debtors, can solve faster and with much less vexation than the credit manager who insists on doing the whole job himself. When used properly a collection agency can be an effective arm of your credit department.

2. *Kinds of collection agencies.* Collection agencies vary according to their methods of operation and their links to industry.

    a. *Method of operation.* A reputable collection agency that fits your requirements should be chosen. An agency should be courteous, firm, progressive in its collection steps, persistent, and practical. Its geographical coverage should be suitable to your markets. The agency should subscribe to the principles of the American Bar Association and not be engaged in or pretend to be engaged in the practice of law. If there is a forwarding service, the attorneys to whom accounts are sent on your behalf should subscribe to the rules and rates set forth by the Commercial Law League of America (C.L.L.A.). There are exceptions where the agency will have to forward your account to an attorney governed by local bar rates. You should require that the money your agency or your attorney collects be turned over to you as soon as there is assurance that the debtor's check has cleared. In instances where payment is received by you directly, you should notify the agency immediately. The agency should transmit timely status reports of the account.

b. *Collection agencies' links to industry.* Collection agencies are either private agencies that operate as individual companies, or they are associated with trade groups. Although private agencies can be most effective, those associated with trade groups have the advantage that the debtor knows that reports of his slow paying habits will be transmitted instantly to other suppliers and will be considered in determining his credit rating. This can also have a disadvantage because it could start a "run" of suits against the debtor, forcing some form of financial embarrassment.

3. *Services a collection agency offers.* The first step in an agency collection service is often initiated by the creditor himself. This is in the form of an insert, stamp, or gummed reminder indicating that the account is past due, the firm subscribes to the particular collection service, or the account will be referred to the collection agency if payment is not received. Some agencies and trade organizations provide a series of collection letters to be sent by the subscriber. In other instances preliminary letters are mailed by the agency. There is usually no charge to the claimant if payment is received within a specified time after the initial letter.

The next successive steps vary but usually consist of additional letter and wire demands, which escalate in firmness of tone if there is no response from the debtor. The next step consists of telephoning the debtor to demand payment. If this does not bring results, the account is usually referred to an attorney located in the debtor's area and he reports his progress to the agency, which keeps their subscriber advised.

In urgent situations agencies provide for special handling. For example, one large agency makes use of a wire network that reports results of the collection effort to the claimant within twenty-four hours.

[1202.2.13]   LOCAL ATTORNEY. Placing an account with an attorney for collection is the very last step you can take in an attempt to receive your money. By this time, obviously, retaining your customer's goodwill is of secondary importance. Indeed, it is unlikely that you would ever want to sell this account again. An attorney, nevertheless, is a good method to use for these two reasons:

1. An attorney, especially a local one, will probably know your customer and his circumstances—and will be able to investigate the case personally. This provides him with a knowledge of what pressure can be brought to bear to induce payments.

2. Because the customer knows that an attorney will bring suit on behalf of his client if the customer does not pay, the customer will be more strongly motivated to comply with the attorney's requests. The customer realizes, in essence, that there will be no more collection letters sent, no more telephone calls made. If a suit is necessary, you should be prepared to furnish your attorney with all the substantiating information on the debt. In addition, most attorneys ask to be furnished with advance court costs and a suit fee. As a credit manager you should be familiar with the stages of a contested and noncontested lawsuit.

[1203]   **FOLLOWING THE COLLECTION EFFORT.** Whether an accounts-receivable department is large or small, a close check must be kept on efforts to collect delinquent accounts. Effective collection-checking procedures are, naturally, an extension of the procedures used to notify the credit department that the due date has arrived. These procedures vary according to the size of the company and the number of accounts the credit department must keep track of. Here are some suggested methods:

[1203.1]   **Ledger Cards.** If a credit manager uses a visible index of ledger cards, collection steps can be noted right on them. Smaller businesses may use a simple past-due-accounts control sheet. On it there are spaces for listing past-due accounts and for the credit clerk to indicate the date for each collection action. (See Figure 12.19 for a sample of a past-due-control sheet.)

[1203.2]   **Tickler Files.** A more elaborate checking method can be set up in a "tickler file." This consists of a box with a collection record card made out for each delinquent account. A collection step is noted and the card is advanced to the date when the next action should be taken. If a collection is made before the appointed date, the card is removed from the file. This file simplifies the daily or weekly collection program. A credit clerk merely removes the group of cards slated for action on any date. The clerk then refers them to the credit manager, who orders the appropriate action.

[1203.3]   **Duplicate-Statement System.** This is operated in the same way as the tickler-file system except that every statement is filed according to the earliest due date. At that time the ledger cards are checked to see if a payment has been made and if so, the statement is destroyed or refiled according to the due date of the next item. If payment has not been made, the first collection step should be started.

[1203.4]   **Collection Files.** These are set up when an account is turned over to an

Past-Due Accounts Control Sheet

DATE ______________________

Prepared expressly for subscribers to the services of
COMMERCIAL COLLECTION DIVISION
DUN & BRADSTREET, INC.

NAME OF ACCOUNT	DATE OF FIRST INVOICE	TOTAL AMOUNT PAST DUE	AMOUNT NOT PAST DUE	PAST-DUE				ACTION TAKEN					REMARKS
				UP TO 30	31-60	61-90	91-OVER			BLUE REMINDER	GREEN REMINDER	SENT TO CCD FOR COLLECTION	

FIGURE 12.19. Past-Due Accounts Control Sheet

agency or an attorney. The ledger card should clearly note that the account has been turned over for collection. The effort of the agency is followed up by putting a prompt date on the face of the folder. The date should be determined by the agency's or attorney's previous report. If payment is received, the folder should, of course, be made inactive and destroyed after a year.

[1203.5] **Collection Calendar.** A special calendar is obtained and used specifically to list what action is to be taken on a past-due account if it is not paid on the date indicated.

[1203.6] **Computer Notification.** As more and more accounts-receivable departments have access to computer facilities, more and more collection efforts are made and recorded—according to prearranged schedules—by the computer. Refer to Chapter 8 for a discussion of the computer in collection efforts.

[1204] **EVALUATION OF THE COLLECTION EFFORT.** Regular evaluation of the collection effort is a necessity. As credit manager, you need to know how your department is functioning. Top management needs to be aware of the accounts-receivable situation to correctly judge budget requirements and evaluate sales and credit policies. Salesmen, too, need to know how the accounts they sell pay their bills. For these reasons, you should employ some or all of the methods suggested below on a regular basis.

[1204.1] **Agings.** Agings have become one of the most widely used methods of checking the collection effort and is one of the most effective. A quick glance at an aging schedule tells you the amount (and percentage) of the dangerously past-due accounts (those older than ninety days) and the number of customers each category represents. Comments on those customers seriously overdue are sometimes used to complete the aging report. Agings are now generally taken every month, sometimes using trial balance figures.

[1204.2]   **Collection Period.** The collection period is a simply calculated financial ratio. To find it, divide current accounts receivable plus notes receivable (including discounted notes receivable) by the net credit sales per day. This latter figure, net credit sales per day, is found by dividing annual *credit* sales by 365. In formula, the computation of the collection period is:

$$p = \frac{r}{d}, \text{ in which } d \text{ represents } \frac{\text{annual credit sales}}{365}.$$

In the preliminary determination of d, or net credit sales per day, if the figure for credit sales is for six months instead of a year, the divisor is 182; if for three months, 91. Any reserves for bad debts should be deducted from the accounts and notes receivable to obtain a net figure of accounts and notes receivable for use in this formula. Here is an example:

A manufacturer of women's full-fashioned hosiery sells directly to retail stores. For the last fiscal year, net sales amounted to $1,500,800; the total of accounts and notes receivable in the fiscal balance sheet amounted to $140,230. To obtain the collection period according to the formula given above, $1,500,880, the annual net credit sales, is divided by 365 days, which gives d an average of $4,112 net credit sales per day. The total receivables r of $140,230 are now divided by d, $4,112. The answer, or the collection period p, is 34 days. Here is the way it looks in figures:

$$d \text{ (net credit sales per day)} = \frac{\$1,500,800}{365} \text{ or } \$4,112$$

$$p \text{ (collection period)} = \frac{r}{d} \text{ or } \frac{\$140,230}{\$4,112} \text{ or } 34$$

Another formula one can use is:

$$p = \frac{r \times 360}{s}$$

Where:

p = average collection period in days
r = current total of outstanding accounts and notes receivable
s = total of last year's net credit sales

Or in the example:

$$p = \frac{\$140,230 \times 360}{\$1,500,880} \text{ or } 34$$

No item of receivables can be analyzed without ascertaining the exact terms of sale used by a particular business enterprise. A collection period of 60 days would mean one thing on net selling terms of 30 days and something else on net selling terms of 60 days. Where a concern uses different selling terms for different trades or for different products, such as cash, 30 days, open-account, and installment terms, the analysis of receivables becomes more complicated. Accounts and notes receivable should represent only merchandise sales and should not include receivables for the sale of real estate, fixtures, machinery and equipment or other items.

[1204.2.1]   HOW TO USE THE COLLECTION PERIOD TABLES. These mathematical steps are eliminated by use of the collection period tables (Table 12.2). In the horizontal line of figures on the top of this schedule in bold-face type, find the first three digits, 150, of the sales figures in the example. Then find the first three digits of the receivables, 140, in the vertical column, either at the extreme right or the extreme left of the table. The protractions from these two points intersect at the number 341. The collection period sought is 34.1 days or, rounded, 34 days.

Like all computations with tables of this nature, the place to insert the decimal must be determined mentally. In the first illustration, the answer, as far as the table is concerned, might have been 341, 34.1, or 3.41 days. A quick glance at the figures representing net sales and receivables would show 34.1 days as the only reasonable answer.

Also, where the exact figure in the formula cannot be located on the table, such as sales of $55,500, interpolation must be used to place the collection period for that figure halfway between the collection period found for the receivables figure under the two sales figures, or 550 and 560.

[1204.2.2]   HOW LONG SHOULD THE COLLECTION PERIOD BE? An easy way of determining the health of a company's receivables is to test the collecton period against this maxim: *The collection period should be no more than one-third greater than the net selling terms of a particular business enterprise that normally sells its merchandise on open-book account.* As a formula:

$$p = n + \frac{n}{3}$$

Where:

p = safe average collection period
n = net selling terms

With selling terms of 2-percent discount in 10 days, net 30 days, the collection period should not exceed 40 days. With selling terms of 2-percent discount in 10 days, net 60 days, the collection period should not exceed 80 days. E.O.M. terms can allow from 15 to 45 days and net terms would therefore average 30 days.

If the collection period is more than one-third greater than the average net selling terms, the credit manager should ascertain if sales were abnormally concentrated during the 30 to 60 days preceding the statement date. He should also analyze his receivables to identify past-

TABLE FOR DETERMINING COLLECTION PERIOD

———————————————————Annual Net Credit Sales———————————————————

	101	102	103	104	105	106	107	108	109	110	111	112	113	114
102	369	365	362	358	355	351	348	345	342	338	335	332	330	327
104	376	372	369	365	362	358	355	351	348	345	342	339	336	333
106	383	379	376	372	368	365	362	358	355	352	349	345	342	339
108	390	387	383	379	375	372	368	365	362	358	355	352	349	346
110	398	394	390	386	382	379	375	372	368	365	362	359	355	352
112	405	401	397	393	389	386	382	378	375	372	368	365	362	358
114	412	408	404	400	396	392	389	385	382	378	375	372	368	365
116	419	415	411	407	403	400	395	392	388	385	381	378	375	371
118	427	422	418	414	410	406	403	399	395	392	388	385	381	378
120	434	430	425	421	417	413	410	406	402	398	395	391	388	384
140	506	501	496	492	487	482	478	473	469	465	461	457	452	448
160	579	573	567	562	556	551	546	541	536	531	526	522	517	513
180	605	644	638	632	626	620	614	609	603	598	592	587	582	576
200	723	716	709	702	696	688	682	676	670	664	658	652	646	641
220	795	788	780	773	765	758	750	744	737	730	724	717	711	705
240	868	859	851	842	834	826	818	811	804	797	789	783	775	768
260	940	931	921	913	904	897	886	879	871	863	854	847	840	833
280	101	100	992	983	974	954	955	946	937	929	920	913	904	897
300	108	107	106	105	104	103	102	101	100	996	987	978	969	961
320	116	114	113	112	111	110	109	108	107	106	105	104	103	102
340	123	122	121	119	118	117	116	115	114	113	112	111	110	109
360	130	129	127	126	125	124	123	122	121	119	118	117	116	115
380	137	136	135	133	131	130	129	128	127	126	125	124	123	122
400	144	143	142	140	139	138	136	135	134	133	131	130	129	128
420	152	150	149	147	146	144	143	142	141	139	138	137	136	134
440	159	157	156	154	153	152	150	149	147	146	145	143	142	141
460	166	165	163	162	160	158	157	155	154	153	151	150	149	147
480	173	172	170	168	167	165	164	162	161	159	158	156	155	154
500	181	179	177	175	174	172	170	169	168	166	165	163	161	160
520	188	186	184	182	181	178	177	176	174	172	171	170	168	167
540	195	193	191	189	188	186	184	182	181	179	178	176	174	173
560	202	200	198	197	195	103	101	189	187	186	184	182	181	178
580	210	207	206	203	201	200	198	196	194	192	191	189	187	186
600	217	215	213	211	209	206	205	203	201	199	197	195	194	192
620	224	222	220	217	215	214	211	209	208	206	204	202	200	108
640	231	229	227	225	223	220	218	216	214	212	210	208	207	205
660	238	236	234	232	229	227	225	223	221	219	217	215	213	211
680	246	243	241	238	236	234	232	230	228	225	223	221	220	218
700	253	250	248	245	243	241	239	236	234	232	230	228	226	224
720	260	257	255	253	250	248	246	243	241	239	237	234	232	230
740	267	265	262	260	257	255	252	250	248	245	243	241	239	237
760	274	272	269	267	264	262	259	257	254	252	250	248	245	243
780	282	279	276	274	271	268	266	263	261	259	256	254	252	250
800	289	286	283	281	278	275	273	270	267	265	263	261	258	256
820	296	293	290	288	285	282	280	277	275	272	270	267	265	262
840	303	300	298	295	292	290	287	284	281	279	276	273	271	269
860	311	307	305	302	299	296	293	291	288	285	283	280	278	275
880	318	315	312	309	306	303	300	297	294	292	289	287	284	282
900	325	322	319	316	313	310	307	304	301	298	296	293	291	288
920	332	329	326	323	320	317	313	310	308	305	302	300	297	295
940	340	336	333	330	326	323	320	318	315	312	309	307	304	301
960	347	343	340	337	334	331	327	324	321	318	316	313	310	307
980	354	350	347	344	341	337	334	331	328	325	322	319	316	313
1000	361	358	354	351	348	344	341	338	335	332	329	326	323	320

Receivables (row labels at left)

TABLE 12.2. Table for Determining Collection Period
Source: *Practical Financial Statement Analysis* by Roy A. Foulke

					Annual Net Credit Sales									
115	116	117	118	119	120	130	140	150	160	170	180	190	200	
324	321	318	315	313	310	287	266	248	233	219	207	196	186	102
330	327	324	322	319	316	292	271	253	236	223	211	200	190	104
336	333	331	328	325	323	298	276	258	241	227	215	204	193	106
343	340	337	334	331	329	303	282	263	246	232	219	208	197	108
349	346	343	340	337	335	309	287	268	251	236	223	211	201	110
355	352	349	346	344	341	314	292	273	255	240	227	215	204	112
362	358	355	352	350	347	320	297	277	260	245	231	219	208	114
368	365	362	359	355	353	326	302	282	265	249	235	223	212	116
375	371	368	365	362	359	331	308	287	269	253	239	227	215	118
381	377	374	371	368	365	337	313	292	274	258	243	230	219	120
444	440	437	433	430	426	393	365	341	320	301	284	269	255	140
508	504	500	495	491	487	450	418	390	365	344	324	307	292	160
572	566	562	557	552	548	505	469	438	411	387	365	346	328	180
634	630	624	618	614	509	562	521	487	456	430	405	384	365	200
699	693	686	681	675	670	618	574	535	502	473	446	423	402	220
762	755	749	742	736	730	674	626	584	547	515	487	461	438	240
825	818	811	804	797	791	730	678	633	593	558	527	500	475	260
889	881	874	865	859	852	786	730	682	639	601	568	538	511	280
953	944	936	929	920	913	843	783	730	685	644	608	577	548	300
102	101	999	990	982	954	899	835	779	730	687	649	625	584	320
108	107	106	105	104	103	955	887	828	776	730	690	654	621	340
114	113	112	111	110	109	101	938	876	821	773	730	692	657	360
121	120	118	117	116	115	107	992	926	867	816	771	730	694	380
127	126	125	124	123	122	112	104	975	913	859	812	769	730	400
133	132	131	130	129	128	118	109	102	958	902	852	807	767	420
140	138	137	136	135	134	123	115	107	100	944	892	846	804	440
146	145	143	142	141	140	129	120	112	105	988	934	884	840	460
152	151	150	148	147	146	135	125	117	109	103	974	922	876	480
158	157	156	155	153	152	140	130	122	114	107	101	961	913	500
165	164	162	161	159	158	146	135	128	118	111	105	100	940	520
171	170	168	167	166	164	152	141	131	123	116	109	104	985	540
177	176	174	173	172	170	157	146	136	128	120	113	107	102	560
184	182	181	180	178	176	163	151	141	132	124	117	111	106	580
190	189	187	185	184	182	168	156	146	137	129	122	115	110	600
197	195	193	192	190	188	174	162	151	141	133	126	119	113	620
203	201	200	198	196	195	180	167	156	146	137	130	123	117	640
209	208	206	204	202	201	185	172	161	151	142	134	127	120	660
216	214	212	210	209	207	191	177	165	155	146	138	131	124	680
222	220	218	216	214	213	196	183	170	159	150	142	134	128	700
228	227	225	223	221	219	202	188	175	164	154	146	138	131	720
235	233	231	229	227	225	207	193	180	169	159	150	142	135	740
241	239	237	235	233	231	213	198	185	173	163	154	146	139	760
247	245	243	241	239	237	219	203	190	178	167	158	150	142	780
254	252	249	247	245	243	225	209	195	183	172	162	154	146	800
260	258	256	254	251	249	230	214	199	187	176	166	157	150	820
266	264	262	260	257	255	236	219	204	192	180	170	161	153	840
273	270	268	266	263	261	241	224	209	196	185	174	165	157	860
279	277	274	272	270	268	247	229	214	200	189	178	169	161	880
285	283	280	278	276	274	252	235	219	205	193	182	173	164	900
292	289	286	284	282	280	258	240	224	210	197	186	177	168	920
298	296	293	291	288	286	264	245	229	214	202	191	180	172	940
305	302	299	297	294	292	269	250	233	219	206	195	184	175	960
311	308	305	303	301	298	275	255	238	223	210	199	188	179	980
318	315	312	309	307	304	281	261	243	228	215	223	192	183	1000

Receivables

TABLE 12.2. Table for Determining Collection Period (cont.)

Receivables	Annual Net Credit Sales													
	210	220	230	240	250	260	270	280	290	300	310	320	330	340
102	177	169	162	155	149	143	138	133	128	124	120	116	113	110
104	181	172	165	158	152	146	141	136	131	126	122	119	115	112
106	184	176	168	161	155	149	143	138	133	129	125	121	117	114
108	188	179	171	164	158	152	146	141	136	131	127	123	120	116
110	191	183	175	167	161	154	149	143	138	134	129	125	122	118
112	195	186	178	170	163	157	151	146	141	136	132	128	124	120
114	198	189	181	173	166	160	154	149	143	139	134	130	126	122
116	202	193	184	177	169	163	157	151	146	141	137	132	128	125
118	205	196	187	179	172	166	160	154	149	144	139	135	131	127
120	209	199	190	182	175	168	162	156	151	146	141	137	133	129
140	243	232	222	213	204	197	189	182	176	170	165	160	155	150
160	278	265	254	243	234	225	216	208	202	195	188	183	177	172
180	313	299	286	274	263	253	243	235	227	219	212	205	199	193
200	348	332	317	304	292	281	270	261	251	243	235	228	221	215
220	382	365	349	335	321	309	297	287	277	268	259	251	243	236
240	417	398	381	365	350	337	325	313	302	292	283	274	265	258
260	452	432	413	395	380	365	351	339	327	316	306	297	288	279
280	487	465	445	426	409	393	379	365	352	341	330	319	310	301
300	522	498	477	456	438	421	406	391	378	365	353	343	332	322
320	556	531	508	487	467	450	433	418	403	390	377	365	354	343
340	591	564	540	527	497	477	460	443	428	414	400	388	376	365
360	626	597	571	548	526	506	487	470	453	438	424	411	398	387
380	661	631	603	578	555	534	514	496	478	463	447	433	420	408
400	698	664	635	609	584	562	541	522	504	487	471	457	443	430
420	730	696	666	639	613	590	568	548	529	511	494	479	465	451
440	765	730	699	669	643	618	595	574	554	536	518	502	487	472
460	800	763	731	700	672	646	622	600	579	560	542	525	509	494
480	835	797	762	730	701	674	649	626	604	584	565	548	531	515
500	869	830	794	761	730	702	676	652	630	609	589	571	554	537
520	904	863	825	791	759	730	703	678	654	633	612	593	575	558
540	938	896	857	822	788	758	730	704	680	657	636	616	597	580
560	973	930	889	853	817	786	757	730	704	681	659	638	619	601
580	101	963	920	883	848	814	784	756	730	705	683	662	642	623
600	104	995	952	913	876	842	811	782	755	730	707	684	664	644
620	108	103	984	944	905	870	838	808	780	754	730	707	685	666
640	111	106	102	974	934	899	865	834	806	779	754	730	708	687
660	115	108	105	100	964	927	893	861	832	803	777	753	730	709
680	118	113	108	103	994	955	920	886	856	828	802	776	753	730
700	122	116	111	106	102	984	946	914	881	852	826	798	775	752
720	125	119	114	109	105	101	974	939	906	877	848	821	797	774
740	129	123	117	114	108	104	100	965	931	901	872	844	819	794
760	132	126	121	116	111	107	103	990	956	925	895	867	841	816
780	135	129	124	119	114	109	105	102	982	949	918	890	863	838
800	139	133	127	122	117	112	108	104	101	974	942	913	886	859
820	142	136	130	125	120	115	111	107	103	100	965	936	907	881
840	146	139	133	128	123	118	114	109	106	102	989	958	930	902
860	149	143	136	131	126	121	116	112	108	105	101	981	952	924
880	153	146	140	134	128	123	119	115	111	107	104	100	974	945
900	156	149	143	137	131	126	122	117	113	109	106	103	995	966
920	160	153	146	140	134	129	124	120	116	112	108	105	102	988
940	163	156	149	143	137	132	127	123	118	114	111	107	104	101
960	167	159	157	146	140	135	130	125	121	117	113	109	106	103
980	170	163	155	149	143	138	132	128	123	119	115	112	108	105
1000	174	166	159	157	146	140	135	130	126	122	118	114	111	107

TABLE 12.2. Table for Determining Collection Period (cont.)

Annual Net Credit Sales

350	360	370	380	390	400	410	420	430	440	450	460	470	480	Receivables
106	103	101	970	954	932	908	886	866	846	828	810	792	776	102
108	105	103	100	974	950	926	904	884	863	844	826	808	791	104
111	108	105	102	997	968	946	922	900	880	860	842	824	807	106
113	109	106	104	101	986	962	940	917	896	877	858	839	822	108
115	111	109	106	103	100	979	956	934	913	892	873	854	837	110
117	113	111	107	105	102	999	974	952	929	909	889	870	852	112
119	116	112	110	107	104	101	991	969	948	926	905	886	867	114
121	118	114	111	109	106	103	101	985	952	941	921	901	883	116
123	120	117	113	110	108	105	103	100	980	957	937	918	898	118
125	122	118	115	112	109	107	104	102	100	964	953	933	914	120
146	142	138	134	131	128	125	122	119	116	114	111	109	106	140
167	162	158	154	150	146	143	139	136	133	130	127	124	122	160
188	182	178	173	169	164	160	156	153	149	146	143	140	137	180
209	203	197	192	187	182	178	174	170	166	162	159	155	152	200
230	223	217	211	206	201	196	191	187	183	179	175	171	167	220
250	243	237	230	225	219	214	209	204	199	195	190	186	183	240
271	263	256	250	243	237	231	226	221	216	211	206	207	198	260
292	284	276	269	262	255	249	243	238	232	227	222	218	213	280
313	305	296	288	281	274	267	261	255	249	243	238	233	228	300
334	325	316	307	300	292	285	278	272	265	260	254	249	243	320
355	345	336	326	318	310	303	295	289	282	276	270	264	258	340
376	365	355	346	337	329	321	313	306	299	292	286	280	274	360
396	385	375	365	356	347	339	330	322	315	308	302	296	289	380
418	406	395	384	375	365	356	348	340	332	325	317	311	304	400
438	426	415	403	393	383	374	365	357	348	341	333	326	320	420
459	446	434	423	412	402	392	382	374	365	357	349	342	335	440
480	467	454	442	431	420	410	400	391	382	373	365	358	350	460
501	487	474	461	449	438	428	417	407	398	389	381	373	365	480
521	507	493	481	469	457	445	435	425	415	406	397	388	380	500
542	527	513	499	487	475	463	452	442	431	422	412	404	395	520
564	547	533	519	505	493	481	469	458	448	438	429	420	411	540
584	568	552	538	524	511	498	487	475	465	454	445	435	426	560
605	588	572	557	543	529	516	504	493	481	471	460	451	442	580
626	608	592	576	562	548	534	522	510	497	487	476	466	456	600
648	629	612	596	581	566	552	549	526	514	503	492	482	472	620
668	649	632	615	599	584	570	556	544	531	519	508	498	487	640
688	669	652	634	618	603	588	574	560	548	536	524	512	502	660
710	690	671	654	637	621	606	592	578	564	552	540	528	517	680
730	710	690	672	655	639	624	609	594	581	568	556	544	533	700
752	730	710	692	674	657	641	636	611	598	584	571	559	548	720
772	750	730	710	693	675	659	644	628	614	600	588	575	563	740
793	771	750	730	711	694	677	660	645	631	616	603	590	578	760
814	791	769	750	730	712	694	678	652	647	633	619	606	593	780
845	812	790	769	748	730	712	695	679	664	649	635	622	609	800
855	832	809	788	768	749	730	713	696	681	665	651	636	624	820
876	852	829	807	786	767	748	730	713	697	682	667	652	639	840
896	872	849	826	805	785	766	747	730	714	698	683	668	654	860
918	882	867	846	824	803	784	765	747	730	714	698	684	669	880
938	913	887	865	842	821	801	782	764	747	730	714	699	685	900
960	933	907	884	862	840	820	800	781	764	748	730	714	700	920
981	953	928	904	880	858	837	817	798	780	762	746	730	715	940
100	974	947	922	898	877	855	834	815	796	779	762	745	730	960
102	994	967	942	928	895	873	852	832	814	795	778	761	745	980
104	101	988	961	936	914	891	870	850	830	812	794	777	760	1000

TABLE 12.2 Table for Determining Collection Period (cont.)

					—Annual Net Credit Sales—								
	490	**500**	**510**	**520**	**530**	**540**	**550**	**560**	**570**	**580**	**590**	**600**	**610**
102	760	745	730	718	703	690	677	665	654	642	631	621	610
104	775	760	744	731	716	703	691	678	668	655	644	633	622
106	790	774	759	745	730	717	704	692	679	667	656	645	635
108	805	789	774	758	744	730	717	702	692	680	668	658	646
110	820	804	788	772	758	744	730	717	705	692	681	670	658
112	834	818	802	786	772	757	744	730	717	705	693	682	670
114	850	833	816	801	785	771	757	743	730	718	706	694	682
116	864	848	830	815	799	784	770	756	743	730	718	705	694
118	880	852	845	829	814	798	784	770	756	744	731	718	706
120	894	877	860	843	827	812	797	783	769	755	743	731	719
140	104	102	100	983	965	946	929	913	897	882	866	852	838
160	119	117	115	112	110	108	106	104	102	101	990	974	957
180	134	131	129	126	124	122	120	117	115	113	111	110	108
200	149	146	143	140	138	135	133	130	128	126	124	122	120
220	164	161	158	155	152	149	146	143	141	138	136	134	132
240	179	175	172	169	165	162	160	157	154	151	149	146	143
260	194	190	186	182	179	176	173	170	164	163	161	158	155
280	209	204	200	196	193	189	186	182	179	176	173	170	168
300	224	219	215	211	207	203	200	196	193	189	186	183	170
320	238	234	230	225	221	216	213	209	205	201	198	195	192
340	253	248	243	239	234	230	225	221	218	214	210	207	204
360	269	263	258	252	247	243	239	235	231	227	223	219	216
380	284	278	273	267	262	257	253	248	243	239	234	231	228
400	298	292	287	281	276	270	266	261	256	252	248	243	239
420	314	307	301	295	290	284	279	274	270	265	260	255	251
440	328	321	315	309	304	298	293	287	282	277	273	268	264
460	343	336	330	323	317	311	306	300	295	290	285	280	275
480	358	350	343	337	331	324	319	313	308	302	297	292	287
500	372	365	358	351	345	338	332	326	321	315	310	304	300
520	387	380	372	365	359	352	346	339	333	327	322	317	312
540	402	395	387	379	372	365	359	352	346	340	335	329	324
560	417	409	401	393	386	379	372	365	359	352	347	341	335
580	432	423	415	407	400	392	385	378	372	365	359	353	348
600	447	438	429	421	413	405	398	391	384	377	371	365	359
620	462	453	444	436	427	420	412	405	397	391	384	377	371
640	477	468	458	449	441	433	425	417	410	403	396	390	383
660	492	482	472	463	454	446	438	430	423	415	408	402	395
680	507	496	487	478	468	460	452	444	436	428	421	414	407
700	522	511	501	492	483	473	465	456	448	441	433	426	419
720	536	526	515	506	496	487	478	470	461	453	446	438	431
740	552	541	530	520	510	500	491	483	474	466	458	451	443
760	566	555	544	533	523	514	504	495	487	478	470	463	455
780	581	570	558	548	537	527	518	508	500	491	483	475	467
800	596	584	573	562	551	541	531	522	512	503	495	487	479
820	611	598	587	576	565	544	554	535	526	516	507	599	491
840	626	613	601	590	578	568	557	547	538	529	519	511	502
860	641	628	616	604	592	582	581	561	551	542	532	524	515
880	655	643	630	618	606	595	584	574	563	554	545	536	527
900	671	657	644	631	620	608	597	586	576	566	557	548	539
920	685	671	659	646	634	622	610	600	589	579	569	560	550
940	700	686	673	660	648	636	624	613	602	592	582	572	563
960	715	701	687	674	661	649	638	626	615	604	594	584	575
980	730	715	701	688	675	663	650	639	628	617	606	596	586
1000	745	730	716	702	689	676	664	652	640	629	619	608	598

(left vertical label: Receivables)

TABLE 12.2. Table for Determining Collection Period (cont.)

Annual Net Credit Sales

620	630	640	650	660	670	680	690	700	710	720	730	740	Receivables
601	591	582	573	564	556	548	540	532	525	517	510	504	102
613	603	594	584	576	567	559	550	543	535	528	520	514	104
624	615	605	595	586	578	569	561	553	545	537	530	523	106
636	626	616	607	598	589	580	572	564	555	548	540	533	108
648	637	628	618	608	599	590	582	574	565	558	550	542	110
660	649	639	629	620	610	601	593	584	576	568	560	553	112
672	661	650	641	631	621	612	604	595	586	578	570	562	114
684	672	662	652	642	632	623	614	605	597	588	580	572	116
695	684	674	663	654	644	634	625	616	607	599	591	583	118
707	696	685	674	664	654	645	635	626	617	609	600	592	120
824	811	799	787	775	763	752	742	730	720	710	700	691	140
943	927	913	898	885	872	859	846	835	823	812	800	789	160
106	104	103	101	996	982	967	953	939	926	913	901	888	180
118	116	114	112	110	109	107	106	104	103	101	100	987	200
130	127	125	123	122	120	118	116	115	113	112	110	109	220
141	139	137	135	133	131	129	127	125	123	122	120	118	240
153	150	148	146	143	141	139	137	136	134	132	130	128	260
165	162	159	157	155	153	150	148	146	144	142	140	138	280
177	174	171	169	166	164	161	159	157	155	152	150	148	300
188	186	183	180	177	175	172	170	167	165	162	160	158	320
200	197	194	191	188	185	182	180	177	175	172	170	168	340
212	209	205	202	199	196	193	190	188	185	182	180	178	360
224	221	217	214	210	207	204	201	198	196	193	190	187	380
235	232	228	225	221	218	215	212	208	206	203	200	197	400
247	244	240	236	232	229	225	222	219	216	213	210	207	420
259	255	251	247	243	240	236	233	230	227	223	220	217	440
271	267	263	259	255	251	247	244	240	237	233	230	227	460
282	278	274	270	265	262	258	254	250	247	243	240	237	480
295	290	285	281	277	273	268	264	261	258	254	251	247	500
306	302	297	293	288	284	279	275	271	268	264	260	256	520
318	313	308	304	299	295	290	286	282	278	274	271	267	540
330	325	320	315	310	305	300	296	292	288	284	280	276	560
342	337	331	326	321	316	311	307	303	299	294	290	286	580
353	348	342	337	332	327	322	318	313	309	304	300	296	600
365	360	354	349	343	338	333	329	324	319	314	310	306	620
377	371	365	360	354	349	344	339	334	330	325	321	316	640
388	382	376	371	365	360	355	350	344	340	335	331	326	660
401	394	388	382	376	371	365	360	355	350	345	340	335	680
412	406	399	393	387	382	376	371	365	360	355	351	346	700
424	417	411	405	398	392	387	381	376	370	365	360	355	720
436	429	423	416	410	403	398	392	386	381	375	371	365	740
447	440	433	427	420	414	407	402	396	391	385	380	375	760
460	452	445	438	432	425	419	413	407	401	395	390	385	780
471	463	456	449	442	436	430	423	417	412	406	400	395	800
483	476	468	461	453	447	440	434	428	422	416	410	405	820
495	487	479	472	464	458	451	444	438	432	426	420	414	840
506	498	491	483	476	468	462	455	448	443	436	430	424	860
518	510	502	494	487	480	473	466	458	452	446	440	434	880
530	522	514	506	498	491	483	476	470	463	457	450	444	900
542	533	525	517	509	501	494	487	480	473	467	460	454	920
554	545	536	528	520	512	505	497	490	483	477	470	464	940
565	556	548	539	530	523	515	508	500	493	487	480	473	960
577	568	559	550	542	534	526	518	511	504	497	490	483	980
589	580	571	561	553	545	537	529	521	514	505	500	493	1000

TABLE 12.2 Table for Determining Collection Period (cont.)

	—Annual Net Credit Sales—												
	750	**760**	**770**	**780**	**790**	**800**	**810**	**820**	**830**	**840**	**850**	**860**	**870**
102	497	490	484	478	472	466	460	454	449	444	438	433	428
104	506	500	493	487	481	475	469	463	458	452	447	442	437
106	516	509	503	497	490	484	478	472	467	462	455	450	445
108	526	519	512	506	499	493	487	481	475	470	464	459	453
110	536	529	522	515	509	502	496	490	484	478	473	467	462
112	546	538	531	524	517	511	505	498	492	486	482	475	470
114	555	548	541	534	527	520	514	508	502	496	490	494	478
116	565	557	550	543	536	530	523	517	510	504	498	493	487
118	575	567	560	552	546	539	532	526	520	513	507	501	495
120	584	577	570	562	555	548	541	535	528	522	516	510	504
140	682	673	664	655	647	639	632	624	616	609	602	594	588
160	779	768	759	749	740	731	721	713	704	695	688	679	672
180	877	865	854	843	832	822	812	802	792	783	773	764	756
200	974	961	949	937	924	913	902	891	880	870	859	849	839
220	107	106	104	103	102	100	992	979	968	956	945	934	923
240	117	115	114	112	111	110	109	107	106	104	103	102	101
260	127	125	124	122	121	119	118	116	115	113	112	110	109
280	136	134	133	131	130	128	127	125	124	122	121	119	118
300	146	144	142	140	139	137	136	134	132	130	129	127	126
320	156	154	152	150	148	146	144	142	141	139	138	136	135
340	166	163	161	159	157	155	153	151	150	148	146	144	142
360	176	173	171	168	166	164	162	160	158	156	155	153	151
380	185	182	180	178	176	173	171	169	167	165	163	161	160
400	195	192	190	187	185	183	181	178	176	174	172	170	168
420	204	202	199	196	194	192	190	187	185	183	181	178	176
440	214	211	209	206	203	201	199	196	194	191	189	187	185
460	224	221	218	215	213	210	208	205	203	200	198	195	193
480	234	230	228	225	222	219	217	214	211	208	206	204	202
500	244	240	237	234	231	228	225	223	220	217	215	212	210
520	253	250	247	243	240	237	234	231	229	226	223	221	219
540	264	260	257	253	250	247	244	240	238	235	232	229	227
560	274	270	266	262	259	256	252	249	247	244	241	238	235
580	282	278	275	271	268	265	262	258	256	252	249	246	243
600	292	288	285	281	278	274	271	268	265	261	258	255	252
620	302	298	294	290	287	283	280	276	273	270	267	263	260
640	312	307	303	299	296	292	289	285	282	278	275	272	269
660	322	317	313	309	305	301	298	294	291	287	284	280	277
680	331	327	323	318	314	310	307	303	300	296	293	289	286
700	342	337	333	328	324	320	316	312	308	304	301	298	295
720	351	346	342	337	333	329	325	320	317	313	310	306	303
740	360	355	351	346	342	338	334	330	326	322	318	314	311
760	370	365	360	356	351	347	343	338	334	330	326	323	319
780	380	375	370	365	361	356	352	347	343	339	335	331	327
800	390	384	379	374	370	365	361	357	352	348	343	340	336
820	399	394	389	384	379	374	370	365	361	357	352	348	344
840	409	403	398	393	388	383	378	374	370	365	361	357	352
860	419	413	408	403	398	392	388	383	378	374	370	365	361
880	428	423	417	412	407	402	396	392	387	382	378	373	369
900	438	432	427	421	416	411	406	400	396	392	387	382	378
920	448	442	436	431	425	420	415	410	405	400	395	390	386
940	457	452	446	440	434	429	423	418	413	408	404	399	394
960	467	461	455	449	444	438	433	427	423	417	412	407	403
980	477	471	465	458	553	447	442	436	431	426	421	416	411
1000	487	481	474	468	462	457	451	445	440	435	429	424	420

(Left margin label: Receivables)

TABLE 12.2. Table for Determing Collection Period (cont.)

| Annual Net Credit Sales | | | | | | | | | | | | | |
880	890	900	910	920	930	940	950	960	970	980	990	1000	
423	419	414	410	405	401	396	392	388	384	380	376	372	102
432	427	422	417	413	408	404	400	396	392	388	384	380	104
440	435	430	426	421	416	412	407	403	399	395	391	387	106
448	443	438	434	428	424	420	415	411	407	402	399	394	108
456	452	447	442	437	432	427	423	418	414	410	406	402	110
465	459	455	449	444	440	435	430	426	421	417	413	409	112
473	467	463	458	453	448	443	438	434	429	425	420	416	114
482	476	471	466	461	455	451	446	441	437	432	428	424	116
490	484	479	474	469	464	459	454	449	445	440	435	431	118
498	493	487	482	477	472	467	461	457	452	447	443	438	120
581	575	568	562	555	550	544	538	532	527	522	516	511	140
664	656	649	642	635	628	622	615	608	602	596	590	584	160
747	739	730	722	715	707	700	692	685	678	671	664	657	180
830	821	812	802	794	785	777	769	761	753	745	738	730	200
913	903	893	883	874	864	855	845	837	828	820	811	803	220
995	985	974	964	953	943	932	923	913	904	894	885	877	240
108	107	105	104	103	102	101	100	989	989	969	959	949	260
116	115	114	113	111	110	109	108	106	105	104	103	102	280
125	124	122	121	119	118	117	116	115	114	112	111	110	300
133	132	130	129	127	126	124	123	122	121	119	118	117	320
141	140	138	137	135	134	132	131	129	128	127	126	124	340
149	148	146	145	143	142	140	139	137	136	134	133	131	360
158	156	154	153	151	150	148	146	144	143	142	141	139	380
166	164	162	161	159	157	155	154	152	151	149	148	146	400
174	172	170	169	167	165	163	162	160	159	157	156	154	420
183	181	179	177	175	173	170	169	167	166	164	163	161	440
191	189	187	185	183	181	179	177	175	174	172	170	168	460
199	197	195	193	190	188	186	184	182	181	179	177	175	480
207	205	200	201	192	196	194	192	190	188	186	184	182	500
216	214	211	209	206	205	203	201	198	196	194	192	190	520
224	222	219	217	214	212	210	208	205	203	201	199	197	540
232	230	227	225	222	220	218	216	213	211	209	207	204	560
240	238	235	233	230	228	225	223	220	218	216	214	212	580
249	247	244	241	238	236	233	231	228	226	224	222	219	600
257	254	251	249	246	244	241	239	236	234	231	229	226	620
266	263	260	257	254	252	249	246	243	241	238	236	234	640
274	271	268	265	262	259	256	253	251	249	246	244	241	660
282	279	276	273	270	267	264	262	259	256	253	251	248	680
291	288	284	281	278	275	272	270	267	264	261	259	256	700
299	296	292	289	286	283	280	277	274	271	268	266	263	720
307	304	300	297	294	291	288	286	282	279	276	273	270	740
315	312	308	305	302	298	295	292	289	286	283	280	277	760
323	320	316	313	310	306	303	300	296	294	290	288	285	780
332	328	325	321	318	314	311	307	304	301	298	295	292	800
340	336	333	329	326	322	318	315	312	309	305	302	299	820
348	345	341	337	333	330	326	323	320	316	313	310	307	840
357	353	349	345	341	338	334	331	327	324	320	317	314	860
365	361	357	353	349	345	342	338	335	331	328	325	321	880
373	369	365	361	357	353	350	346	342	339	335	332	329	900
381	377	373	369	365	361	357	354	350	346	343	339	336	920
390	386	382	377	373	369	365	361	357	354	350	347	343	940
398	394	389	385	381	377	372	368	365	361	357	353	350	960
407	402	398	393	389	385	381	377	373	369	365	362	357	980
415	410	406	401	397	392	388	384	381	377	373	369	365	1000

Receivables

TABLE 12.2. Table for Determining Collection Period (cont.)

due accounts and length of time past due, or he should age his accounts to determine what portion is past due and for what reasons.

The second measure to determine the health of receivables is relative. The credit manager can compare his collection period with the period of others in the same line of business. Dun & Bradstreet calculates this ratio for many lines of business (see Figure 9.9 for some recent figures compiled by Dun & Bradstreet on selected industries). These are given as median ratios with upper and lower quartiles (or quarters). To obtain each ratio, the collection periods for the individual businesses in a particular line under analysis were arranged in a graduated series with the smallest number of days at the top and the largest at the bottom. The median period was the period halfway between the top and bottom. The period representing the upper quartile was one-quarter of the way down the series from the top, and the lower quartile was halfway between the median and the bottom. The credit manager, by comparing his collection period with the performance of others in his line, can thus see where he ranks.

[1204.3]   **Turnover of Receivables.** A third method used to measure collection effectiveness is to determine the number of times your receivables turn over within a year (of a given interim period) and to compare that with others in your industry or your performance of a preceding year. The turnover rate is easily found by dividing total annual credit sales by the receivables (minus bad-debt reserves) that appear on the closing balance sheet. As a formula it can be expressed:

$$rt - \frac{s}{r}$$

Where:

rt – receivables turnover
s = annual credit sales
r = outstanding receivables

It goes without saying that the more rapid the turnover rate—the better the collection effort.

[1205]   **SPECIAL COLLECTION PROBLEMS.** As credit manager, you will encounter, from time to time, the collection problems described below. You will find the solutions suggested helpful in cleaning them up.

[1205.1]   **Checks Returned for Insufficient Funds.** In spite of the existence of bad-check laws, you will not uncommonly receive checks that are returned by the debtor's bank because of insufficient funds. There are various procedures you can follow. One is to write a letter to—or telephone—your customer and explain to him that his check has not cleared. Inform him that you will present his check again within a specified number of days. Instruct him to deposit sufficient funds to cover the check. When the time has elapsed, resubmit the check for collection. If the customer refuses to make the check good, of course, you are presented with a serious collection problem and an agency or attorney should be considered. Find out if the customer does not have the money or if he is registering some kind of complaint through his action. Your collection efforts to follow will be determined by the situation that does in fact exist.

[1205.2]   **Unearned Discounts.** Unearned discounts should actually only occur once, if at all, for each customer you have. Often, however, credit men are plagued by this problem. The best solution is to develop a firm, no-nonsense policy on this issue—and to stick to it. You may allow a new customer the benefit of the doubt on his first order, but on all succeeding ones, deposit the check and immediately bill him for the unpaid amount. What is not paid should be considered past due.

[1205.3]   **New Orders from Past-Due Accounts.** Your response to this problem will depend upon the individual customer, his financial health, the reason he is past due, how much is past due, and the amount of the new order. You will also consider how important you are to this customer as a supplier. Your credit policy should provide for the examination of each case on its own merits. The credit manager must decide whether the account will be good for its money, when, and if he is prepared and willing to wait. Often the mere threat to hold future orders is enough to produce payment. At other times, the credit manager will work out a procedure whereby the customer pays off the past-due portion of his bill on an installment basis but continues to buy in reasonable amounts on open-account terms.

[1205.4]   **Disputed Accounts.** You should decide what action to take as soon as you discover the account is in dispute. Measure principle and company policy with the practicality of the situation.

Is there a return of merchandise involved? If so, would you be able to resell it? Is the dispute open to a compromise? If so, weigh the merits of your case against projected litigation time and expense.

[1206]   **INSOLVENT ACCOUNTS.** Insolvency, as defined in the Bankruptcy Act, occurs "whenever the aggregate of [a person's] property, exclusive of any property which he may have conveyed, transferred, concealed, removed, or permitted to be concealed or removed, with intent to defraud, hinder or delay his creditors, shall not, at a fair valuation, be sufficient in amount to pay his debts." Simply put, insolvency occurs whenever a person or a company does not have enough money to pay the bills that are due and does not have sufficient liquid assets to realize the money needed to pay them.

[1206.1]   **Duration of Insolvency.** You will recognize, from the preceding definition, that insolvency could be a temporary situation that the advent of the selling season, a bank loan, collection of receivables, etc., could remedy; or it could be a desperate, more permanent situation that could not be corrected by any reasonable action of the debtor or his creditors. Depending upon the situation that exists, you can decide upon your course of action in dealing with your insolvent customer. In addition, you would consider the intentions of the insolvent debtor as evidenced by record or indication of criminal activity or past failures, if any.

[1206.2]   **Rehabilitation of Insolvent Accounts—Out of Court.** If your customer is merely in a temporary state of insolvency, your object should be to help him through this period of difficulty, to help him avoid future financial crises if possible, and to collect your money as quickly as possible without inflicting permanent damage on the customer—and thus losing a potential customer forever. Working with a committee of other unsecured creditors, therefore, you might work out one of the following arrangements with the insolvent debtor:

[1206.2.1]   EXTENSIONS. An extension is an agreement between the debtor and the creditor for the debtor to pay the amount owing over a longer period of time than provided by the original terms of sale. A general extension occurs when all creditors of a debtor agree to postpone the due date of monies owing to them according to a schedule satisfactory to all. Generally, an agreement for extension should be signed by all creditors.

[1206.2.2]   SETTLEMENTS. Settlements occur when the creditors of an insolvent debtor agree to accept less than the full amount owing to them. The agreement must be signed by all creditors. The method the debtor will use to pay the sums agreed to will vary according to his financial situation and general reliability. Any method—promissory notes, endorsed notes, postdated checks, immediate cash payment—may be required by the creditors.

[1206.3]   **Liquidation of Insolvent Accounts—Out of Court.** Sometimes, of course, the financial condition of an insolvent account is so critical that nothing can be done to rehabilitate him. Still, the costs and complications of court proceedings may be avoided by an out-of-court liquidation of the assets of the debtor. This is generally done by having the debtor assign his assets to an adjustment bureau or other creditors' committee, which liquidates them and distributes them to creditors on a pro rata basis. Obviously, it is essential that creditors work through a reliable credit association or other organization to avoid any fraudulent losses. Moreover, you should recognize that there must be thorough analysis and accounting of the debtor's position so that proper decisions can be made by the creditors. Generally, the committee of creditors, working with an accountant, is responsible for this aspect of the problem.

[1206.4]   **Legal Proceedings Involving Insolvent Accounts.** Arrangements may also be effected under the Bankruptcy Act through court-supervised rehabilitation or liquidation, usually through extensions or composition settlements.

[1206.4.1]   EXTENSIONS. Extensions are agreements between the debtor and his creditors that the due date for the money owing to the creditors is postponed to some time, generally specified, in the future. A general extension, as you have seen, occurs when the creditors of a debtor agree to postpone the due dates of monies owing to them according to a schedule satisfactory to all. The commitment of the debtor to pay the money at that time can be guaranteed by notes, and interest could be paid. This is the least damaging arrangement it is possible to make, from the debtor's point of view. As a creditor you should be certain that your chances of recovering your money are improved by an extension.

[1206.4.2]   COMPOSITIONS. Compositions are agreements whereby the creditors of a debtor agree to write off as losses a certain portion of the money owing them if they can be assured of payment of the remainder. This can be paid in installments with interest or as lump sums.

PROCEDURE FOR EFFECTING ARRANGEMENTS. The procedure for effecting the arrangements described above (as well as "any plan of a debtor for the settlement, satisfaction or extension of the time of payment of his unsecured debts upon any terms") is contained in the Bankruptcy Law, Chapter XI, whose major features are summarized below:

1. *Petition.* The debtor files an original petition (unless a bankruptcy proceeding is pending, in which case he files a petition before or after the adjudication) stating that he is insolvent or unable to pay his bills as they come due and stating the provisions of the arrangement that he will propose to his creditors. At the same time, he must supply a statement of his affairs and his creditors.

2. *Bankruptcy judge (referee).* The courts will generally then refer the proceeding to a bankruptcy judge. He will handle the case.

3. *Meeting of the creditors.* Shortly after the petition is filed, a meeting of the creditors is held, at which time the referee will rule on the claims of the creditors and accept their written acceptances of the arrangement, if available. At this meeting, if acceptances have been given, the referee may also designate a receiver or trustee who will be responsible for distributing any consideration that the debtor may deposit, and the money necessary to pay monthly debts. The creditors may also select a committee (see below).

4. *Arrangement.* The arrangement may include any of the following provisions:
   a. Provisions for treatment of unsecured debts on a parity, one with the other, or for the division of such debts into classes and how they are to be handled.
   b. Provisions for the rejection of any executory contract.
   c. Provisions for specific undertakings of the debtor during any period of extension provided for by the arrangement, including provisions for payment on account.
   d. Provisions for the termination, under specified conditions, of any period of extension provided by the arrangement.
   e. Provisions for continuation of the debtor's business with or without supervision or control by a receiver or by a committee of creditors.
   f. Provisions for payment of debts incurred after the filing of the petition and during the time the arrangement is in effect.

5. *Committee.* The committee, if one is appointed by the creditors, may have the following responsibilities:
   a. To examine the conduct of the debtor's affairs and the causes of his insolvency or inability to pay his debts as they mature.
   b. To consider whether the arrangement proposed by the debtor is for the best interests of the creditors and is feasible.
   c. To negotiate with the debtor concerning the terms of the arrangement and to advise the creditors of its recommendations with respect thereto.

d. To collect and file with the court acceptances of the arrangement proposed.

6. *Confirmation of the arrangement.* The court will confirm the arrangement if it is satisfied that:

   a. The provisions of the law have been complied with.

   b. It is for the best interests of the creditors and is feasible.

   c. The debtor has not been guilty of any of the acts or failed to perform any of the duties that would be a bar to the discharge of a bankrupt.

   d. The proposal and its acceptance are in good faith.

[1207]   **BANKRUPTCY.** Bankruptcy occurs in several different situations as outlined by the Bankruptcy Law. In all cases, however, your job as credit manager is to secure the money owed to your company from the liquidation of the bankrupt's assets.

[1207.1]   **What is Bankruptcy?** A bankrupt is a person against whom an involuntary petition or an application to revoke a discharge (i.e., revoke a previous release of a bankrupt from all of his debts that are provable in bankruptcy) has been filed or who has filed a voluntary petition or who has been adjudged a bankrupt. The petitions will assert, or the judgment will have found, that the bankrupt has committed an act of bankruptcy.

[1207.2]   **Acts of Bankruptcy.** According to the Bankruptcy Law, acts of bankruptcy by a person shall consist of his having:

1. Concealed, removed, or permitted to be concealed or removed any part of his property, with intent to hinder, delay, or defraud his creditors or any of them, or made and suffered a transfer of any of his property, fraudulent under the provisions of the act.

2. Made or suffered a preferential transfer.

3. Suffered or permitted, while insolvent, any creditor to obtain a lien upon any of his property through legal proceedings or distraint and not having vacated or discharged such lien within thirty days from the date thereof or at least five days before the date set for any sale or other disposition of the property.

4. Made a general assignment for the benefit of his creditors.

5. While insolvent or unable to pay his debts, as they mature, procured, permitted, or suffered voluntarily or involuntarily the appointment of a receiver or trustee to take charge of his property.

6. Admitted in writing his inability to pay his debts and his willingness to be adjudged a bankrupt.

[1207.3]   **Who May Become Bankrupt?** As a credit manager, you should know that individual proprietors, partnerships (including limited partnerships), and corporations may all be declared bankrupt. The procedures vary somewhat for each case and you should consult your attorney on the particular situation with which you are faced.

[1207.4]   **Duties of the Bankrupt.** According to the text of the Bankruptcy Act, the duties of the bankrupt include the following:

[1207.4.1]   ATTEND MEETINGS. Attend the first meeting of the creditors and specified other meetings and proceedings.

[1207.4.2]   COMPLY WITH ALL LAWFUL ORDERS OF THE COURT.

[1207.4.3]   EXAMINE PROOFS OF CLAIM. Examine and report to the trustee concerning the correctness of all proofs of claim filed against his estate.

[1207.4.4]   EXECUTE PAPERS. Execute and deliver such papers as shall be ordered by the court.

[1207.4.5]   EXECUTE TRANSFERS. Execute and deliver to the trustee transfers of all his property in foreign countries.

[1207.4.6]   REPORT EVASIVE ATTEMPTS. Immediately inform the trustee of any attempt by his creditors or other persons to evade the provisions of the Bankruptcy Act.

[1207.4.7]   PREPARE PROPERTY SCHEDULE. Prepare and swear to a schedule of his property, showing the amount and kind of property, the location thereof, and its money value, in detail; and a list of all his creditors, including all persons asserting contingent, unliquidated, or disputed claims, showing their residences or places of business, the amount due to or claimed by each of them, the consideration (proof) thereof, the security held by them, if any, and what claims, if any, are contingent, unliquidated, or disputed; and a claim for such exemptions as he is entitled to.

[1207.4.8]   SUBMIT TO EXAMINATIONS. Submit to an examination concerning the conducting of his business, the cause of his bankruptcy, his dealing with his creditors and other persons, the amount, kind, and whereabouts of his property.

[1207.4.9]   PREPARE INVENTORY. Prepare a detailed inventory showing the cost of his merchandise and property that he has as of the date of the bankruptcy.

[1207.5]   **Discharges under Bankruptcy.** Except for corporations, simple adjudication as a bankrupt will normally operate as an application for discharge of most debts upon surrender of property. Courts will grant a discharge in most cases unless the bankrupt has committed a criminal act or has failed to fulfill his duties under the Bankruptcy Act.

[1207.6]   **Contested Bankruptcies.** An individual, partnership, or corporation is entitled to a jury trial if it contests the claims made in the petition.

[1207.7]   **Bankruptcy Judges.** Once bankruptcy is adjudged, a bankruptcy judge (or judges) is appointed by the court. Their duties are as follows:

1. Give notice to creditors of the proceedings.
2. Prepare and file the schedules of property and lists of creditors required to be filed by the bankrupt or cause the same to be done when the bankrupt fails, refuses, or neglects to do so.
3. Examine all schedules of property, lists of creditors, and statements of affairs, and cause such as are incomplete and defective to be amended.
4. Furnish or cause to be furnished such information concerning proceedings before them as may be requested by those interested.
5. Declare dividends and cause to be prepared dividend sheets showing the dividends declared and to whom they are payable.

[1207.8]   **Trustees.** At the first meeting of the creditors, the creditors or the court will appoint a trustee or three trustees. The trustee or trustees, who may be assisted by a committee of the creditors, will perform the following duties:

1. Collect and reduce to money the property of the estates for which they are trustees, under the direction of the court, and close up the estates as expeditiously as is compatible with the best interest of the parties in interest.
2. Deposit all money received by them in designated depositories.
3. Account for and pay over to the estates under their control all interest received by them upon funds belonging to such estates.
4. Disburse money only by check or draft on such depositories.
5. Keep records and accounts showing all amounts and items of property received and from what sources, all amounts expended and for what purposes, and all items of property disposed of.
6. Set apart the bankrupt's exemptions allowed by law, if claimed.
7. Examine the bankrupt:
   a. At the first meeting of creditors or at other meetings specially fixed for that purpose, unless they shall already have been fully examined by the referees, receivers, or creditors.
   b. Upon the hearing of objections, if any, to their discharges, unless otherwise ordered by the court.
8. Examine all proofs of claim and object to the allowance of such claims as may be improper.
9. Oppose at the expense of estates the discharge of bankrupts when they deem it advisable to do so.
10. Furnish such information concerning the estates of which they are trustees and their administration as may be requested by the interested parties.
11. Pay dividends within ten days after they are declared by the referee.
12. Report to the courts in writing the condition of the estates, the amounts of money on hand, and such other details as may be requested by the courts.

[1207.9]   **Receivers.** Receivers are appointed by the court to take charge of the property of bankrupts and to protect the interests of creditors after the filing of the petition and until it is dismissed or the trustee is qualified.

[1207.10]   **Meetings of the Creditors.** After a person or company has been adjudicated bankrupt, the creditors meet, under the supervision of the referee or judge, to rule upon matters of their interest and to submit for approval of the judge or referee their claims.

[1207.11]   **Priority in Settlement of Claims.** The Bankruptcy Act provides that revenue derived from the sale of the bankrupt's assets be distributed according to the following priority:

[1207.11.1]   DEBTS THAT HAVE PRIORITY. The bankrupt's debts that are paid before the creditors' claims are as follows:

1. The costs and expenses of administering the bankrupty proceedings.

2. Certain employee wages.
3. Taxes.
4. Those who, according to United States law, have priority, and rent.

[1207.11.2]   PREFERRED CREDITORS. After the debts specified in Section 1207.11.1, 1–3 have been paid, the claims of the preferred creditors are met. Creditors obtain preference in the following ways, according to the terms of the Bankruptcy Act:

1. Transfers of any of the property of a debtor to or for the benefit of a creditor for or on account of an antecedent debt.
2. A lien obtainable by legal or equitable proceedings.
3. Certain classes of preferred stockholders if the bankrupt is a corporation.

[1207.12]   **Corporate Reorganizations.** When a corporation goes bankrupt, the procedures are somewhat different. A summary of the significant features of the Bankruptcy Act as it applies to corporations is given below.

[1207.12.1]   PETITION. According to the provisions of the act, "A corporation, or three or more creditors who have claims against a corporation or its property amounting in the aggregate to $5,000 or over . . . may, if no other petition by or against such corporation is pending . . . file a petition. Once filed, the court will accept or dismiss the petition." The petition shall include the following:

1. That the corporation is insolvent or unable to pay its debts as they mature.
2. The nature of the business of the corporation.
3. The assets, liabilities, capital stock, and financial condition of the corporation.
4. The nature of all pending proceedings affecting the property of the corporation.
5. The status of any plan of reorganization, readjustment, or liquidation affecting the property of the corporation.
6. The specific facts showing the need for relief under this chapter.
7. The desire of the petitioner or petitioners that a plan be effected.

[1207.12.2]   POSSESSION. If the indebtedness of the debtor is $250,000 or over, the court will appoint one or more trustees to take possession, prepare the plan, and administer the estate during the proceedings. If the indebtedness is less than $250,000, the court will continue the debtor in possession or appoint a trustee at its discretion.

[1207.12.3]   STATEMENT OF CONDITION. The debtor, if he continues in possession, or the trustee will file a statement covering the following items:

1. A schedule of the property of the estate, the location, quantity, and money value thereof.
2. A schedule of its creditors of each class, showing the amounts and character of their claims and securities, so far as known; the name and post-office address or place of business of each creditor.
3. A schedule of its stockholders of each class showing the number and kind of shares registered in the name of each stockholder,

and the last-known post-office address or place of business of each stockholder.

In addition, the trustee may, at the discretion of the court, perform any of the following:

1. Investigate the acts, conduct, property, liabilities, and financial condition of the debtor, the operation of his business, and the desirability of the continuance thereof.
2. Examine the directors and officers.
3. Give notice to the creditors and stockholders that they may submit suggestions for the formulation of a plan.

[1207.12.4]   THE PLAN.

1. *Who may file a plan of reorganization.* When there is a trustee, the trustee shall file a plan, taking into consideration the suggestions of creditors, stockholders, and the debtor himself. When the debtor continues in possession, a plan or plans may be filed:
   a. By the debtor.
   b. By any creditor or indenture trustee.
   c. By any stockholder, if the debtor is not found to be insolvent.
   d. By the examiner.

2. *Provisions of the plan.* A plan of reorganization, according to the provisions of the Bankruptcy Act:
   a. Shall include in respect to creditors generally or some class of them, secured or unsecured, and may include in respect to stockholders generally or some class of them, provisions altering or modifying their rights, either through the issuance of new securities of any character or otherwise.
   b. May deal with all or any part of the property of the debtor.
   c. Shall provide for the payment of all costs and expenses of the proceeding.
   d. May provide for the rejection of any executory contract except contracts in the public authority.
   e. Shall specify what claims, if any, are to be paid in cash in full.
   f. Shall specify the creditors or stockholders or any class of them not to be affected by the plan.
   g. Shall make provision for compensating those stockholders who do not accept the plan.
   h. Shall make provision for compensating those creditors who do not accept the plan.
   i. May include, where any indebtedness is created or extended under the plan for a period of more than five years, provisions for the retirement of such indebtedness.
   j. Shall provide adequate means for the execution of the plan, which may include:
      (1) The retention by the debtor of all or any part of its property.
      (2) The sale or transfer of any part of its property to one or more corporations theretofore organized or thereafter to be organized.

(3) The merger or consolidation of the debtor with one or more other corporations.

(4) The sale of all or any part of its property, either subject to or free from any lien, at not less than a fair price, and the distribution of all or any assets, or the proceeds derived from the sale thereof.

(5) The satisfaction or modification of liens.

(6) The cancellation or modification of indentures or other similar instruments.

(7) The curving or waiving of defaults.

(8) The extension of maturity dates and changes in interest rates and other terms of outstanding securities.

(9) The amendment of the charter of the debtor.

(10) The issuance of securities of the debtor or such other corporations for cash, for property, in exchange for existing securities.

[1207.12.5]   CREDITOR-STOCKHOLDER PRIORITIES AND APPROVAL. The Bankruptcy Act provides that for the purposes of compensation, the creditors and stockholders of a corporation be divided into classes "according to the nature of their respective claims and stock." The plan must then be accepted by or on behalf of creditors holding two-thirds in the amount of the claim filed and allowed of each class and, if the debtor is not insolvent, by or on behalf of stockholders holding the majority of stock of each class. Once this is done, the plan can be confirmed by the courts and executed.

Note: The Commission on the Bankruptcy Laws of the U.S. has submitted recommendations in the form of a proposed Bankruptcy Act of 1973. This could result in significant changes in the existing Federal Bankruptcy Act.

[1208]   **ADJUSTMENT BUREAUS.** As you will have observed from the proceeding material, bankruptcies are complicated and costly undertakings. They are also time-consuming. In order to avoid the legal entrapments of bankruptcy, therefore, credit men throughout the country now use the services of adjustment bureaus whenever possible.

[1208.1]   **Makeup of Adjustment Bureaus.** Adjustment bureaus are organizations which are often part of the National Association of Credit Management. They are staffed by experienced lawyers and credit men.

[1208.2]   **Function of Adjustment Bureaus.** The function of an adjustment bureau is to supervise extensions and compromise arrangements for the benefit of trade creditors or, if bankruptcy is inevitable, to supervise the liquidation of the debtor's business assets for the benefit of creditors without the debtor's having to declare bankruptcy or have an involuntary petition filed against him.

[1208.3]   **Procedures Followed by Adjustment Bureaus.** Adjustment bureaus supervise meetings of creditors and debtors, assist in development of extension and compromise plans, and, in the event of liquidation, are assigned the debtor's assets for sale and subsequent dispersal of the proceeds.

[1209]   CREDITORS' LEGAL AIDS. Creditors are protected by the law in various situations. Most of this protection is derived from the Uniform Commercial Code, Article 2, which governs sales. The major features are summarized below for your benefit:

[1209.1]   **Contracts.**

[1209.1.1]   FORMAL REQUIREMENTS, STATUTE OF FRAUDS. The provisions of the Uniform Commercial Code provide that, in general, a contract for the sale of goods for the price of more than $500 must be made in writing and signed by the buyer, or an uncontested confirmatory letter sent by the seller within prescribed time limits for the contract to be enforceable.

[1209.1.2]   GENERAL FORMULATION OF CONTRACTS. The U.C.C. provides that:

1. A contract for sale of goods may be made in any manner sufficient to show agreement, including conduct by both parties which recognizes the existence of such a contract.
2. An agreement sufficient to constitute a contract for sale may be found even though the moment of its making is underdetermined.
3. Even though one or more terms are left open, a contract for sale does not fail for indefiniteness if the parties have intended to make a contract and there is a reasonably certain basis for giving an appropriate remedy.

[1209.2]   **Creditors' Remedies under the Uniform Commercial Code.** As outlined by Webb and Bianco in the *Uniform Commercial Code Handbook* (Holt, Rinehart and Winston, Inc., 1969), the creditor's or seller's remedies can be separated into (1) his remedies against the *goods*, (2) his right to recover *damages*, and (3) his right to *cancel* the contract.

[1209.2.1]   REMEDIES AGAINST THE GOODS. The seller's remedies against the goods consist, basically, in his right under the law to withhold delivery (formerly called the unpaid seller's lien) or stop delivery of goods to an insolvent customer who will not pay in cash, or a customer who has otherwise breached the contract. The creditor has the further right to reclaim from an insolvent customer and sell any goods in that customer's possession if the seller does so within the time period prescribed by the law.

[1209.2.2]   RECOVERY OF DAMAGES. Again as outlined by Webb and Bianco, the seller may institute legal proceedings against an insolvent customer or one who has otherwise breached a contract after resale of the goods to recover monetary damages consisting of expenses, incidental damages, and the difference between the contract price and the resale price. Legal proceedings may also be instituted to recover damages when the seller does not accept the goods.

[1209.2.3]   SELLER'S RIGHT TO CANCEL THE CONTRACT. The Uniform Commercial Code also provides that the seller or creditor can cancel the contract when it is breached by the buyer. Thus, unpaid bills in violation of a contract give the seller the right to cancel it.

INDEX